A Reconstructed World
A Feminist Biography of Gertrude Richardson

The first biography of Gertrude Richardson (1875–1946), *A Reconstructed World* reveals her key role in the development of feminism and pacifism in England and Canada and her remarkable accomplishments as both an activist and a writer.

Born in Leicester, England, and raised in a working-class family, Richardson emigrated to northern Manitoba in 1911. She was influential in the women's and peace movements in both countries. Devoutly religious, she challenged orthodoxy and worked outside the mainstream churches for peace and social justice. She was the co-founder of one of the earliest suffrage groups in Manitoba and was a key activist in peace movements during the Boer War and World War I. She also served as an information centre for international antiwar news and during World War I ran an internationally focused women's peace crusade from her farmhouse through the mail and newspaper columns.

Richardson was also a gifted writer and poet. She wrote on a variety of issues in the women's movement for British and Canadian newspapers and magazines, including *Woman's Century*, the magazine of the National Council of Women of Canada. However poor health, both mental and physical, interfered with her work and prevented her from achieving the recognition attained by her feminist contempories, such as Nellie McClung.

Richardson's protests against war, her indictment of militarism, and her call for women and men to stand together for justice are powerful messages that are still important today.

BARBARA ROBERTS is professor of women's studies, Athabasca University.

Gertrude Richardson in Leicester, c. 1899.

A Reconstructed World

A Feminist Biography of Gertrude Richardson

BARBARA ROBERTS

McGill-Queen's University Press
Montreal & Kingston • London • Buffalo

© McGill-Queen's University Press 1996
ISBN 0-7735-1394-9

Legal deposit second quarter 1996
Bibliothèque nationale du Québec

Printed in the United States on acid-free paper

This book has been published with the help of a grant from the Social
Science Federation of Canada, using funds provided by the Social
Sciences and Humanities Research Council of Canada.

McGill-Queen's University Press is grateful to the Canada Council for
support of its publishing program.

Canadian Cataloguing in Publication Data

Roberts, Barbara Ann
    A reconstructed world: a feminist biography of Gertrude Richardson
    Includes bibliographical references and index.
    ISBN 0-7735-1394-9
    1. Feminists – Canada – Biography. 2. Richardson, Gertrude,
    1875–1946. 3. Women pacifists – Canada – Biography. I. Title.
    HQ1455.R53R63   1996   305.42'092   C95-920915-8

This book was typeset by Typo Litho Composition Inc.
in 10/12 Palatino.

Contents

Acknowledgments

In the more than ten years I have been researching Gertrude and her peace comrades, I have benefited from help from more than a hundred people. I have acknowledged a number of them in earlier publications about feminist peace activism in the endnotes to this book. I am grateful to them variously for information, analysis, inspiration, access to material, and hospitality. I am also grateful to Frances Rooney for good editing, and for loving Gertie too.

As usual, David Millar has been a valuable source of scholarly and personal support. I particularly appreciate his patience and tact; not until January 1992 did the word "boring" ever pass his lips in connection with my mention of Gertrude.

I am especially grateful to our parents. I have appreciated their generosity, loving kindness, and information about some of the periods discussed in this book. Graham Millar has shared his wonderful memories. Mildred Millar has been in addition an exemplar and feminist comrade. As I get older, I understand more of the extent of my own parents' gifts to me, especially their message that I have something to contribute to a better world. I drew on my father's medical knowledge for interpreting Gertrude's health information, and had looked forward to further intensive discussions with him about specific issues, but he died before I wrote the final manuscript. My mother's inquiring spirit and happy disposition have rubbed off on me; I appreciate my luck in being her daughter more than I can say. This book is dedicated to Charlotte Ruth Bowman Roberts and to the memory of Paul Curtis Roberts.

Introduction:
In Search of Gertie and
the Mother-Hearts

I first "met" Gertrude Richardson in 1984. In January 1918, from the Richardson homestead near Swan River, Manitoba, hundreds of miles north of Winnipeg, she had written to Saskatchewan farm women's columnist Violet McNaughton: "Here I have often felt so alone. There is dear Mrs Thomas and Miss Beynon and a few others but we are all so far apart. There is Miss Laura Hughes of Toronto and a number of socialist women there, and some in Vancouver, – but oh, there must be very many more – if only I could find them." I had just begun to discover this small group of women, scattered and isolated, who worked for peace in wartime, who had felt their way carefully through the old suffrage networks to find each other and give support.[1]

I had begun to research the history of Canadian women's peace activism, focusing on women who opposed the First World War. For several years I had been very much involved in the antinuclear movement, and in the early 1980s when I lived in Winnipeg I had been a member of a support group (a "spirit-raising group" as one of us called it) made up of women who were working in peace and social justice movements. We named it "Croneys" and I was never sure whether that was a misspelling or a pun. We found it difficult to do peacework; hard to speak out, hard to stand up against officialdom, hard to work with some of the men in the movement, hard to think about the unthinkable. In those days we feared that the big question about nuclear war was not, "Will it happen?" but, "When will it happen?" We had to try to stop it, but to make sure it was really stopped, we had to change the ideas and systems that underlay nuclear war. These included militarism, inequality, sexism, macho governments, macho populaces, reliance on what Ursula Franklin calls the "threat system," and so on. We wanted to remake the world. That led us to tackle a reconstruction of the social order, which was even more daunting than the antinuclear work.[2]

By then my scholarly research also reflected this interest in feminist perspectives on a peaceful world. What were the most common forms of violence in the world and how could they be eliminated? One answer now seems obvious, but then it was startling to claim that violence against women was a peace issue. In 1981 I had undertaken a massive survey of research on various forms of violence against women, and soon thereafter began to publish in the area of peace studies.[3]

My work in women's peace history came about for two distinct but quite straightforward reasons. First, I felt some disjuncture between two fundamentally important parts of my life: scholarship and activism. I was involved as a scholar in feminist peace research, and it was deeply satisfying, politically, spiritually, and intellectually, to feel that I was using my capacities for a purpose to which I was committed. But my historian was left out. I wanted more congruence in my intellectual and activist lives. Second, I wanted to find resources that would make it easier for us to do feminist peacework. We found it painful and frustrating to confront the magnitude of the problem and our own limitations to understand and change the situation. Both in the short term and the long term, we wanted to remake the world. I knew we weren't the first. Who were the earlier peace feminists? How had they found sustenance and courage for their work? What in their circumstances made it harder or easier to do peacework? What barriers did they face and how did they overcome them? I decided to start with the Great War.

In a folder labelled "peace," I found the January 1918 letter from Gertrude in Violet McNaughton's papers in the Saskatchewan Archives. Who was this Gertrude Richardson? I mentioned this to Linda Kealey who was researching early socialist women. "I know her," Linda said, "she's turned up in *Canadian Forward*, I'll send you the references." Slowly, as I pieced together the network of antiwar feminists of that period, I accumulated more information about Gertrude. She was from Leicester in the industrial Midlands of England, born in 1875 to a working-class family. She and her family were Radicals, dissenters, part of a lively cultural, intellectual, and political milieu; they had been pacifists during the Boer War. She was a poet, and for years had written regular columns for a Leicester newspaper. She had been a suffragist in England. Her personal life was a mystery at that point, but she had come to Canada in 1911 and married a Manitoba farmer. In Canada she was a suffrage leader, and had been involved in social-ist circles. She was a pacifist during World War One, and had organ-ised a Canadian women's peace group. She had links to the Women's International League for Peace and Freedom (WILPF). Her feminism, socialism, and pacifism were based on religious convictions. Like many feminists of her day, she wrote in maternalist terms. She wrote to "sister women" and "women with mother hearts," and spoke of the "brothers and sisters of the new humanity" in the *Canadian For-ward* columns that Linda Kealey had told me about. Gertrude's out-cry against the war, her indictment of militarism, and her call for women and men to stand together for justice against all odds were akin to the strongest calls to peacemaking that I saw in the peace movement of my own time. I wanted to find out more about her.[4]

My intention was (and still is) to write a history of Canadian women's peace activism in the twentieth century; at first, Gertie was just one of the gang – Gertie and the Mother-Hearts. During the 1980s I was an academic migrant worker, every couple of years moving to a new city, a new contract. I took advantage of this situation by re-searching peace women in each place; very handy for the overview I planned to write. Everywhere I went, someone knew someone; a long-dead activist, another researcher, a source. Dozens of people helped me; other academics, neighbours, political comrades.[5]

While I was in England for another project (related to the Peace Tent at the 1985 Nairobi Women's NGO Forum, itself part of women's international peace networking) in January 1986, I went up to Leices-ter, Gertrude's home town, and found out more about her family. I found hundreds of her published columns and poems in the Leicester papers. I made a long list but could afford only a few photocopies. By then I was living in Halifax and researching Nova Scotia paci-fists; Gertrude would have to wait.

In 1986 I used a small research grant from the Canadian Research In-stitute for the Advancement of Women to go to Swan River, Manitoba. I remember that trip so vividly; my friend Sue loaned me her car and I drove out from Winnipeg on a perfect September day, through wheat fields, swatches of green fallow, low hills, the countryside I had grown to love while living in the prairies between 1980 and 1985. "You can al-most see the life before you in the land ... behind you as you pass," I sang along with my new "Prairie Spirits" audiotape. I felt connected to those who loved and worked this land, as Gertrude had. "There's nothing like the freedom of looking over miles of land," sang the tape, "Something about the Prairies strangers just don't understand."[6]

In Swan River local historian John Booth introduced me to Isobel McKay, whose mother had been a suffragist with Gertrude. Isobel took me around, gave me the names of relatives and friends. I talked to a host of people who had known Gertrude or her family, or whose parents had; I read the local paper, investigated local history sources, and talked to Gertrude's adopted son. I went to southern Manitoba to meet her nieces. One biographical clue led to another.

Gradually I came to understand what an important figure she had been in her day. She illustrated the importance of religious conviction as a basis for social action, overlaps between farm, suffrage, peace, and socialist movements, and the international connections between Canadian and other pacifist women. She was fascinating as a writer: a keen observer of rural life in the settlement period and a lively reporter of the campaign for woman suffrage in Manitoba. I set out to do an edited collection of her writings, with a substantial biographical introduction, thinking it would be impossible to find out enough about her to do more.[7]

An Athabasca University research grant allowed me to send away for more photocopies of her published material, and piece together enough information for an application to the Social Sciences and Humanities Research Council. Thanks to their two-year grant and release time from the university, I was finally able to pursue what had by then become an obsession. My partner, also a historian, teased me about Gertie and the Mother-Hearts, my facetious working title. It sounded like good material for a musical, David said, or a detective novel. Or maybe a good name for a rock group. After five years of nibbling at the edges, it was time for a feast. Suffice it to say that I went here and there to dig up more information. I made the first major trip back to England to dig in archives and dusty repositories.

Academics and others were generous with their help. Leicester University had put me in touch with Linda McKenna. A Victorian studies specialist, she knew local history and women's history, and she was willing to work on Gertrude. I spent weeks in Leicester, Gertrude's home town. Linda put me in touch with other researchers. Historians are notorious for gossip sessions about long-dead people and events, strange sounding to outsiders, which are often the key to interpretation of sources. I gossiped with David Nash who filled me in on the socialist and labour scene that had been the backdrop for Gertie's peace activities. Linda's friend Karen O'Rourke, whose field is women's religious history, also knew a lot about medical issues, and her analysis was of critical importance. I met Malcolm Elliott, a historian specialising in Leicester; he helped me with such topics as housing and neighbourhoods and the social concerns of religious groups. While in England I met Jill Liddington; Jo Vellacott had put me on to Jill. I saw Sheila Rowbotham; all three had done crucial work on the peace movements that formed a background for Gertrude. These historians put me in touch with others and smoothed the way for access to archival material, private papers, and chats about various individuals and groups of Gertrude's day. (I have specific thank yous in the footnotes throughout the book for some of these.)

As I am a Quaker (and I suspected that Gertrude or her brother Horace, who was a Christian Socialist and a conscientious objector, might have been), I had written to Leicester Quakers to inquire about accomodation, and Annette and Oscar Wallis offered me the use of their house while they were away in the States. Thanks to them, I was no longer a visitor, but a resident who could share in the Meeting and neighbourly hospitality. In addition to their house, they bequeathed me their circle of friends, so I enjoyed the friendship and hospitality of Malcolm and Jenny Elliott and neighbours Anne and Malcolm Gregson.

I needed to get to know Leicester, to understand Gertrude's milieu. I could see why she liked it so much. I found out about her circles and their activities, and walked the streets to see where she had been. Linda took me through Gertie's old neighbourhood, one afternoon (they thought it cold; compared to Edmonton's minus 40° c I thought it was lovely). We trudged through miles of streets spotting Gertrude's old addresses. We could see traces of the old Leicester, and get a better sense of her everyday world. And the food! Despite what I had heard about English cooking, the food was wonderful. Gertie no doubt shopped at the outdoor market (the oldest continuous one in the country), and so did I. Gertie must have eaten sandwiches made with baps (rolls), or maybe had tea at Fenwick's department store as a treat; me too. To do my duty as a researcher, I forced myself to sample the wonderful pork pies for which Leicester was famous, and which Gertie had learned to duplicate for New Year's Day family feasts in Manitoba.[8]

Sometimes my own experiences overlapped uncannily with Gertrude's. In Bradford, I held the Women's Social and Political Union (WSPU) suffragette ribbon and button and the Independent Labour Party (ILP) medal that belonged to my great aunt Nance Bowman, of whom I had only vaguely known. I spent the day going over family trees with Gertrude's nieces Olive Burrell and Margaret Bailey in Scarborough, not far from the Newcastle area where my grandfather Charles Bowman grew up. Keith and Jean Twilley filled in Gertrude's family details; Keith's grandfather Frank Twilley had been one of Gertrude's younger brothers. Family trees were important in the research. There was also a mystery to solve. A family member thought that Gertrude's first marriage had been hasty, and had produced a child who had died soon after birth. However vague the information, it required a serious search. I spent days at the registry offices in Leicester and Loughborough scanning parish birth and death records for several decades. We found no baby, but there was lots of excitement and wild speculation, digging through registers with the staff. I was later able to confirm that there had been no child, nor had the wedding been hasty.

Some of the *déjà vu* was political. The Gulf War began while I was in Leicester; my research made the war more upsetting. With the local peace coalition I stood in a peace vigil at the clock tower, and knew it had been the scene of similar vigils by Gertrude's peace groups. I spent a day reading accounts of tumultuous antiwar meetings in 1900, and that afternoon in the Market Square I realised that the Corn Exchange building I was passing was one of the sites I had been reading about. I sat in Meeting for Worship on a Sunday morning with Quakers seeking a response to the 1991 war, having spent the week reading records of similar meetings during the Boer War and the First World War. Was it all going to repeat again, war after war? Had all that pacifist work been for naught?

In London it was a thrilling experience to sit for days at L-15, my spot at the blue-leather covered circular desks in the reading room of the British Museum where Karl Marx and Virginia Woolf had worked. On a later trip I spent hours in the Marx Memorial Library reading peace society minutes written by Gertrude's comrades. I found periodicals and suffrage records in the British Library and the Fawcett Library, and searched divorce and annulment registers at the Public Record Office. Sometimes the links with Gertrude were tenuous, but lacking family archives, they were all there was.

I freighted home cartons of notes and photocopies to Edmonton, with more to come. I knew a lot more about Gertie's life and times than I had ever hoped to learn, but there were still big gaps. It was not until the summer of 1991 in Manitoba that the final pieces fell into place. I talked over what I had discovered in England with various family members who had previously given me information. Gertrude's niece Connie MacDonald had recently found Gertrude's sister Florrie's photo album from 1897, and a another stack of family mementos; Connie's daughters Peggy and Myra helped me go through them. Gertrude's other niece Dorothy Twilley Shewfelt once again dug into her records and her family memories of her aunt. She arranged for me to obtain copies of medical files that contained essential biographical material, without which a full biography of

Gertrude would not have been possible. I remember Dorothy also for a generous heap of seeds for the stunning pink poppies in her garden; now they bloom in my own. Her sister Joan, who had died suddenly in 1987, had organised copies of Gertrude's writing and other mementos; Dorothy's son Grant Shewfelt photocopied the material and sent it to me. Joan's husband Bob Wallcraft helped me sort through the storage drawers in the little museum founded by Dorothy's and Joan's father Fred Twilley. We unexpectedly turned up a rich collection of family letters.

In Swan River, Gertrude's son Eric Richardson went over his childhood recollections in light of the English material I had found, and made it possible for me to see some useful local legal records. He gave me two patience plants, packaged for travel. The original cuttings had come from Muriel Spicer, who with Isobel McKay had helped me with interviews in 1986. Muriel's mother-in-law and Isobel's mother had been suffrage comrades of Gertie's. I visited Gertrude's grave one last time, but by then I was too tired to feel much except longing to go home. After a final stopover in Brandon at a nurses' reunion, to talk to nurses who had worked in a hospital where Gertrude was a patient in her later years, I headed home, ready to write.

When I began writing in earnest that fall, I thought I was going to do a biographical introduction to an edited collection of Gertrude's writing. Before I had gone to England, Mandy Jenkins had painstaking typed hundreds of Gertrude's journalistic pieces, poems, and some fiction onto disks. I had combed Gertrude's work for clues, and had made elaborate look-up lists, now scribbled over with notes. I had accumulated several boxes of material, the fruit of eight years' work. Now I was stuck, tongue-tied. How to untangle a life?

I started when Gertrude and her widowed mother (her father had died after being struck at a Boer War peace rally in 1900) crossed the Atlantic to settle in Swan River with Gertrude's brother Fred and sister Fannie and her family. The brief story grew ridiculously long. Gerry Hallowell, history editor at the University of Toronto Press, read four chapters and reassured me that I could do a full scale biography. The project was redefined in several respects then. Now it would be a full length biography. I took a deep breath and kept writing. By the end I was sick of her.

Gertie and the Mother-Hearts did not seem like a joke, once I had started writing. Sure it sounded like a rock group, but that was not much help at the computer every day. Biography is hard to do, especially when the person is obscure and her life is not well documented. Much of my historical training seemed irrelevant – or inappropriate.

As my frustration in the early 1970s with Donald Creighton's biography of John A. Macdonald had showed me, biography was as much a product of the biographer's creative imagination as it was of the character and circumstance of the subject. I didn't want to have creative imagination, but was beginning to admit that there was no alternative. I devoured biographies, detective fiction, and novels about biography, and worried about how to do it. Novelist Isobel Colegate's fictional character Catherine Hillery expressed similar qualms about the biography she was struggling to write about fictional political figure Neil Campion:

The truth was, she had lost her belief in biography. She used to think that if you read a book about someone you would have a pretty good idea of what they were like. It now seemed to her that was not so at all. You would have an idea of what someone else thought they were like ... She had the facts of Neil Campion's life, more or less, and she had the opinions of various people who had known him ... if she were to create – to invent in fact – a portrait which was a composite of these various opinions, it would presumably ... become the ... "real" [version] ... It was possible that her biography might be the only one ... She would have fixed him, pinned like a butterfly in the collecting box of history, in perpetuity. How could she take it upon herself to do such a thing to a fellow human being?[9]

Liz Stanley and Ann Morley faced similar questions in their biography of suffragette Emily Wilding Davison, best known for dying from injuries after flinging herself in front of the King's horse at the Derby races in 1913. They point out that the process of research and writing is an essential part of feminist biography, so the feminist biographer should explain fully about her hypotheses, gaps, assumptions, and so on. At first I was sold on the idea of describing all my blind alleys and false scents, but reading their book I kept forgetting which scenarios turned out to be wrong and which proved correct. Scratch that idea; I would compromise. But I did retain another of their key points: women live and work in social, political, intellectual, cultural networks; the woman's families, friends, and comrades are crucial components of any feminist biography. I have written not only about Gertrude, but about her family, her comrades, her circles.[10]

Gertrude's and my relationship has gone through a number of stages. It had been pretty one-sided, all along; I had the power to define her, to control her, to create her as I chose. When I began to write, I wanted to exercise that authority only in my selection of her writings. I had planned to ignore her poetry. But as I grappled with gaps in my information about periods or issues in her life, I had to scrutinise her writings and anything else I could lay my hands on and try to read between the lines and otherwise look for clues to piece together guesses about what she was doing or thinking. That's when I had to come to grips with her poems; they were less transparent than the prose, but still revealed something that I was able to see. (Others will see more, I hope, when they take up her writings.) Inevitably I intruded more and more in her story; yet, ironically, the more actively I intruded, the more I was forced to confront parts of her that were not comfortable or easy for me to be embroiled in. For example, the religious beliefs that led her political activism. It seems idiotic to me now that I expected to understand her without gaining a sympathetic undertanding of the religion that was so fundamental a part of her life, especially when she got into trouble as a consequence of putting her religious principles into practice. Yet when I first met her, I automatically deflected her Christian references; I did not take them in or take them seriously, except to note that they were pervasive. In an edited collection, I would not have to talk about Jesus all the time, Gertie would do it. But as a biographer, I had to try to understand what her religion meant to her. If I didn't have to learn to believe in him, I certainly had to learn to accept that she did, and do the best I could to see what that meant.[11]

When I decided to write, I wanted to make sure as many people as possible found out about Gertrude and had access to her life and work, so we could use her as a resource when we need inspiration or a sense of connection with a tradition of decency and commitment and passion for justice and peace. Yet it seems a very chancy undertaking, now that this book has become a biography. Investigators in the mysteries I read often rehearse multiple interpretations of facts about individuals and their actions, then choose the most plausible interpretation. They usually have to invent some of the facts to fill in gaps. Reconstructing Gertrude's life, I was engaged in the same process. Fictional private investigator Catherine Sayler, nonplused when a meeting with a suspect reveals his innocence, mused about my own fears: "We sat quietly for a few moments. I watched the man whom I'd thought about day and night for the last two weeks. I knew more about him than I knew about most of my friends. I'd assembled information, examined his character under a microscope, and struggled to understand what made him the man he was. From all that, I'd constructed a scenario that was rational, logical, and on the one point that mattered, totally wrong."[12]

The omniscient historian or biographer finds it hard to avoid the pitfalls of constructing an ideological discourse, to use Dorothy Smith's description, when the biographer's version of truth outweighs that of the original teller of the tale. I have tried to construct an old-fashioned narrative, despite being unsure that a narrative really is possible, these postmodernist days, when subjects reputedly do not exist and supposedly nothing ever really happens. As fictional detective Catherine Sayler says after her conversation with her suspect, above, "We go through life getting only part of the story, and from that part we construct meaning. If it 'makes sense,' we believe it. Truth doesn't have a whole lot to do with anything." Have I told the truth about Gertie? Although Mariana Valverde's sensible advice about analysing social discourses "as if subjects existed" resonates for me, my approach has been a bit Luddite. I'm not primarily after truth, or facts (whatever they are), but something more elusive: I think it is understanding. I've tried to reconstruct Gertrude's world, in hopes that understanding her world will help us understand and reconstruct our own.[13]

Abbreviations

ANZWVA	Australian and New Zealand Women Voters Association
BDWSU	British Dominions Woman Suffrage Union
BMHC	Brandon Mental Health Centre
BPS	British Peace Society
CCF	Co-operative Commonwealth Federation
CF	*Canadian Forward*
CO	conscientious objector
COIB	Conscientious Objector Information Bureau
CPR	Canadian Pacific Railroad
CRIAW	Canadian Research Institute for the Advancement of Women
CSA	Canadian Suffrage Association
CTF	*Canadian Thresherman and Farmer*
DORA	Defence of the Realm Act
EFU	Equal Franchise Union
ELFS	East London Federation of Suffragettes
FOR	Fellowship of Reconciliation
FSC	Friends Service Committee
GGG	*Grain Growers' Guide*
ICW	International Council of Women
ICWPP	International Committee of Women for Permanent Peace
IODE	Imperial Order of the Daughters of the Empire
ILP	Independent Labour Party
IWSA	International Woman Suffrage Alliance
IWW	Industrial Workers of the World

LCW	Local Council of Women
LP	*Leicester Pioneer*
LPS	Leicester Peace Society
LSS	Leicester Secular Society
MFP	*Midland Free Press*
MSA	Military Service Act
NAC	National Archives of Canada
NCF	No-Conscription Fellowship
NCWC	National Council of Women of Canada
NEFU	National Equal Franchise Union
NUWSS	National Union of Women's Suffrage Societies
NUWW	National Union of Women Workers
PAM	Provincial Archives of Manitoba
PEL	Political Equality League/Political Education League
SAB	Saskatchewan Archives Board
SACC	South African Conciliation Committee
SDP	Social Democratic Party
SR *Star*	Swan River *Star*
STWC	Stop-the-War Committee
TLC	Trades and Labour Council
WAWSA	War Against War in South Africa
WCTU	Women's Christian Temperance Union
WFL	Women's Freedom League
WILPF	Women's International League for Peace and Freedom
WIL	Women's International League
WLA	Women's Liberal Association
WLF	Women's Liberal Federation
WLN	*Western Labor News*
WMS	Women's Missionary Society
WPC	Women's Peace Crusade
WPP	Woman's Peace Party
WSPU	Women's Social and Political Union

Gertrude, Fannie, and Horace.

Gertie and Eliza in Leicester, c. 1910.

Fannie, Fred, Connie, Eliza, John, and Gertie, c. 1911.

Florrie, c. 1897.

Horace, c. 1910?

Robert and Gertie, probably 1912.

Eric, Robert, Jim, John; Gertie, Connie, Fannie, probably summer 1918.

Gertie and Eric, c. 1919.

Postcard from Roaring River, Christmas 1919: Jim, Robert, Edith, Eric, Gertie.

Connie, Jim, Fannie, Mac, Jackie, Edith, Robert, Gertie, Eric, Fred; probably
New Year's Day 1921.

Roaring River Suffrage Association picnic at Livesey's, probably 1912.
Aggie Richardson (behind fence), Fannie, Alice Cox, Gertie, Margaret Martin,
Grace Shaw.

SUFFRAGE PETITION FORM

Will any lady who will take around a petition form kindly let me know at once? The time is passing, and all must be ready by October 1st.

We are expecting shortly a visit from a representative of the Women's Christian Temperance Union, when public meetings will be held in Swan River and Minitonas. There will also be a general gathering of the Swan Valley branches of the Political Equality League of Manitoba. Petition forms will be brought to any address for signature on request. Do not let us content ourselves, dear women, with merely caring for the physical needs of our dear brave soldiers. Let us work for a reconstructed world, where war, with all its attendant horrors shall never more find place, the new world of brotherhood, the kingdom of God on earth.

Gertrude Richardson.
Swan River *Star*
Friday, 27 August 1915

1 Destined For "True Womanhood": Working Class Girlhood, Middle Class Education, Radical Social and Political Milieu (1875–1901)

Gertrude Twilley was born in 1875 into a working class family in Leicester, England, a manufacturing town of about 110,000 people. Formerly a hosiery centre, by then the boot and shoe industry, still largely composed of relatively small family firms, had become the major focus of the city's economy. Light engineering was another growing sector. The diversity of the local economy and its employment opportunities (hosiery employed mostly women, boot and shoe mostly men) underlay a period of growth and prosperity after the 1860s. Leicester had been a Roman town, and was the seat of the county; at the centre of the Midlands regional railway network, 150 kilometres northwest of London, it also developed as a regional shopping and service centre. In Gertrude's day the town was solidly Liberal; a former centre of Chartism, it boasted a strong labour movement, and until the switch to separate Labour representation in the early twentieth century, its Liberalism was so permeated by labour that for many, the two were synonymous. Although its public health history had been dismal, by 1875 the city's death rate was the lowest of any manufacturing town in England.[1]

The Twilley family went to Leicester via Syston, in Lincolnshire; they were earlier from around Bourne or Spalding. Gertrude's grandfather William Twilley was settled in Leicester by the early nineteenth century. He and Matilda Cox married in 1834. He was a bootmaker and his son, James William, born in Spalding in 1847, was trained in the boot and shoemaking trade. William Twilley reportedly was a "hearty man who lived to an advanced age," although he was "inclined to be intemperate" sometimes (he was not a total abstainer). He died of a bowel obstruction. Of Matilda Cox, I know nothing, save that she was reputed to be "an even tempered woman." The Twilley family were dissenters. They were listed as Congregationalists on the marriage certificate for Gertrude's parents James Twilley and Eliza Richardson, when they exchanged vows at the London Road Chapel in 1869.[2] Between 1870 and 1886, the Twilleys had eight children, seven of whom survived. Gertrude Matilda was the third. The first child, Florence Annie, was born in 1871, followed by Wilfred Ernest two years later. Gertrude was next in 1875, then Fannie Elizabeth in 1877, Frank Charles in 1880, Frederick Arthur in 1882, Lewis Edwin, who lived only a few months, in 1885, and the last child, Horace Gladstone, in 1886.[3]

The Twilleys were probably better off financially than many working class couples. James worked as an elastic web weaver, one of the highest paid jobs in the shoemaking trade. Web weaving was in a decline by the 1880s, but James Twilley had managed to flourish. He made the transition to self-employment as a boot and shoemaker, probably sometime in the 1870s. There are several possibilities. He may have been part of a group of web weavers who formed a producers' cooperative to supply webs to manufactures and to the new Cooperative Wholesale Society's boot and shoe factory. Or perhaps he was one of those squeezed out of web weaving by changing styles and technology. His training as a boot and shoemaker stood him in good stead. He may have made the transition by outworking; finishing work was often put out to small shops in that period, and the practice survived into the 1890s. Sewing machines could be rented, the cost based on the number of pieces sewn, so someone with little capital could set up as an outside worker or independent boot and shoemaker.[4]

By 1880 James was working for, or in partnership with, boot and shoemaker William Wray, who had been in business for at least two decades. The 1881 census lists Twilley as a "shoe factor" which suggests he may have been a middleman, coordinating the putting-out for a small manufacturing business. By the late 1880s, James Twilley had taken over the whole business (or at least, his partner's name disappeared from the city directory listings of the business and the 1891 census lists Wray as "living on own means"). At some point, according to family stories, James Twilley had signed a note for a man who defaulted, and he lost everything. They had the business at home, but the bailiffs seized the Twilleys' equipment (which they must have owned) and supplies. The family was plunged into poverty and had to start over.[5] Was William Wray the defaulting man, or had the partnership with him represented starting over? The court records containing bailiffs' orders are lost, so there is no way to be sure. It seems likely that the disaster occurred between 1881 and 1891. The 1891 census lists Twilley more humbly as a shoemaker, and shows that the children had been put to work in the business.[6]

Eliza Richardson Twilley, who was born in 1849, had come from an unusual family, even for the period; her father John Richardson had married three times, and Eliza was from the third batch of children. The family may have been a bit better off than the Twilleys, or at least some of them may have been. Eliza's father was an engineer and her brother William Horatio, who stood up for her at her wedding, was a wholesale confectioner. Her father was much older than her mother; her mother may have died in childbirth, for Eliza spent some time in an orphanage, according to her granddaughters. Despite this, Eliza was a healthy, cheerful sort, with a streak of adventure. Her granddaughters recalled family stories about the poverty days; Eliza was always keen to move house, and would be on the lookout for a better place, as if it were a lark. The family moved frequently (as did other working class families), but stayed in the same neighbourhood. It must have been quite the enterprise to move a large family. Eliza was described years later by her daughter Fannie as "very even tempered [and] healthy"; she had a gift for seeing the funny side of things. Fannie and Fred were like that too, but Gertie, like her father, was more inclined to earnestness.[7]

From various sources, I gathered an impression of Eliza as the sort of person who was sunny and optimistic, relatively tolerant of childish misbehaviour, and less strict than James. Fred's daughters had grown up on stories of family discipline. They told me that when the kids were bad James would spank them but the fiercest punishment was to send them off to bed with no supper. But James was very active in religious, community, and political affairs, and he frequently went off to meetings in the evening. After he went off to the meeting, Eliza would take supper to the bad child of the moment. James Twilley loved his children dearly and wanted to do right by them. He was stern and had a hot temper, but he didn't stay angry long. His son Fred remembered, "He was the most upright, unselfish, God-fearing man that ever I have known in my life. I have seen him stand on a chair outside his shop in Waring Street and expose 'bookmakers' and others. Though my father was poor, everybody honoured him." But James was also a worrier. Fred said, "I believe my father shortened his life by worry. He really did have things to worry about but the worry didn't help him at all but only hastened his death." However pressed he was at times, he was very concerned with the children's wellbeing; he "worshipped" Eliza, his granddaughters told me.[8]

The Twilleys lived in a section of Leicester called "Highfields" by the time Gertrude was born, a new suburban area built up after 1870, noteworthy for medium-quality housing, a mixture of villas and terraced (row) houses meant for the better-off working classes and the lower middle classes. Few of the Twilley addresses still exist; urban renewal has eradicated two of the earliest streets entirely, and at several other house numbers the original terraced or semidetached houses have been replaced by larger buildings. Nevertheless, parts of Highfield still convey a sense of the Twilley neighbourhoods. Most of their addresses were terraced houses: block-long rows of two storey townhouses, with small gardens in the rear.

Today's renovated and more comfortable and attractive versions retain the typical layout. The front room was usually directly inside the door from the street; an inner room connected to the kitchen, sometimes with another small room behind, at the rear of the house. The present-day upstairs generally has two bedrooms and a bathroom, but in Gertrude's day, the toilet was outdoors at the bottom of the garden. There would have been three bedrooms, none very large, shared by several children. Gertrude and her two sisters shared a bedroom; Fannie and Florrie slept together, but Gertrude was a restless sleeper much troubled by insomnia, at least by the time she was in her teens, so she slept in a separate bed. The boys presumably shared another bedroom, and the parents took the third, sharing it with the current baby. Later, when the older children moved away, the Twilleys, like many other working class families, took a lodger, who probably shared the boys' bedroom. In many such places, the front room was kept for formal occasions, and the main living room was the middle room next to the kitchen. However, a large and lively family may have used all the rooms for everyday. The family were emphatically respectable and deeply religious, but they were not necessarily stuffy. It is a safe estimate that there was a lot of reading, studying, and praying in the house and probably a lot of laughing, too, since at least two of the children were notoriously funny as adults. The Twilleys belonged to the better-off strata of the working classes, at least before they were wiped out by the defaulting borrower, and even after that, they maintained respectability. They were quintessential improvers, eager to take advantage of educational and cultural opportunities, and, in cities like Leicester, formed part of a lively intellectual, religious, and political milieu.[9]

Information about Gertrude's childhood is fragmentary. She was not a particularly robust baby. Gertrude said years later that her mother had not been well during the pregnancy, and the birth had been difficult. Gertrude suffered from the usual childhood diseases (which could be fatal) such as measles, whooping cough, and scarlet fever, and during one illness had convulsions. (Her siblings were also at risk; Fannie, for example, had rheumatic fever as a child.) Gertrude was raised Congregationalist, and with her siblings regularly attended Sunday School and other church activities at the London Road church where her parents had married and Eliza Twilley's brother William Horatio Richardson, the wholesale confectioner, was a deacon. Sunday School in Gertrude's day often included serious instruction and study, and she soaked up anything that came her way. She was a highly intelligent and sensitive child. "She suffered deeply because of human sorrow and was grieved beyond words on hearing a missionary tell the story of how the Chinese prevented the growth of their children's feet." She was carefully brought up, and led a sheltered life. The strict parents (probably primarily James) did not approve of such popular entertainments as the theatre, for example. Gertrude was protected from seamier aspects of life, or from any hint of indecency, in ways that tend to be ascribed to the Victorian middle classes alone: "I always had one of my brothers or numerous male cousins as escorts," she recalled. Her parents were apparently active in their community through their church and other groups, almost certainly including temperance groups. She later described them as of "noble character" and "suffer[ing] poverty in order to assist the social outcasts of their native city," although there is no hint of the nature of their implied charitable activities. The London Road church was substantial in several senses of the word, seating over 1300 people. Its members included a number of wealthy manufacturing and commercial families. The Carnall family, for example, owned ironmongeries and dealt in cutlery, stationery, and haberdashery. John Carnall was one of the original church trustees, and served as treasurer from 1879 to 1908; his descendants held that office until the 1950s. His daughter was one of Gertrude's Sunday School teachers. John Carnall made an impression on Gertrude; she wrote in 1914 on hearing of his death, "Memory takes me back to the days, when, as an imaginative little girl, his keen eyes always made me think of fire and swords." Her brother Fred's more prosaic recollections were of Sunday School and visiting preachers.[10]

Gertrude and Fannie went to a nearby church-run elementary school on Friars Lane. Gertie did very well in school; it was easy for her and she enjoyed it. In 1887, when she was twelve, she wrote an entrance exam and won a scholarship to the prestigious Wyggeston Girls School, a day school established in 1878 with 150 pupils, modelled after Miss Buss' North London Collegiate and Camden schools for girls. Wyggeston headmistress Ellen Leicester had worked with Miss

Buss and had hired two more Buss teachers to open the new school. The pupils were sorted by age and grade, had regularly scheduled (and academically rigorous) classes, and top quality teachers who were experts in their subjects and dedicated to teaching girls. The school accepted students ages seven to nineteen; fees began at 10 s. for girls under thirteen; with £2 pounds 15 s. 10 p. being regular term fees (music, singing, and dancing were extra). These fees were well beyond the means of working class parents, even the better-off artisans.[11]

Although it was a day school, Wyggeston attempted by various means to produce the closeness and a sense of community that characterised the new girls' boarding schools. The curriculum included science, mathematics, classics, modern languages (teachers were from France and Germany), literature, current events, history, and various other subjects, and also fine sewing, and (by virtue of the school rules and social occasions) middle class etiquette. There were various clubs, centred around a mix of academic and social activities, and the students enjoyed school teas, theatrical performances, cozy get-togethers with teachers, field trips, and other up-to-date activities prescribed by feminist education. The school magazine, the *Wyggeston Girls' Gazette*, reflected the school's official and unwritten curricula, the teachers' and pupils' interests, and also the privileged lives of most of the pupils. The students sat for various high school exams and school leaving exams, including the Oxford and Cambridge Locals (established for boys in the 1850s and opened to girls in the 1860s, to test students against national standards), international school prizes, the South Kensington exams in math, mechanics, chemistry, physiography, geology, botany, other exams in the fine arts and music, the University of London matriculation exams, and so on. Although there were women's colleges at Oxford and Cambridge by then, and women were allowed to attend lectures and write the exams, neither university awarded women degrees until after the First World War. The less prestigious University of London, however, allowed women to take any of its degrees (women could write London exams after attending Oxbridge if they wanted an actual degree). These students benefited from the struggles of the previous generation for reform of girls' education, and improvements in women's access to higher education.[12]

Although most of the Wyggeston girls came from middle and upper class families, a number of working class students attended on scholarships.[13] Gertrude's maternal cousins Ada and Charlotte Flude were also students, and their father was a framework knitter (a hosiery worker). Ada and Charlotte became pupil teachers, a common strategy to earn a living while continuing to get more education and better credentials. Pupil teachers could compete for scarce five-year paid apprenticeships, combining classroom experience and teacher training classes, at the end of which they were elementary school teachers; they were supposed to save money to pay for further training (but some had to contribute to family support and could not save). At age eighteen they could write the exams for the few Queen's Scholarships to go to a teachers' training college. Many also took classes at night or at other adult education institutions, hoping to upgrade to an appointment in a better elementary school, a post in one of the strong academic girls' high schools, or even a headship of an elementary school; some might hope to become school inspectors. A very few were able to gain a university education; scholarships were scarce and costs could be prohibitive. (Fees for a residential college at Oxford for the three terms of eight weeks each were about £100 in Gertrude's day.) However, as Martha Vicinus points out, "an ambitious girl could study for an external degree from the University of London and rise to a respected position." Working class women who taught could be better off than those in other occupations, who typically had such low pay and long hours they were often too tired and poor to manage any further education.[14]

The new girls' schools were typically middle class, and although it was assumed most girls would marry and raise families, they were prepared for a variety of possibilities. The schools could give girls the tools to enter the lower ranks of the professions (such as elementary school teaching, although this was more attractive to working class women) or the respectable white collar jobs open to women, or, for those who could find the means, to prepare them for university entry. A university education could in turn give young women a chance for community living (to absorb communitarian values) if they lived in a residential college, for individual intellectual and spiritual development, and a source of inspiration that they could draw on over the years for renewal and comradeship as they went about their business in the world serving God's purpose, "mankind," or, for some, womankind. Indeed, it was the first generation of university-trained women who ran the new girls' schools of the type Gertrude attended in the 1880s. The girls' schools reproduced some of the features of the universities, such as the challenging curriculum and solid academic programs, but most notably the deliberate inculcation of a sense of social responsibility and wider citizenship in their students. As Martha Vicinus points out, girls' schools promoted a kind of doublethink. On the one hand they taught public duty (as opposed to family duty), which might mean staying single, living in a community of women, working in a serving profession, but on the other hand, most girls would find their life's work in family settings, rather than in careers outside the family, so they had to be prepared to carry out that work in ways that were consistent with the new women's agenda. Political activism was one of the ways to contribute found by middle and upper class married and single women.[15]

The handful of working class girls who were bright enough and lucky enough to gain entry into these schools got a middle class orientation thrown in along with their academic and community training. In some ways this was a useful thing to gain: the presumption that they had the right to learn, to think, and to explore; a sense of entitlement mixed with and conditional upon duty; and a sense of efficacy, that they could accomplish something, they could make a difference. For most working class girls, such lessons about efficacy might be learned at higher cost in often-lost trade union or socialist struggles, and despite the fact that there were both a thriving working class intellectual life and widespread tradition self-education, the chances for intellectual exploration and challenge were few and far between for females. But this middle class approach was based on fallacious assumptions about the availability of resources. It was very unusual for a girl from Gertrude's background to have her opportunities (and virtually impossible for a girl lower in the class strata). Working class girls normally did not have enough money to pay the school fees, and even if they had scholarships, these did not cover all the costs. Assuming that the family could afford to forego the daughter's earnings, they still probably would not have money to pay for necessary incidentals, let alone optional items. Gertrude's father, she said, "was so good, and loved me so much. When I had my scholarship to Wyggeston High School, he sold his ring to buy me a watch." When she was ready to write exams and had to travel out of town to do so, her family could not afford the train fare. In one instance, Gertrude recalled years later, Lewis Rodhouse, a rich saddlery owner and father of another Wyggeston girl some years younger than Gertrude, "paid my train fare in order that I might enter for a certain examination."[16]

Gertrude did well at Wyggeston, and apparently fit in with the other girls, for she maintained contact with a number of them for most of her active adult life. Her family was genteel, although poor, and the school was strictly but sensibly run and frivolity disallowed, so Gertrude probably did not have to behave much differently at school than at home. She may have been a bit of a snob, or maybe it is more accurate to say she was a bit stuffy. Fannie's daughter Connie remembered hearing that when Gertie would encounter her younger sister on the street, Fannie at that time was such a ragamuffin that Gertie would sometimes pretend she did not know her. (Ah, grubby little sisters! But Fannie was forgiving; she told her niece Dorothy years later that Gertie was "sedate.") Disaster struck when Gertie was fifteen; she became very ill with tubercular adenitis, a form of tuberculosis of the adrenal glands. She wrote years later, "I had abscesses in the glands and was very sleepless for 2 or 3 years and had to have an operation on my neck." She was saved by an operation by the eminent local surgeon Sir Charles Marriott. Whether her Wyggeston connections helped her to get access to him, or whether this was a routine part of his charity practice is not certain. It saved her life, but she bore scars on the right side of her neck the rest of her life. Although she may have hoped to stay at Wyggeston longer, she did not return. Whatever her original plans, by the time she recovered from her illness she had to think about earning a living.[17]

Gertrude trained to be a seamstress; not just any seamstress, but a highly-skilled "costumier," if her later self-description was accurate. Her choice of occupation was not surprising, as dressmaking appealed to many working class or lower middle class girls who wanted respectable work; daughters of artisans, farmers, and tradesmen abounded in the trade. It could be done at home, thus it was genteel, compared to factory work. The demand for clothes had increased due to middle class prosperity and cheap machine-made cloth and lace. Some working women were also customers, especially single women keen on fashion. But freelance dressmaking was a precarious living.[18]

Linda and I were unable to learn where Gertrude trained. There are several possibilities. During her last year at Wyggeston, the school magazine recorded a demonstration by Mrs Conquest of the Scientific Dressmaking (or Dress Cutting) Association. Perhaps training was arranged through her. Another possibility was a technical school. According to the city directory, the municipal technical school taught dressmaking in 1895; the listing for 1887–88 does not specifically mention dressmaking, but it may have been offered. The school was intended for working class children who had completed school and were ready for technical training; it followed the South Kensington Science and Art regulations and was considered among the best in the country, according to city directories. Or Gertrude may have apprenticed with a dressmaker at a local workshop; this was the most common practice, and her sister Fannie later implied that this had been the case. She may have combined a traditional apprenticeship with evening or daytime technical courses. Wherever she took it, her training lasted two years. She found the sedentary nature of her sewing days unpleasant after having regular physical exercise at Wyggeston school, but enjoyed her work, and must have gained satisfaction from her skill.[19]

Gertrude apparently had tried to continue her studies after she left Wyggeston, although it is not clear whether this was before, during, or after her dressmaking training. She planned some career of service to the poor, although she did not record the field in which she would serve: teaching, social research or social work, home mission work? Any of these could express her religiously based vocation. She could have studied at night school, been tutored by a family friend or someone from her Wyggeston circle, or studied on her own. There had been a free municipal library since 1870, so she had relatively good access to books and newspapers beyond those her family owned (and the Twilleys apparently were great readers, especially of improving books, judging by comments from family members and other evidence). Since she stayed in touch with Wyggeston friends, she probably had access to their families' libraries, which could have been substantial – but this too is speculation. There were places she could take classes; for example the Working Men's College in Leicester admitted women after 1880 and the fees were low, only a penny a class (although the subjects were fairly elementary). She may have tried to write more examinations during this period (although the reference to this is ambiguous, from a Canadian family member who was probably unfamiliar with English practices and may have been referring in any case to the examinations she wrote while a Wyggeston student). A later biographical sketch says, "Her deep sympathy with the enslaved gave her no rest, and in order to be of greater service she made an exhaustive study of social conditions." But whatever her mode of study, "her thirst for knowledge was stronger than her frail body, and resulted in a physical breakdown which necessitated the relinquishing of her studies, with intense regret." The nature and timing of her collapse is unclear, but she did suffer from "brain fever" when she was eighteen or twenty-one; this was a commonly used term for meningitis, some strains of which can be fatal. Although she remained intellectually active all her life, she never again attempted systematic academic work. Perhaps what her health could not support was the double burden of work and study. Most working class women faced that barrier, and most could not overcome it.[20]

Gertrude worked at home dressmaking. Despite her top-of-the-line title (and skills, probably), she likely did a range of sewing from prosaic household linens, servants' clothing, and workaday garments for working and middle class families, to special occasion dresses. She may have got some business from the middle class families and friends of her Wyggeston classmates; a family member in Canada told me he thought she had sewed in middle class homes. However, Gertrude's own comments suggest she worked at her parents' home; it is possible she went out to measure and fit, but did the cutting and sewing at home, although that was not the usual pattern for home-based dressmakers. She apparently was able to earn enough money to contribute to household expenses. At some point Gertrude bought her own sewing machine, a modern portable, hand-cranked, with a smart wooden cover/carrying case. She also could buy the odd luxury. She bought Fannie a book for her sixteenth birthday in 1893, a miniature Bible study guide that she inscribed, "May He who gave you to that world / Your wandering footsteps guide, / And give you heavenly grace and power, / That you may serve Him every hour, / Whatever may betide." (The Twilleys often gave each other books, so perhaps they were not considered luxuries.)[21]

By the 1890s, the older Twilley children were grown up. The activities of the children illustrate how complex the class/status situation was for this family, who straddled the boundary between working class and lower middle class. The boys learned to work in the family boot and shoemaking business (except Fred, who was left handed), although only Frank stayed with it in later years. Florrie, the oldest daughter, married Charlie Davie 11 September 1897, in a Baptist ceremony. She remained in Leicester and saw her family often. Florrie was lovely, intelligent, and very musical. We were able to find out virtually nothing about her education, although Fred did say in a letter years later that Florrie had spent four years with rich U.S. cousins in Boston (from the Richardson side). Other references to this family suggest they had visited Leicester sometime between 1890 and 1895. We know Florrie was in Leicester in 1891; if, as seems likely, she had returned to Leicester with her cousins by then, it is possible she had gone to school in the States in the late 1880s. We know little about her activities. She worked as a hosiery machinist in a factory (as did at least one of her Leicester cousins) at the time of her marriage. At twenty-six Charlie Davie was a year older than Florrie. A few weeks before their marriage Florrie had given Charlie an expensive photograph album, which I saw at her niece Connie MacDonald's in Brandon, Manitoba in June 1991. There were several shots in the album of Charlie and his chums in military uniform. Charlie was handsome, clean-cut looking. But Florrie may have married down a bit; Charlie was working as a railway porter at the time (British railway workers had excellent job security but low wages). His family came from West Coventry, his father was a warehouse worker. Gertrude did refer later to Florrie's having a "little business" of some sort; she may have kept working as a hosiery machinist after she married, although the most common pattern by then would have been a switch to outwork. Various evidence shows Florrie was interested in religious and political questions, although it is not clear how this interest translated into action.[22]

Gertrude's younger sister Fannie, born in 1877, had moved a step up when she married John Livesey in 1895; they had settled in his home town of Bradford, where he worked as a clerk. By 1896, Fred was fourteen and presumably out of school (if not earlier); he went to work in an office. The family needed the earnings of all its members. It may have been about this time that Gertrude and her mother did homework for a hosiery company, Cooper and Corah, to try to make ends meet. Fred later wrote on a photograph of the factory in a Leicester guidebook, "Mother and Gerty did outdoor work for these. I used to take the stuff in my noon hour." (Fred does not say if he was in school or had gone to work, so it could have been earlier.) They probably sewed seams of stockings, the most common form of hosiery outwork by then. This was a widespread working class strategy to increase family income; women married to artisans did not normally do it. Sometimes wives would seam only long enough to earn the cost of a specific item the family needed (winter boots, for example), but others were at it steadily for normal living expenses.[23]

Although times were tough economically, the period also offered exciting changes and opportunities. The oldest brother Wilfred had become involved with the Salvation Army, established in Leicester since the 1870s, and although he may have worked in the family shop for some years, he had moved out by 1891 and may already have gone into the Army. The family had attended the London Road Congregational church for years, and some of them continued to do so, but they did join Wilfred in Salvation Army activities at times. Fred recalled, "Oh, the Christmases I used to be out with the Salvation Army blowing a cornet." He had mixed feelings about the organization, especially in retrospect. Years later he recalled "the joy of welcoming back the erring ones to the fold," saying he "used to envy the returning lost sheep and sometimes wished I could leave the ranks of the ninety and nine for a bit. Brother Kay used to get into the ring and say 'Thank God I'm saved and happy. I have fifteen children and am on my happy way to Heaven.' Some good honest people in the Army but very droll. Splendid thing the Army is for a certain class."

Fred apparently did not consider himself or perhaps his family, as belonging to that class. "I don't think I would care much for the old-fashioned noisy Salvation Army meetings as a regular thing. There is so much circus noise about it and so much idiocy … There is such a large place in the world for just such an organization as the Army that it will not be me to ever feel above going to hear them or belonging to them," but he preferred a quiet service. "I believe, though, that the Army have the best system of making Christians because they exact a more exacting life of their followers than the ordinary church. Doers of the Word and not hearers only."[24]

Wilfred was not the only Twilley to be attracted to dynamic new religious movements; Gertrude, along with some of her maternal kin, got involved with a Baptist church which had been established by the charismatic preacher Frederick Brotherton Meyer in 1880, with William Fullerton in the pulpit since 1894. Melbourne Hall Evangelical Chapel possessed an attractive and imposing building, and groups for every imaginable evangelical activity. There were classes and lectures, groups for studying, for Bible women (lay women who operated neighbourhood mission rooms and did home visiting), for young people, older people, mothers, singles, marrieds, teachers' preparation. There were off-site Sunday Schools and Bible classes, roving groups called "moral and spiritual ambulance corps" in working class districts on Saturday nights breaking up fights, helping people, and preaching. They did prison work, ran halfway houses and a job service for unemployed men (window cleaning, messenger service), formed a Christian Police Officers' Association (they already had annual police and wives' teas), a Gospel Purity Association to protect girls, and a deaconess order. By 1897 there were 2500 members and the church magazine had a run of 4,000 copies. Melbourne Hall's membership crossed class lines; founders included substantial manufacturers and merchants and working class people.[25] Gertrude became a member in December 1897, along with John Leonard Dexter, a young cabinetmaker who was a lodger in her parents' house.[26]

Victorian middle class girlhood emphasized purity as a basic component of femininity; being ladylike, sensitive, gentle, and kind, usually meant being kept in the dark about anything remotely sordid, such as human sexuality.[27] Gertrude's ostensibly working class upbringing was remarkably similar in this respect, although she may have had some basic information about human reproduction in her biology and health classes at school. She "was delicate and did not reach puberty until nearly 16," she reported. She began menstruation at age seventeen, on the late side but within the normal range for girls of the day. Unfortunately her menses were extremely painful. "My mother took me to see a doctor and he said I was suffering from congestion of the ovaries and should be better when I married. My mother did not tell me what he said for a long time, and I was not engaged to be married anyway." In those times, girls were discouraged from exercising during menstruation, so there was little to do but suffer through these interludes. Gertrude apparently still felt some of the aftereffects of her bout with T B of the adrenal glands, and had difficulty sleeping in any case, but painful menses made it worse. As a consequence of the pain, she wrote, "I acquired what I now know to be a very sinful habit, but which at the time seemed to bring on the menstruation, and also to help me to sleep … I was deeply religious, and never thought that the habit of rubbing myself to produce a peculiar sensation was a sin against myself and everyone and God."[28]

Although Gertrude was uninformed about sex, she was not kept entirely unworldly; in this respect her upbringing was unusual for a sheltered girl. When she was in her late teens, her father gave her books about sin and vice.[29] One was W.T. Stead's *The Maiden Tribute of Modern Babylon*, a muckraking investigation of child sexual slavery, indecent in its subject matter. Stead had developed his talents as a crusading journalist while the editor of a small northern newspaper, and had become allies with Josephine Butler in her campaign to repeal the infamous Contagious Diseases Acts, before taking over the *Pall Mall Gazette* in London. Stead, Josephine Butler, Bramwell Booth (head of the Salvation Army), and a handful of other reformers had formed a private "Special Commission" to investigate juvenile prostitution in London. As part of their investigation, and with help from Salvation Army members, Stead had developed a scheme to buy a little girl, in order to dramatise the extent to which children were ill protected and easy prey for dissolute men. He published his findings as a series in his *Pall Mall Gazette* in July 1885, and thereafter in pamphlet form. The sensational exposé was part of a campaign to get legislation passed to raise the age of consent above its level of age twelve. Salvation Army officers were directly involved in the campaign; Wilfred Twilley may have been among those circulating petitions, and General William Booth distributed Stead's series from the Salvation Army headquarters. No doubt the Salvation Army connection played a part in James Twilley's decision to give Gertrude the book. But so might have the conjunction of politics and religion in Stead's analysis. A devout Congregationalist, he had written that democracy and socialism would have to combine with religion to try to bring this dreadful exploitation of children under control.[30]

James Twilley obviously wanted to prepare his daughter for the adult world. Although the subjects were indelicate, their treatment within the evangelical reform tradition rendered them acceptable for a soldier of Christ, albeit a carefully reared young woman. If my reading of her comments about her studies of social problems is correct, he may also have wanted to help her prepare for her life's work.

Gertrude later referred to Josephine Butler as a heroine; her family may have been supporters of Butler's campaigns for some time, although it is not clear whether Gertrude knew of Butler before the Stead booklet. Gertrude may have encountered the Contagious Diseases Acts repeal campaigns through her study of social problems.[31]

There were also personal reasons for acquainting Gertrude with information about human sexuality. By then she probably already had her first sweetheart, Willie (she does not give his last name), to whom, she said, she was true for over three years until he "just found someone prettier." She had several other brushes with romance, all without doubt extremely decorous and probably carefully chaperoned. Until she was twenty-one, she was oblivious to the possibility that she herself might be touched by the sinful practices that others were trying to eradicate. But that year, she wrote, "I got a book, as I knew absolutely nothing of life. I had never left home, never worked out, except for the two years learning to sew, never discussed sexual subjects, never heard a coarse joke or an impure word … In this book, I read, *to my intense horror*, a reference to the dreadful act [of masturbation] to which I have referred, and no words can describe the shame and horror which I experienced. I dared not tell my mother, and I know my father would have killed me if he thought I had done any wrong, as he was so good, and loved me so much." It was the end of innocence, for she had been innocent despite her reading. "I knew so much in theory," she said of that period, but her knowledge had been impersonal. Eventually she managed to forget "the early habit I so loathed ever since I had come to realize its licentious character [and] still believed I was a pure maiden." Whatever her regrets, her life was full, and probably happy.[32]

Gertrude married John Leonard Dexter 30 October 1899; she was 24, he 26. The wedding took place at Melbourne Hall, William Fullerton officiating. It may not have been a large and posh affair, but it was very properly done. Gertrude was dressed in a dove grey silk gown, wore a veil with an orange blossom wreath, and carried a shower bouquet; since she made all her own clothing (and probably most of her family's), her gown was no doubt lovely and most fashionable. Her new husband was from a middle class family that had moved relatively recently from the nearby countryside (where his father had been a farmer, according to the boy's birth certificate) into the town of Loughborough, about thirty kilometres north of Leicester, but a short distance by train. At the time the young couple were married, Gertrude's father-in-law was a cashier. The senior Dexters lived in a substantial two-storey mock tudor detached house with its name, "Rose Cottage," and the date of its construction, 1889, carved in a stone plaque above the front door. The house was surrounded by a fenced garden, in a pleasant area of town. How the son came to know Gertrude and lodge with the Twilleys is a mystery; nor is anything known about his training and employment at that period. However, a skilled cabinetmaker was in the better-paid segment of the working classes. The young couple lived for a time in "Gimson's Cottages," terraced housing built by the owners of a nearby works for their employees in 1878, on the edge of Highfield where the Twilleys had lived for decades. These were model working class dwellings of the period; Josiah Gimson (1818–83) had been an Owenite in his younger days, and was a leading local socialist and reformer, a model employer of the benevolent paternalist type. The houses were two or three storeys, with a parlour, living room, and kitchen on the ground floor, and bedrooms upstairs. How Leonard Dexter came to this address is not clear. He or his brother George Cecil, who had previously lived next door, may have worked at Gimson's Vulcan Works, which had opened in 1878 and employed about 350 workers to produce machinery and tools for manufacturing footwear, hosiery, and elastic web weaving, and household hardware and decorative iron casting. But by 1900 the cottages were not exclusively occupied by Gimson workers. Whatever the case, the newlyweds were not the sole occupants of number seven; they probably rented rooms. By January 1900 they had moved to another terraced house in the same neighbourhood, just across Spinney Hill Park from her parents; this is one of the family's addresses that can still be seen today.[33]

The marriage should have gone well. "My health at the time was fairly normal (as I supposed) and I had forgotten the early habit I so loathed ever since I had come to realize its licentious character, but I still believed I was a pure maiden and longed for marriage and children," Gertrude recalled. She had thought her husband shared her views, but he "told me he had no desire for children." The young couple "never lived together as husband and wife, only in the same house [and] the marriage was *never* consummated." Gertrude wrote, "Leonard told me that he had committed a sin that made him unworthy of being a father for a time – but I could sleep in his arms like a child ... I was frightened and unhappy." His refusal to consummate the marriage and his vague explanation are probably indications that he had venereal disease acquired through prostitutes who were infected by their customers; if that was the case, then he was unusually decent in refraining from infecting his wife and siring congenitally infected children. However, what is harder to understand is why he got married in the first place. There had been no hint of this situation before they married: years later she commented, referring to her readings on vice, that she had known "so much in theory, it is strange how I was deceived." But Gertrude had other crises to deal with that demanded her time, energy, and courage. The Boer War had begun three weeks before her wedding day, and Gertrude had quickly become a key figure in Leicester of the most radical antiwar group, the Stop-The-War Committee.[34]

The Boer War began 9 October 1899, after months (indeed years) of provocation and posturing. British leaders and most of the British public made patriotic noises about British liberty and high principles, but it was an imperial war between Britain and the Boer white settler South Africans, fought for ignoble reasons using shameful methods; "natives," as they were called, did not figure in the official view of the conflict except as the subject of white propaganda. The official line was that "the Boers posed a threat to the global security of the British Empire," as Richard Rempel says. The Tory government had split the Liberal opposition by appointing Imperialist Liberal Alfred Milner as High Commissioner to South Africa in 1897, so united party opposition on principle (or opportunism) was tactically impossible. Most religious denominations supported the war. Hugh Price Hughes, editor of the *Methodist Times* and himself a strong imperialist, estimated that 75 percent of Methodists were prowar; Quakers were officially antiwar (and supposedly Baptists but they did little as a body and Gertrude's Melbourne Hall supported the war); Congregationalists split; and a few from other churches joined the antis. Socialists and labour were split. (It is misleading to speak as if these were separate and distinct groups; Liberals, socialists, labour, and dissenters overlapped.) Passions were high in England; jingoism was the typical outlook, and those few who openly opposed the war did so at their peril.[35]

Gertrude was one of them. Her working class family had been part of the Liberal anti-imperialist movement of the late nineteenth century based in the dissenting churches and associated with Cobden, Bright, and Gladstone: anti-imperialist in their own eyes, although as James Hinton points out, free trade pacifism in a Pax Britannica world depended on "a firm belief that Britain's destiny was to serve the universal interests of [hu]mankind." Although I have little information about James and Eliza Twilley's views, there is one unmistakable piece of evidence: they named Gertrude's youngest brother Horace Gladstone Twilley (and this in 1886, four years after Gladstone had sent troops to occupy Egypt and caused some Radicals to speak of a lie in the soul of Liberalism).[36]

The antiwar response was rapid, largely from those who had been engaged in trying to prevent war from being declared; Quakers, for example, continued their letters, petitions, and protests. In Leicester, Charles Wynne, Independent Labour Party (ILP) leader and member of the local Quaker meeting presented a peace petition to the mayor and tried unsuccessfully to get him to call a town peace meeting. On the day war was declared, more than 34,000 Britons had already signed a petition for a peaceful settlement of the Transvaal dispute. Some socialist groups held protest meetings, and antiwar speakers were prominent on the agendas of working-men's clubs. Radical and Lib-Lab opposition politicians and women's groups and pacifist clergy spoke out. Of the three major antiwar groups, the Transvaal Committee predated the war by several months, the South African Conciliation Committee (SACC) was formed 1 November 1899, and the Stop-the-War Committee (STWC) was officially founded 24 December 1899 (the latter two groups were publicly launched in January 1900). This latter was the most radical and least rational and respectable in its activities, but jingoist hostility was so strong that even the most timid and polite opposition to the war caused riots, so differences of style and tactics are not particularly important here.[37]

W.T. Stead was a main force behind the Stop-The-War Committee; his bulletin *War Against War in South Africa* (*WAWSA*) began 20 October 1899 to circulate news of the activities of the antiwar campaigners who later formed the STWC. Richard Price has speculated that a determinant of whether a city had SACC or STWC as its antiwar focus depended on the presence of a strong Social Democratic Party branch; but in Leicester SACC and STWC worked together under the aegis of the local Peace Society. The Leicester Peace Society became a branch of the STWC in January 1900, although its members had been working as individuals and as a loose network since the outbreak of war. It was not affiliated with the British Peace Society (BPS), which dated back to earlier in the nineteenth century. The British Peace Society "kept its head down" as Jill Liddington puts it, and did not take a large part in the pro-Boer campaigns. Its situation in 1899 was complicated by the fact that well-known jingoist Hugh Price Hughes was a Peace Society vice president at the time. However, in December 1899 the BPS did send out 35,000 peace letters urging clergy to preach against war, and individual members and a few local branches were active.[38]

Some Leicester peace activists had previously been involved in W.T. Stead's Peace Crusade of 1898–99 in support of Tsar Nicholas II's proposals for developing international negotiation mechanisms that led to the Hague Peace Congress of May 1899. Stead had visited several European leaders to solicit their support for the tsar's proposals, and found little willingness to make a commitment. Deciding to focus on popular support, Stead printed a million broadsheets and produced a weekly newsletter called *War Against War* for several months, to publicise the objectives of the upcoming congress.

In December 1898 Stead launched his "International Peace Crusade," asking fellow citizens to sign up for a holy crusade for peace to culminate in a large conference in London on 1 March 1899. The rhetoric and networks were those of the evangelical dissenters, the methods were those of mass canvass, and the intended audience was popular and cross-class, rather than narrowly influential. A special committee was set up to attract working class support; the committee wrote a labour manifesto, which 500 men and women from the labour movement signed, and set out step-by-step suggestions for organising local support, making it clear that expenses would be paid if necessary. Stead wrote an appeal urging a similar committee to be set up to carry out a special campaign among women; women were working locally, he said, but there was no nationwide effort by that constituency. Apparently no national women's committee came of this, although the Women's Liberal Federation (WLF) circulated information in support of the Crusade and asked its members to participate. Women were active in supporting the tsar's proposal, and Ellen Robinson of the Peace Society had spoken in Leicester late in 1898 during her tour to publicise the Hague Congress. A town meeting was called in Leicester in aid of the Crusade in November 1898, and a meeting sponsored by the Independent Labour Party was held on 28 January 1899, featuring various prominent labour leaders. Leicester names appeared in Stead's Crusade newspaper.[39]

Although it is difficult to determine whether the Crusade had any real impact beyond the already converted, many large meetings were held, thousands of signatures were gathered, and it was a heartening experience for Crusade supporters. Because this campaign has not attracted much attention from historians, I know little more of its activities or how it fit into popular support for the establishment of dispute settlement mechanisms (for there was indeed such support in several countries, particularly amongst women's organisations such as the International Council of Women). Historian Douglas Newton concludes that there was widespread trade union support for the 1899 Hague Peace Conference. Stead attended the Hague peace congress as an observer from May to July 1899, published weekly reports to the tsar, and covered the congress extensively in the *Review of Reviews*, his current affairs digest. He was optimistic about prospects for peaceful settlement of international disputes; in 1899 there were over 425 peace organisations globally, forty-six of which were in Britain. In some British towns the Crusade groups established John Bright

League locals to carry on peace activism; although Leicester was not among those listed in the initial account of their founding, some activity may have continued there too. I have no direct evidence that Gertrude was involved in Stead's first Peace Crusade (certainly several of her Stop-The-War Committee comrades had been), but it seems likely, given her family's previous admiration for Stead, and their overlapping circles of religious and social concern.[40]

Gertrude was, she later said, the first woman to join the Stop-The-War Committee when the Boer War was declared. She meant in Leicester, presumably; her early STWC membership may imply pre-existing links. Stead's papers are not available or have been destroyed, so it is not possible to trace Gertrude's relationship with him, despite the efforts of Stead's biographer Joseph Baylen to find this evidence.[41] The information in *War Against War in South Africa* shows that she occupied a key position in Stead's STWC organisation. He set up a network of local collectors from among his contacts early in the war to distribute antiwar materials and collect signatures on stop-the-war petitions to the queen; a list of the official contacts appeared in the 5 January 1900 issue of *WAWSA*, and Gertrude was listed as his Leicester collector. By then she had sent in thirty completed antiwar memorials, quite a feat considering the intense hostility such views encountered.[42]

The Leicester end of the antiwar campaign can be followed through letters in the local papers, especially the *Midland Free Press* (*MFP*), the radical Liberal paper whose editor was one of the few that gave space to peace material. Editor Edwin Crew was personally opposed to the war, but he did not agree with the position of the Stop-The-War Committee. "Stopping it under present conditions is impossible. Going on with it may lead to our destruction as a nation, stopping it certainly would," he wrote. "Turning back would be the beginning of the end of the British Empire." Nonetheless, he printed STWC and other antiwar news, as well as the usual local labour, socialist, Liberal, temperance, cultural, political, and war news.[43] The antiwar material in Crew's paper illustrates the composition of the antiwar movement in Leicester, and thus, of Gertrude's associates in this period. The significance of these associations and the ideas of the antiwar movement for Gertrude extended far beyond the Boer War period; she would draw upon its lessons and themes for the rest of her life.

Information on particular women antiwar figures is scarce, but some were to be found in Liberal circles. There were two national Liberal women's groups. The Women's Liberal Association (WLA), which had a local branch in Leicester, did not officially protest the war until the mainstream Liberal party began to do so in the spring of

1901. Leicester WLA members were also active in the more radical Women's Liberal Federation (WLF), with 60,000 members nationally. The WLF was virtually unanimous in opposing the war, and on 10 October 1899 the officers had signed a national petition protesting the war and sent petitions out to the local associations for circulation. The WLF had been involved in "a frenzy" of antiwar activity since September 1899 which continued until war's end; a number of local branches contributed funds and workers to the STWC. Little has survived of the WLF records, and Leicester activities are not well documented, but some information can be found. For example, local peace activists Edith and Catherine Gittins were part of the Leicester WLA; at occasions such as the annual local WLA garden party, Catherine Gittins and others reported on WLF council meeting antiwar discussions.[44]

It is easier to find out about the men involved. One key figure in the local movement was William Wicks, a greatly beloved elderly temperance worker, a Unitarian active in adult education, who was well known as a writer and speaker and famous for his kindness. Wicks was a frequent correspondent on antiwar issues; he wrote that anyone who claimed to be a Christian and supported the war was a hypocrite and humbug. He lamented the lack of opportunity for refusing to pay war taxes. Wicks publicised the antiwar petitions that Gertrude was circulating. His granddaughter Nellie (who often recited at temperance and other cultural events) was also involved, contributing a poem entitled "And the devil laughed!" which criticised imperialist ambitions.[45]

Another influential figure in the peace movement, and in Gertrude's later life, was Congregationalist minister J. Ernest James. Like other antiwar clergy, he argued that the war was unchristian, and that Christians must act. In November 1899 he preached on the "criminal indifference of Christian men and women" as a factor in the failure of efforts to settle the Transvaal issue by peaceful arbitration. Each person had to take a share in the responsibility for the war, he said, quoting Lowell's dictum that "guv'ment aint [sic] to answer for it / God'll send the bill to you." He warned against callous fatalism, and urged his listeners to watch intently for the right moment to intervene to stop the war. In another sermon James attacked the prowar clergy's misuse of clever theological arguments to persuade their followers that it was acceptable in God's sight to support the war. It is not the soldiers who are to blame, he said, but rather "we Christian men and women who have employed them" to break commandments. If it were true that God advocated war, then "atheism would be my only refuge," he declared, but it was not true. War was antithetical to communion with God: "To tell me that a soldier can surrender himself to the lust of slaughter and yet retain through that experience the spirit of Christ, is to make a statement which my credulity will not accept." To claim that war was compatible with Christianity was a heresy. James had support for his views within his church; when one member objected, James offered to resign, but his management committee and the congregation as a whole refused to accept it. He was also admired in the broader community.[46]

Did Gertrude hear, as well as read about, these sermons? She shared James' views, and wrote in a similar vein for many years. She certainly heard nothing like this in her own church, Melbourne Hall. There were individuals who were antiwar, but William Fullerton preached support for the war. Gertrude was disgusted and angered; she ceased attending. Through the antiwar movement she became involved with local socialist groups, and as she put it, she "ultimately concluded that many atheists were better Christians than the professors of that faith," notably those with whom she became affiliated through the Stop-The-War Committee. "I found in these what I had vainly looked for amongst the Christians of my acquaintance."[47]

The Leicester Secular Society (LSS) was an important centre for pacifists in Leicester during the Boer War, providing a meeting place, institutional resources, and several leaders. The Secular Society was, as its name suggests, secular, but it was also one of the most important intellectual, cultural, and political groups in Leicester. Manufacturers, large and small merchants, labour leaders, socialists, ordinary workers, reformers of every stripe were represented in its membership. Others who were not official members attended its frequent public lectures and other events. Many Leicester socialists and labour activists were religious, in fact it sometimes seemed that dissenters made up the bulk of groups like the ILP. Leading Quakers, Baptists, Unitarians, Congregationalists, and for that matter, Anglicans, to name a few, appeared among the ranks of the left. Quaker Charles Wynne, for example, was Secretary of the local ILP, Wycliffe Congregational Church Committee member Archibald Gorrie was also on the ILP executive, and Anglican Lewis Donaldson was active in Christian Socialist, antipoverty, and unemployed groups for years.[48]

The Secular Society welcomed their religious comrades, as long as they did not try to foist their religious beliefs on the secularists; indeed, a bust of Jesus was included in the five figures of great representatives of Humanity that graced the face of the Secular Hall. Edith Gittins, a Unitarian, was a frequent speaker and led LSS discussion circles; William Wicks, another Unitarian, was also a familiar lecturer on history or social questions. Secularists attended some Christian events; for example, the Secularists' newsletter noted that several young members attended a lecture series at the Christian Social Union, and the Secularist organiser gave lectures at the young men's Christian Reform Society in 1900–01. Especially during the war, their shared antiwar commitments overrode doctrinal differences. The Secular Society was established in Leicester in 1853, and their large and modern Secular Hall, with a seating capacity of 600, many meeting rooms, a library, and even a swimming pool, had been open for eighteen years by the time the war began. Sydney Gimson, one of Josiah's sons (and a former Unitarian), was a key figure in the LSS and was also active in the antiwar movement. Most secularists were pro-Boer and the Secular Hall regularly played host to antiwar lectures and meetings. The organiser (today he might be called the coordinator or executive director) of the Secular Society, Frederick James Gould, had been an evangelical Christian with years of Bible study behind him when he became a secularist; he was a teacher in East London schools, had long been active in community and political affairs, and was an authority in "moral education" (which we might call "peace education") by the time he arrived in Leicester in 1899. He was to become an important figure in Gertrude's life, his influence enduring long after the Boer War brought her into his ambit through peace meetings and other Secular Society events.[49]

During the early weeks of the war when peace activists worked individually and often in isolation, Gertrude and her sister Florrie wrote antiwar letters, and got hate mail back. "The usual jingo epithets" included one letter saying "she was a cross-breed between the Irish Fenians and a pig." Initially, Florrie was more outspoken in print. Her husband Charlie Davie was a reservist and was called up within days of the declaration of war, and shipped off to South Africa. Florrie had, Gertrude later wrote, "very strong convictions of the unrighteousness of that war, and would not accept any of the money provided for the relief of soldiers' wives – except that part of her husband's pay to which she was legally entitled, and which was paid by the Government. All the rest she called 'blood money.' " Florrie had been involved in socialist antiwar activities on the war's eve. Just before its declaration she had written to the *Morning Leader*, the sole London daily to oppose the war, whose editor Spencer Leigh Hughes was an "old friend" of the Twilley family (but I have no information on the friendship or its origins). "Why should we encourage in the nation what we punish in the individual? The man who kills his fellow man, no matter how great the provocation, is punished by death on the gallows or a long term of imprisonment," she wrote. "What a glorious nation we are! We use our brains and spend our time trying to invent something more deadly, to kill men off a little more quickly, so that we can gain their territory. The financier and the politician looks upon South Africa and beholds in it a goodly pleasant land. He cares not that the way to it is paved with blood and corpses, tears, cries, groans and broken hearts. Let the politicians and the capitalists who will benefit thereby themselves go to the front ranks and fight if they think they are right." Hughes persuaded Florrie to write a series of articles on the plight of reservists' families, for which she was paid a modest sum; these appeared during the first few months of the war.[50]

Gertrude joined the war on the editorial page of the Leicester *Daily Post* in December 1899. She had been circulating W.T. Stead's peace petitions and must by then have made contact with other antiwar comrades, but this letter is apparently the first time she spoke publicly on the issue. In it she set out her credentials and grounds of argument: elite education, community respectability, patriotism and loyalty to British principles and traditions. She wrote in response to a prowar letter, asking as a former Wyggeston pupil the right of reply. "There is no truer Englishwoman in her Majesty's wide realm than I," she wrote, "but when patriotism becomes but another name for bloodthirstiness it is time to choose another word for loyalty to our country." The British were attempting to rob the Boers of their homeland and the Boers were fighting courageously in its defense. "It is cowardly and spiteful beyond all expression to vilify and slander those men, who like our own brave soldiers, have but risen at duty's call and gone forward to battle." Gertrude too had almost certainly been working with local antiwar socialists, most likely under the auspices of the local Secular Society. She made use of a theme often found in socialist lectures, a debate about social Darwinism. Local socialist thinkers were ambivalent about evolution theories; on the one hand they were scientific, but on the on the other they were used immorally to justify imperialism and inequality. "But it is ever thus, the weakest will go to the wall and the strong and powerful nation will exult in its triumph. But other nations now dead and dying, have gone on for a time, subjugating and sundering and who knows but our turn may come. While cathedrals are decorated with bullet-riddled banners and our little ones are trained to curse their enemies how may we expect the right to overcome?"

She identified the role of inequality at home in promoting imperialism abroad: "The Uitlanders were certainly much better off than the majority of men in England. Why have our young men gone out [to work in the] Transvaal? We all know why – because they could earn a living there, whereas, in England, our boasted free and glorious country, they could do little more than starve." The British were not willing to extend their fine principles to the Boers, expecting foreigners in Britain to abide by British law but not accepting that the same expectation was legitimate in South Africa; "I suppose the Boers have no right to the great principle we admire in our own countrymen," she wrote. "For their religion and their land they will shed their best blood, and I, for one, am not afraid to say that I consider this war to be an unholy, unjust and altogether unnecessary one ... What we want is the riches of the country, in spite of all the protestations to the contrary and it matters not that the blood of a few thousand of our and their men shall be poured out, so that the British flag shall fly proudly over the South African Republic and the Orange Free State. But we are paying a fearful price after all."[51]

There were several outraged replies in the letters page and privately. Gertrude wrote again early in January 1900:

Our country is engaged in a disastrous war, our brethren dying in South Africa, falling in an unworthy cause. The spirit of hate has taken possession of our land, towards those who for the moment we call our enemies. But by some at least, the shame of our country's crime is felt and we bow our heads in deep humiliation. Where is the spirit of charity? Where is the voice of the Christian church? ... If the glory of our empire depends on the sword, then it would be better for that glory to depart. There was a time when a story was told with pride about our great Queen when asked, what was the secret of our country's greatness, taking a Bible and telling the Ambassador that was the secret. But that day has passed away and we look to the power of arms, the number of our army and navy, and our man-slaying weapons, to bring us empire and greatness. After 1900 years of Christianity, at the close of a long and glorious reign, we have returned to what at best is but a relic of barbarian times, the murder of man by his brother ... The homes of our land are desolated, women and children helpless and alone, many of our lives shadowed by hourly anxiety for dear ones at the battle's front. And yet the war fever remains unabated. Women, otherwise tender and true are injected with the awful hate and children in our streets play at "killing Boers." We must cease to talk of "Christian England" for the spirit of Christ has departed from us. Even among the leaders of religious thought the war is tolerated ... I wish I could express myself more emphatically but I can only say I am filled with horror at the awfulness of this iniquitous war and with deepest sorrow at my beloved country's intoleration and blindness.[52]

Later that month a meeting of the Leicester STWC was held to unite local peace workers, an antiwar resolution passed, and the STWC joined with the local SACC to plan joint Peace Society activities. Peace Society members also continued their work in their own groups: by then, local Quakers Charles Wynne, Charlotte Ellis, and Alex Wilson were circulating peace appeals. As many as 30,000 antiwar pamphlets and leaflets were distributed in Leicester during the first fourteen months of the Peace Society's work. In the days before radio and television, and even after the spread of mass market newspapers (which usually represented a political party), groups depended on broadsides and leaflets to get their message across. The peace committees (and the prowar committees) printed many thousands of pamphlets and broadsheets. One study found that a prowar group, the Imperial South African Association, distributed 500,000 pamphlets in 1899 alone. But pamphlets distributed were not necessarily pamphlets read; public meetings were crucial methods of communication and recruiting. The Leicester Peace Society held its first public meeting in the Co-operative Hall on 20 February 1900. The invited speaker was S.C. Cronwright-Schreiner, an English South African journalist (and husband to the well-known writer Olive Schreiner, whose name he took). He had been a war correspondent for the Manchester *Guardian*, working behind the Boer lines. He came to England in January 1900 at the invitation of antiwar groups, to give lectures on the situation. The Leicester meeting had strong support from a number of important constituencies; twenty-three Trades Council members were conspicuously present. STWC members William Wicks and Jabez Chaplin, socialist city councillor and LSS member, were also prominent on the platform; Chaplin was in the chair.[53]

The Leicester meeting was the "most uproarious" ever held in the town. Prowar bullies forged tickets and packed the inside of the hall, where more then a third of the crowd were "violently hostile and were there with the purpose of wrecking" the meeting. The organisers found out about the forged tickets too late to issue new ones. As a stopgap measure they had hired police guards who were supposed to admit only those who had "endorsed" (i.e., genuine) tickets; the guards were either inefficient or intent upon sabotaging the meeting. Cronwright-Schreiner reported that rowdies "came armed with dangerous and offensive missiles, with the fixed object of breaking up the meeting"; he thought some of them had been paid to do this. Once the disruption started, the police did not intervene effectively and were more in sympathy with the bullies than the meeting organisers. At one point a police officer was observed leading a disruptive chorus. The standard disruptive tactic was to sing patriotic songs ("God save the Queen," "Rule Britannia," and "Soldiers of the Queen") so loudly that speakers could not be heard. Rowdies also threw eggs, flour, and chunks of wood. Not all the prowar listeners were there with the intention to prevent the speakers from being heard; some planned to listen, debate, and then attempt to amend or defeat the antiwar resolution that the meeting would almost certainly attempt to pass. However the rowdies made that democratic method of dealing with disagreement impossible to carry out. Cronwright-Schreiner succeeded in getting across part of his message in a question and answer session, but was reduced to speaking to reporters seated in the front rows; the hall became so noisy that most of his comments were lost. Various other speakers had tried, with no better luck. The antiwar resolution was moved and seconded and passed. Eventually the mood became so threatening that women left the hall. Outside the hall an even larger crowd cheered and heckled and passed an antipeace resolution, then went off to the pubs to celebrate. The local press carried an account of the meeting's disruption but little was made of the forged ticket tactic, except in the *Midland Free Press*, which commented upon an accusation that just as the Boer War was caused by "lying, forgery and fraud," so were those methods used to disrupt the meeting.[54]

Who were the rowdies? That question would be asked often in the early months of 1900, as dozens of meetings were disrupted, and those who dared to speak against the war were harassed and sometimes assaulted. The rowdies in Leicester were mostly younger men and well-to-do middle aged men. In other cities they were sometimes university students. These were not simply spontaneous working class mobs. As Richard Price says, "The recurrent feature of a small group of middle-class men and youths deliberately" creating a mob disturbance at peace meetings was "unmistakeable." A meeting of the Leicester Trades Council a week later came to the conclusion that a good portion of the rowdies had been tipsy. It is noteworthy that antiwar supporters were at pains to speak of their patriotism, their support for the brave boys fighting, and their contributions to the fund to support the reservists' families; Gertrude's lifelong pacifism would reflect this distinction between the wicked policies and greedy elites that caused war, and the courageous sacrificial lambs who were sent to fight it.[55]

A week later MP and labour leader Keir Hardie spoke to a crowd of a thousand at another peace meeting at the Corn Exchange, held by the Leicester ILP. This time the organisers were forewarned and managed to prevent infiltration by jingoists. The meeting went off peacefully, with sharply critical stirring speeches and an antiwar resolution passed without trouble. Other antiwar activity continued in the town; the Reverend J.E. James preached an antiwar sermon to the representatives of Leicester's Adult Schools at the organisation's quarterly meeting, without incident. Prowar speakers in turn took the opportunity to impugn the motives and conduct of antiwar groups at their own meetings, but no large public prowar meetings were held in this period. A "Limp" (Liberal Imperialist) meeting was held but the attendance was small. The letters page of the *Midland Free Press* featured accusations that Cronwright-Schreiner had been in the pay of the Boers, rejoinders, and criticisms of the war, capitalism, and jingoism.[56]

Gertrude's sister Florrie figured in the debate. Responding to a particularly sharp speech at a prowar Constitutional Club meeting, she attacked the Limps and Tories in a rousing letter that illustrates the complexity of the debate on the war and its impact on the working classes. She pointed out that many working class people were "blinded by khaki" and that political careers would be made and parliamentary seats gained through jingoism. Issues of principle were clouded by opportunism, she argued.

Probably it would do the workingmen of England good to go back a little time to the days of their forefathers and then see which they would prefer, Liberalism or Toryism. I remember driving with a friend of mine through a village in the South of England. The village was owned by one man and every tenant in that village was obliged to belong to the Church of England. When the countryman votes for the Liberal party it is because he knows what he is voting for, not for Imperialism abroad but for freedom at home.

It is the fashion at the present time for supporters of the government not only to attack the principles of Liberals but also to criticise their persons and habitation … As I am a woman and not a voter, it might be thought that I have no right to speak. But Imperialism is no respecter of persons or sex, it not only invades the country but it invades the home; it drags from the hearth the women who are perfectly contented to do their duty in a sphere that is rightly their own. The breadwinners are taken, the mothers are left to bear a double burden for themselves and their children. Then the working men complain that the women do their work and help to lower wages. And finally, Imperialism means that God has created thousands of men for the express purpose of being slaughtered. Contact with men and women of other races and colour led me to the conclusion that the Anglo-Saxon had not a monopoly on all that was good; a policy of Imperialism is only another name for national suicide. The Nonconformist mission is to uplift and ennoble our weaker brethren, in the same spirit that our Master did, and for what we do we have good authority. Old-fashioned Nonconformists get their authority from an old-fashioned book but we call it the New Testament.

Gertrude's husband may also have been involved in the antiwar movement. The *Morning Leader* listed some of the names of those who had written antiwar letters there was no room to print; the name John Dexter appears in a lengthy list in February 1900, although no town is mentioned.[57]

W.T. Stead wrote in mid-March 1900 that twenty-eight antiwar meetings across the country had been disrupted and broken up, the local press often inciting the attacks. "It must be noted, however, that no person was killed at any of these demonstrations, although many had cuts, concussions, and broken bones." Although there had been no major disruptions in Leicester following the Cronwright-Schreiner debacle, bullies still patriotically harassed and assaulted those who spoke out against the war. The attacks usually were verbal, but in some cases threats of violence were carried out.[58]

The war came closer to home for the Twilleys late that March; James Twilley was struck on the head by a cane or umbrella by a jingoist as he was rising to speak against the war at a meeting. He went home and lay down for a rest, as he felt shaky. He died a few days later, according to family stories. The coroner found his death was caused by heart failure. Exactly what happened is not clear. A biographical article on Gertrude said her father was "mobbed … for taking part in a peace meeting, badly mauled by the tools of Capitalism and dying a few days later of a broken heart." His son Fred said years later that his father "got terribly knocked about," but the attack was not discussed in the newspapers, nor was it or anything else about the war mentioned in the report of testimony at the coroner's inquest. Presumably Eliza did not press the connection, for reasons that are far from clear. Perhaps, given the hate mail that Gertrude had received (and Florrie may have fared no better), it was too dangerous. Shop windows had been smashed for displaying peace signs, and mobs had attacked private homes of peace leaders in some cities. Aside from sorrow, there were grave consequences for a family that lost its chief breadwinner: what was Eliza Twilley to do? She was listed as proprietor of the business for several years following her husband's death. However, given her age – she was over 50 – it seems unlikely that she helped make the shoes. Frank could keep working in the family boot and shoemaking business, Fred had a job, Horace was by then fourteen and probably working, whether at boot and shoe work or in the yarn business. They would help her, but if times had been hard before, they must have been harder then.[59]

Gertrude's life must already have been difficult enough, given hostility against peace activism, and her father's death doubly painful for its circumstances. But her marriage had also come apart by the spring of 1900. "A few months [after their marriage], my husband stole from the Church and was written out. I could not bear the shame but tried to work and keep him, for I believe he loved me, as far as it was in his nature, and I certainly loved him ... and though he disappeared and I do not know where he [was] I ... never ceased to pray for him." Gertrude was, to say the least, stunned by this turn of events. John Leonard Dexter was removed from the Melbourne Hall Church Roll on the recommendation of the elders, 27 June 1900. Without knowing anything about his circumstances it is impossible to guess what he took, or why, or what their relationship was like.[60]

Florrie had her own problems at this time. Aside from any opprobrium she faced for speaking out against the war, she also had to cope with being a reservist's wife. Gertrude later wrote about one experience:

A certain lady (well-intentioned no doubt) visited the home of another soldier's wife, who happened to be a friend of my sister's. Here, she found a pretty, well-kept home. looking around the dainty little parlour, she remarked, "You will not need help at present. You can sell your piano and many other things." "I do not wish to part with my home," was the broken-hearted reply. My sister's indignation knew no bounds. Soon afterwards, the lady visited her, and my sister, knowing who she was, remarked: "You are Lady So-and-So, are you not? I suppose you are the woman who insulted the lady down the street. I presume you have come to insult me also. Would you be good enough to leave my house at once?" I hope the lady learned the lesson my dear sister intended, for the days of patronising charity are fast passing away from us.

Florrie had some kind of small business or other paid work to keep her afloat; in fact, she "had a nicer home for her husband to return to than the one he left," Gertrude reported. Florrie had no children to support. For those who did, things could be grave indeed and they had little choice but to accept patronising charity if it were offered.[61]

Not surprisingly, the suppression of dissent caused free speech to become an issue after March 1900. Heckling in Parliament was one thing; but breaking up legal public and private meetings and assaulting speakers and members of the audience was another. Local authorities seldom intervened effectively, often seeming to support the mobs by their inaction. Indeed some local authorities openly supported jingoist mobs. Local newspapers encouraged disruptions (although they denied they urged violence) by saying that antiwar statements should not be allowed and anyone expressing such unpopular and provocative opinions invited attacks and deserved what they got. Meanwhile, supporters of the war condemned the Boers for alleged failures to support British liberties, the securing of which for

Britons in South Africa was an object of the war. Of course not all proponents of the war agreed that the rights of opponents should be suppressed, but neither the government (as a debate in the House of Commons made clear) nor prowar leaders were prepared to do anything to prevent that from happening. Such lapses of logic were pointed out in antiwar pamphlets and from platforms, to the extent that public platforms could be secured, as hall rentals were refused to antiwar groups by owners who did not want their property trashed by mobs. Nonetheless, antiwar activity in Leicester continued. As Charles Wynne had reported to the annual meeting of the Socialist Quaker Society that May in London, "The South African war overshadows everything in Leicester."[62]

Florrie remained involved in editorial page debates. Her letter of early May 1900 defending the soldiers and attacking the imperialists illustrated the Radical and Nonconformist analysis typical of a good part of the movement. She wrote,

Some days ago I saw in my morning paper two pictures: one was the picture of a tent full of British soldiers lying stiff and cold in Spion Kop. I know what my impressions were at the time I saw the illustrations and I must confess they have undergone no change. I thought those men were "murdered." [Another letter writer] wants to know "who are the murderers." There is a text in the Sacred Writings which reads thus: "He that hateth his brother is a murderer," and we find that in the majority of cases it is not a spirit of hatred and revenge that animates our soldiers; it would however be a very wonderful thing if among so many thousand of our soldiers there were not some who forgot for a time what "civilised warfare" means. The cry of "Avenge Majuba" is not the cry of the solder; it is the cry of the "Yellow Press," it is the cry of the men who tried to introduce the seven days newspaper, the men who would rob us of our greatest blessing, the "day of rest." These are the men whose hearts are bowed down with sorrow because of the woes of the "Uitlanders" and the oppressions of the "natives," the men who at present appear to be the masters of the Press and of public opinion not only in England but in South Africa. Not only have our soldiers proved themselves to be brave, they have also shown us that they are not lacking in chivalry. It was the colonists who jeered at the Boer prisoners when they were passing on their way to exile, not the soldiers; it is the colonists who are clamouring for compensation for themselves and disenfranchisement and confiscation of property for their enemies; it is the colonists who are proposing that the farms should be taken away from the rebel Dutch and given to the Loyalists. Loyalty with them is not a matter of sentiment; it must be made to be what the "colossus" calls the British flag, a "commercial asset."

Was Florrie a STWC member? Her few letters suggest such was the case, but no records are available.[63]

During the summer of 1900 there were open air peace meetings every Sunday evening in the market place in Leicester, reportedly with "no trouble." The ILP held another peace meeting at the corn exchange featuring Harold Rylett. The Secular Society held a number of antiwar meetings in the spring and summer of 1900: Ernest James and Thomas Adcock spoke on militarism, and Emily Hobhouse and E. Mallet of the SACC spoke on conciliation. Hobhouse had just orchestrated a unique and successful peace meeting for several hundred prominent women in London, the concluding resolution of which was an expression of sympathy for "enemy" women.[64]

In the midst of these clashes and high feeling over the war, Gertrude fell into despair. She had good reason: her father's death, the stress of antiwar work in an atmosphere of hatred and threat, and her husband's unforeseen disgrace, which could not help but taint her name too and humiliate her among the Melbourne Hall congregation (who had been her community of peers for many years, despite her recent disgust over their prowar views). All this became too much to bear. Frightened, miserable, she got sick. "The doctor said I had nervous depression and I stayed with a sister for a few weeks – but she did not understand, because I could not open my mind, or tell anybody what was troubling me," Gertrude wrote years later. Not surprisingly, her sister Fannie concluded Gertrude had a miscarriage and was too upset and embarrassed to tell anyone. "The June after [the wedding] I attempted suicide by hanging myself with a clothesline." Although her family tried to take good care of her and help her back to health, she did not perk up. Goodness knows there was little to be optimistic about, personally or politically. By the end of the summer, a new issue had arisen: atrocities in the conduct of the war. The British were seizing livestock and crops and burning farms to prevent noncombatants from providing food and supplies to their Boer menfolk who had taken to the countryside after a series of defeats, and turning out the farm women and children to survive as best they could on the veld without adequate food, clothing, or shelter. This was a violation of conventions on the conduct of warfare, but the British hid behind technicalities to claim it was legitimate. Legitimate or not, the authorities attempted to deny or conceal the details of their farm burning policies and activities.[65]

The general election of October 1900 confirmed the majority support for the Tory war policy (and the effectiveness of Tory tactics such as a large election poster with the slogan "Radical traitors in correspondence with the enemy," or the use as a campaign slogan of the accusation by the mayor of Mafeking: "Every seat lost to the government is a seat sold to the Boers"). But as more information became available about the farm burnings (and about routine looting of Boer private homes by British soldiers), criticism of the war increased. There was reportedly somewhat less intolerance of pro-Boer opinions, perhaps a greater willingness to listen, in some locales. The Leicester Peace Society held several well-attended meetings that autumn. There is no record of these local discussions of the war, but it is evident that in Leicester as elsewhere, atrocities were a major topic. They were often denied or downplayed. Some people defended the policy as necessary to shorten the war, but as one WLF member said, "If the burning of farms could be called a terrible necessity, we might resort to anything, even to the poisoning of wells and any mortal thing in order to sweep out our enemy from their own country."[66]

The farm burnings were bad enough, but they led to worse. Homeless women and children were illegally herded into refugee camps set up by the British for that purpose. This was done perhaps partly out of humanitarian motives, and it no doubt was seen as a necessity, but the camps were set up for the express purpose of tucking away the families where they could not be in contact with their menfolk fighting with the Boer commandos. The British denied that the women and children were prisoners. This situation might have been unremarkable, as wars go, and forgetting the question of how these noncombatants had become refugees in the first place, but the British set up and ran these "concentration camps," as they were called, so incompetently (presumably incompetence rather than deliberate policy) that the nonprisoners died in droves. Emily Hobhouse had started a women and children's relief fund, and herself went off to South Africa early in December 1900 to assure the funds were properly used and to investigate conditions, sailing on the same ship as Quakers Joshua Rowntree and a nephew of Liberal MP John Ellis, who were travelling for a similar purpose.[67]

Despite official waffling, the Leicester Peace Society decided it had enough evidence to issue an appeal in December 1900, describing the violation of British promises made early in the war, the contraventions of international law, and the mistreatment and imprisonment of noncombatant women and children. "No ends can justify these means ... [this] disregard of truth, international law, and humanity," the appeal said. Such tactics were "more damaging to British prestige than any defeat." The appeal had been signed by more than a hundred "representative men and women of our town," in addition to the thirteen names published. The antiwar *Morning Leader* had sent J.M. Robertson to investigate the concentration camps, and he spoke at numerous public meetings about his discoveries after he returned in December 1900. One of these lectures was given to a packed hall at the Leicester Secular Society, on 6 January 1901. F.W. Rogers commented concerning the event, "A crowded house gave attentive hearing, and this change in the local attitude to such questions was significant of much." Robertson used lantern slides to illustrate his presentation, "Imperialism in Action." His audience were electrified, horrified, and if Sydney Gimson's reaction is any indication, badly shaken by Robertson's revelations. The lantern slides made his claims more difficult to disbelieve, and the human suffering involved more difficult to forget. Although I have no evidence that Gertrude attended Robertson's talk, it would be surprising if she had not, given her close involvement with the Peace Society. If Gimson was shaken, Gertrude would have been severely upset.[68]

Early attempts to publicise concentration camp conditions and death rates had been dismissed as inaccurate or mere propaganda, but in February 1901, John Ellis, who had eyewitness information from his nephew, raised the issue in the House of Commons. Despite government shilly-shallying, within a few weeks official information began to dribble out. On 24 May 1901 Emily Hobhouse returned from her tour, and when the government refused to make real improvements to conditions, she published a lengthy report detailing the dreadful conditions in the camps and the resultant thousands of deaths of women and children caused by overcrowding, exposure, and inadequate sanitation and diet. Her report was given to each MP and widely circulated through the WLF, SACC, and other networks, and several journals reprinted excerpts; Hobhouse herself went on a speaking tour. "The effect was electrifying," as Jill Liddington says. Joshua Rowntree's report was also circulated. Gertrude surely must have read Hobhouse's report or similar material. Like others, she must have felt heartsick that the government and British soldiers could have done this, the populace supported policies that led to this, and the peace movement failed to arouse the conscience of the nation sufficiently to stop it. In addition, there was talk of the possibility of conscription, and local peace activists agitated in opposition.[69]

Another severe blow was the death of William Wicks, who had been a stalwart of the Peace Society, and apparently also to Gertrude personally. Wicks died 5 June 1901; the *Midland Free Press* was filled with tributes and reminiscences for more than two weeks. Gertrude contributed a memorial poem, commenting, "I knew him best as a member of the Peace Society, but for all his noble work he deserves the honour of all his townsmen and women." The poem has little to recommend it in a literary sense, but is interesting for what it reveals of her views of his work and reward. The first three stanzas follow:[70]

Called above – to a high sphere, a hero has left the field,
No more in the cause of peace or truth, his trusty sword to wield;
No crown of laurels adorns his brow, no place in the roll of fame,
Midst loud acclaims of a country's voice, is assigned to his honoured
    name.

He has lived in the strength of the loving God – His foes to overthrow,
And drink and crime have staggered oft, at his true and well aimed blow.
But his work is done, and a gap is made in the ranks that fight with sin,
And those who are left must harder strive, that the Prince of Peace may
    win.

We need not weep as we speak his name, for his work was nobly done,
And the crown he wears in the shining land has been bravely, grandly
    won.
He has followed the steps of the holy Christ, and the part of right hath
    trod,
Fulfilling the glorious mission of a man in the image of God.

Gertrude's message was one of hope and peace, victory in the struggle. But Gertrude herself was fast losing hope and peace in a struggle of her own.

2 Defeat And Victory: Collapse, Recovery, Respectability (1901–11)

Gertrude had been living at home with her mother since the summer of 1900; it had been a painful time for her, and she became increasingly upset after April 1901. About the time that William Wicks died early in June, she began to fall from distress into illness. By the end of that month, she was in a terrible state, and for a week had been extremely agitated, unable to sleep or eat or put a coherent sentence together. Her worried family decided that Dr Shearer, the family physician, should take her to the Leicester Borough Asylum for the Insane on the outskirts of the town. The construction of Towers Hospital (as it is known) had begun in 1867, and by 1901 there were several substantial buildings, a farm area, and pleasant treed grounds. "Lunacy reform" in the late Victorian period led to more humane treatment in public asylums catering to the working and lower middle classes. Victorian cures for mental breakdown emphasised moral perspectives. "Moral management" was the favoured treatment: a carefully structured and highly controlled daily routine in a calm atmosphere and pleasant surroundings. Feminist psychiatric history tends to focus on the social construction of mental illness in Victorian middle class women, which does not fit Gertrude's circumstances very well. Nor does it resolve the ambiguity in debates about organic factors in mental illness. However, it is helpful in understanding Gertrude's probable treatment at the Leicester Asylum. As Elaine Showalter notes of this approach, the ideal was that the medical superintendent of the asylum "felt affectionate concern for his patients that filled his days with religious purpose and emotional satisfaction." Although the ideal was not necessarily applied, it does sound as if that were the case from Gertrude's perspective. She admired Dr Baker, the medical superintendent whom she later called "God's Good Man." Long after her recovery, she believed that he cared for her wellbeing, kept him posted on her doings, and sought his advice. She stayed in touch with him for many years.[1]

Discovering information about Gertrude's illness helped to solve a crucial research puzzle. I had learned from Canadian sources in 1986 that Gertrude had been ill about this time, but knew no details. One family member had overheard things as a small child that suggested Gertrude had been seduced by a smooth-talking young cabinetmaker at whose middle class and rather grand family home she was sewing, and there had quickly been a shotgun wedding, to the dismay of his family. This person thought that there had been a difficult childbirth and the child had died, at which point the inlaws had sent Gertrude home, saying there was no need for the marriage to continue and they would have it annulled. However, church records subsequently had shown that to the contrary, John Leonard Dexter had been a lodger in the Twilley household and that he and Gertrude had known each other for several years before they married. However, a difficult childbirth or stillbirth remained a possibility. Family members mentioned a mental breakdown of some sort; I speculated it might be postpartum depression. But Gertrude's Towers Hospital admission form suggested otherwise: the brother (no indication of which one) who had given the intake information had said he thought her marriage had never been consummated. This explained why registry office staff had been unable to find information on a possible child of her first marriage. Later sources indicated there had been no child.[2]

The details of the hospital stay are scanty. Regulations required that a patient's biography, occupation, family and medical history, and condition must be recorded within seven days after entry; there were to be weekly reports for the first month, monthly reports thereafter, and so on with diminishing frequency, supplemented by additional reports in the case of anything unusual. Although these reports do comment on her behaviour, outlook, or reactions, they rarely say what circumstance gave rise to these; for example they may say she was upset but not about what, or that she worked industriously, but not at what. Thus it is very difficult to judge if she was sad, for example, about something dreadful that really happened or something imaginary. Given that she had been a dissident, the lack of contextual information in the record makes the question of what was "normal" still more troubling. When she went into the hospital, the medical certificate noted, "She suffers from acute mania, cannot carry on any rational conversation, rambles from one subject to another, imagines she can see angels." Gertrude wrote many years later of this period that she was "most intensely happy. I thought I was going to Heaven and passed through states of great rapture, and saw visions of entrancing beauty."[3]

Once admitted, the asylum staff noted that she danced and sometimes flung bits of clothing about. She was affectionate to the nurses, but sometimes tried to strike them. Despite her incoherence, she was clear that she did not want to be called Dexter, but Twilley. She did not sleep or eat well for the first month she was in hospital. But by the end of August, the record noted that she was much better, "orderly and industrious, working in an intelligent fashion," although still overtalkative. Notes for the remainder of the summer comment on her improved health, and by the end of October the file said that she had put on weight, behaved in a "rational and intelligent way and is usually industrious," although she still seemed "rather talkative and emotional in her manner" at times. Just before Christmas they noted continued wellbeing, but added, "Is a little troubled at times." This sounds straightforward but reveals little. There were chaplaincy services, and patients were allowed library access and visitors, but the record does not show how often Gertrude availed herself of these. What subjects caused her to become emotional in her manner or troubled? If she regularly read newspapers and magazines and talked to visitors, then she may have been aware of the suffering and death of thousands of Boer women and children in concentration camps; this issue was widely discussed within the Liberal Party and in various periodicals and dailies. If she were upset about this, would the staff have considered this reasonable and a sign of normal health, or of excessive emotionality? But she may have been more or less cut off from current events; during periods of upset, she almost certainly would have been.[4]

Early in January 1902 Gertrude was released for a month's trial. But she returned after a week, saying she felt depressed and suffered from headaches and other assorted ailments. Well into spring and summer she reportedly remained easily upset and had headaches, although by early August she was again described as orderly, rational, intelligent, and only occasionally troubled. She went home again in October 1902, but after two weeks, according to the case file, she decided she was still too depressed and wanted to go back. For several weeks, she was "in a very silent state and seldom speaks. Says she shall never be well again." It was not until February 1903, according to the case notes, that she was "brighter." She was not well physically, and had ceased to menstruate some time before, the notes said. It is possible she had become very thin, as concern about her eating habits appears throughout the record, and in July 1903 the record noted approvingly that she had gained some weight. At that time she still had periods of feeling quite depressed, according to her case file, and although she was usually cheerful, the file said, she told the staff that she would "never be as she was formerly."[5]

Although the records rarely mention her activities, it is clear that she was not idle during her illness. The entry for 11 November 1903 noted, "She has a very high degree of intelligence and is capable of writing poetry and prose of a very remarkable kind. Employs herself at sewing." Until the spring of 1904, according to the records, she went up and down, sometimes cheerful and working well, other times quite gloomy or depressed. "She says she has lost all her natural feelings and has no affection for anyone," noted the entry for 25 April 1904. Three months later, the entry commented, "Frequently very depressed, she has a desire to obtain impossible objects." But it does not say what she got depressed about or what she longed for that she could not have. Conversations with angels? A university education? World peace? Health and happiness? That November, the entry expanded on this observation: "She gets very depressed at times and always appears to be striving after some ideal existence that she is unable to obtain. Sometimes expresses a wish to commit suicide but she never makes any attempt. Is industrious and intelligent. Is in fair bodily condition." She got worse still at the beginning of 1905. She had been spending most of her time writing poems, but had become "too excitable to do anything. She sings and chatters and sometimes insults people." She slept badly, and got thinner again. For the remainder of the year she was in bad shape, very upset, closer to acting on her suicidal feelings, verbally abusive, and at one point in January 1906, smashed the crockery during an argument in which she stood up for another patient (the question in dispute is not recorded). Yet by the end of January 1906 she seemed to be fine. She was "discharged as recovered" 2 May 1906 and went home to begin her life again.[6] Care had been more or less custodial. The staff tried to encourage patients to eat and sleep well, take moderate exercise, and occupy themselves in pleasant and useful routine. They recorded no medications except aloe (perhaps for constipation) and iron for amenorrhea, and the occasional sedative at night; if there were any treatment, it probably consisted of kindness. As she said later, "I had nothing but kindness from everyone ... I recovered completely."[7]

What was all this about? Given the upheavals in her religious, political, and personal life from the fall of 1899 until she entered the hospital in June 1901, there was plenty to push her over the edge. Her case record is not much help, offering only ambiguous clues. For example, Gertrude had rejected her married name and by implication her marriage. She was caught in an impossible situation: she could not have a normal or even superficially respectable married life, given her husband's apparent unwillingness or inability to carry out his part. But neither could she resume her single life as if the marriage had never happened. As far as the state was concerned, she was married to him.[8] She apparently did not eat for some periods: recent studies of anorexia nervosa in the Victorian period have stressed the complex meanings and sexual implications of appetite and the lady-likeness of physical weakness and illness in Gertrude's time. Was the death of William Wicks another last straw, recalling her father's death, and coming as it did on the heels of concentration camp revelations that struck at the heart of her ideals of British decency? But stress alone may have been enough: her earlier illnesses suggest that her endocrinological system may have been damaged, and perhaps the stress of the war years and her personal circumstances exacerbated previous damage.[9] Was she unable to be pragmatic (or so we usually judge it) about what was do-able, or what she had to settle for, whether this was on behalf of society or just herself as an individual? And was what she had to settle for a reasonable and fair arrangement? Was she really "crazy" for all or part of this time? Why did she get well? The more I read and think about this, the less I feel able to say what happened. But for years to come she was apparently fine, or at least she never recorded any recurrence of her illness, whatever its cause and cure had been.

It is not possible to tell whether any of her published poems were among those written during her stay in the asylum, although I have a hunch some were. One poem excerpted below seems especially likely, given that she had seen angels during her hospital stay: "God's Angels," published in the *Midland Free Press* in October 1907:[10]

Not all in Heaven God's angels dwell, But here on earth below,
Where suffering bows the weary head, And poverty and woe,
Clothed – like their Lord – in human form, Like Him, they live to bless,
And make Love's flowers to bloom anew, In earth's vast wilderness.

I saw, within a place of pain, One move with gentle tread;
No wings he wore of radiant light, No halo crowned his head;
And yet I felt, as by the beds Whereon the sick ones lay
He stayed to comfort and to heal – An angel passed that way.

For there, beside the shrouded form, Another stood to weep,
And whispered, as the eyes grew dim, "This is not death, but sleep":

And, as she wept for grief of mine Mourning my loved one gone,
It seemed that round her brow so calm, A crown of pity shone.

In vision I can see them stand With calm and holy eyes,
There in the Golden Land of God, Glad with a great surprise:
Where Christ shall say to all His own – "Ye did it unto Me,
Come, share with Me my Father's Throne For all Eternity."

Gertrude began to publish her poems after her recovery, they appeared regularly in the *Midland Free Press* after March 1907. Most were on religious subjects. Some referred to Bible stories or figures in the history of Rome or Greece, but whatever the purported topic, they usually contained a lesson. Was she paid for the weekly poems? Regularly published writers generally were paid, and such contemporaries of Gertrude's as the ILP's educational reformer Margaret McMillan made a good part of her living from socialist newspaper articles. But it seems likely that Gertrude was not paid for poems, although she may have been paid for the few articles she contributed in this period.[11] She and her mother lived with the Twilley sons, but she still had to earn her living. Legally, John Leonard Dexter was required to support her, although he apparently did not. She continued to be known as Gertrude Dexter, but according to her later comments about this period, she never saw Dexter again after early 1900, and had no idea of his whereabouts. She may have resumed dressmaking, although she never referred to it in her published pieces.[12]

The poems above all are religious expressions, revealing in religious terms Gertrude's view of herself and her place in the world. She had a passion for justice, and her experience of a living faith permeated everything in her life. This is very difficult to understand for someone (like me) who neither experiences things that way nor lives in a world where the radical Christian imperative is a norm. There has been relatively little in my historical training to support taking seriously the Christian part of Gertrude's outlook, thus making it difficult to interpret. It seems to me that she would have seen her poetry as a gift from God, and felt that she must use it to further His plan. She wrote to comfort, she later said, and readers' responses show that she succeeded. But she also wrote with authority. There is a difference between giving comfort (a proper womanly function), and giving leadership, taking on and exercising religious authority. Given her life circumstances, relative youth, gender, and marginalisation, her conviction and her authority are remarkable. In extreme cases Gertrude had not the slightest difficulty speaking out against wrongs (such as wartime slaughter or the apostate church), but that is not the same as the sort of everyday authority exercised by a minister of the gospel. Although she came from a tradition where the individual is supposed to be directly tuned in to God and there had been important women preachers, by the time she was writing the situation was more formal and there were also strong taboos about women preaching and exercising authority over men, to say nothing of class and other hierarchies. I doubt that she thought of herself as exercising her own authority over anyone, but I do think she saw herself as expressing God's will and carrying God's message. It was He whose authority she expressed, not her own. She wrote of her own lack of authority in ways that underscored the social gospel message of justice. As she wrote to a critic, "I only try to comfort, in the only way I can, my sorrowing fellow-creatures whom I love. I am only a woman. No power is given to me or to any others of my sex to make juster and more beneficent laws, so that the lives of the less fortunate in the great family of humanity might be made happier and more beautiful. Even were I rich, or great, or powerful, I could not touch the fringe of the terrible injustice – the appalling inequality so apparent to us all – since the cause lies beneath the surface." For her, the message of Jesus was clear, and it was in radical opposition to many of the powerful institutions of the day. Not coincidentally, many women social reformers had come to a similar situation in the evangelical movement in the early nineteenth century, finding that they had to reject mouse-in-the-corner behaviour because they were called by God to do His bidding.[13]

Gertrude's poems were sermons. She was an adherent of the "new theology" associated with the controversial and immensely popular Reverend R.J. Campbell, minister at City Temple Congregational Church in London from 1903 to 1915[14] (a movement similar to that which came to be known as the Social Gospel in Canada). The new theology posited that Christian faith can best be expressed by loving practice, and the Kingdom of God should be brought about on earth by Christians following Christ's admonition that "whatsoever ye do unto the least of my brethren, ye do it unto me." Gertrude preached the gospel of applied love, a gospel of compassion, forgiveness, and human responsibility to care for each other as brothers and sisters of the same family. Although her poems may not appeal to today's taste, nor be outstanding as literary works, they are good examples of their day, and some are powerful and moving. Some of her poems are stirring, cheering, and radiant with joy and triumph. However, it bears repeating that her typical poem of this period was religious, devotional, often sentimental, and inspirational. The power of love (for or from God or Christ) to overcome suffering and pain, the importance of faith in God's plan for humanity, the ultimate Glory to come when

all were gathered to Him, and the contribution made to human betterment by those individuals who throughout history acted as God's
angels, were her most frequent themes.

Her tone was often melancholy; at best, she had a gift for great em-
pathy and compassion, but at worst, she came close to being a whiner.
"Must I always voice the anguish of a weeping, mourning world?"
she wrote; "May I never sing the joy-song with its triumph over
pain? ... Oh I cannot sing the joy-song while the world around me
weeps."[15] As she said of herself, if she were in "some world of glory"
surrounded by "radiant beings [and] golden light stream[ing] o'er the
glorious throng," and "if just outside there wept one outcast soul:

> To me, a gloom would darken Heaven's day,
> And o'er celestial skies the storm-clouds roll.
> I know that all above the angel's hymn,
> My soul would hear the weeping of the lost,
> And I should see a vision – veiled and dim –
> Of weary ones all anguished, tempest-tossed,
> Till I should cry (I know that He would hear
> Who reigns majestic, on the rainbow-throne)
> 'Oh god, my Father, let me bring them near,
> Thy children wander, all bereft and lone.' "

The concluding lines describe her sense of her task:

> "So I would walk, through all the scenes of strife
> And help to point the weeping to the stars,
> And I would seek to gladden human life
> And for the captives, rend the prison bars."[16]

Not all poems were gloomy. "Laborare Est Orare," excerpted below, suggested that doing good unto others makes a body feel better,
and is a good remedy for "a crushing weight of woe." This may also
be her prescription for healing her own despair.

> Are you tired and heavy laden? Is your soul with anguish sore?
> Are you shrinking from the roughness Of the way that lies before?
>
> Do you look around for comfort For your aching heart in vain?
> Are you crushed beneath the burden Of a ceaseless, hidden pain?
>
> Would you know the surest healing For a crushing weight of woe?
> Go and bear another's burden, And your own will lighter grow.

There are hearts around you breaking, For the world is full of grief;
Shower your wealth of love upon them, And to you shall come relief.

Tears of sorrow – anguished, blending – Loving hands can wipe away;
Bleeding wounds need gently binding, "Those who toil are those who
   pray."

And the path before shall brighten, Skies – so tempest tossed – grow calm;
You shall know the wondrous comfort Of a precious, healing balm.

Once there lived a King amongst us, Healing suffering with a touch;
In the thanks that wan lips murmur, You shall hear His "Inasmuch."[17]

Gertrude was active in two major movements for change during
this period: peace and woman suffrage. When her poems contained
political messages or comments on current political issues, they were
frequently on peace themes. She had become reinvolved with the
Leicester Peace Society in 1906, and used its name when she signed
her Christmas poem that year. The Peace Society's activities centred
around promoting reduction in military spending, and various forms
of peace education. They organised annual Peace Sunday observances in Sunday Schools, and special services in a different local
church each year. The group met at the Wycliffe Congregational
Church. Pastor J. Ernest James had been outspoken as an opponent of
the Boer War and continued to play a prominent role in the society.
Other members of the executive were drawn from the same church,
and from the Unitarians and Quakers. Some were also active in the
Leicester Secular Society, socialist and labour groups, and the Liberal
Party; temperance, aid to the blind, women's, and suffrage connections are also evident. Gertrude knew many of the members from
school days and Boer War peace campaigns.[18]
   Despite the disquiet many people felt over the Boer War concentration camp atrocities revealed by Emily Hobhouse and others, once
the war ended in 1902 the peace movement dwindled. Historians are
not agreed about the relative proportions of militarist versus antimilitarist sentiment in Britain, nor indeed about the continued existence
of any substantial network of the latter. However, there were pockets
of peace activism around such issues as militarisation of the curriculum, in particular the proposal to model the physical training program in British schools after the British Army's infantry drill. The
infantry drill version of the program was eventually withdrawn,
but there were also attempts to institute peacetime conscription and
universal military training for men, and various other facets of

"preparedness," as peacetime militarism was called. The peace movement was generally disorganised; the ILP socialists were critical of arms profiteering and conflict of interest (links between the military, the government, and armaments contracts) but neither systematically opposed the use of war to settle disputes nor supported disarmament, and the pacifists were not necessarily anticapitalist and did not ally themselves in general or as a matter of policy with socialists or with the labour movement. In Leicester there seems to have been somewhat more unity in the peace movement, perhaps because of the links between religious radicals, socialists, and secularists. However, despite the fact that some key figures remained active in peace issues, there was little public interest.[19]

There were periods of increased enthusiasm. The second Hague Peace Conference was held from mid-June to mid-October 1907, and the issue of armaments grew contentious in Britain during this period, culminating in debates about a major naval armaments race in 1908 and 1909. The Liberals had won the 1906 election, but it was the Limps, the Imperialist wing, that dominated the party and the government, especially after Henry Campbell-Bannerman died in 1908. He had been the Liberal leader during the Boer War, and on the anti-war side.

In November 1907, Gertrude's poem "Within the Shadow," excerpted below, was published.

In amaze I looked, around me on a sorrow-stricken world
Half in fear I looked above me as the clouds of gloom unfurled;
And I wondered why the evil seemed to triumph o'er the good,
And to ride to unblest conquest through a path all red with blood.

For I saw them press the thorn-wreath on the brows of marble-white,
Till the soul within me shuddered at the horror of the sight:
And I heard their mocking tauntings as the true and holy died,
Like the One who came before them, scorned and pierced and crucified.

And I saw the weary toilers, martyred in the marts of gold,
Sacrificed to Gods of Mammon like dumb cattle bought and sold;
And I saw the little children die for lack of daily bread,
And I wept with suffering mothers when the tiny forms lay dead.

With a great and awful vengeance God is coming to the world,
Downward, from their long usurping shall His enemies be hurled;
And their prayers shall be unheeded, God shall speak in majesty,
"Ye have crucified my children, ye have done it unto Me."[20]

The poem's imagery and moral ferocity are more typical of her wartime poetry, and it may have been written during the Boer War despite its publication date. My own suspicion is that she wrote it while she was a patient in Towers Hospital. The poem illustrates; her profound moral outrage that those in power inflicted suffering on others out of greed and indifference; the religious conviction that typifies Gertrude's pacifism; and the extent to which she took for granted that a world organised on Christian principles would include not only peace but social and economic justice, and those who controlled the "marts of gold" would no longer be able to treat "weary toilers" like cattle. Gertrude speaks from the rich socialist community traditions of the 1880s and 1890s, and she is a reminder that in some locales these prevailed beyond that period.[21]

Gertrude later wrote a poem dedicated to the Hague Peace Conference, but it is a much tamer affair than "Within the Shadow." The Hague poem was published in July 1908 during the early stages of the great naval arms race between Britain and Germany that became such a hot issue in British politics. Later that year she wrote a prose piece on the same theme, commenting that however noble the wars of earlier days may have seemed or been, "we live in other days, in days when wars are planned and waged for sordid gain. Yet still, we take our swords to God for blessing-our swords so soon to be dyed with a brother's blood ... My friends, this world is in our hands. It is for us to say whether or no the Prince of Peace shall take his throne and reign. We may crown and enthrone Him, or we may disrobe and dethrone Him. Words of worship are all meaningless. 'If ye love me keep my commandments.' 'A new commandment I give unto you, that ye love one another.'"[22]

Secularist and educator J.F. Gould was a major influence on Gertrude during this period. Since April 1899 the secretary and organiser of the Leicester Secular Society, he had likely been a Boer War comrade of hers. Gould had written in his 1899 "History of the Leicester Secular Society" that some secularists thought that a "religion of humanity" could help people to bring about better moral and material conditions in life, and they were interested in a "better earthly life," not in some hereafter. The Secular Hall featured speakers on positivism and the religion of humanity, resembling the Social Gospel or Christian Socialism minus the Christ. Gould's evangelical Christian background equipped him as a translator; he could, for example, pick useful bits from Christian teachings, such as the importance of moral purpose and consistency in the character of St Augustine. Although Gertrude did not discuss attending meetings at the Secular Hall, she certainly must have done so during the Boer War, and it is evident from some of her writings that she was also there in this later period. Gertrude did not become a secularist, or give up Christianity (although she quit the Melbourne Hall Chapel), but accepted some aspects of the positivism central to Gould's thought.[23]

Gould spoke on such themes as "The Human Meaning of the Eucharist," drawing on William Morris' comment that "Fellowship is heaven." Gould used Christian themes that must have been familiar to most of his audience, because many if not most secularists came from some religious background, to illustrate the positivist vision of a vehicle for human community and transformation. Gould said, of the Eucharist, "Bread was the staff of life, but bread eaten together by friends and comrades stood for life, democracy, and morality." His lecture, according to the report in the *Midland Free Press* "described the working class clubs which were widespread at the time of Christianity," and their public meetings over meals, "the guests at which were animated by a common purpose," as the source of like Christian rituals. "The element in the Eucharist which had a real moral was this," according to Gould: "The ceremony of the Lord's Supper made men and women feel that they were united in a bond of brotherhood, in a holy fellowship or communion; that they were not wandering units, not lonely individuals, each living in a little world of his own pain and pleasure, but social units, members of one another, co-operators, kinsmen, and perpetual companions." Gould argued that a better "Ideal" than the Christian was that of "Humanity." It included "the ideal of fatherhood, considered apart from the errors of the father; of motherhood, freed from the weaknesses of the mother; of neighbourly usefulness, devoid of the faults of the individual neighbour. Humanity gave us our life, nursed us, and watched over us. It handed down to us the language of our lips, our books, our science, our morality. Before this ideal of Humanity we forgot we were craftsmen, tradesmen, masters, servants, learners, teachers; we remembered only that we were men and women, and we learned to respect each other; and mutual respect was the foundation of the true democracy."[24]

Gould had also brought in Malcolm Quin, a Newcastle "Missionary Priest of the Church of Humanity," who had spent part of his youth in Leicester and had some early association with the Society in the early 1870s, to lecture on religion and its alternatives on 10 March 1901 at the Secular Hall. Quin argued that the purpose of religion was to promote human unity by means of love. Positivism also aimed at this, by focusing reverence toward the "nobler life of all human beings in the past ... to which we owed all that we possessed of value," that could be represented as another sort of Supreme Being. Positivists advocated regular worship and prayer during which "we

should ... commemorate, or call up before the imagination, the greatness of the life of humanity, and pour forth our desire to become
purer, more loving, more wise and courageous." This would help
people develop their ability to "conduct human life to the realisation
of ideals" desired by the religious and ethical secularists alike. Gould
did not find the term "religion" off-putting, but some other secularists did. By 1908 Gould believed there had been sufficient interest
aroused locally to establish a Church of Humanity. But Sydney Gimson and some of the other directors of the Secular Society were unwilling to have a church of any stripe set up within the society, so it
was decided that Gould would resign his post. A farewell tea was
held at the Secular Hall for the Goulds at the end of April 1908. The
Church of Humanity opened in rooms nearby in High Cross Street
shortly thereafter.[25]

The extent of Gertrude's involvement with the Church of Humanity is unclear. She wrote about two services she attended, one in November 1908 (probably her first visit), and the second on New Year's
Eve; however, she may also have gone at other times. She was favourably impressed by, and indeed, shared a number of, their ideals and
values. Despite the professed agnosticism of the positivist church,
"the eternal Spirit was there, the Spirit that under all names and all
forms of thought or worship lifts up the hearts of men to ever-higher-
ing ideals." However she found the idea of a short life followed by
nothing but "darkness and death" too desolate to accept. "By whatever name we call the great good Father of us all, it is He who upholds us, who speaks to our spirits, who leads us each in varying,
differing ways, until the dawn of the eternal day when all seekers after truth will be one." Whatever her qualms, she enjoyed it enough to
spend New Year's Eve there, "greatly honoured to be present." The
service on that occasion celebrated the dead, all those men and
women who have lived and died and given their gifts to those who
lived after them. She especially liked the hymn sung to the tune of
"Angels of Jesus": "Friends, in whose eyes we looked awhile ago, /
Come to our hearts, in spirit language telling, / All that your deeds
among us used to show; / Friends long departed, friends ever dear, /
Stay in our sacred thoughts this last night of the year." Describing the
sermon, she commented, "I am glad to meet with those who, while
their thoughts and beliefs are unlike mine, have yet some sweet and
holy dreams in common with me, blended with the charity that covers many sins. Intolerance and bigotry have done so much to blight
the world – it is sweet to remember that we are brothers and sisters,
who must for awhile dwell together upon this earth, fulfilling in our
turn our share of building and moulding, our part in preparing the

earth for the reception of those who shall follow us." She especially appreciated the remembrance service, for to her, she wrote, the dead were not really dead, and she expected to meet them again in the life after death. Meanwhile she appreciated their inspiration.[26]

A number of Gertrude's poems and prose pieces reflect Church of Humanity themes and a continued association with J.F. Gould in the ensuing period. Shortly after the New Year's Eve visit, Gertrude described a dream during a much earlier illness. She had flown to the top of a mountain, where, surrounded by singing glowing beings, she had seen far below "a long streaming line of men, women, and little children."

What is this? I asked of the angelic being beside me. "The Procession of Humanity" was the reply. How long I gazed I know not, for before me passed the people of all the ages, and all the climes, the people of every kindred and tongue that had ever dwelt upon the face of the earth. And in their eyes I looked and understood, for there were martyrs and saints, and holy women, and the "common people," the singers, the poets and the dreamers, the sufferers and the sinners, the high and the low, the kings and the priests, the small and the great, "a multitude whom no man could number."[27]

She wrote also of heroes who led Humanity forward, usually at "fearsome sacrifice." These were "the sweet and true, the pure and good and noble [who] have sought before us for the starry way." In every age, she believed, ordinary men and women lived exemplary lives and by their example were "redeemers of the world." Redemption had its price, and some sins were too terrible to be redeemed. In an allegory entitled "The Angel and the Seer" she, the "Seer," described a collection of "redeemers:" there were "here a thinker, there a toiler at the forge, there a statesman and a warrior, a fair, sweet, woman, pure and chaste as a star beam, a pilgrim, bent and sorrowful, and round them each a radiance as of Heaven." These "chosen ones of earth" were surrounded in glory, but their hearts were wounded and bleeding. The meaning of the vision, the angel explained, was "that by love and suffering alone, the earth may [be] redeemed, that by love and suffering alone, Earth's sin may be forgiven, for so hath God ordained that for the guilty still the innocent must die." Did that mean that all humanity's sins would be forgiven? The angel took on a terrible power and answered, "No cry of suffering unjustly borne, no wail of woman's broken heart, no anguished moan of holy trust betrayed escapes the ear of Eternal Justice. Know then, Oh Man, all sin shall be forgiven, save only the sin against love."[28]

Although her poems and prose pieces on the subject of heroes and redeemers were redolent with pain and martyrdom, Gertrude did write a few with happier elements. Her poem "Requiem," excerpted below, is representative of these.

> I will sing a song of triumph for the great and good of old,
> All who ever sought to crush the power of wrong,
> For the heroes and the martyrs, for the fearless men and bold,
> Though a wild, low, thrilling wail runs through my song.
> I will voice the world's thanksgiving for the breakers of this chain,
> For the freers of the captive and the bound,
> For the tender and the gentle ones who bore their load of pain,
> For the sweet pure lives whose fragrance breathed around.
>
> I will sing, and Heaven's own music from the harp-land high above
> Shall be wedded to the soul within the song!
> For I sing of lives of beauty, lives of saintliness and love.
> Lives of holiness – unnoticed in the throng.
> Men who fought for truth and freedom, men who died for faith or land,
> Men who bore aloft a snow-white flag of peace –
> I will sing with soul and passion for the theme is great and grand,
> And the echo of the song shall never cease.
>
> I will sing of gentle mothers, who in giving lives to earth,
> Have in silence and in pain laid down their own;
> Tears will echo through the singing, sweet the solemn hour of birth,
> Tender sweet the memories of the loved ones flown:
> I will sing of lovely women who on battle plains of blood,
> Gently knelt the wounded warrior's hurt to bind;
> Sing of countless noble women, great, heroic, pure, and good,
> And my song shall hush the wailing of the winds.
>
> Oh! the wailing in the music; oh! the madness in the song;
> Then the triumph strain that echoes in its joy.
> I will sing, the wind shall carry all the joyous notes along,
> And shall soften all the weeping tones that cloy.
> For the great and good and holy, for the brave and sweet and true,
> For the tender and the noble and the strong;
> I will sing a song of gladness, fresh and bright as morning dew,
> While a triumph-ring shall echo through my song.[29]

If Humanity needed heroes, how were these to be found? Gertrude believed that ordinary people could be helped to cultivate the good within themselves. She was a fan of Gould's work in moral education; education was crucial to remaking society. As a socialist, Gould believed there must be a moral as well as economic transformation in society. Gould and other Secularists put great faith in human capacity to reason; they did not mean a narrow rationalism, but defined the faculty broadly, to include feeling. Feeling plus Reason were together the key to solving human problems. Education was the key to training people to care and to use feeling and reason. Gould had been elected to the Leicester School Board in 1900, campaigning on the abolition of religious instruction and the implementation of "moral instruction" that would inculcate the highest of human virtues. Gould had twenty-five years of elementary school teaching experience (from 1871 to 1896) with the London School Board; he had been a freethought lecturer and writer since 1882, specialising in secular and socialist Sunday Schools for adults and children. Since 1888 he had been writing on secular methods of moral and ethical education, and had been a founder of the "Moral Education League." An editorial (presumably by Edwin Crew) describing Gould's background, written around the time of the 1900 school board election aptly called Gould "an Agnostic parson." Indeed, Gould referred to the Secular Society magazine, *The Leicester Reasoner*, as "the only Freethought Parish magazine in the world."[30]

Gould's moral education curriculum included teaching such things as self-respect, truthfulness, kindness; history of human goodness and invention; the nature of justice; principles of liberty; the state and citizenship, cooperation and peace, and "social and political equality of the sexes." Although Gould's insistence that schools should be secular was controversial, his methods of moral education were generally accepted as pedagogically sound (and indeed, were based on modern teaching methods used by elementary education leaders in various countries). At Gould's initiative, in 1901 Leicester schools had inserted weekly "moral instruction" lessons into the curriculum, to supplement the ineffective Bible lessons (which they refused to eliminate as Gould had proposed) as a method to train children in moral judgment. Each session dealt with the application of its theme at the level of "Family, Country, and Humanity." Gould wrote moral education lessons for children in the Secular Society's magazine, *The Reasoner*, and children's stories in the *Midland Free Press*. He was an indefatigable classroom demonstrator of his methods, and often taught or spoke at teachers' training institutions or in private settings. In one such demonstration held in London, he taught a lesson on "respect" to a class of twelve students in front of an audience of adult observers, one of whom was a journalist for the Manchester *Guardian*.

"He coaxed the children into deductions, and delighted them with a sense of their participation in a matter of fascinating importance ... When the children filed out ... we sat down to a cold analytical appreciation of what had been done," the favourably impressed correspondent reported.[31]

Gould also taught children in the Secular version of Sunday School. Gertrude wrote about one of his Sunday afternoon classes at the Secular Hall: "Full of interest from beginning to end – and touching everywhere the highest ideals of practical love and duty – there was not one dull moment. Anecdote, legend, historical fact, followed each other, blending harmoniously ... I am so glad I was allowed to be there – to listen – and to learn that there are better methods of teaching high knowledge than those usually employed." She compared Gould's teaching and concern for the children to those of Jesus, and referred again to her version of the teachings of positivism. "For, by whatever name we call it, the gentle spirit of humanity is one throughout the ages – finding expression in the lowly service of the early saints – and in all the love and sweetness, all the kindly deeds and gentle words that have blessed and comforted the lives of others, from the beginning until now."[32]

When the debate on militarism in the schools grew heated in 1908 and 1909, so too did Gould's approach become controversial, for his moral education was founded on internationalism and what today would be called "peace education." Gould was then embroiled in an attempt to get the Leicester School Board to remove military maps supplied by the Navy League, from Leicester schoolrooms. He proposed a motion at a late June 1909 education committee meeting: "That the Elementary Schools Sub-Committee be requested to remove from the schools all Navy League maps, on the ground that such maps are suggestive of party politics, and are out of harmony with the principles of international peace which should be fostered by the school-training." He and his colleague Councillor Hill argued that the supporters of the maps wanted children to learn "that material wealth and naval supremacy were the glories of England – for such is the distinct message of the statistical tables printed on the maps." These were not the values that children should be learning. "I quoted the Bible, 'Blessed are the peacemakers,' 'Peace on earth, goodwill towards men,' but all in vain," Gould reported. "With remarkable heroism [the Rev. A.M. Harper, Mr Mantle Hubbard, and others who voted against Hill and me] rode roughshod over the pacific principles, and joyfully supported the Navy League. If they will keep up their courage and proclaim Naval supremacy doctrines next Christmas Day, we shall see great things," wrote Gould.[33]

Gertrude was an enthusiastic supporter of attempts to remove the offending maps from schoolroom walls. In the same number of the *Midland Free Press* as her report on Gould's Sunday School class, she published a lengthy poem "dedicated to the two councillors who desire the abolition of war-maps in the schools." A hostile reaction from a reader who objected to her associating Christ with a man who was antichristian drew her more directly into the fray. Her reply further illuminates her relationship with Gould and his religion of humanity:

I know the Son of God. I listen to his words. And I hear Him say "Love one another." He does not tell me to ask what my fellow-creatures believe, or even what they are. Yet I look for the image of God in the faces of the men and women I meet, and sometimes I find it. I do not find it often in those who most loudly proclaim their loyalty and allegiance to Him. And indeed I believe that if Christ came back, the very men who are eternally singing His praises would be scouring the forests for the orthodox kind of wood on which to crucify Him! It is a very possible thing that some who do not call themselves Christians at all are nearer to the heart of God – and dearer – than many who do. And I think the Angels at the gate of Heaven will not look out for orthodoxy – but for human love and charity which is divine.

Gertrude's breach with institutional Christianity had not healed. She believed that applied love plus justice equalled the will of God on earth, and Christians were called to bring that will into being.[34]

The second major cause to which Gertrude was committed during this period was the woman suffrage movement. Indeed, it eclipsed the peace movement in the frequency and intensity with which issues arose and events took place. Like many English towns during this period, Leicester was a site of considerable agitation over the issue of women's rights. Artist and suffrage activist Sylvia Pankhurst had spent some weeks in Leicester in the summer of 1907 talking to and sketching women boot and shoe workers, and holding numerous Women's Social and Political Union (WSPU) suffrage meetings.[35] The suffrage movement was in full swing by 1908. The militant WSPU was growing very rapidly, as were the newly established Women's Freedom League (WFL, split from the WSPU in October 1907) and the moderate ("constitutionalist") suffragists of the National Union of Women's Suffrage Societies (NUWSS), whose members often were radical in their social change objectives although they did not approve of the suffragette tactics. Suffragettes had been going to prison since 1906; their tactics were the subject of controversy, as was the woman suffrage question itself. Various suffrage groups held meetings in Leicester, often unscheduled open air efforts where one or more speakers would hold forth and attract a crowd. For example, there was a very large meeting in the Market Square in Leicester on 30 July 1908. Typically several local women would preside over such a meeting, joined by an organiser or a big name on tour.[36]

Reactions to these events were mixed. Women (and some men) flocked to the movement, but hostile spectators could and did assault suffragists and suffragettes alike, and the authorities could not be relied upon to protect speakers or deal with assailants (almost invariably male). Some of these attacks were little more than the low level rough stuff common at political meetings, but in many cases there was an element of viciousness and an intent to injure not found in male attacks on male political speakers. A more innocuous attack might be to throw food at speakers; when Leicester's Agnes Clarke and London WSPU executive committee member Nellie Martel (who had been involved in the suffrage movement in Australia) spoke at a meeting at Northampton Square, Clarke was hit with an orange thrown by a (male) shop assistant.[37]

Gertrude was deeply interested in woman suffrage, and saw the struggle for the vote as a crusade. The vote was important both as a matter of the natural rights of freeborn Englishwomen and as a tool with which women could right wrongs and help to reconstruct society along more humane and decent lines. Gertrude did not write directly about the issue at great length, but it permeated a number of her poems and surfaced in some of her prose pieces. She did not then discuss her membership in any particular branch of the movement, except to say that although she was not a militant suffragette she had great admiration for their courage and willingness to martyr themselves for a holy cause.

In Leicester as in many towns, however, sectarian niceties were not always crucial at this juncture; local suffrage organisations might include members of the Pankhursts' Women's Social and Political Union, Charlotte Despard's Women's Freedom League, or Millicent Fawcett's National Union of Women's Suffrage Societies. Whatever the disagreements and rivalries at the top level, the rank and file seem to have worked together to a large extent, particularly in this early period. These three major groups joined others, such as the Men's League for Women's Suffrage, in publishing news in a magazine called *Women's Franchise*, "a record of the women's suffrage movement." The magazine records a variety of suffrage activities in Leicester, shows growing membership in all groups, and describes large crowds at events. The summer of 1908 was also the beginning of the suffrage tradition of huge processions. In London in June 1908 there was a procession and meeting at Royal Albert Hall drawing over 12,000 women from the WFL and NUWSS, followed eight days later by a monster meeting at Hyde Park organised by the WSPU that drew crowds estimated at up to 500,000. The suffrage processions, featuring banners, costumed representations of historical figures, university graduates in their academic gowns, and marchers organised by occupational or geographical groups, emphasised women's history and women's contributions to culture and human advancement. They promoted a sense of entitlement and justifiable pride in womankind. They were spectacular performances. Not least, they demonstrated that suffrage was a live issue, whatever the disagreements about strategies and tactics.[38]

It is not clear how Gertrude came to be involved with the suffrage movement. Many of her associates were strongly prosuffrage. R.J. Campbell, the "new theology" minister whom she so admired, was a suffragist associated with the Women's Freedom League. She may have met Sylvia Pankhurst during her 1907 visit; Gertrude's later writings show that the two were in touch for some years. Gertrude knew Dorothy Pethick (sister of Emmeline Pethick-Lawrence), who lived in Leicester and organised for the WSPU. She knew constitutionalists Edith and Catherine Gittins, and Isabel Ashby, from the Peace Society. The Secular Society contained numerous advocates, and women, including radicals such as Annie Bradlaugh Bonner, were regular speakers at the Secular Hall (although not in numbers equalling their male counterparts). F.J. Gould had lectured on Mary Wollstonecraft, the rights of women, and the importance of women's access to education at the Secular Hall in February 1900. Gould's final lecture in his 1907 summer series had highlighted women's special qualities and advocated giving women the vote ("as women, not as ratepayers") as a way of getting those qualities into "politics, industry and education." He believed, "Women would in the future bring a new moral factor into politics, and in the church of tomorrow they would be honoured as the representatives of the spirit of Humanity. That spirit was symbolised by the figure of the mother with the child in her arms."[39]

Gertrude also had allies at home, in her mother and her youngest brother Horace. While saying he was not a suffragist (presumably meaning that he was not a member of any suffrage society), Horace wrote to the *Midland Free Press* defending the militants against their detractors. Although information about Horace's activities during this period is sketchy, he was by then in his early twenties, and may have already been working as a commercial traveller for a woollen firm, a position which took him all over the country and to Europe. He likely was already attending the radical Wycliffe Church, fashionable among the avant-garde for its intellectual and cultural activities. Wycliffe minister J. Ernest James, mainstay of the peace movement, was active in a number of progressive causes. Horace underwent a conversion to socialism sometime before 1910; likely his circle and Gertrude's overlapped, and their shared Christian Socialism was one of the bases of the special closeness that would sustain both of them in unforeseen difficult periods in the future.[40]

Another influence was that of the young clergywoman Gertrud von Petzold, the first woman ordained minister in England to win a full-time appointment to the pulpit of a regular congregation. Von Petzold was inducted into the ministry in 1904 following her theological training and completion of requirements for the M.A. at Manchester College, Oxford; she wore her academic gown at the ordination ceremony. She was appointed to the pulpit of Leicester's newly built Narborough Road Free Christian Church, a prosperous church with a large congregation. Von Petzold was an attractive young woman with a clear voice, a slight accent, and a scholarly preaching style; she was modern in her ideas, theologically, socially, and politically. She was a daring appointment in that respect, and in her youth, but especially in her gender, for there was some doubt about the readiness of the congregation and the public to accept a woman minister; however she had powerful backers in the management committee (and powerful detractors). Her uniqueness attracted attention and crowds attended her services. She had a large following of young women. Von Petzold was active in a variety of community and social groups and kept a finger in every pie in the church. She brought current issues into the regular concerns of the congregation; for example she set up a Sunday afternoon lecture series for men, featuring prominent speakers on social policy and social reform topics. She herself appeared as a speaker at various Leicester venues, lecturing on such scholarly topics as Dante, and on more immediate questions such as peace and international arbitration. Von Petzold was also a keen suffrage supporter, and helped to organise and appeared at a number of suffrage events in Leicester, notably a mass women's meeting in March 1908, a "splendid success." She also spoke at open air meetings, appearing, for example, on an impromptu stage (a lorry) in the marketplace with visiting WSPU speakers. Eventually her detractors gained the upper hand and she left Leicester.[41]

Gertrude had admired von Petzold, recalling in 1913, "I remember how impressed I was when I first heard Rev. Gertrud von Petzold preaching at Narborough-road ... Her dignity and grace and beauty have remained with me – an abiding memory, and I can still hear at times her voice, with its pretty touch of foreign accent, as she said,

'Only upon some cross of pain or woe / Each son of God may lie. / Each heart redeemed from self and sin must know / Its Calvary.'" Still later Gertrude recalled "She spoke ... many memorable words to me ... Miss von Petzold is a very great woman, whose work is not yet done – indeed, scarcely begun."[42]

There is also some evidence from Gertrude's collection of newspaper clippings that she was acquainted with another suffrage militant, writer Agnes Clarke, a follower of von Petzold who wrote regularly in the *Midland Free Press* about the minister's doings. Clarke later published an autobiographical novel about von Petzold's Leicester years; it describes Clarke working behind the scenes to organise support for von Petzold, even persuading her brother to ask von Petzold to officiate at his very fashionable wedding. Gertrude may have known Agnes Clarke through Wyggeston School circles; an Agnes Kate Clarke, born 1873, was a student there from 1880 to 1888. Isabel Ashby, whose friendship with Horace Twilley lasted into the 1930s, had also been a Wyggeston student in the 1880s, had attended von Petzold's church, and was a friend of Agnes Clarke's.[43]

Alongside Clarke's literary efforts and reports on von Petzold, the *Midland Free Press* ran her reports on suffrage doings. Clarke was a WSPU member. In the spring of 1908 the WSPU were campaigning against the government in by-elections, and were criticised by a *Midland Free Press* temperance columnist, "Semper Fidelis," allegedly for jeopardising the government's temperance bill. Clarke responded at length to his attack; the two carried on a running battle for several weeks in the letters page. Although most of Clarke's writing was political rather than personal, she did from time to time write about her own reactions to events in which she participated: one such article described her feelings of outrage, dismay, and helplessness as a spectator to the sentencing of suffragettes in a London police court. She also wrote about a visit to the rural home of an elderly suffragette, "loyal Liberal gentlewoman though she was," whose allegiance had been given to the WSPU because there had been no progress after decades of ladylike and respectable efforts. Many WSPU events Clarke participated in were in fact quite staid and ladylike. In August 1908, Clarke co-chaired a meeting organised by the WSPU featuring a lecture by historian Miss F.E. Macauley on the historical and contemporary status of women; Macauley also spoke to a combined meeting of the Adult Schools during her visit to Leicester.[44]

A major Leicester suffrage event in the fall of 1908 was a large demonstration at the Temperance Hall held in October. Although Gertrude does not mention the event specifically, she may well have been there. There was an afternoon exhibition of the banners carried at the

WFL-NUWSS June meeting followed by an evening meeting featuring various worthies, including the Reverend Lewis Donaldson, Ramsay MacDonald, and leaders from the two suffrage societies. A Lancashire cotton worker and labour activist working as an NUWSS organiser, Selina Cooper, represented the working women's constituency. This latter group had been the focus of some activity by all societies, and working class women were the backbone of the movement in the north. In Leicester, Edith Gittins (who had helped to organise the October demonstration) was on the executive of the local branch of the National Union of Women Workers (NUWW), which had protested in July 1908 against the light sentences meted out to men who assaulted women and children, while those who committed offences against property were more heavily punished. "We feel as Englishwomen that everything possible should be done, by punishment and by publicly expressed detestation of offences against the persons of women and children to make the roads of England safe for the daughters of England to walk on," they concluded. Gittins was one of those opposed to the tactics of the WSPU, fearing they alienated potential supporters. Clarke of course did not share this view, and the two sides had snide comments about each other from time to time. Clarke referred, for example, to women "who wanted the vote but would risk nothing for it – they preferred the safe policy of conciliation." However, she added, "The incumbent of a country parish leads a less strenuous life than the missionary on the West coast of Africa. Yet both are 'Christians.' "[45]

Solidarity was important in the face of antisuffrage arguments (even those of the apparently chivalrous sort) that women did not need the vote, that they would be worse off with it because they would lose men's protection. One antisuffragist wrote that voteless women had "considerably more rights than men, and are a great deal better off, more womanly, and more worthy of the respect, consideration, and protection of men without the vote than they would be with it." Women were already the real citizens, men their loving vassals concerned with passing legislation to create conditions suitable for worthy noble women to live under, he argued. Whatever their stripe, suffrage activists would all snort at such specious claims.[46]

There is some evidence to connect Gertrude with the Women's Freedom League, despite her own nonmilitant inclinations, primarily her championing of Daisy Lord. As the militants were sent to prison in ever larger numbers, they were exposed to prison conditions about which middle and upper class women normally knew nothing. On occasion the plight of particular prisoners was brought to public notice as a consequence of this exposure. One such prisoner was Daisy

Lord, a young servant who had been sentenced to death for killing her illegitimate newborn; her sentence was commuted to life imprisonment. Her cause was taken up by the Women's Freedom League. WFL branches publicised the case, and the WFL woman suffrage caravan that visited dozens of villages and towns in the summer of 1908 also circulated petitions for further clemency. On 5 September 1908, Gertrude published "An Appeal" in the *Midland Free Press*, asking readers to sign the Daisy Lord clemency petition. "Think of it – women whose lives are full of sunshine – mothers with sweet and beautiful daughters, all sheltered from the shadow of sin, and while your hearts dwell upon the thought of what this child's life might have been – come forward and help us in our endeavour to get her sentence at least reduced," she urged. Her appeal was accompanied by "Virginia's Cry," a lengthy poem excerpted below, comparing Daisy Lord (and the suffragettes, by implication) to the persecuted woman from Roman times (this poem really ought to be read aloud in order to appreciate the full impact of Gertie's declaiming and thundering!):

Oh, for the power and passion that in the days of old
Rang through the souls that God had formed in such heroic mould!
Oh, for a clarion voice to reach the farthest bound of earth,
A voice of strong command to still the revelry and mirth;
Far greater wrongs cry out to-day in our fair English home
Than by the flowing Tiber in the ancient days of Rome.
To-day, Virginia, unavenged, is sold to curse and shame,
Then left to bear the cruel weight of her dishonoured name.
To-day, a weeping mother in a hideous dungeon lies,
Where wrongs could pierce the very heavens, and rend the veiling skies,
On her – all frail and trembling – so sorrow-filled and lone,
Is laid the condemnation of our nations and our Throne!
Betrayed – and left to suffer! what woe could equal this?
Oh! none save His who knew a "friend's" betrayal "with a kiss,"
'Tis strange to stone the victim and to let the wronger free,
'Tis passing strange – this "Law" of ours – this "Law of Liberty."

Now, no Virginius – fatherlike – can save her from the snare,
Can ye not hear her anguished cry while fangs of wolf-hounds tear?
Is this the "justice" England boasts? The justice stern and great,
That stands beside the balance-scales an Arbiter of Fate?
No! She would lift the victim up, and hurl the monster down
Who dared to take from womanhood her pure and royal crown.
Shall we not follow where she leads, though lone the way and long?

For only by a briary path the good shall conquer wrong.
Yes, we must leave the fields and flowers and gird us for the strife,
Till nevermore our hearts shall weep o'er one poor broken life,
Till nevermore the sins of men on trusting women fall,
Till nevermore a life unborn is laid beneath a pall,
Till nevermore the shadow falls ere yet the day had dawned,
Till nevermore an open grave for fragile lives has yawned.

Oh! men who dare to make the laws ye bid us to obey,
We will not rest in calm content while friends shall tear their prey;
Ye shall not bar in dungeons foul the victim in her pain,
For on your heads the sin shall rest with all its crimson stain.
Come down! your hands too long have held the sceptre and the sway,
Come down! your thrones are all defiled, for faster men make way,
The cry of anguished womanhood through centuries has rung
Profounder than the bitter cry by Roman poet sung.
And we will lift the victim up, and bind her wounds, so deep,
And bid her tortured spirit rest and sing her grief to sleep,
And we will burst the prison door and set the captive free;
We do not fear your cherished "Law," it is iniquity!
For men and women great and good shall cast your sway aside,
And you, beneath their chariot-wheels, shall groan as on they ride;
Oh shame! oh shame a thousand-fold, that ever doom shall fall
Upon a maddened mother and a babe beneath a pall!
Oh, for the power and passion that in the days of old
Rang through the souls that God had formed in such heroic mould.[47]

Early in October 1910 the Women's Freedom League held an immense demonstration in London to protest Daisy Lord's sentence. Gertrude wrote a rather lurid article, introduced by an excerpt from suffragette Vera Wentworth's piece "Prison Horrors," which described their Holloway experiences and mentioned Daisy Lord, wherein Gertrude compared the women in Holloway to the revolutionary martyrs imprisoned in Russia. In enlightened England such things were not supposed to happen, Gertrude wrote, yet in Holloway, where "many of the best women of our country have suffered vile indignities," poor "half-demented" Daisy Lord was sequestered behind a crimson curtain. "And this is England in the 20th century – humane, enlightened, civilised, Christian England! Shame on the laws that suffer such horror to exist, shame on the men who made them, the nation that upholds them! Shame on the silent voices, the folded hands! Shame on the Christianity that traduces every maxim and ethic of its Divine founder! Shame on the Crown and the Empire, the high and low, the rich and poor, alike allowing and uncaring. 'How long, O Lord, how long?'" she melodramatically concluded.[48]

Not surprisingly, a reader objected with some justice to her "sensational letter," adding that the suffragettes got off lightly. Gertrude's response, entitled "Christ and Womanhood," reminded readers that Christ had invoked, and would do so again were He to reappear, His higher authority to forbid the application of harsh manmade laws to "a woman such as I have pleaded for, a woman with a blighted womanhood, a ruined life laid waste, and … He would reply again 'He that is without sin among you, let him cast the first stone at her.'" She wrote of the present system of justice, "The teaching of Jesus … does not suit the world today. It is not His word they preach, but some strange fabric of religiosity they have built up around His name." He was murdered by "the laws of man … [and] there is little doubt the women who, weeping, watched beside His cross were jeered upon, and deemed 'hysterical.' Let us watch beside it still, and share the sufferings of all the wronged and bleeding sons and daughters of the Most High, till God's just vengeance falls." The same correspondent replied, pointing out instances of illogic in Gertrude's "sermonette," as he called it, but antisuffragist cold logic could do little against the holy cause of woman suffrage then filling the pages of the *Midland Free Press* and the streets of Leicester and other English towns.[49]

Most of Gertrude's written contributions to the suffrage campaign were highminded poems about women's nobility of character, deservedness of fair treatment, and ultimate triumph in the divine scheme of things. Like Miss Macauley and other feminists who had gained an education, like Gertrud von Petzold who preached the message of God's kingdom on earth, Gertrude put her gifts to the service of "the cause." Gertrude's poem, "The Death of Hypatia," excerpted below, is a fair example. She began with a biographical caption: "Hypatia, teacher of Greek philosophy, daughter of Theon, brutally murdered by fanatical monks at the foot of the altar in the Church at Alexandria, fifth century." She prefaced the poem with Charles Kingsley's description of the scene: "She shook herself free from her tormentors, and springing back, rose for one moment to her full height, naked, snow-white, against the dusky mass around, shame and indignation in those wide clear eyes, but not a stain of fear. With one hand she clasped her golden locks around her, the other long white arm was stretched upward toward the great still Christ, appealing – and who dare say in vain? – from man to God."

> The lady, a queen of classic lore, went forth to her student-hall,
> The wisdom loved of the sages old held mind and soul in thrall;

Her litter passed through the crowded street, she heard no noise of strife.
Nor dreamed that fiends in the guise of men were hunting for her life.

Is it best to draw the curtain-veil o'er the hideous crimes of men?
Or to tell how the hell-hounds stripped the robes from the noble woman
    then?
How they tore and mangled marble limbs at the very feet of Christ,
While the great Hypatia's unstained soul soared up to Eternal Tryst.

They tell us the days of martyrdom have passed with the long gone years,
That freedom reigns in this land of ours, that the slaves may dry their
    tears;
While yet in their loathsome dungeon-dens there are noble women cast,
And the crimes of this newer, later day, are greater than crimes long past!

You may chain them down to your prison floors in the holy name of God,
Yet know, ye men of this day and hour, that the path by women trod –
The path of suffering bitter scorn in the holy cause of Right –
Will end in the perfect majesty of a hard won crown of Light.

Though ye have no care that with mortal pangs a woman gave you life,
And that women bear the holy names of sister and of wife,
God reigns above and His arm outstretched is ever above their heads,
And His love o'er the path of thorns and tears the great good Father sheds.

I think he cares Who laid aside His crown for the bitter Cross,
And I think He looked at the joy beyond when He chose the gall and dross:
Oh shame! that ever the sons of men in the name of the Great and Good,
Should strive to tear the royal crown from the brow of womanhood.
    (Dedicated to all women who can suffer for the truth.)[50]

Other poems offered positive examples. "Per Ardua Ad Astra"
spoke of the woman scholar, a "seeking soul" who spent many years
"at the Shrine of Light" in the pursuit of knowledge and the development of wisdom, seeking to understand the mysteries of that "House
of Gold." Summoned by God to "heed the pleadings of My children
as they roam," she spent the rest of her life teaching children, blessing
the weeping, counselling those who would stray. "Here was Wisdom,
greater than within her House of Gold," Gertrude wrote of the life
dedicated to teaching and helping rather than to isolated ivory tower
scholarly pursuits. The woman dies one night over her books, and her
soul rises to "perfect Knowledge, through struggle to the Stars." One
clear message is that ministering to human need, teaching, counsel-

ling, and caring, is of greater value in the eyes of God than is the monastic life of the disengaged scholar. This view confirms Gertrude's choices in life, her ideal (her early plan for a life of social service, for which she intended to prepare herself by intense study), and perhaps her actual life, teaching and consoling through her poems. I think it also is an affirmation of the work of educated women for social reform and women's suffrage, an expression of her admiration for them, and an indication that she identified with them in their quest for "spiritual regeneration, and moral right," to use the formulation of Martha Vicinus. Vicinus has provided an acute analysis of the element of "extraordinary idealism that found its fullest expression in the utter sacrifice of self for the cause" that animated the suffragettes and many other suffrage activists. Although Gertrude did not abandon her other concerns in favour of suffrage activism, she did see the suffrage struggle as a holy cause. A few years later when her changed circumstances placed her in a setting where she was propelled into more public activism, her English experience in the suffrage movement was invaluable as training for leadership. At that time she would describe the movement as God's main purpose for her life.[51]

By late 1908 Gertrude's poems increasingly dealt with issues of economic justice and the failure of social policy to avert hunger and want. She addressed poverty and suffering as religious issues, in that she took as literal instructions Christ's teachings: "Love one another," "Feed my lambs" and "Whatsoever ye do to the least of my brethren, ye do it unto me." As she understood this last point, "God comes down with every life new given, as with the Christ adored." Mainstream Christianity certainly did not make these their priorities, she noted. A Christmas poem entitled "God With Us," excerpted below, discussed this theme in polite terms:

"Lo! I am with you always," said the Saviour,
"With you until the end of all the days;"
I wonder if He loves the chants and praying,
        And oft repeated praise.
I think if we would feed the little children
He would rejoice, Who came to be a child,
And we should win a smile of rarest beauty
        From His sweet eyes so mild.

I think He must be tired of all the preaching,
And weary of the endless organ peal –
Such thoughts as these will come without my seeking,
        And o'er my spirits steal.

I think that there would be an endless Christmas,
It would not pass with dying of the year,
If we would only look around for Jesus,
    Oh! we should find Him – here![52]

She was less polite in other verses such as "Ye Did It Not: A Dream," excerpted below, about the failure of organised Christianity to practice what Christ had preached.

The guests assembled at the banquet-table, The table of the Lord,
In clouds of flame from Heaven there came an angel, Bearing a shining
    sword;
"Stay!" and the people by the holy altar, Waited with bated breath,
While silence fell o'er all the vast assembly, A silence – as of death.

"I see your symbols of my broken Body, And of My poured out Blood,"
The Master spake in accents sad and anguished, As in His Church He
    stood;
"Yet where are they for whom I left the Glory, The tempted and the sad?
Where are the weary and the sorely-laden? I lived to make them glad.

Ye have not sought the widow in her sorrow, The orphan in his woe;
Ye have not broken bread to feed the hungering, And yet I taught you so –
In wintry winds, unclothed, the poor and needy Bow, shivering, to the
    blast,
And in your loathsome dungeons dwell My loved ones, All bound and
    fettered fast."
And now, upon that Face, so calm, so holy, An awful anger grew:
While terror, such as earth had never witnessed, The weeping people
    knew:
The Master spake His words of condemnation, There, in the Temple dim;
And not a soul who dared a prayer to whisper, Who dared to answer
    Him!

"Take ye your symbols of my tortured Body, Ye who have crucified;
Fitting your emblems of a bleeding Saviour, Who by your sin has died:
Still do ye nail to crosses rude and rugged, The child of want and woe;
Still do ye leave to die in shame and anguish The lambs I cherished so.

Ye are not Mine – My children love and suffer, My children seek the lost,
And fold to hearts all filled with tender pity The sinner, tempest tossed";
An awful wail through all the Church resounded, A wail of deep despair;
For Christ had come, the Christ of love and justice, Had come to judgment
    there;

"I know you not," He said, then passed in silence, While wailing rent the air.[53]

Unemployment and poverty were by then the subject of heated public debate, as the provisions and administration of the poor law were called into question. A depression had increased unemployment and produced large numbers who had to apply for relief or starve, and the Poor Law Guardians responded in some cases with punitive measures to "test" the legitimacy of claims or exclude some from relief. She wrote indignantly in May 1909 of the Guardians' harshness, "A poor man has been sent to prison for a week because he did not accomplish the 'task' set him by the [workhouse] authorities. A number of other and younger men have been sent to prison for a still longer period." Gertrude's poem excerpted below, "Christ at the Workhouse," critiqued the callous treatment of the poor. It was introduced by the appropriate Bible verse: "Inasmuch as ye have done it unto one of the least of these, My brethren, ye have done it unto Me (Matthew 25–40)." In the poem, Jesus turns up anonymously at the workhouse, hungry and tired; the next morning,

They bade the Lord when He rose from sleep Bend down to His heavy toil,
But He saw around Him eyes that weep, And hands that had tilled the soil:
And a great compassion filled His soul For His brethren in their woe,
And He yearned that their lives should be glad and whole, That comfort
    their hearts might know.

Then a wonderful radiance touched His brow, It gleamed as the Sun at
    noon;
His sweet voice spoke, but so soft and low – Like a child's when it craves a
    boon:
"Ye know Me not, or your crowns and thrones Would be laid at My feet
    to-day,
You have bidden your Saviour to break your stones, Your Saviour – to
    whom ye pray!"

"I came all poor, that My soul might learn The love ye would show to Me;
I came in need, that your hearts might yearn O'er My woe and poverty: "
"These, these are Mine," and a nail-torn Hand Swept round like a sweet
    embrace,
O'er a weeping group in a "Christian" land For whom there is found no
    place.[54]

Although Gertrude did not write explicitly about the various policies proposed to deal with the depression, her poetry shows she was involved in political battles over the issue. Her poem entitled "To Arms!" described a "clarion call ... sounding throughout the night," and called to battle "My brothers, men of England! of the race and name and clime." "Shall children die of hunger?" she asked, "I hear them cry for bread / And will ye starve the children that the rich may heap their gold? / And will ye starve the mothers, too, God gave them to enfold?" She continued, "The world is looking on us now, oh, brothers will ye choose? / And crown the lofty aims and high, the mean and low refuse? / Our land is OURS, God made it ours, we will not bend the knee, / We will not yield our heritage to Greed and Tyranny." The concluding stanza contained the lines, "Oh! for a pen of living fire to write across the sky, / 'To arms, ye true and faithful, prepared for Truth to die.' / Ye angels of the Highest, lend your music to my song, / That once again the pure and true may crush the power of wrong, / to arms! To arms! save England! Let the good and righteous reign, / The hymns of joy may yet resound instead of cries of pain." The battle in question was the general election of January 1910, precipitated by the House of Lords' refusal to approve a Liberal budget which provided modest sums for social services and proposed to tax land sales. In March of that year, Gertrude wrote further about these issues in a piece called "Love and the World," which described her meditations upon the human soul while sitting in church. "We are not small but great, we children of earth. Not puny are we, but mighty, not ignoble but noble" in seeking the best and the highest, the Angel Love. "And bitter cries have risen from the earth, seeking to reach some mystic throne where love and justice reigned since ever human eyes looked up to find a God," she wrote.

We dream of a Day when the forces of the universe shall be hurled with resistless power against the forces anew that bear men down to loveless toil, that chain them to tasks unending that gold may be reaped by the proud, that drag fair womanhood to the market to be exploited, that rob the children of bread, and the poor of home, that change this fair world to a vast shambles and a market-place, and cast out of the city to the rubbish-heap the frail and the weak. There is comfort in the thought that One loved us once. "Whoever tries to uncouple the religious and the social life has not understood Jesus," says one. And there is hope for a world that still remembers Him.[55]

Further insight into Gertrude's views can be found in those of her brother Horace, who had become involved in poor law reform. The government had appointed a Royal Commission on the Poor Law which brought in its (split) report in 1909. The minority report, by far more popular (judging by number of copies sold) than its majority counterpart, had been much influenced by Fabian Socialist thinking, and more or less written by Royal Commission member Beatrice Webb and her husband Sidney. The minority report recommended the abolition of the poor law (the majority report wanted to change its name), a devolution of its powers to the county or municipal council level, an emphasis on prevention of destitution (rather than on relieving it once it occurred), and a national scheme for reducing unemployment. The Webbs founded the National Committee to Promote the Break-up of the Poor Law to create public support for the minority report's recommendations; in April 1910 a meeting was held in Leicester to found a local branch. It was organised by *Midland Free Press* editor Edwin Crew, active in the Wycliffe Congregational Church; the Reverend F. Seaward Beddow, a follower of R.J. Campbell and soon to succeed J. Ernest James as minister of the Wycliffe Church; Anglican priest Lewis Donaldson, a Christian Socialist leader much involved with the cause of the unemployed and active in the Church of England Franchise League; suffragist, Unitarian and Leicester Secular Society member Edith Gittins; and Secular Society leader Sydney Gimson. This may have been where Gertrude met Donaldson of whom she later said that upon first seeing him she was "struck ... by his fearlessness and loyalty and when I got to know him I liked him better still." Gertrude and Horace would have been supporters of this group.[56]

Horace had by then been converted to socialism, most probably during the public debates about the minority report, and had been discussing his conversion in the *Midland Free Press*, hoping to influence other Christians. Horace's letters on social problems had previously appeared in the Free Speech page of the paper, and as late as January 1909 he had argued there against socialism, "the seed of which is envy." But Horace had been exposed to George Bernard Shaw, Walter Rauschenbusch (whose writing Gertrude also admired), no doubt had been involved in discussions with Gertrude and possibly socialist members of the Wycliffe Church, and may have heard speakers brought in by Donaldson and others, and sometime late in 1909, something clicked. His "tardy realisation" of the extent and unfairness of inequality, he explained, "has convinced me of the pressing necessity of revising and reorganising Society." He saw society as divided into the wealthy, who wanted to keep the status quo, the middle classes who wanted mild legislative reform, and the disinherited, who created the wealth but were cheated out of their rightful heritage. "We who work for a better day for our poor disinherited brothers, those who, under the present conditions must depend upon the scanty bounty of more favoured fellow creatures for existence, we desire only that they should come into their own." His announcement of his conversion triggered a debate, and in a subsequent letter he clarified his position. "It is certain that Socialism would make it easier for us to obey the Master," he wrote. "I, personally, am convinced that any improvement we may contemplate, must come from a union of Christianity, the doctrine of love, and Socialism, the science of justice." But the Christian churches did not carry out their proper doctrine: "The so-called Christianity preached by many of our denominational bodies, has done absolutely nothing in the way of a definite campaign, to uplift the poor. Something, therefore, must be done to make true Christianity known, the Christianity that implies Socialism." Now, the "greatest desire of [his] life" was "the growth of ... Socialist Christians."[57]

But it was not just a religious question for Horace, he was also intellectually captivated. "I can count about twenty friends of mine who are ardent Socialists," he wrote a few weeks later, "and when I want an intellectual, when I require a mental refreshment, I just get right away into their company." Horace predicted that continued inequality, poverty, misery, and injustice would lead to inevitable revolution in Russia, and believed socialism was the way to avoid a similar situation in England. "It is not the doctrine of vagabonds and shirkers, but of men who love their fellows, men of intellect and highmindedness ... It is not folly to say that the brightest of the minds, especially the young minds, of this beloved country of ours are flocking to its banner. Assuredly a brighter day is coming." Horace and Gertrude shared a fundamental outlook. For him too, it was a question of conscience. "I am a Christian, an active, ardent Christian worker; I assert that Christianity implies Socialism, that the Bible and the ministry of Jesus, preached from beginning to end a deadly warfare against vested interests and monopolies." A Socialist, he said, was "a lover of his fellows [and] ... a lover of Justice."[58]

Not all the Wycliffe Church's social commitments were the subject of political controversy; it was the centre of a charitable organisation for helping the blind, in which many peace activists were involved. Gertrude began to write about their undertakings during 1909. It seems likely that she was regularly attending Wycliffe Church, perhaps with Horace, and that may have given her a closer exposure to the group. Gertrude had already known a number of prominent Blind Society members from her involvement in the Leicester Peace Society. Hamilton Donisthorpe had been a member of the STWC; he attended Blind Society meetings as a representative of the Adult Schools Union in 1901, and was Honourary Secretary of the Society in

1908. His daughter Jessie, whom Gertrude knew as a temperance advocate, was also involved with the Blind Society. Donisthorpe and his wife had been on the platform at the tumultuous Cronwright-Schreiner meeting of 24 February 1900. The society had been founded in 1893 at Crew's initiative, originally linked to the Women's Guild of the Wycliffe Church, shortly after James had become minister. The Blind Society organised social events and outings for the blind, administered various schemes to provide limited financial aid, warm bedding and other items, and coordinated a system of free medical and dental care donated by the Society's "honourary consultant" physicians and dentists. In 1900 they had built several cottage homes with large flower and vegetable gardens, where thirty-four blind residents could live with help from a sighted housekeeper for each cottage. The society was supported by donations from various groups including cooperatives, trades unions, Bible classes, adult school classes, and employee groups at various workplaces, and numerous individuals who gave money, materials, and services. Gertrude formed lasting friendships with some of the cottage homes residents. Her involvement with the Blind Society probably consisted of attending their meetings and functions, and befriending blind members. Without knowing anything about the lives and interests of her blind friends, the basis for the friendships is unclear.[59]

Despite debates and a good deal of attention to poverty and unemployment remedies at the municipal level, the big issue in 1910 was woman suffrage. There had been hopeful signs; the Liberals had lost their majority and needed Labour and Irish votes to pass legislation. Asquith had promised to grant woman suffrage. Immediately after the January general election the WFL and WSPU publicly declared a truce with the government to allow the government to pass woman suffrage without losing face. A compromise Conciliation Bill was drawn up by an all-party committee, proposing to give the vote to approximately one million women who were qualified under the municipal franchise; that is, women who occupied business premises paying more than ten pounds a year rent, and women householders (which included renters, even of a single room; but would exclude most married women). With considerable reluctance (as its provisions were neither universal nor on the same terms as men), suffrage groups eventually accepted it on the condition that it would be passed during the current sitting of Parliament. Despite opposition in the House and no government backing, the bill passed second reading 299 to 190, but was sent back to a committee of the whole, that is, back to the House to be debated again. The government refused to give it a place on the agenda before the summer adjournment.

Suffrage groups decided to wait until the autumn sitting before re-
voking the truce, and meanwhile campaigned even harder to show
MPs there was tremendous support for the bill. However, various
cabinet ministers refused to promise their constituents they would
put the bill through. The militants established a deadline near the end
of November, and planned to end the truce with a big splash, if it became obvious that nothing could be done. In Leicester as elsewhere,
plans were made to send delegates to form part of a great deputation,
which would no doubt end in the usual roughing up of women by
the police, arrests, and spectacular abuse in prison. That is more or
less what happened; the issue of the conciliation bill was left hanging,
the government refused to pass it in the autumn session, and another
general election was held in December 1910. Asquith wriggled his
way through another Parliament the following year with another version of the conciliation bill without passing woman suffrage.[60]

Despite these dramatic events, Gertrude's involvement is usually
inferred by her pieces, rather than described; a mention in passing of
speaking to a group of women at a meeting, no details given. Nonetheless, her published comments on women's suffrage and womanhood are worth examining in some detail, for the light they shed on
her views, and by extension, those of her Christian Socialist – Radical
milieu. Her April 1909 poem "Womanhood" portrays Gertrude's
ideal. "Woman" was to be beautiful, pure in soul, gentle, loving, tender, strong, patient, faithful, courageous, hopeful, chaste, mighty "that
her wondrous power / Silent [and] vast, might move a wondering
world, / Leading to heights of grandeur and of truth / Blessing and
blest, the Daughter of His love." She was to be "free as the singing
wind" so no one could stand between "her soaring soul" and God.

> Yet from the vision of such grace I turn …
> I see the Wrong that reigns above the world,
> Holding in chains the Daughter of the skies;
> Across the sea, in fair and sunlit lands …
> I see her crushed, insulted, scorned and bound:
> Is it that she, like Christ – God's holy Son,
> Must die, a sacrifice, to save a world?
> God made her sweet and fair and full of love,
> And yet oppression spoils His holy work,
> And robs her of her loveliness and grace.
> And here, in this sweet land – this land of light,
> Where Freedom, crowned with stars, lifts high her head,
> I see her weeping, grieved and sore distressed,
> Lifting sad eyes to where, on lofty throne,

Blinded indeed, unseeing Justice dwells:
I hear her pray – unheard? Ah! never this
While God, Who made her, reigns above the Heavens.
God sees – as once He saw His Son-Beloved
Bow low His head to cruelty and shame.
And high above the watching angels bend,
Touching earth's broken hearts and grief-crushed lives –
Teaching her tear-dimmed eyes to look Beyond
To where the stars shine, glowing, white and calm,
And God will lift again His arm of power,
Smite the oppressor, raise the frail and weak,
Until again the Daughter of His love
Shall stand erect, in God-like majesty,
Gracious and great; a crown upon her brow,
With none to stand between her lofty soul
And His Who formed and made her sweet and fair.[61]

The theme of suffering for redemption is again present, the comparison of women's rights activists with the sacrificed Christ, ready, if that is what is required, to die to save the world. But stronger still is the assertion that the natural laws of the universe created and ruled by God ordain freedom and majesty for Woman, and presumably for ordinary women made by Him in His Daughter's image. Like John Donne whose poetry used the image of the legs of the compass, the *dernier cri* of science of his day, Gertrude mixed astronomy and religion to demonstrate the rightness of her vision. Such uses of science were frequent, by reformers and their opponents. For example, Gertrud von Petzold did this in her sermons and talks, such as her December 1910 address on "The Meaning of Evolution" in natural history, government, and religion. "The God of evolution, of infinite space and time, was a greater God than the anthropomorphic Deity of the Book of Genesis," she said. The scientific laws of evolution applied to government: "The primitive form of government based on physical force merely had in the course of centuries developed into government based on the consent of the governed, and approached more and more to the democratic ideal. That government should be of the people, for the people, and by the people. The principle of evolution could also be traced in international history, and they were learning more and more to realise the principle of universal peace between nations; that humanity ought to be one large family on earth." Von Petzold's conclusion united science and religion in ways familiar to Gertrude's readers: "In its ultimate nature evolution was a divine law, tending towards the spiritual uplifting of mankind."[62]

Gertrude's article, "A Defence of Womanhood," was a response to antisuffrage views expressed in the *Midland Free Press*. Women did not need to "claim equality," she said, "Woman has always been the equal of man." Of the few women who had been famous, she wrote that women had been two-thirds of Christian martyrs of early days, that queens had done no worse than kings. But, "What of the armies of loving mothers, whose self-sacrifice can never be computed, of tender wives, of faithful sisters and daughters? What of the crowds of frail, gentle, women and girls, toiling day by day to earn their bread and to help in supporting their homes? The days are past, long past, when woman's part was to be protected and cared for. In most cases she must face the world, just as does her brother." True men would always be chivalrous, but the system when women treated men as lords was long gone. "Gentleness, sweetness, and purity are not synonymous with weakness. We seek no mastery, we desire none, but we will yield to none." She refuted the old claim that suffering in childbirth was a punishment for original sin. In the Christian context, suffering in childbirth was women's equivalent of Christ's suffering on the cross to redeem the world, and like his pain, theirs earned women a "royal crown ... the greatest of all crowns, a very crown of life."[63]

Gertrude reversed the traditional notions of purity and sexual morality wherein the victim was contaminated and guilty. "It is not true that true women would turn away in horror from their sisters whom men presume to call 'fallen.' Good women would fold about them loving arms, and shield them from the evil travesties of men who had wrought their ruin." Men were not automatically entitled to reverence; those who were noble earned reverence, but others did not deserve it; "There is no virtue in being born a man ... Many men are unworthy to breathe the same air as the woman, who in all faith and pure trust gives herself a living sacrifice." Alluding to ravages of venereal disease spread by unchaste men, Gertrude wrote: "How I wish I could paint a picture! Oh, that I could take you, you who have as yet no reverence for womanhood, and show you lives ruined and laid bare, broken, bleeding hearts, reason tottering upon her throne, and in our terrible Palaces of Insanity dethroned forever! I would bid you look upon suffering unspeakable, and there learn reverence at least." This is a bit ambiguous: she may be saying that the false chivalry based on women's subordination leads to such outrageous suffering by the innocent and it should be replaced by true reverence based on mutual nobility and equality. Or, she may be saying that hideous suffering entitles the sufferer-victim to reverence. There is a theme of woman-as-victim-betrayed here, unquestionably, but she is arguing, I think, for a wider recognition of nobility, from women who would by any standards be entitled to reverence, to those women who because of their class and loss of "virtue" would not normally be considered entitled. "God bless the noble women of the world – of our land – from the Royal Queen-Mother, weeping for her dead, to the toiling girl wrestling to conquer trust betrayed and show a brave, bright face to the world," she wrote. A woman's place, Gertrude concluded, was not, as St Paul mistakenly claimed, as "a servant, but a ministering angel, when she is true to her highest self."[64]

Gertrude was not unique in her focus on women's holy mother-hood as a legitimation of women's demands for the rights of citizens, and more. Such references were mainstays of the votes for women movement, especially among the militants but also among some male supporters. "One thing must be conceded by the enemies of the movement – the spirit that actuates the women is a holy flame," wrote Agnes Clarke early in October, likening the militants to the saints. Men who supported woman suffrage shared this view, she said, and quoted a poem by John Masefield (later poet laureate), enti-tled "First Fruits," from the WSPU magazine *Votes for Women*. His mother had literally created him, Masefield wrote, and now dead, she could not see what he had done with her gift. If her grave could open and she could see him now, what would she think? "What have I done to keep in mind / My debt to her and womankind? / What woman's happier life repays / Her for those months of wretched days; / For all my mouthless body leached / Ere birth's releasing hell was reached? / What have I done, or tried, or said, / In thanks to that dear woman dead? / Men triumph over women still, / Men trample women's rights at will, / And man's lust raves the world untamed, / O grave, keep shut, lest I be shamed." Masefield was a member of the Men's League for Women's Suffrage, a broadly based group whose members came from diverse occupations and political affiliations.[65]

One of Gertrude's rare accounts of a suffrage event concerned her Leicester drawing-room encounter with an unnamed suffragette who had been in Holloway Prison. A report in the same issue by Agnes Clarke on a visit by Adela Pankhurst to Leicester suggests that it was Pankhurst whom Gertrude met. Clarke's article gives a sense of the highly charged atmosphere of courage and sacrifice that surrounded the suffrage issue in Leicester. Gertrude was almost certainly in the midst of this on several occasions in these years. Clarke described the reaction of local activists to the government's attempts to avoid a con-frontation by rescheduling the opening of Parliament, and the bravery of the women who were willing to risk injury by participating in such violent activities as attempting to gain admission to a minister's office to present a petition. Clarke cited a conversation with an another suffragette who was gradually becoming paralysed from spinal damage caused by being hit and kicked by Liberal stewards during one such attempt. "Have you never interrupted a Cabinet Minister's meeting? If not you must have seen it," the suffragette replied to Clarke's suggestion that the blows must have been accidental. "Stewards deliberately hit us with their fist, or knock us down. Several kicked us while we were lying on the ground." Other such incidents were described. "A great many men joined the League for Women's Suffrage [after such occasions] because they realised for the first time what it means to be unenfranchised in this country." Her own injury did not matter so much, the suffragette said, the cause was so important and the leaders so worthy that she held it a privilege to be able to do something. Clarke commented, "If this is not heroism, what is?" Pankhurst's lecture was no doubt also dramatic, featuring lantern slides of sweated workers and of the suffrage campaign.[66]

Gertrude's epiphanic description suggests that she met the visitor at someone's home during the day (Pankhurst's public lecture was at night). It sounds as if the two of them were alone for the moment; they sat by the fire, the suffragette embroidering a sash or banner in the WSPU colours of purple, white and green. The account emphasises the suffragette's femininity, grace, and refinement. Gertrude affected a naïve tone: she had heard, she wrote, many descriptions of suffragettes depicting them as "unwomanly beings, lacking in truly feminine refinements – in short, as strange monstrosities, aping and envying men." But this woman had not been at all like that. The suffragette spoke quietly and matter of factly about her prison experiences, "counting it as an honour to suffer that others might not suffer, just as one did long ago," Gertrude reported, alluding to Christ. "A great indignation filled me with a sense of more than personal wrong." A small child came in, the suffragette caressed it, and Gertrude thought about "that same form, so womanly, so naturally loving," in coarse prison clothes, the graceful hands sewing heavy mail bags. "Resuming her seat she spoke with loving re[v]erence of those great women who are the leaders of the movement which is going to take away from one-half of the human race the badges of serfdom and of slavery. She looked out the window, the Sun was shining, and as her eyes caught its rays they, too, shone with the light of a great purpose, of resolution and of sacrifice." Gertrude wanted to wish her Godspeed, she said, but was too choked by tears to speak further. "And I am glad and proud to be a woman," Gertrude concluded. Gertrude's earlier writing also shows that she greatly admired the militants, although she said consistently over the years that she was a suffragist, not a suffragette.[67]

Nineteen ten was also a banner year for the local peace movement. Years of quiet work on the part of the peace society came to fruition in the selection in 1909 of Leicester for the site of the Sixth British National Peace Congress to be held in June of the following year. The Leicester Peace Society had laid the groundwork with annual peace events, had distributed vast amounts of literature, and taken some part in F.J. Gould's campaign against militarism in the schools. LPS leaders had participated in International Peace Conferences including the 1908 conference held in London, and in National Congresses. They had networked with local sympathisers and with peace societies in the region to form a "strong and influential Reception Committee" to support their invitation to the National, and then to plan the congress. LPS leaders had circulated executive offices among themselves over the years, but they unanimously elected J. Ernest James to preside over the society during the National Congress. In preparation for the great event they intensified their efforts to draw in participants from other organisations; meeting minutes early in 1910 recorded the presence of delegates from such organisations as the Women's Labour League, the Amalgamated Society of Railway Servants, various Adult and Sunday Schools, and the Tool Makers Society.[68] The Congress was a success, with good crowds in attendance at public sessions. The opening sessions of the Congress featured local and other MPs, the Mayor, peace activist city councillors such as George Banton and Jabez Chaplin, and clergy such as Anglican Lewis Donaldson. Although Gertrude was not an executive member or official delegate from any of the participating societies, she did refer in later years to having attended peace meetings in this period and doubtless took part in the public events.[69]

J. Ernest James died in October 1910. He had been in frail health for a number of years, and may have entered his final illness by the time of the National Peace Congress meetings in June 1910, as it was LPS secretary Sydney Gimson and executive member Edith Gittins whose names appeared in newspaper accounts of the proceedings. With James' death Gertrude lost a key figure in her life. He had been an inspiration in the peace movement during the Boer War, had continued as a leader in the Peace Society, the Blind Society, and other groups in which Gertrude was involved. James had preached a gospel of loving service: individual responsibility for solutions to social problems the necessity for suffering to bring about social progress the socialism of Jesus. Gertrude's notions of the social imperatives of applied Christianity are echoed in James' sermons. Gertrude had often visited the Jameses at their family home, Rood House, in nearby Rothley; she was almost certainly among the hundreds of friends and comrades who attended his funeral. James had been more than a political comrade. She kept his photograph on her table for years. Leader, exemplar, teacher, friend, and probably also mentor, he had been one of her heroes of humanity, a "great brother-saint." He left his wife, two sons, and four daughters. His eulogies referred to his outspokenness, his compassion, and his courage. He had been fearless in the peace movement, and in general lived according to "an exalted ideal of Christian citizenship," as one of his funeral sermons put it. "He was his brother's keeper. Humanity was to him a vast brotherhood, and consequently he held it to be a violation of the golden rule for a Christian man to neglect a duty which affects the common good. He prayed earnestly 'Thy will be done,' but he felt that unless he laboured to establish that kingdom of righteousness, peace, and joy on earth, the prayer was not a Christian prayer." James had been universally admired and respected, and much loved. His successor Seaward Beddow appears to have been cut from the same cloth. "Preached in" to his pulpit at the Wycliffe Church by R.J. Campbell himself, Beddow would continue James' tradition of outspoken advocacy of pacifism and social justice, and would be a mainstay of support to the Twilley family in years to come.[70]

Sometime around the end of 1910, the decision was taken that Gertrude and her mother would go to Manitoba to join Gertrude's brother Fred and sister Fannie and her husband and daughter. It is not at all clear who took this decision, or why. It certainly was not Gertrude's idea; she did not want to go. There were a number of reasons to go to Swan River, from Fred's and Fannie's perspective. Fred was a bachelor and lonely. It would be better for him to have his mother and sister there. Aside from the family attractions, British newspapers had for years been flooded with articles describing the Canadian northwest as a desirable ground for settlement, even for English city women, if they were healthy and sensible. Gertrude and Eliza were certainly not the targets of such recruitment efforts, but these did establish a climate of information that made it seem at least possible to live in Manitoba. A number of Leicesterites had settled in the northwest; a son of Eliza's older sister Elizabeth Richardson Shirley, Arthur Shirley, had homesteaded in the Roaring River district where Fred and Fannie lived, just south of the town of Swan River, as had another Leicester family the Twilleys knew, May and Edward Minchen. Although no letters survive for the early period, later letters of Fred's indicate that the family wrote frequently. Fred was a wonderful writer; his later letters contained vivid reports of the doings of family and friends, local characters, community life, flora and fauna, and glories of the setting and the seasons. Fred also sent samples of local items; leaves and flowers, local newspaper clippings, and several pairs of moccasins. There may also have been reasons why it would be difficult for Gertrude and Eliza to continue in Leicester. Horace may already have been thinking about getting married, and that may have raised questions about Eliza and Gertie's livelihood and whereabouts; would they live with Horace and his wife? The other brother Frank was already married and living on his own, while continuing to work in the family boot and shoe business. But the fact is, I have no information about why they decided to go, if indeed it was actually Gertrude and Eliza who decided.[71]

In April 1911 Gertrude and Eliza left Leicester to go to Liverpool and thence to Canada. Gertrude had surely made the rounds of familiar places and friends, most likely feeling a mixture of excitement and dismay, probably mostly the latter. Friends had given her farewell gifts. Gertrude left England intending to go home for a visit in a few years' time. There was much to look forward to; women would get the vote, it was a matter of time. Social reform was in the air, and despite disagreements over the extent of changes to such institutions as the poor law, it was clear that even the Liberals would do much that was useful if the Tories could only be kept at bay. She would miss seeing a number of things she cared deeply about come to fruition, but at least she could feel optimistic. And in the daughter land, there would be fascinating sights and new experiences. Editor Edwin Crew had given Gertrude a huge sheaf of excellent quality paper and arranged for her to supplement her poems with regular articles about her experience; Gertrude would have her own column, or as good as, for the *Midland Free Press*. That may have been cold comfort as she left her beloved Leicester behind that April, not knowing what lay before her.[72]

3 New Destinies: Emigration, Settlement, Farm Wife, and Feminist Leader (1911–14)

Gertrude's destination was Swan River, in northern Manitoba. The town lies in a rich, sheltered, well-watered valley with deep black loam soil, just east of the Saskatchewan border, between the Porcupine Mountains to the north, the Duck Mountains to the south, about 800 kilometres north and west of Winnipeg. In 1898 when the survey was done and the area opened for settlement, the government erected a huge tent for settlers (on the West Favel River near Minitonas, about fifty kilometres from the railhead at Cowan) and the shacks that sprang up around it were called "Tent Town." This functioned as a staging area for homesteaders who wanted to leave their families and equipment and travel light to select their claim, which then had to be registered in Dauphin, 120 kilometres away. The "town" was supplied from Dauphin, or from the railhead when wagons could get through. Although most early settlers were Canadians, English, or Americans, there were also 1,500 Doukhoubours, many of whom hired out as labourers. The railway from Dauphin had been extended into the Swan River Valley and the town of Swan River created in 1899, about thirteen kilometres from Minitonas. By the time Gertrude and her mother arrived in 1911, the Swan River area had become a Leicester enclave of sorts. The Twilley clan were supplemented by various others including May Minchen, a friend who had settled there with her husband Edward in 1903, had kept in touch with friends at home, and introduced Fred in 1912 (via mail) to her Leicester friend Edith Watson, whom Fred would later marry.[1]

Incorporated in 1908, by 1911 Swan River was a reasonably well provided frontier town.[2] The town offered three main streets for shopping and businesses; these featured a railway station, grain elevator, flour mill, livery stables, boarding houses, cafes, hotels (one was a temperance hotel), blacksmith, harness shop, butcher, banks, a lawyer, farm equipment agency, hardware and general stores, banks, druggist, grocer, funeral parlour, poolroom, and a milliner. A twelve-bed cottage hospital was built in 1902, one of the series the Victorian Order of Nurses established in western Canada on a cost-sharing basis with the communities. As was usually the case in the development of community services, women's groups had been active in fundraising.[3] The hospital was staffed by a matron, an assistant, and several student nurses. The town had at least one doctor by 1901. There was a school in town and others were built in the outlying areas. The local newspaper, the Swan River *Star*, was founded in 1900.[4] Several churches were active; the Presbyterian church, built in 1900, seated 225. Each church had its women's organisations, such as the ladies' aid and the missionary society. Although much of the Valley went dry on local option around 1908, Swan River had a liquor outlet in the Commercial Hotel (the entire valley went dry in a wartime provincial referendum in 1916). Some settlers had pianos (for example Gertrude's sister Fannie Livesey) or organs and other musical instruments in their homes; a municipal band was established in 1912. Picnics often featured musical entertainment. Churches had music. In short, it was not the culturally bereft, lonely frontier of the horror stories warning ladies not to go West.

Despite all these amenities, life in the newly settled West was difficult for women like Gertrude. As her sister Fannie Livesey later wrote to Fred's fiancée Edith Watson, "There is certainly much in this country that is very hard for English women, many things that even our husbands do not see or understand, and to anyone fond of life and excitement it would be intolerable, as home has to be everything here, there are really no outside interests, and to a newly married couple it will certainly be a testing time, but what others have done you can do."[5] There was such a diversity of social, religious, cultural, and political activities, so much took place in the home, and so many areas of life and society were deemed the proper concern of "housekeeping," that this focus on the home was not as confining as it sounds from Fannie's letter. The work for women involved in this home-as-everything community, however, was extremely heavy, much more so than in an English city of the time, with its shops and services.

Gertrude and the rest had followed Fred, the first Twilley to go to the Swan River Valley. He and the other Twilleys settled in the Roaring River District, a few kilometres south of the town of Swan River. Fred had left Leicester as a twenty year old and gone to Ontario to learn farming after landing at Halifax in March 1902. In Leicester Fred had worked in an office in a shoe manufacturing company; he had come to Canada with a friend from work. Their employer had given them money and told them they could have their jobs back if they changed their minds (as the friend later did). "I thought I was very brave as so many scare stories were prevalent regarding this country at that time," he wrote to Edith Watson, who was a shop clerk in Leicester at the time they began corresponding.[6] After two and a half years in Ontario, Fred was ready to put into practice his plan to obtain land of his own. He went West on a harvest excursion in the fall of 1904; discouraged by anti-English feeling and an announcement in Winnipeg that no more harvesters were needed, he took a train north and disembarked at Gladstone, for no particular reason but the name. Finding no work there, Fred caught the next train for Swan River, where his cousin, who had for a time worked on the CNR in the dining cars, had homesteaded after his marriage. Fred worked for a general store, hauling wood and supplies around the region, installing pumps, and acting as a jack of all trades; by 1907 he was the manager, "farming as a side-line." In 1911 at his mother's urging he quit the store to farm full time, but periodically helped out at the store in Swan River and a branch at Durban.[7]

Gertrude's older sister Florrie had come out next, arriving in 1905 to keep house for Fred. At the time, Florrie was still married to Charlie Davie, who had turned out to be less than a good husband. Florrie had been on good terms with him at some point, but the relationship had deteriorated. The precise nature of his sins is not clear; Fred later said that Charlie drank heavily, and Fannie also thought Charlie was a no-good. Charlie had come back to Leicester after demobilisation of the reserves, and in 1902 he may have been a shopkeeper, according to the ambiguous information in the city directories. In 1904 he was listed as a bootmaker at the Twilley Brothers shop, and also lived at that address, according to the voters' list. It is conceivable that his earlier work experience had been in the boot and shoe industry, but there is no evidence for that. At any rate, Florrie considered it impossible to maintain a home with him. She decided to join Fred, and also worked at a store in Swan River, probably where Fred did. Charlie Davie was going downhill fast by then; in 1906 his listed occupation was "Private, Northamptonshire Regiment, Army Reserve, and a hawker [peddlar]." He died at age thirty-six in the workhouse infirmary

30 August 1906, of "malignant disease of the lungs and liver." By then Florrie and Fred had been joined in Manitoba by Fannie and John Livesey and their daughter Connie, who settled next door to Fred.[8]

The closeness of family, the contacts with customers, must have helped Florrie to accustom herself to the life, for she reportedly was happy there. She wrote home about how she appreciated the beauty of the setting. The isolation of the Roaring River district prevented her from attending church regularly, but she made do with the religion page of the newspaper, called "The Quiet Hour," which contained the weekly International Sunday School lesson and various inspirational writings. It is not clear what part Florrie might have played in the community as it became better established. Fred described her as "very clever all round." My own impression of her from her few Boer War writings is of a brilliant intellect, less sentimental than Gertrude. She was very musical, as were several of her siblings, and presumably cultured, but seems less self-consciously refined than her sister. However, that can only remain idle speculation. Florrie died suddenly 26 November 1907 of kidney disease. May Minchen wrote that Florrie appeared in excellent health during a visit a few days before being taken ill. The Liveseys had "no idea it was at all serious; they sent for the doctor, as she did not improve and he brought her to the hospital ... this was on Friday and early Tuesday morning she passed away." At the time Florrie fell ill, Fred had been working in Durban some fifty kilometres away. He walked home to visit her and arrived at the hospital only to be told she had died and he must remove her body as they urgently needed the bed. Fred carried Florrie in his arms to the funeral home. Fred was devastated. "We were so happy," he said. "It was a long time before I took interest in things again."[9]

Gertrude and her mother followed hundreds of thousands who crossed the Atlantic in those years, although since Gertrude and Eliza travelled cabin class they did so more comfortably than most. (They also avoided any possible trouble at the immigrant inspection station, since cabin passengers were not subject to the same severity of inspection as the steerage passengers; given Gertrude's medical history, this was just as well since she was probably a prohibited immigrant.) Gertrude's accounts of the voyage mark a new stage in her writing career. The editor of the *Midland Free Press*, where she had for years been a featured poet and occasional commentator, had asked her to write a description of the voyage from Leicester to Swan River and then to contribute regular columns on life in the new country for Leicester readers. This places Gertrude's work in the genre of travel writing, which was immensely popular during the Victorian and Edwardian eras; by 1910, as Susan Jackel points out, there were a good hundred such books published by Britons. Although Gertrude was to write as an emigrant rather than a traveller, in newspaper columns rather than a book, the conventions of that genre nonetheless apply to a great extent to her writings. The purposes of travel writing were to educate the reader about conditions of life in the colonies, and of course, to entertain. Jackel cautions that although these writings were often autobiographical in form, narrated from a first-person perspective, they were not necessarily autobiographical in intent. Jackel points out to readers of Georgina Binnie-Clark's reissued 1914 volume *Wheat and Woman* that it is difficult to be certain that the "I" in the narrative "is primarily self-revealing or self-creating: whether we are dealing here with the confessional tones of the autobiographer, or the plausible but largely fictive revelations of an artfully-projected narrative persona."[10] Although the Binnie-Clark volume tends toward one end (the fictionalised end) of the spectrum and Gertrude's more straightforward and repertorial columns the other, the caveat is still worth remembering. However, I have taken Gertrude at her word about events, and I have been relieved to find over the years that when there are other sources for Gertrude's experiences, reactions, or ideas, they have tended to be consistent with her published versions. Gertrude's columns on the voyage and the new country began to appear in the *Midland Free Press* on the third of June 1911.

Gertrude and her mother left Liverpool in late April 1911 and officially entered Canada as landed immigrants in Halifax some two weeks later. Gertrude enjoyed the voyage (her first trip on the ocean) more than she expected, given her sadness at leaving. She appreciated the excellent and beautifully served meals, and was surprised by the "wonderful beauty of the water glistening beneath the rays of the sun. Now black and silver, now blue and crystal, now green and gold, or so it seemed to me." Mercifully lightly touched by seasickness, she spent long hours on deck. "The sea gained steadily a great fascination for me. I shall love it forever," she exclaimed. She attended church services in her own class and elsewhere, enjoyed a hymn-sing, various musical entertainments, was saddened by a baby's sea burial, and gladdened by another's birth and by the fresh-faced idealism ("underneath the fun and mischief and apparent carelessness ... earnest transfiguration") of the young men. The ship put in at St John's to unload cargo, and Gertrude and her mother took advantage of the break to visit churches, buy postcards, and chat to the inhabitants. The landing at Halifax went smoothly, cabin passengers being troubled by only the slightest of formalities before being permitted to disembark, go through customs, and proceed to the train station for the next five-day leg of the trip.[11]

The rail journey to Montreal took thirty hours; Gertrude and Eliza spent the four-hour layover sightseeing near the station, viewing the Mary Queen of the World Cathedral with its life-sized statues high up on the outside walls, modelled after Rome's St Peter's Cathedral. They travelled for two days and nights on to Winnipeg in CPR tourist class (rather than the less comfortable colonist cars), but delays at sea made them miss being met. They stayed overnight at the Brunswick Hotel on Main Street until time for the CNR to Swan River. Despite the length of the journey, Gertrude was impressed by the scenery (its quantity as much as its quality), and also by the courtesy she saw men showing to women (getting up to open train doors and such). This "augurs well for a new and virile country" she concluded. They disembarked before dawn at Swan River, population 574, and rode out into the countryside to the Liveseys' house in an open buggy, "in ideal weather, all opening out into beauty." Gertrude was home, the "strange veiled future ready to unfold."[12]

Whatever the amenities of the town of Swan River only a few kilometres from the farm of John and Fannie Livesey where Gertrude and her mother lived after their arrival on the 12th of May 1911, it must still have been a considerable shock to a woman from an English city to find herself in such a setting. Yet Gertrude seemingly liked it enormously from the beginning. Although she later admitted she had not wanted to emigrate, the columns she wrote about her early experiences in Swan River reveal fascination and admiration. This was not the primitive backwoods of Susannah Moody's day, or even the rough setting encountered by Tent Town pioneers. As Fred said, "The pioneer work is done ... we have now quite a nice little circle of our own and also our Canadian neighbours are very nice and the most of them refined." A few days after her arrival, Gertrude attended a nearby wedding with seventy-five other guests, held in the bride's "typical Canadian home, built of logs, very picturesque, spacious and comfortable." Gertrude was impressed by the sacredness of the ceremony (unexpected to her in a home wedding), beautiful wedding gown, the elaborate wedding feast cooked by the two mothers, the music (played by a local band), the "tasteful and numerous" presents. She was "filled with admiration at the cleverness of Canadian ladies who are able to do such splendid cooking and do everything else that comes their way without any assistance." She found the entire experience "all very new to me – but I enjoyed everything very much," she added. The day ended with a drive home in the soft summer air, the way lit by fireflies (and apparently blessed by a scarcity of mosquitoes). Her mixed emotions about the event could describe her feelings about her new life: pleasure, but a hint of sadness, "sadness of gates passed, doors closed ... the mystery of untrodden paths, unopened years, a cloud veiled future."[13]

The natural beauty of the area was a source of delight. Gertrude found the open stretches of the prairie countryside, the flowers, the fields of ripening grain, the wildlife, the extravagant sunsets, strikingly lovely. As she said, quoting a hymn about gold-adorned fields, joy ringing in the hills, valleys so thick with corn they too sang, she had never understood the meaning of such hymns as she now did, surrounded by the "lavishness of God's goodness to earth." Her writings convey her sense of ripeness, of God's bounty, of trust in the earth and her continuing blessings. (Later that year, she would draw reassurance about immortality and ongoing creation, from the seasons: the death of flowers and the onset of winter, surely followed by spring's renewal. "I am learning that there is no death," she wrote.) She enjoyed her experiences that summer of easy hospitality, the inclusiveness of social events, "much visiting and many picnics" in which she immediately took part. The impressive spread at the wedding was echoed in the abundance of the typical fare, cakes, pies, salad, sandwiches, seemingly without end, prepared by the women and set out for all to share pot-luck at picnic suppers. Everyone who could get there (and as she remarked, nearly everyone had teams of horses for transportation and in any case there were neighbours to hitch rides with if need be) was welcome. She noted that servants and hired hands were treated as household members, that "ladies" were not leisured but took pride in their hard work and skill and were no less "dainty" for it. There was a lesson about partnership between God, nature, and humankind in much of what she saw, and nowhere more than at harvest time. The harvest was "the touch of the Father's hand upon the labour of mankind ... There were [sic] no harvest but for the miracle of the master. Yet the labour of man is great and worthy and noble. I love my toiling brothers and their hand and brain are earth's true royalty," she concluded. Abundance, classlessness, justice, and brotherhood were creating something new, good, and divinely ordained, thus inevitable.[14]

This mixture was expressed in her poem "The promise of hope," that fall, excerpted here.

There shall rise new dawns of beauty o'er the darkness of the earth,
Sweeter than the breath of Spring-tide, purer gladness comes to birth
For the world is looking upward, truer faiths and better creeds,
With the glow of light upon them come to meet the people's needs.

Thrones of monarchs all shall perish, pomp and power of earth shall fail
Yet the soul of truth and beauty o'er the wreckage shall prevail:
Gladly shall the poor and needy hear the message Hope shall bring,
That the Father, high in Heaven, looks alike on slave or king.

It is manhood that is royal – manhood noble, true and strong,
Manhood hurls aside oppression, rising great o'er tyrant-wrong!
And the song of Hope grows louder as she watches from above,
Calm and pure above the tumult, while the changeful ages move.

Captive-chairs are ever falling, everywhere the people sing,
Of their new-found hope and courage as their gladdest song they bring:
'Mid the golden waves of sunset, or the rose-hued clouds of dawn,
All the music of their anthem is the glory of the morn!

There must be the minor-echoes, but they make the music sweet,
And they lift the soul for ever to the One with nail-pierced feet –
One who taught the earth to triumph o'er the gathering hosts of wrong,
One Who filled the world of weeping with the glory of the song![15]

Gertrude was curious about her new neighbours and impressed by the ethnic mix of the region. She wrote lengthy and sympathetic descriptions of the history and culture of native peoples, Doukhoubours, Galicians, and Scandinavians for her Leicester readers. However sympathetic, these accounts reflected the stereotypes (and settlement and assimilation policies) of her time. Her discussion of the Galicians focused on the need for and methods of assimilation; the column on Scandinavians referred to Queen Alexandra's Scandinavian ancestry, the great cultural contribution of the sagas, and the industry, cleanliness, and respectability of their emigrants to Canada. Of the native peoples, she commented that "less than twelve years ago this valley was the abode of Indian tribes," but despite her tendency to side with the oppressed, she apparently did not find any oppression here. Indeed, she commented approvingly, "The Indians are well cared for by the Dominion government, lands being retained for their habitation and other lands being reserved so that the profits may assist in providing for Indian families." Of the Scandinavians she commented, "I am glad to be in a country where races blend as brothers." Likewise, despite the supposed flaws of the Galicians, their presence was a positive and necessary part of a higher purpose: "To blend into one great family the long-estranged brothers of the human race. From the blending together of the nations of the world fair fruits of love shall spring forth and blossom." According to the

"visions of the ancient prophets ... we shall rise to greater understanding as the great race of mankind sweeps on its ever-upward
course." She admired the communitarian practices, hard work, pacifism, and gender equality she saw amongst the Doukhoubours, and
described their controversial leader Peter Verigin as a "Moses of his
people."[16]

Like many evangelical liberals, Gertrude viewed Canada's settlement experience as a divinely guided harbinger of international cooperation and human enlightenment; she was intrigued and hopeful.
She looked toward the "growing commonwealth of humanity," as
Brian Fraser describes it, to bring about the "progressive realization
of the Kingdom of God on earth." It is noteworthy that whatever her
assessment of the amount of work needing to be done by or on each
"race," her religious-based belief in humanity's progress toward
unity and peace was the final arbiter. Thus she could have written in
any of these vignettes her concluding lines in the Scandinavian piece:
"I pray that God may open the gates of the nations of the earth, cast
down the vessels of war and teach us all to live in peace and love together, so that for the whole earth there shall dawn a holier day."[17]

The Empire was an instrument of this divine process. In a poem for
the new King's coronation, she wrote,

And for the wide dominions where Britain's flag bolds away,
We kneel beneath Heaven's canopy in humble prayer to-day;
Give peace within our borders, O Prince of Peace Divine,
That Love may reign in Glory, and righteousness may shine ...
We thank Thee for our country's power spreads where suns ne'er set.
We pray Thee that Thy holy law our hearts may ne'er forget ...
We thank Thee, that a woman's hand once held a holy sway,
And sweetly lifted England up to greet a nobler day –
We thank Thee for a King who bore aloft a flag of peace,
And strove to herald in the age when strife of man shall cease.

British rule was not tyranny, the throne need not tumble nor the Empire fall, and her vision of hope was at that time unclouded by any
analysis of British imperialism as a wicked system antithetical to democracy. This is particularly striking in contrast to the analysis, which
she ardently supported, of the Stop-the-War Committee of her Boer
War days, and that which she would come to consider during the
First World War.[18]

Gertrude's first Canadian Christmas was noteworthy for extreme
cold (minus forty-nine degrees Fahrenheit, cold even for northern
Manitoba). She missed Christmas carollers and the Christmas morn-

ing postal delivery. She was comforted by cards and letters from "Home," enjoyed the bittersweet familiarity of family observances of holiday meals and songs, and for the most part experienced her recollections of similar festivities as happy memories rather than painful nostalgia. She enjoyed the Sunday School concerts and "Christmas tree" parties (one complete with Santa arriving through a window to distribute the children's presents). Post-Christmas socials followed similarly attractive patterns: sleigh bells, beautiful winter scenes coming and going (the travelling luckily not too uncomfortable), new friends, new games, music, high spirits, good conversation, and good times. She was amused at a Bible-class social by the custom of having men serve the supper (that the women had provided, of course). Gender-reversal play was featured at a Valentine's party too; men were instructed by rhymed notes to carry out typically feminine tasks such as darning a sock, and the winner was given a prize. The novelty and beauty of the winter landscape captivated her, the "snow dazzling bright, shining like jewels all around"; this theme recurred in her prose and poetry during that first winter season.[19] Travel by sleigh was romantic, especially in the hours past midnight, under the "holy radiance" of the clear winter stars. She wrote of trees coated with hoarfrost, of snow crystals glistening in the moonlight in that "sweetly silent world."[20]

At home in Leicester, seriousness and high-minded refinement perhaps did not go hand in hand with frequent partying. As she said, commenting on the sharp changes in social activity according to the season, "There is more visiting done and social life of all kinds in winter than in England, and correspondingly less in summer," when everyone is too busy. "The winter is long, yet social events fill up the months, relieving it of dullness … The 'Valentine Party' is an institution here, and is great fun." The typical winter whirl included carnivals (there was an outdoor rink on the Swan River), fancy dress balls, dances, receptions, and parties for specific holidays; there were more serious-minded events such as bazaars and various meetings, but most of these included a social component, and fun was predictable if not compulsory. In Swan River, the Twilleys and particularly Gertrude had risen in status. In Leicester, however admirable Gertrude's education, acquaintances, literary and intellectual accomplishments, and cultural and political interests, she could never rise higher than the margins of the lower middle class; her own and her family's occupations and poverty were those of the working classes. In Swan River she was among the most cultured and respectable community members, and these too were expected to participate in fun and silliness, which had probably not been a regular part of Gertrude's adult life.

Here there were not the tightropes of class and her own personal history to walk; if she had felt she carried liabilities, she could shed them, while her accomplishments shone in this new setting. As she later commented about a discussion with a woman in nearby Minitonas who had been there since pioneer days, "The lady ... also seemed much amused at the class distinction of the older countries. It is really not possible for these people to understand it, and I sincerely hope it will be long before it finds its way into Canadian life. No woman here is ashamed to work, unless it is someone who comes from the 'Old Country.' Housewifery is an art, and people are proud of being proficient in that art." Granted that there was frequently hostility against the useless and snobbish type of English immigrant, the English settlers in the Swan River area do not appear to have that held against them, perhaps because they were competent and hardworking. Gertrude may have been much concerned with being ladylike and refined, but she also enthusiastically accepted the new rules, did her best to acquire the necessary knowledge and skills, and took part in whatever came her way. She in turn was accepted and admired. She blossomed in this "lovely Land of Snow" that first winter.[21]

Gertrude was in her element in her new home. As Fred wrote a year after her arrival, "She has made a host of friends. She is a very good speaker and has already got the first suffragette [sic] society in Manitoba (or in the West for that matter) well under way with herself as President and my other sis as Sec." Fred exaggerated slightly, as Gertrude was not the organising force behind the society, but her involvement (whatever its extent) in the English suffrage movement certainly helped to get the local group started. In March 1912 she was invited to speak at a Grain Growers' Association (GGA) meeting in support of woman suffrage; the Manitoba Grain Growers' Association had adopted a prosuffrage position in 1911. The GGA meetings (and just about everything else in the little rural area a bit south of the town of Swan River) were regularly held at the schoolhouse seven kilometres' drive from the Livesey farm. The principal speaker was William Sifton, one of the earliest settlers, retired in Minitonas since 1910, but still active in community affairs and a staunch proponent of women's rights. Sifton argued that women's contribution entitled them to the vote. He emphasised the importance of women's influence in refining men in the West, and defended the English militant suffragettes. Gertrude was asked to discuss the situation of women in England, and the progress made thus far by the various wings of the suffrage movement. The Roaring River Suffrage Association was founded on the spot, Gertrude unanimously chosen as president, her sister Fannie as secretary, and local leaders Mrs Alice Cox,

Mrs Margaret Knox Martin, and teacher Miss Grace Shaw as the executive committee.[22]

The Roaring River Suffrage Association was one of the earliest suffrage associations in the province, its members claiming it to be the earliest (unaware of the Icelandic association), and established a week before the Winnipeg Political Equality League (whose minute book begins on March 29), it put Roaring River women on a par with their city sisters to the south. Its membership included men and women.[23] It was moderate in its outlook and tactics, as were Canadian suffragists generally. Suffragists' views of the militants differed in sophistication, but antimilitance did not go hand in hand with antisuffrage. Member May Minchen wrote to her Leicester friend Edith Watson, "We have some nice meetings ... Are you in favour of [woman suffrage], of course not with the Militant Suffragettes, I often wonder if it is all true what I read in the papers here, if so they act as if they are crazy. I do hope they will get the vote, it is only right, and I believe in homesteads for women, I don't see why they should not have the same opportunities as men."[24] Fred Twilley echoed the moderate position: "The suffragettes are having a wild time over there aren't they ... I really can't see the wisdom of violence. I quite believe the present government is the one to whom the advocates of universal suffrage can look with the best chance of success, but not with such methods."[25]

Getting to the monthly suffrage meetings could be difficult. Gertrude commented, "The roads have been almost impassable ... a heavy hail storm prevented punctuality" at a May 1912 meeting. "We seemed to be driving through rivers of water and seas of mud, alternately ... the poor horses, they were struggling so hard. The badness of the roads made the load so heavy, they kept stopping and seemed to look back at us reproachfully." Spring usually brought a period when it was very difficult to travel, the ground being a morass of mud too wet for wheels and too warm for snow runners. Yet people longed for the brief spring season and rejoiced in the warmth and new growth; despite the slackening of social life, once the seeding was done there were numerous summer festivities, the most common of which was the picnic.[26] The woman suffrage group held a community picnic near the Liveseys' house that June, featuring ice cream, lemonade, assorted snacks, foot races, a tug of war, and a baseball game (women against men, the latter winning. The sorrow of defeat was assuaged somewhat by a gift of ice cream from the winners to the losers.) The day was topped off by a big potluck supper, and recorded for posterity in photographs taken by Fred.[27]

Picnics were frequent in the summer months, to celebrate various holidays, commemorate anniversaries (such as the Pioneers'

Re-union picnic Gertrude attended in 1913), or for community organisations to recruit members and raise funds. Gertrude's initial enjoyment of them was perhaps enhanced by their exotic flavour (compared to Leicester city life). She attended many, and described several in her columns for the Leicester paper. Hard on the heels of the 1912 suffrage picnic was the big community picnic celebrating Dominion Day (the 1911 celebration had been rained out). Gertrude viewed the celebrations as a triumph for the Empire, marking Canadian "loyalty to the British flag." People entered the flag-decorated town from all over the district, dressed up for the occasion; there were speeches, pony races, athletic competitions and games, refreshment booths, and meals served by the Hospital Ladies Aid. (In 1913 the Ladies Aid charged $.36 for a full meal.) The food was prepared and brought in by the Ladies Aid members and other women in the community; in 1913, for example, Gertrude brought three pies and a quart of cream for them. A typical menu included cold sliced meat (this was bought in town, not donated), potatoes, salads, pickles, bread, butter, pies, cakes, fruit, tea. Tea water was heated on portable gas stoves. The 1912 celebrations were noteworthy for the prominent participation of native peoples of the area; Gertrude was impressed by the splendid costume of a local chief, the physical beauty of some of the children, the pipe smoking of some of the women, and the prowess of the men at horsemanship and footraces. The day ended with a pow-wow, "a national dance among the Indians, of great significance to them," Gertrude reported.[28]

Gertrude did what she could to retain her Leicester ties; she wrote regularly to friends. She learned Braille and set her poems in Braille, in order to correspond with some of her blind friends from the Wycliffe Society for the Blind. However, she found plenty to do in her new home. She lost no time in becoming involved in Presbyterian church activities such as the Ladies Aid, and the Women's Missionary Society, which met monthly in members' homes in and around Swan River. Gatherings usually began with Bible verses and prayer, society business reports, followed by an educational presentation on a foreign or home mission theme, concluding with refreshments. The Society held various fundraisers such as sales or concerts, to support mission work. One was based on the biblical tale of "talents"; each member spent $.25 on material to make something to sell, the proceeds to be reinvested and the cycle repeated for a set number of weeks, at which time the earnings would be paid into the fund. Gertrude made tea aprons, eventually paying in $2.00. The local paper records that she read a paper on missions to the Society in May 1912. Gertrude was enthusiastic about mission work among the "foreigners" settling in Canada, as part of the progress of humanity toward unity in "peace and love and mutual service."[29] For the fall 1912 harvest fete, she helped the group cook hundreds of ears of corn in huge pots suspended over open fires, supplemented by cake, ice cream and tea. The event featured dainty table "linens" (paper serviettes were used), Japanese lanterns, gipsy costumes for the servers, and music by the newly founded community band. She noted approvingly that there was good attendance by members of other denominations, and took it as evidence that the ecumenical spirit promoted by the Presbyterian minister had taken root in the town.[30]

In the fall of 1913 she hosted a WMS meeting to hear a report of the presbyterial (equivalent of the annual general meeting) which had been held in Dauphin; one of the group's delegates was the bank manager's wife, who had come to the valley about the same time as Gertrude. Gertrude enlivened the traditional "plain tea" (only bread and butter and plain cake were usually permitted) with corn on the cob that she had grown. The minister and his wife stayed on to supper; they often visited, and discussed books and newspapers, which they exchanged. These sorts of activities, combining religious, intellectual, political, and social interests, were indicators of Gertrude's place in the community. She was praised for, and justifiably proud of, her acquired skills of housewifery, and admired and appreciated for her intellect and cultural and political sophistication. She was elected president of the Women's Missionary Society for 1914.[31]

Gertrude had began to publish poems and other items in the local paper in the summer of 1912, a year after her arrival. Her first substantial contribution was a lengthy article on the education of adolescent boys. The article is an interesting mix of the traditional and the radical in its style and content. It features the sentimental and devotional Christian rhetoric found in her poetry, and admires the role in England of excellent teaching based on religion in elite boys' schools in shaping leaders of the Empire. It also advocates F.J. Gould's advanced notions about education based on reinforcement of the good as a means of extinguishing the bad in boys' habits and nature, discusses the Comteian positivist moral education theory and practices of the Moral Education League, and describes her friend Gould's methods.[32] Her tone is that of the expert, knowledgeable and quietly assured; Gertrude clearly felt at home offering leadership on this topic. This is suggestive of how rapidly she was accepted as a community leader; at least in the eyes of the editor and Presbyterian minister Andrew Weir, Gertrude was part of the intellectual and cultural elite. She was presented by him as an educational authority, and even more strongly and consistently as a writer of the highest literary standard. Remarking on her kindness for contributing poetry, and explaining she was modest on the subject, Weir touted her "literary accomplishments." He wrote that "her work has been given a very high place in literary circles in England," hinting at royal readers: "During the past few months she has received special cards of thanks from the Hon. Charlotte Knolleys, Private Secretary to Queen Alexandra, for contributions in memory of the late King, Edward the Seventh."[33]

Within months of her arrival in Swan River, Gertrude was being courted by Robert Richardson. Robert was a good catch. Among the earliest settlers in the valley, by 1903 at age twenty-six, Robert had cattle, horses, pigs, a granary, log stable, and log and frame house, surrounded by a rail fence. When Gertrude met him, he was an established farmer, well respected in the community. A tall, handsome man remembered by his nieces as gentle and kind, he was involved in numerous local organisations, active in the Presbyterian Church, and the superintendent of Sunday Schools for the Swan River Presbyterian Church, where he taught a Bible class. By November, Gertrude was attending church with the Richardsons: given the distance and the mode of winter travel (a horse-drawn sleigh complete with bells) and the scheduling of the services (afternoon Sunday School, evening service) this activity provided excellent opportunity to get to know each other.[34]

Robert's cultural attractions included a fondness for poetry, of which he could recite a large repertoire. Fred Twilley later wrote, "Our famous reciter here is Robert Richardson. He can 'chew the rag' for hours ... Our friend Bob can recite until he is blue in the face." Robert is remembered as a rather solemn and deliberate person. He had very little formal schooling but was self-taught in a number of areas; his son Eric recalls that Robert figured out how to make the complicated calculations for angles for roof building, for example. He was politically active, especially in the local Grain Growers' Association, and interested in social issues. In January 1914, for example, he gave a paper at the annual meeting of the GGA entitled "Why We Allow the Present Conditions as Affecting the Masses, to Exist." Robert's brother James, who lived with him and their sister Maggie, was equally nice, but very slow moving, and handicapped by a stutter. Bird-like, fast-moving Gertrude was an opposite type, but she and Robert shared interests in literature, deep religious convictions, an earnest commitment to social responsibility, and were well matched in many respects.[35]

The possibility of marriage to Robert raised a number of issues for Gertrude. As she later wrote, she longed for her own home, children and a normal family life, but was uncertain about the propriety or legality of a second marriage.[36] There were sound practical reasons for marrying in general and marrying Robert in particular. He was an established farmer, a landowner (he and Jim together had 480 acres by 1912), and if he was not especially well off, he was certainly no worse off than most others in the area. She was a seamstress and writer, neither of which was a secure or lucrative occupation. On her own, she could never hope to afford land or a home.[37]

Fred's experiences farming show that more was needed than hard work. As Fred wrote to Edith, "It is hard work and expensive work breaking land for cultivation that has been forest and never seen the plow." He explained, although "it is possible to make a living and more besides on the few [twenty-five] acres we have had arable," many farmers were crippled by debt. Fred's share of the grain profits for years went to Winnipeg to pay off the debt for a second quarter section of land he bought (with John Livesey). "We have splendid farms and I hope it will not be such an outlay every year," but as it stood in 1913, "our expenses are about sixty dollars yearly and not very much return." Fred like many other farmers relied on the sale of hay, wood, butter and eggs and an occasional animal to make a living during the years he was paying off the debt. Gertrude wrote to Edith, "But in this great country of infinite possibility there are times when the money stringency is acutely felt. There are reasons for this that are difficult to explain to English people, but so much must be invested in land, implements and stock. And interest charged on working capital is tremendously high." [38]

Although western settlement was based on the idea that any man could get a homestead, this was not so for women. The Canadian government had deliberately barred single women from access to homesteads in order to force them to marry. As interior minister Oliver had told agricultural expert and suffragist Cora Hind, "To admit women to the opportunities of the land grant would be to make them more independent of marriage than ever." Would single women have rushed to take up homesteads and refused to marry but rather competed with their male neighbours? All other things being equal, women could make good farmers; but given the system of discrimination in access to homesteads or the money to buy land, all other things would never be equal for the majority of women. Since few Canadian women had the choice to be farmers rather than farm wives, often the only land to which they could gain access was their husband's. Never mind that it was his, not theirs, in law and fact during his lifetime, and theirs after his death only if he chose to bequeath it to them; that was the closest most women could come.[39]

Gertrude's situation was predictable. Single women were generally scooped up and quickly married in the West; this phenomenon was discussed in the immigration and settlement literature of the period, whether government, imperialist, or even feminist in origin. British emigrationist reformers of all stripes advocated empire-building or nation-building or whatever their term, through the emigration, marriage, unpaid work, and family influence of British women. Of course the fact that by 1911 there were 1,300,000 more women than men in Great Britain no doubt added to the attractions of this solution. The middle class spinster was the favoured empire-builder, but respectable working class women were also greatly desired fodder, especially if they would work as domestics while settling in. Gertrude, with her working class origins and middle class education, outlook, and pretensions, lacking robust health, and beyond the prime child-bearing years, was not the typical woman envisioned to fill this role, but nevertheless she was being called to service.[40]

Susan Jackel has pointed out that a disproportionate number of middle class British women emigrated to Canada in the period just before the First World War, and they "introduced a perceptible skew into the demographic makeup of Western Canada at a crucial time in its social formation … The significance and impact of these women extends far beyond the question of numbers." Jackel argues that a significant factor in the particular flavour of western consciousness of social issues of the period was the active presence of these women. Hence the influence of a de facto network of middle class British women emigrants was at work in such phenomena as the great interest in the English suffrage movement (including the militants), the invitations extended to English suffrage leaders to tour Canada, the visibility of British women in Canadian women's organisations, the prominence of British-born leaders, the importance given to a wide range of educational and training opportunities, the interest in housing, public health and sanitation, and so on. More broadly, Jackel speculates about the pervasiveness and efficacy of the "civilising mission" of British middle class women in the West, for example in the promotion of cultural activities, reading, and writing. The flood of British immigrant women's fiction and nonfiction writing about the western experience, a genre of immense popularity (due in part to the Canadian government's intense propaganda campaign to attract immigrants), is another example. Jackel comments on the relish with which many of these women realised the vast possibilities of the west for freedom of all sorts: "space, latitude, movement" for the gentlewoman chafed by English restrictions. This was no less a factor for Gertrude, with her acquired gentility; she was able to be comfortable in the relative classlessness in Swan River in a way she never could have been in Leicester. She could enjoy the attributes of gentility without the restrictions. Marriage further confirmed her solidly respectable status, if it needed additional confirmation. She could be normal without sacrificing freedom, the restrictions of marriage being significantly less than those of class, her anomalous marital status of spurious widowhood (for so she was apparently known in the community, although it seems likely that this description was introduced by Fred or Fannie before her arrival), and her economic marginality as a husbandless woman.[41]

Gertrude's sister had mixed feelings about the proposed remarriage; Fannie believed that Gertrude had miscarried during her first marriage, and she may have thought Gertrude could not have children as a consequence; she was afraid there were leftover legal entanglements, and thought it wasn't fair to Robert.[42] It is unclear whether Gertrude and Fannie discussed this openly. Evidence is fragmented and not wholly consistent; two of Gertrude's few surviving letters contain references to her decision. "He wanted to marry me and I felt very happy indeed, and we became engaged," she wrote in 1924. "I was thirty-seven, but regularly menstruating, and hoped I could have children."

She wrote for advice from a physician she had known in England, with whom she had stayed in touch. He replied that there was no reason she should not marry, and he hoped she understood all that marriage implied (i.e., sexual intercourse), given the circumstances of her first marriage. It is not clear what information Robert was given about her first marriage; he must have known that it was unconsummated. According to Gertrude, Robert had consulted a lawyer and their minister; because her account is ambiguous as to the identity of the advice-giver, it is worth recording in full. "Mr R. called upon a lawyer, and consulted the Minister of our church – and in July 1912 we were married by Rev. Mr Bowman in Winnipeg – the license being issued by Mr Brown at the City Hall. He said we were justified as the other marriage was a strange one and we had not met for eleven years – but he wished me to say I was a widow, and I would not do that. However, he said the marriage would be perfectly lawful – and wished me every happiness."[43] "He" in the second sentence could refer to Andrew Weir, James Bowman, or perhaps Mr Brown. Writing in late 1939 about the same events, she described discussing the decision with her mother and the minister of the church, with the same result: "Everyone who knew all there was to know thought it right for me to marry." The minister could have been Weir or Bowman. In any event, she followed their advice. She married Robert Richardson 25 July 1912.[44]

Gertrude settled happily into married life, to all accounts. Fred wrote, "They seem very happy and contented. She is learning to drive the horses and nearly broke the gate today when turning in."[45] In addition to the heavy load of domestic work faced by every farm wife, she continued her writing and her political work. Fred teased her about this latter; to Edith he wrote, "You know my sister Gerty [sic] is the Mrs Pankhurst of the movement here and when she 'cuts loose' on mere man I point out to her that it didn't take her very long to 'freeze on' (Canadian parlance) to one here." (He added, "Yes, I'm sure you would like my sister if you met her. You would like both of them and Mother too. I am proud of all of them.")[46] At least Gertrude did not face the primitive conditions and isolation of women on the open prairies. Neighbour May Minchen wrote, "We are fortunate to what many poor women are, those away on the prairie, many miles from a doctor, it is heartrending to read some of the letters the poor creatures write to a Ladies Page in our Free Press. It is a splendid page, I always read it first, I find such help in it ... Most of them are English, and often tell what part they come from, which makes it doubly interesting, and the pluck of some is wonderful."[47]

Gertrude apparently loved it, saying of her new life and new home, "I am very happy here. It is sweet and restful, living away from the noise and bustle and loneliness of the big cities. All the people here are very kind, and I find my life increasingly interesting in this new land." Despite her content, she still had moments of nostalgia and homesickness, and she missed her friends from England. She corresponded with them, exchanging clippings and information about organisations and causes that had involved her in her Leicester days, and the new ones in Manitoba. She was very fond of her family. Gertrude and Robert lived five kilometres from town, and a few kilometres away from her mother, Fannie, and Fred, and although it was too far for daily visits, she did go up periodically to visit her mother for a few days, sometimes hitching a ride on a farm wagon. "I saw her go by on a load of hay," May Minchen noted.[48]

Living conditions were comfortable, for a farm wife of the day; she and Robert built a new house in the fall of 1912, and while it was not luxuriously furnished in the urban fashion, it was attractive, and had the necessities of modern rural life. She called their home "Ingleside," after the British middle and upper class manner. The family spent holidays together, of course, Christmas Day at the Liveseys' and New Year's Day at the Richardsons'. There were additional and frequent opportunities for visits with family and friends, to the point that Gertrude sometimes found difficulty in getting her columns written for the Leicester paper. Rural telephone lines were installed beginning in the summer of 1913; Fannie got hers in June 1914, and Gertrude shortly thereafter (for $20 yearly). There had been telephones in town since 1908, and the valley was hooked up to long distance service around 1910. A Mrs Livingstone and her daughters ran the phone exchange after 1913, handling about seventy lines. Gertrude and Fannie were able to have the early service in the countryside because the line ran close to their house; as soon as all the Twilleys were hooked up, Gertrude could also keep in touch by phone.[49]

Gertrude had mixed feelings about the phones; they were a convenience, but with their poles and wires they "interrupt the beauty of the landscape and bring echoes of the great noisy world into this quiet spot." They seemed to stand for the "Great Juggernaut of Progress," to symbolise the spirit of competition; she hoped for a new spirit of "brotherhood and love" to displace heartless industrialism. This was romanticism, but practical, too, and part of her critique of inequality and exploitation in the England. As she said of the satisfaction she felt from harvesting and putting by the produce of her vegetable garden, "If I had known how nice it is to gather the vegetables and things, I would have had a garden when in England. But I forgot, there is not any room, unless one happens to be rich." She realised that unemployment, poverty, and misery existed in Canadian cities too, but added, "There are no evidences of want in this beautiful Valley. People own or are buying their farms, and if one met a farmer and his hired man out together, it would be impossible to know which was the one and which the other. Workers are looked up to – not looked down upon, and there is no surplus labour … In the country men are always wanted. In the cities are found the same evils that curse older countries."[50]

There was lots to write about. Gertrude's introduction to farm housewifery coincided with a period of rapid expansion of government-funded systematic rural adult education in the province, managed by the Manitoba Agricultural College. The provincial government had established a network to support agricultural development, and after 1910, encouraged the development of Home Economics groups among farm women in the rural areas. These groups, which served a social and educational function, met regularly and discussed various topics related to women's work in the home: child care, sanitation, nursing, gardening, preserving, cooking, and so on. They also discussed various community and political issues, and undertook civic betterment projects. Information about their doings was provided in the women's columns of the monthly *Canadian Thresherman and Farmer*, a staple in farm living rooms, including

Gertrude's. The magazine also featured regular educational features on various agricultural, economic, and social topics. Gertrude took her new job of farm housewifery seriously and was interested in the various sources of information about the role of the "home-maker" as it was called by then. She approved of the inclusion of household arts and household science in the agricultural college curriculum, and appreciated the outreach services of the college.[51]

One innovative method used to promote public education on farm and home subjects was the agricultural train. The initial train project had been a dairy train in the summer of 1910; in 1911 two trains were equipped and the CPR and CNR ran them on their lines, staffed by agricultural college extension teachers. These travelling classrooms and showrooms visited 146 stations in 1912, stopping for three-hour visits in towns and villages, normally giving a morning, afternoon, and evening session in three different settlements. The train visited Swan River in June 1912 and Gertrude was in attendance. There was a home economics car; Gertrude attended a lecture on trees, flowers, and plants tested at the experimental farm and found suitable to grow in the region and another on medicines and nursing practices for home care of the sick. There were demonstrations on infant care. Another car taught butter making and home preserving, another had displays of grains and grain products, and lectures on how to get rid of weeds. Aside from the direct educational benefits derived from the trains' visits, the contacts made by train home economists Miss Black and Mrs McCharles were useful for the development of women's groups in the communities.[52]

In the spring of 1913, an extension worker came up to help found a branch of the Home Economics Society in the Swan River area; Gertrude was amongst the early participants. The founding meeting was held on a member's screened veranda, beginning with a presentation on the societies' aims and procedures, by a "lady professor" of Household Science at the Agricultural College. After the new branch was properly equipped with an executive and a dues-paying membership, the group moved to the kitchen for a nutrition lecture and a cookery demonstration, after which the group ate up all the demonstration dishes. Subsequent meetings followed the format of business meeting, lecture, demonstration, and refreshments. An early program featured a member who had been the matron of the local hospital before she married a local man; she gave a talk and demonstration on "Home Nursing." Topics were usually practical or had some practical application. However, they were not restricted to rural issues; for example, a fall 1913 meeting featured a paper on "Women in the business world," discussing women workers and also the responsibility of housewives to show a sympathetic interest in their husbands' business affairs (and thus increasing their influence). Recipes were frequently exchanged; Gertrude made use of these in preserving and cooking, and passed some of them on to her English readers. The group usually met in town, about 16 of its 32 members typically attending during the busy summer and fall months. It planned various useful community projects such as sewing classes for schoolgirls. Its earliest accomplishment was to set up a "Rest Room" for the use of rural women while in Swan River. The Rest Room provided a clean, quiet, respectable haven, a place to rest for a bit and have a cup of tea, during day trips to town. The Society carried out various fund raising activities to support the Rest Room; one was a "cooking exchange" wherein members prepared food and brought it in to be sold: Gertrude brought a squash pie, jar of pickled beets, and a dozen ginger cookies.[53]

The suffrage movement occupied a major part of Gertrude's attention. The Roaring River society attempted to reach beyond the converted and invited "antis" to come to their meetings and exchange views.[54] The society continued to work closely with the Grain Growers, mixing business and pleasure in such events as a "Poetical Social" held at the schoolhouse. The evening programs included "songs, dialogues, instrumental music and a Monologue" (performed by Fred Twilley), a "rousing speech on Direct Legislation," interspersed with organ accompaniments. The ladies provided the supper. Secretary David Reid (whose wife was a member) reported, "It is impossible to get along without the ladies. The members of the Women's Suffragette [sic] Association were there in force, but nothing of a militant nature was noticeable. On the contrary they acted the perfect lady, bestowing every kindness and attention on the men, and seeing that nothing was left undone that ought to be done to make our social a success. By all means let us men get down to business and demand the vote for women."[55]

The issue of suffrage militancy surfaced repeatedly during 1912 and 1913, sometimes in a teasing way as in that account by a supporter. Militant suffrage tactics, police brutality, and the persecution, imprisonment, and forced feeding of the militants by the authorities, were constantly in the British headlines. By the summer of 1912, thousands had been arrested, there were 102 suffragettes in prison, ninety of whom were being forcibly fed by painful and dangerous methods. Most men and women probably would not accept militant tactics in Canada but there was sympathy nonetheless. Grace Shaw, the schoolteacher who was a cofounder of the suffrage society, wrote a lengthy article in the local paper in February 1913 on the issues. She argued that it was historically and logically impossible to expect intelligent women to sit back quietly and submit to injustice perpetrated by a government in which they were denied a voice. Movements against autocracies always were greeted by complaint, whatever their methods, she wrote. Moreover, suffragists who disliked militant tactics were still determined to maintain solidarity with the militants and keep the movement united. In Canada, hopefully militancy would not be necessary. Women had tried to get government to remedy unjust situations, only to be ignored. Shaw concluded sarcastically that women must never become unladylike or unwomanly by objecting to this state of affairs. At least one individual in Swan River had direct experience of suffragette groups in England. The Victorian Order of Nurses hospital matron, a Miss D. Higgins, who came out in the spring of 1913, was a suffragette, probably a member of the Women's Freedom League, since she read their newspaper. It is not clear if she had herself been in prison, but she commented once, upon seeing Gertrude's new calf bottle fed, that it reminded her of suffragettes' forced feedings.[56]

Gertrude became involved in controversies in the local paper over the activities and treatment of the militant suffragettes in the Old Country. The arguments are interesting for what they suggest about local feeling on the issue (generally prosuffrage), but also as evidence for ties between the local group and the English movement, ties strengthened by Gertrude's personal links. Writing "as an English lady ... conversant with the facts," Gertrude denied that militant tactics were hindering the suffrage cause. Describing the history of the suffrage movement, she emphasised the continuing rapid growth of the National Union of Women's Suffrage Societies, the abandonment of (Liberal) party politics by women in favour of nonpartisan tactics, and the increasing prosuffrage activism of men. Persecution of women would do no good for the antis; God's purpose would prevail, and those who tortured the noble women would someday repent. She portrayed the eventual suffrage victory as the remedy for "abominable inequalities of the laws of every land, the shameful unspeakable traffic – the very thought of which defiles the soul, the exploitation of adolescent girls in the labour markets, the corruption and rottenness cling to political life – all shall be swept away in the new days that are coming. Down the centuries the cry of anguished womanhood is ringing: we will not listen and take no heed, but rise to the call of God." Gertrude accused the Church of apostasy, teaching false doctrines of male supremacy as if they were the word of God. She warned, "Let [the church] take heed, and learn from the past what is the terrible vengeance of the Most High on the oppressor.

Yet truth eternally shall triumph." Her religious arguments about the rightness of the cause recall Martha Vicinus' reminder that "joining the WSPU meant joining a spiritual army," and that militants saw their activities as spiritually (or divinely) inspired, and their suffering as martyrdom for the noblest of causes.[57]

Her letter brought a law-and-order response from former Londoner H.W. Middleditch, who claimed Jesus would not have liked the militants' methods. Women whose hard work and great ideas inspired their "great men" would not have been able to influence these men if instead of gentle forbearance they had "gone about destroying property and endangering lives." (He admitted the "men have got the glory.") The voice of the people should triumph, he said, and if the people were asked they would be strongly against the militants. He argued that the proper place for the militants was in a lunatic asylum; they were fanatics bringing shame on womankind, they should instead busy themselves helping the poor, and Gertrude was wasting herself as their champion.[58]

Gertrude responded that until women had the vote and were heard in government, the suffering of the poor and evils of many kinds would not be eliminated; she referred to Josephine Butler's work against the Contagious Diseases Acts as an example of what would be done. Butler "accomplished more for the triumph of goodness than any council of statesmen in the last century," she claimed. Exhortations to gentleness rang hollow in the face of oppression and injustice: Jesus was "not always gentle, but awful in His terrible wrath poured forth on all oppressors." Grace Shaw also challenged Middleditch's assertions, pointing out that women had tried to promote reforms but were not listened to by the men who controlled government, and that it was illogical to call women's revolt treason or anarchy when they struggled against unjust laws they had no part in making.[59]

Gertrude's allies included young social gospeller William Irvine, follower of Salem Bland and J.S. Woodsworth (who was later to be an Alberta leader in the farm and socialist movement and a CCF co-founder). In 1911 he was a divinity student at Wesley and Manitoba Colleges, the Methodist and Presbyterian joint program institutions which later became United College and is now the University of Winnipeg. Students did summer placements, a combination of job and internship, at isolated churches. Irvine also worked in lumber camps, where he focused on the "social" in social gospel, and ran discussion groups instead of prayer circles. He was a good fiddler and a good sport, and became very popular with the workers. He married Adelia Little, 29 December 1910 in Swan River. They had become engaged while he boarded with her family during a summer assignment at the

Methodist church in Shellbrook, Manitoba; he switched to the Presbyterians because the Methodists did not allow students to marry. He took time off from school to earn money as a supply minister in the area; he also worked evenings in the drugstore in nearby Togo, Saskatchewan, where they moved in January 1911, and hired out as a harvest hand to supplement his supply minister earnings and save enough to return to school in the fall of 1912. Irvine served the Presbyterian church at Minitonas in the summer of 1913; he left for his final year that fall, and did not again serve in Swan River Valley churches after his graduation in 1914. During the summer of 1913, Gertrude and Robert became friends with Irvine, and visited back and forth. The friendship survived Irvine's departure from the valley, and Gertrude visited during her rare trips to Winnipeg. A "brilliant orator," Irvine drew crowds to his lectures on socialism and other topics in the Minitonas Town Hall and elsewhere. Gertrude and Robert attended his farewell sermon, "Is it possible to be a Christian under existing conditions?" Gertrude was receptive to Irvine's call for all to "work for an ideal state – the setting up of the Kingdom of God here on earth."[60]

Gertrude found Irvine a ready ally in her public debates about militant tactics. Irvine responded to Middleditch's accusations of anarchy, criticised government violations of British liberties, and argued that it was inconsistent to claim that God meant women to be men's helpmeets, then deny women the means to help their men go about God's business (such as eliminating suffering, injustice, and exploitation). If Middleditch believed in the voice of the people, Irvine said, it seemed odd for him to refuse to allow the people (including women) to have that voice. He argued that if working women and the wives of working men could vote, they would sweep away "the present system of injustice." This was precisely what the antis feared. The antis were trying to protect their own ill-gotten gains, unjust privilege, and shameful immorality, Irvine argued.[61]

Confrontation in the press was a minor part of the activities of the suffrage group. Educating themselves was one goal, educating others was another. As Grace Shaw wrote years later, "My two years there educated me. I wrote Mrs Carrie Chapman Catt, several years at that time President of the International Suffrage Association. She responded with an engaging blessing and many armfuls of literature. Our members in the midst of pioneer patching, gardening, preserving, milking, baking bread, and making butter, achieved something of a world consciousness. Petty things fell into place." The Roaring River group was also in touch with the Winnipeg Political Equality League and various Canadian and British suffrage groups.[62]

The suffrage group held the first picnic of the season in 1913, and it was very much a Twilley family affair. Fred built the poplar branch-covered, blue and gold refreshment booth (which also did a brisk business in badges). Fannie, Eliza, and Gertrude (the president) played prominent parts in the proceedings. People arrived in buggies and wagons, loaded with food, wood to build the tables and benches, and barrels of ice. The events of the day began shortly after 2 PM, with speeches by pioneer William Sifton (who had inaugurated the group at the Grain Growers' meeting the year before), William Irvine, who had decorated his buggy with "Votes For Women" placards, and the mayor of Minitonas, with Gertrude as the emcee. Speeches were followed by mountains of food (including ice cream) served at "indescribably dainty" tables, topped with tea brewed in huge kettles over open fires tended by Robert and another man, this being men's work. Such an event entailed a great deal of work on the part of the women from the sponsoring group, not only in food preparation but in its service; there were three sittings at this picnic. As Fred wrote to Edith Watson about a snapshot he sent her of the event, "Some of the ladies seem very busy and you would have soon been in the thick of it if you had 'popped' over." The event drew wide community support; in her description of the picnic, Gertrude remarked that she doubted the Swan River suffragists would ever be badly treated, a sharp contrast to the experience of suffragists in Leicester who had been recently harassed in the town square. "Our Society is non-militant, because militancy is unnecessary, but not anti- militant. If necessary we too, would fight for right and justice," she added. The day concluded with baseball, races, and games. The picnic was a success financially, too: it reportedly raised more than $45.[63]

In the fall of 1913 the Roaring River group invited Lillian Beynon Thomas from the Winnipeg Political Equality League to unite the two (and Gertrude thought, the only) Manitoba suffrage groups into one organisation, and to give talks on woman suffrage in Swan River and Minitonas, the two nearest towns. Lillian Beynon Thomas, well known as "Lillian Laurie," a farm journalist specialising in women's issues, was an excellent drawing card. The events were great successes. Eliza Twilley made the bunting to decorate the hall in Swan River. The meeting in Minitonas was preceded by a grand reception in the town hall, featuring the best white linen trimmed with royal blue and gold (the association's colours), flower centrepieces, fine china, and a ladylike tea with sandwiches and dainty cakes, formally served by ladies and girls in white dresses with suffrage rosettes. Gertrude explained in her report to English readers that an inordinate amount of work by the women had been required to prepare all the basic ingredients from which the fancy foods were made, to say nothing of transporting all the linens and china long distances into the town and setting everything up. After the reception the group split into several smaller groups to go to supper (they had too many invitations to stay en bloc) at various homes until time for the evening meeting.[64]

Presbyterian minister Peter McLeod, who was the first speaker, chaired the meeting in Minitonas. Gertrude also spoke – on "Woman's Sphere." Thomas described the legal position of women in Manitoba, particularly concerning the dower law and family property rights. She described women's complete lack of legal claim to their husband's property no matter what their contribution to its prosperity over the years, and spoke of a particularly blatant case where a deserted wife struggled to support her son who later became successful; upon the son's early death, the husband showed up and confiscated the son's bequest to his mother, and was perfectly within his rights to do so. The meeting was followed by yet more tea at the home of the Reverend Mr McLeod, and a long drive back to Gertrude's house where Lillian Thomas was staying. The local paper commented approvingly of the Minitonas meeting. "Her remarks were enthusiastically received. A notable feature of her address and one that male politicians might well follow, was the total elimination of all mud slinging, although the subject dealt with was of so highly controversial a character." The Swan River meeting, chaired by William Irvine, went equally well, despite rumours that there would be opposition. The association was especially gratified that all the ministers but the Anglican were present. Gertrude was impressed by Thomas; judging by subsequent events, the feeling was mutual.[65]

Fall is harvest time, and the "hungry horde" of harvesters come around. "Every house wife is glad to see them come to thresh and glad to see them go away again as they eat a lot of grub," Fred explained to Edith. In Gertrude's time, local harvesting was done by threshing crews (made up mostly of men from the valley) who moved from farm to farm, about twenty men, thirty horses, and various machines to separate the grain from the straw and chaff, and wagons to carry the grain to the elevators in town. Women went to help neighbours feed the crews. The 1912 harvest was a frightening and exhausting time for Gertrude; newly married, she was inexperienced and uncertain about how to cope with feeding the hungry workers. The weather was bad, the threshing prolonged, and the crew at her house for nearly a week, that first summer. By the next year she was an accomplished farm wife and could face the event with more equanimity. She wrote to Leicester readers, "You may

imagine our home for a little while converted into a huge restaurant –
with me as cook, waitress, and mistress combined." For days before
the event, she cooked and cooked. That year Gertrude was nearly indeed mistress and sole worker, for at first she could not get anyone to
help her; Fannie, who normally would come, was busy with her own
crew, and the neighbour Gertrude had just helped was ill. Luckily her
mother was able to work with her. They fed the workers fourteen at a
sitting (although their crew was slightly smaller than the neighbours'
because their hay was stacked rather than stooked). In two days Gertrude and her mother used forty pounds of beef, as well as large
quantities of ham. Supper was not served until dark, and consisted of
enormous servings of beef, potatoes, mashed turnips, pickles, raisin
pies, iced fruit cake, bread, butter, scones, and tea. They got up at five
to make breakfast: fried potatoes, ham, cold beef, pickles, biscuits,
bread, butter, crackers, cake and fruit, and tea; dinner at noon was
roast beef, boiled potatoes, cabbage, beets, pickles, bread, biscuits,
butter, cranberry tarts, blancmange with cherry sauce, and tea. Supper the second night consisted of roast beef, fritters, potatoes, gravy,
pickles, bread, butter, biscuits, sponge cake with coconut frosting,
fruit, cranberry jelly, cheese tarts, and tea. The remaining meals were
similarly huge. Setting up, especially for multiple sittings, was a big
job, and washing up was "endless." Feeding a threshing crew required planning, energy, knowledge, and skill. Nearly every item of
food was grown, processed, and prepared by Gertrude. Not surprisingly, she was proud of her competence. As well, she continued to be
fascinated by the threshing "outfit," machines, horse teams, and the
coordinated work of the men.[66]

The harvest was an inspiration, too. "I am full of wonder as I think
of the providence of the kind, good Father of us all. There is abundance, lavish abundance, plenty for all, and the most unobservant
student of economics cannot fail to see that somewhere the blunder-
ings, perhaps the cruelty and selfishness of man, prevent its distribution along the proper channels. Let us who care arise and demand
that what God gives to His people be not withheld from them." But
God's bounty was not enough; by December she was explaining that
times were bad in the valley and some men were working in lumber
camps for board and room. Farmers who sold firewood for cash (like
Fred) were losing their market to coal. The wheat crop had been plentiful, but prices were down. "Men and women all over the world
should earnestly and carefully study economic problems," she urged,
"in the hope of finding a solution to some of these. For God is so lavish and bountiful, so good and kind to us all. It is our duty to learn, to
understand, to read the signs of the times … as God's people ever

have done, to prevent calamity." She announced that her future columns would focus less on the personal, more on social and economic problems of the country; the broader context of country housekeeping was demanding more of her attention.[67]

The opening event of the winter "season" for the Roaring River suffrage group was a big social and concert in November 1913; the evening included a debate on "militant tactics." However unsettling it might be to engage in public wrangles about militancy, however contentious the issue, the group did not hesitate to use it in an attempt to engage public interest. In December they held a concert in the Minitonas Town Hall, with *Mrs Northbrook's Daughters*, a two-act play featuring a cast of nine, written by Gertrude. Suffrage campaigning was respectable; public events were presided over by teachers and ministers, and membership grew nicely. Suffrage campaigns infiltrated other societies in Swan River; in December 1913 the Literary Society held a debate on the topic "woman suffrage for Great Britain and Canada," featuring Gertrude among the "for" speakers. Her side won.[68]

Gertrude's holiday season was a happy one that year, filled with community and family festivities, spiced by cards and remembrances from dear friends at "home." Family news was good; Horace's new business in Leicester was to be launched in the New Year, and he and his partners were sure it would do well. He had been a commercial traveller for a woollen house for some years, and knew the business well. His old firm had offered him a substantial raise to stay on, but he wanted to be independent. Horace and his young lady hoped to marry later in the new year, and talked about settling in Canada. Meanwhile Horace was enjoying singing in a holiday production of *Elijah* at the splendid De Montfort Hall, and the future looked bright, Fred wrote to Edith. Gertrude, Fannie, and Eliza outdid themselves, and every gathering featured mountains of food, which Gertrude described in her *Midland Free Press* columns: heaps of roast chickens and pork, vegetables, and assorted jellies, pickles, relishes, cakes and pies and puddings. The Twilley family were joined by their friends the Chrichtons (the Minchens usually came too but were elsewhere that year) at the Liveseys', for feasting, presents, and happy talk. Fred gave his mother an easy chair, and John gave Fannie a wringer washing machine; other small gifts were exchanged. (Fred and his sisters usually gave each other a kiss, he wrote to Edith.) Fred reported that he took the feasting part very seriously: "Edith, I ate so much on Christmas Day that I had to refuse the dessert. Don't tell anybody." By that New Year's Day (always at Gertrude's house) she had perfected her version of the pork pie for which Leicester was renowned.

Her description of the lavish spreads added, "So you see, in spite of the financial stringency now depressing Canada, we are not in any danger of starving. There is always plenty and to spare in farm homes, even though we do not see much actual money at times. We read of the strain and stress, and it touches our lives, but the touch is an indirect one. We are warm and well provided for in our snug homes, and well able to tide over times of difficulty. But my heart goes out to the lonely ones in the cities, and I am full of fear for the girls who lose their employment in office and store in the cold winter season. Many, I know, are English, and have been tempted here by the alluring prospect of higher wages, unable to understand, until the experience actually comes, the higher cost of living and clothing in a new country." Although she believed the country would recover, and might even learn something from the experience, she was concerned about urban suffering in the meantime.[69]

Gertrude's visibility in the Manitoba feminist movement increased substantially in 1914; this was made possible by a visit to Winnipeg which permitted her to meet key leaders in person. In November 1913 she had accompanied her husband to Winnipeg where he was a delegate to a Presbyterian Synod meeting; she heard C.W. Gordon preach ("Ralph Connor" the well-known novelist), and enjoyed an address by the incoming moderator, the Reverend James Bowman, who was the Immigration Hall chaplain in Winnipeg, and the clergyman who had performed her 1912 marriage ceremony. Another highlight of the Synod was an address by Salem Bland. There were no women delegates, and no other women attended the sessions. Gertrude sat through every one (reassured by Dr Gordon that she was welcome), except when she accompanied their hostess (Gordon's former secretary) to a Women's Foreign Missionary Society meeting nearby. While Gertrude was moved and inspired by the addresses and proceedings of the men's Synod (for so it was), she was still more pleased to be able to visit Lillian Thomas for lunch the day after the business part of their trip was concluded. At the Thomas home Gertrude met suffrage notables such as Mary Crawford, Nellie McClung, and Francis Marion Beynon, founders and core members of the Political Equality League and several other feminist groups in the city. They took her to an afternoon meeting of the Women's Press Club and introduced her to other feminists whose writings she had read and admired. The final evening she and Robert spent with the Irvines; she predicted that he had a "great mission to perform."[70]

That winter Gertrude enjoyed the carnival-like social whirl of fancy dress evenings, parties, sleigh rides, teas, and meetings, meetings, meetings. A recent amenity in the town was a movie theatre; its early programs seem to have included enough highbrow material to avoid any qualms about sin or frivolity (Bible scenes, Shakespearean play excerpts). The severe cold made it hard to get around, as "however well clothed we may be the atmosphere enwraps us in a chill enfolding that seems to pierce through and through." What must it be like for poor people who could not dress warmly? "Sad tidings reach us of distress in the cities," she wrote. Christmas dinner from a soup kitchen was "heartbreaking in this great country of riches, and resources." But the cities were far away and winter in the Swan River area was noteworthy for scenes of breathtaking beauty. Gertrude's initial fascination with these continued. She wrote of "a perfect fairyland ... trees outlined against the dark blue mountains ... covered with frost ... [like] white coral. As we were driving to Church, I was awed and quieted by the exquisite loveliness."[71]

Her enjoyment of rural life is a recurring theme in these years: "I think it is lovely to live in the country. The beautiful white snow with the sun shining on it, the snow-birds and prairie chickens, the little white rabbits that run away at our approach, everything is so pretty. When [Miss Higgins] visited us she stood looking out of our west window at the glorious sunset, and turning round with its light in her eyes, remarked that she had never seen anything in all her life to equal the beauty of Canadian skies and sunsets. My sister, who died here – at that same Hospital – wrote to us of their magnificence just before she passed away, so that invests the sunset-sky, for me, with a sacredness that can never pass away."[72]

Yet country life did not mean bucolic isolation: "Social life of every kind is varied and interesting," she wrote. "The [nearby] town [of Swan River] is peaceful and quiet as an English village. There are no hideous mills or factories, no loud hooting noises, only the music of the train-bells and the pretty cutters with their teams of horses bearing the people enveloped in furs to their business at the banks and stores." Her columns also described more mundane but livelier moments, such as a bridal shower for the church organist (featuring a canopy filled with small gifts, which was designed to collapse onto the bride as she entered the room), and the post-honeymoon at-home reception. At the reception, the bride wore her wedding gown, and her wedding party served an ample tea to guests. Despite the informality and openness of most social events, Swan River ladies preserved some vestiges of the custom of formal calling, with ladies having their at-home days and leaving a trail of calling cards in their wake.[73]

Gertrude was re-elected to a third term as president of the Roaring River Woman's Suffrage Association in March 1914, and the group looked forward to a year of intensified activity. The membership had more than doubled in the previous year, and revenues had been high enough to bring in Lillian Beynon Thomas, rent halls, donate and send delegates to the provincial Political Equality League (PEL), and buy the necessary supplies for their functions and activities.[74] Gertrude also remained active in church affairs, and was recruited as a last-minute speaker at an ecumenical Sunday School convention (involving Presbyterians, Methodists, Anglicans) held in Swan River.[75] Gertrude joined the inner circle of feminist writers in Canada when she was invited to become a contributor to the leading women's magazine, the monthly *Woman's Century*, an organ of the National Council of Women of Canada (NCWC). She was probably invited initially, because of her position in the provincial suffrage movement, to send reports on Manitoba, but she would soon become more than a regional reporter. The magazine had been founded by the Scottish Jessie Campbell MacIver, who had migrated with her lawyer husband and five children to Toronto, and become involved in the National Council of Women. MacIver published the first issue in May 1913, and operated the magazine largely as a family enterprise, her husband and children contributing money and wrapping and addressing the issues at the dining room table. She wanted it to be a women's magazine that would educate women about public issues and necessary reforms, and provide a forum for a wide range of women's groups. The NCWC at the time had a few pages each month in *The Canadian Magazine*, but as the council grew it needed more space to discuss issues and pass on news about "the progress of Canadian womanhood," as Press Convenor Bessie McLean Reynolds put it. In April 1914 the NCWC made *Woman's Century* their official organ, and gradually took over the ownership, with MacIver remaining as the managing editor.[76]

All these activities and achievements paled in significance by comparison to the upcoming provincial election campaign, which would lead Gertrude to a new intensity of commitment to the cause. There was a partisan flavour to the proceedings, as it became evident that the provincial Liberals were on God's side in this election. The Liberals came out in favour of woman suffrage so the Political Equality League suffragists backed them. The Roaring River group had in any event decided to set in motion an organising campaign to establish suffrage groups all over the valley, beginning with nearby towns. The demands of this campaign offered a variety of challenges and expanded Gertrude's sphere of operations. Gertrude and others started organising at Ravensworth, a forty kilometre drive; attendance was good, enthusiasm high, and many people signed suffrage petitions and joined the Roaring River society. The Roaring River women did not leave for the return trip home until 1 AM, which must have made for a nerve-wracking journey, given that several sections of the way were steep, and although there was abundant snow some snowdrifts were deep enough to cause detours, the snow was soft, and conditions were poor for the sleigh.[77]

Shortly after the Ravensworth trip, hospital matron Miss Higgins and Mrs Sims, the wife of the Liberal candidate (who was elected in 1914) asked Gertrude to form another suffrage group in the town of Swan River itself, the Roaring River meetings being inconveniently distant. Although Gertrude had mixed feelings about making suffrage a party issue, at least the Liberals had made a commitment to justice. Or rather, the Liberals had promised that if they received a petition signed by numbers of women equalling 15 percent of male voters, justice would triumph. Feminist groups all over the province were thus encouraged to redouble their efforts. Gertrude duly spoke at the meeting and was elected honorary president of the new Swan River Political Equality League (her mother held the equivalent office of the Roaring River society), the actual president being Mrs Sims.[78]

Gertrude's columns for the late winter, spring, and summer of 1914 referred often to the issue of suffrage militancy. Events in England were making the news, and the intensified campaign in Manitoba made the English situation a hotly debated topic. Matron Higgins had kept Gertrude up to date on the English campaigns; indeed, their shared commitment to suffrage appears to have formed an important basis for their friendship. She passed on to Gertrude various issues of the suffrage papers, ranging from the Freedom League's *The Vote* to the journal of the Church of England Franchise League.[79] Even in the heat of the campaign, Gertrude did not believe that Manitoba feminists would ever be subject to the same "bitter opposition" or harsh treatment faced by the Englishwomen. Whatever anti-suffragist Premier Roblin might do about the vote, he at least received the delegations with respect, and the opposition Liberals included prominent suffragists. Apparently Gertrude's disbelief was shared; she repeated a story Miss Higgins had told her of several local men who, when finally convinced that the stories about physical mistreatment of the suffragettes were accurate, exclaimed that they could not understand how their English fellow men could tolerate such a thing, and it certainly would never be tolerated in Canada. Gertrude agreed, adding, "Of course the whiskey and money interests are fighting woman suffrage, but they are doing it in an outwardly polite manner." Patriotically (if somewhat inconsistently) she added, "I think Canadian women are too much like American women to submit to indignity or disrespect."[80]

Nevertheless, there remained those who were "horrified" at the tactics of the English militants, and expressed that horror in discussions of the current election campaign. Soon after Gertrude's address to the Swan River audience who formed the new society, she resorted to the letters to the editor columns to discuss the issue. Thirty women had died because of harsh prison treatment, she said; how could she not defend them? She referred to an appended (but not reprinted) extract from the *British Medical Journal* which contained testimony from prominent doctors about the torture-like methods of forced feeding. Although it is not clear who sent her this material, her use of it does underscore her ongoing links to the British movement. The medical journal article was part of a campaign by a small group of British doctors who attempted to use their social position and medical expertise to shame the government into stopping its abuse of imprisoned militant suffragettes. The lines were not that clearly drawn at the local level between the various suffrage societies and tactics, and in any case the violent treatment of the militants was unacceptable, whatever the differences of policy at the national level. Gertrude was not atypical in her overlapping suffrage group loyalties, and her continuing willingness to defend the militants and their tactics, whatever the risk of being tarred with the same brush. She asked critics to think if they would be willing to undergo such treatment, and said that the provincial PEL's position was to refrain from criticising any English suffragist. However, she added, Nellie McClung and Lillian Thomas believed as she did, that the bravery of the militants had won a lot of recognition for the cause they and other women espoused.[81]

The summer of 1914 was filled with campaigning. The annual suffrage picnic featured an address by the local minister and Liberal candidate William Sims, followed by a basketball game between the suffragists (in pale blue and white uniforms) and the Minitonas town team and the usual spread of food.[82] The highlight of the summer campaign was a visit from Nellie McClung, who had moved to Winnipeg in 1911 and had quickly become a key figure in the suffrage movement. Now she was stumping for the Liberals. McClung wrote that she would gladly come because of her friendship with Gertrude, whom she had met through Political Equality League connections; McClung and her husband stayed with the Richardsons.[83] McClung's visit occasioned two "glorious gatherings," one in the afternoon for women, and a public meeting at night; the Sims' automobile carried the party from a family noon meal at Gertrude's to the Presbyterian church for the women's meeting. Gertrude described the afternoon talk as "the most wonderful speech ever made in my hearing to a gathering of women."[84]

From Gertrude's description, McClung must have made quite a powerful impression on her audience: her discourse was filled with "unanswerable arguments, unchallengeable facts, sound logic," and a moving discussion of "saddest, most heart-breaking problems," which McClung persuaded her listeners they all had some responsibility to correct. "There were tears in many eyes ... the deep hush of solemnity broken only by the sobs of some who were listening to terrible truths for perhaps the first time in their lives." Gertrude, who did love a good martyr, was especially heartened by McClung's sympathetic comments on the heroism of the English suffragists "fighting for womanhood so grandly," who, "filled with the spirit of the martyrs, were willing to die for the cause so dear to them." Gertrude hoped that McClung's visit would create more sympathy for the English movement, and thus remove some barriers to the success of Manitoba women.[85]

Gertrude's account of the afternoon session concluded with a discussion of the food at the tea. "A most sumptuous repast was prepared." Gertrude's frequent discussions of food signified more than her own delight. As she explained to her Leicester readers, she talked about Canadian meals "to make this letter agree with the title [Housekeeping in Canada], and also to show the magnificent hospitality of the Canadian ladies." Women prepared and served food; to offer such sumptuous hospitality was a mark of their skill, the richness of their personal and household resources, their power in the household and in the community, and their choices about how those resources should be used. It is of course noteworthy that this hospitality was put to use for the support of women's work of social transformation: a feminist interpretation of "housekeeping" indeed, wherein women have the sacred duty and the sacred right to intervene. As she said earlier that year in a discussion of the intensified campaigns for the provincial election, "God bless the world's homemakers! God bless especially those whose eyes are turned outward from the sacred precincts of the sweet home-sanctuary to see the world's sin and misery and care and sorrow – whose hearts leap up in answer to the call, whose hands are quick to toil, whose voices are sweet to comfort." Gertrude was big on duty – the more sacred the better. In the happiest periods of her life, joy and duty coincided, and duty brought more than just its own reward. Of course she must have considered herself lucky, greatly blessed, to have her own home in which to do her duty, for the circumstances of her earlier life had seemed to eliminate this possibility. Yet she could write, "My life is a very full and busy one. I do all my own work and sewing, and try to make a happy home for those around me. And yet, I feel God gave me other work to do and I should do wrong if I failed in this." Part of her duty was surely to write her columns, for she had great faith in and a high opinion of newspapers as a force for good. "I think the day will come when Editors will take a high view of their work and responsibility. To me it would be as sacred as the pulpit, since like the latter it is a strong force in the making of ideals and the promulgation of creative thought." Might not columnists share in this great work? A fair number of Canadian feminists of this period were journalists; Winnipeg circles were especially rich in this occupation. Even making allowances for Gertrude's tendency to sacralise and sentimentalise, she and her housewife colleagues (some of whom practised additional callings) were doing holy work.[86]

McClung's evening address was no less a performance, as she spoke to what Swan River *Star* editor Weir judged to be "probably the largest indoor gathering any political speaker ever faced in Swan River." She began with a reading from her 1910 book *The Second Chance* (wherein, among other things, Pearlie's family gets a second chance in life by getting set up on the land) as a warm-up. Then, blessed by an introduction by the Methodist minister, she spoke to great effect on "The New Chivalry."[87] McClung was an attractive woman who was a remarkable writer and superb political thinker, but this was the least of her abilities: "Her personality attracts long before her voice is heard. But when she speaks! It is not easy to do justice to her power." One of the great speakers of the period (in a class with the great nineteenth century Methodist revivalists Dwight Moody and Charles Spurgeon, to whom she was often compared), McClung could captivate an audience in ways that we who have neither the religious convictions, idealism, nor listening habits of that generation find it impossible to envision. As Gertrude said, "There were people of all shades of opinion present, but nothing but praise of her has yet been heard." Mr Weir agreed: "From the moment she stepped on the platform one could see the most critical in the audience willing to give her the benefit of all doubts. When she had spoken a very few minutes the entire audience was captivated … It is doubtful if Mrs McClung has more than one or two equals as a platform speaker in the province."[88]

McClung was a role model for Gertrude, who placed her in exalted company. "Thank God for such noble women, of the type of Elizabeth Fry, and Florence Nightingale, and Josephine Butler, whose home cares and home affections do not absorb their hearts, but whose hearts, yearning with wonderful mother-love, take in the sorrows of the world. These are the true home-makers, the daughters of God upon whom the mantle of the old-time prophetesses has fallen." The evening was truly epiphanic for Gertrude, who sat on the platform in support of McClung, wearing her black and yellow "Votes for Women" emblem. "This is the first time I have worn it in public, but my courage has been strengthened, and I am going right on, in this and all other work my Heavenly Father has commissioned for me to do. Will all women who read this pray for me, as I am deeply impressed with the need of the prayers of women at this time." In the years to come Gertrude would draw on that moment, as her own "commission" as one of the new prophetesses led her into opposition with some of the sisters and comrades upon whom she had counted so heavily.[89]

Premier Roblin's visit to Swan River shortly thereafter coincided with Dominion Day celebrations; he inveighed against the Liberals' plan to ban booze and give women the vote, but McClung was a hard act to follow. Gertrude was not much impressed, and his visit only made her long the more to be active in the fray. She knew that her colleagues were working full tilt in Winnipeg. Her growing enthusiasm for public activity is evident in her discussions of the progress of the campaign. It is not exaggerated to say that she saw this enthusiasm as divinely inspired. This view is made explicit in Gertrude's discussion of the election campaign activities carried out by her colleagues in Winnipeg: "I wish I could be there," she says. "But it is my duty to carry on the work and hold the fort here in this western valley. This is very clearly God's will for me and I pray that I may be faithful. May Christian women everywhere rise to the new duties awaiting them, since to us as to our husbands and brothers Christ said: 'Seek ye first the Kingdom of God.' We cannot do that if our whole souls are engrossed in dusting chairs and cooking pies and attaining a broader outlook on life will not make us any less efficient home-makers." Despite the note of defensiveness in this (and she surely must have heard criticism of the "women belong in the home" sort during the campaign), it is clear that she regarded feminist political activism as commanded by God, a higher duty than those commanded by men and women.[90]

Suffrage militance continued to be a hot issue for Gertrude's Leicester readers during the summer of 1914, and she received numerous letters pro and con. Although she was quick to say that she was not herself a militant, she consistently defended them, saying that such drastic actions had been necessary historically to bring about reforms, and that it was better to follow God's laws than to submit wrongly to unjust laws. She refuted condemnation of the militants. Far better, she said, to investigate the reasons that "refined ladies" were willing to take such actions, than to condemn them. For

Gertrude the militants' illegal actions against property were not against God's law; when faced with evils, "God did not value property or life ... he poured down brimstone and rained down fire on evil cities of old." On a more personal note, she commented, "I honour them all as the greatest of our race, because I can understand. I know a great deal about them – the reasons – so dark and terrible – for many of their actions." She compared the militants to Christ on the cross, and their condemners to the mob. Her notions of accountability and complicity in injustice were articulated in this discussion: "Why I sorrow is because I think of the sufferings of these poor women, and remember how the mob and rabble still cry 'Crucify.' I refuse to be identified with that mob. There are some people I despise more than those who hammered the nails into the weary feet and tireless hands of Jesus, and these are those who stand aloof, and in their self-righteousness and hypocrisy 'did not agree with Him.' History repeats itself. Jesus died by the hand of the Law. These ladies are dying by the hands of the Law." But God was "keeping watch above His own," she warned.[91]

In subsequent columns she wrote of Presbyterian liturgical defender Jenny Geddes, the Chartists, the Bread Rioters, and Florence Nightingale as examples of rebels who flouted law and propriety and risked much for the sake of justice and reform. Nightingale, now a hero, had been vilified – in terms similar to those hurled against the suffragettes – when she went out to nurse. Gertrude's comments about tactics were a critique of gender and class convention as much as of law. As she pointed out, if Nightingale and other ladies chose to live idle, useless, and proper lives, few would say anything against them. The restrictive notion of women's proper sphere was contrary to Jesus' teachings, Gertrude believed. It was not Martha, "the very 'womanly,' very careful, very prudent, economical housewife [he] commended," and "here is an eternal answer to those who would outline what is called 'woman's sphere.' Woman's place is at the feet of Christ, now as then, till her time of learning is accomplished. Afterwards, her place is where He is – where He was." The true woman must cry woe upon "those who torture the children of God." As much as Gertrude "deplored" the destruction of beautiful homes, churches, and works of art, she deplored more the "ruined lives for which our laws have no remedy, laws in which there is no trace of the tender, pure souls of womanhood." As an example of the evil permitted by sexist laws, she cited a recently publicised case of an eleven-year-old Burmese girl bought as a sex slave by a British rubber planter. Gertrude was terribly upset that she and other women could do nothing to protect little girls like these, "a sweet little sister of mine," and such cases made her more determined to persevere by whatever methods were necessary to obtain power for women to enable them to change the legal system. "May God forgive those who criticise women who are suffering torture and death to bring an end to things like this," she concluded.

Not all Gertrude's Leicester readers were persuaded by her logic. A letter from "Observer" to the editor published in the following week's issue characterised Nightingale as a "sweet soul" who did "so much good" in Crimea, but the reader "could not see what she had to do with militant suffragettes." Gertrude "must be a very emotional person." Although "Observer" conceded that women should have the vote, that should exclude the militants who did not deserve the vote: "Not such women as militant suffragettes who commit these outrageous crimes."[92]

Although the Liberals did not win the 1914 election (Swan River candidate William Sims was elected, however), they did manage to reduce the Tory majority. The suffragists were disappointed, although some believed that women soon would gain the vote in any case. Despite the outcome of the election, the campaign had been important for Gertrude, as it broadened her acquaintance and gained her an important place among the Manitoba suffragists, introduced her to several of the Winnipeg socialists (for example, she wrote of Fred Dixon's win and impending marriage to "suffragette" Winona Flett) who would be key figures in the antiwar movement, and strengthened her conviction that speaking and writing about "the cause" was her sacred duty to God and womanhood. She prayed for God's blessing on all motherhood, she wrote, and for tenderness and compassion to fill all women's hearts; for her, women's maternal capacities and experience created a concomitant duty to act for social redemption and reform. For those like herself whose personal circumstances made them able to act, the duty was yet more pressing: "May God ... teach us all to live to save and serve and comfort, in the thankfulness for our own blessedness and happiness and safety."[93]

4 Sisterhood Divided: Suffrage and the War (1914–17)

Like many of her feminist associates, Gertrude was horrified when World War One broke out. Women were widely assumed to be more peaceful than men, and morally superior. The prewar women's movement generally favoured peace, and considered war and militarism to be features of the barbaric and outmoded way of thinking that excluded women from full citizenship and from access to decision making in society and government. Nonetheless, in Canada as in the other belligerent countries, the organised women's movements split between a majority who took a patriotic stand, and a minority who retained their pacifist convictions. Gertrude, most of her Roaring River suffrage colleagues, and several of her Winnipeg feminist friends had believed that the vote for women would make war impossible.[1]

Gertrude's columns in the Leicester paper for the first few months of the war describe mixed reactions in the valley. She wrote of her dread for the local men who had signed up to fight without any real understanding of what they were in for. She was touched by the support for England that she saw around her in Swan River, and was particularly pleased by news that Canada was to contribute a million hundred-pound bags of flour for the English poor, that they might not go hungry when the inevitable inflation set in. Gertrude remembered hearing stories from her aunties, who had been children during the Crimean War (1854–56). Her family had shared in the "bitter suffering of the poor," and her "grandmother [cut] the bread into slices – that all might have some – though none could be allowed sufficient to satisfy hunger. May God grant that these things may not be repeated," she concluded. There is a strong sense of bafflement in her comments, of disbelief that such a thing could have come to pass. She believed in the goodness and common sense of ordinary people. If the ordinary little people, the "good people" of the world had their proper say, surely wars would not happen. They were caused by the "military power that like a dragon raises its hydra-head in every land." Why would men who normally would try to save each other's lives now kill each other? How could women "be found who in so-called patriotism … rejoice that other women's sons are slaughtered?"[2]

Gertrude was not alone in this reaction; although it is impossible to know how many women opposed the war (and this has been little explored by historians), many were reluctant to allow their men to enlist. "So many women refused consent that as early as August 1914 one senior officer was prompted to remark, 'If Canada is to maintain her independence the Canadian soldier must do his duty and his wife should not restrain him from selfish motives.'" Leaving aside for the moment the issue of whether it was selfish of a wife or mother to try to prevent her husband or son being injured or killed, some women may also have intended that their men be prevented from injuring or killing others (or to put it in a maternalist perspective, from killing the loved ones of other women).[3]

Locally, the Women's Missionary Society, of which Gertrude was then president, convened a meeting for all women in and near Swan River to pray for peace. At least some of the women of the area had qualms about the war. The president of the Anglican women's society had lost a brother during the Boer War. Others seemingly believed war incompatible with Christianity, or at least sought refuge in religious hopes. At the women's peace prayer meeting, "very quiet and solemn," Gertrude read a paper called "Women in Time of War," and the group prayed and sang hymns such as "Peace, Perfect Peace." Gertrude wrote, "The only command Jesus left us is that we should love each other." God surely could not want such things to happen. Those "men of blood" who started the war would surely be called to judgment for their evildoing.[4]

In early September 1914, Gertrude went to Dauphin, 130 kilometres away, as a WMS delegate to the Presbyterial meetings; while there she attended a service of intercession called by the mayor at the request of the town's churches. The ecumenical service offered prayers for the rulers, armies, and people of countries on both sides of the conflict. Women and children were the greatest sufferers in war, one clergyman reminded the congregation. Another spoke of the Holy

City described in Revelations "as the triumph of Christian Democracy, when all war shall be impossible." The Reverend Dr Samuel Crothers Murray, head of Home Missions for the Presbyterian Church, noted that while masses of people rallied to the flag, "yet apart there stands Christ, with His White banner of Peace, and it is so hard, oh, so hard to get young men and women to join the army that fights under that standard." The "white banner of Jesus is being trampled in the dust ... the nations bearing his name are at each other's throats," lamented Gertrude.[5] Back in Swan River, although flags and portraits of the Royal Family appeared quickly in shop windows, there were worry and sorrow as well as enthusiasm. Several Swan River churches established weekly ecumenical peace prayer services, held at each church in turn.[6]

There had been a debate over peace versus preparedness within the Presbyterian Church, partly in response to Prime Minister Borden's attempts to fund naval rearmament. The Peace Manifesto drafted by John MacKay of Vancouver and circulated nationally early in 1913 had urged that every effort be made to avoid war, as its catastrophic effects would be unfairly borne mostly by the working classes. A peace resolution had been debated and passed at the 1913 General Assembly and the Presbyterian magazine discussed the pacifist fundamentals of progressive Christianity. James A. Macdonald, a key progressive leader who had moved from the ministry into church publishing and thence into the editor's seat of the Toronto *Globe*, was an admirer of W.T. Stead, the leader of Gertrude's radical antiwar group during the Boer War. But now, few Presbyterian clergy expressed qualms about supporting the war. Although Murray continued to mourn the war as a "terrible calamity," he did not work against it.[7]

Women's groups who opposed the war and wished to provide help to nonparticipants often decided to do relief work not directly connected to war support; Sylvia Pankhurst's group did relief work among the East London poor, for similar reasons. The Roaring River suffrage group decided to focus on relief of distress in the region; there had been a dry season, crops had been poor in some areas, unemployment was up, and there was an unprecedented possibility of starvation. Although the Swan River Valley was better off than most places, a few families were in serious need even in there. "This is the first time I have been in touch with real poverty since I came to Canada," Gertrude reported. Government aid provided some cattle feed and supplies of food to farm families; the women were going to concentrate on clothing. The local missionary society had undertaken a similar project before the war began, as their annual thank-offering. They had vowed that they would send only clothing good enough for their own families, and had spent extra hours adding finishing touches. In late November, they sent off a huge bundle of warm clothes, to be distributed by a minister. Other women were willing to do relief work to help human suffering of the combatants, such as Red Cross work or nursing, even though they opposed the war or accepted it with greatest reluctance. Miss Higgins, the Matron of the Swan River Hospital, who had become a good friend of Gertrude's, went to nurse at the front. Her sister had written that she was caring for a Belgian refugee in England, a girl whose hands had been chopped off; no doubt such atrocity stories encouraged enlistment. Miss Higgins would be among those who sent Gertrude gory details of the war over the next few years.[8]

Gertrude grappled with the questions forced upon many suffragists by women's general acceptance of the war: would women have stopped it, had they the power? Were women different? "I wonder whether it has struck any that no woman whatsoever has had any voice in the war or in any decisions regarding it ... No woman has been consulted as to the provisioning and clothing of the troops, though in their thousands they are working for their comfort, and toiling to relieve the distress caused by the paralysing of ordinary life and work, as well as all the other havoc caused by the carnage and horror," she observed. Once the war was over, nobody would care about women's contribution, she predicted: one of Florence Nightingale's Crimean War nurses had recently died in a workhouse, completely destitute. Whatever women did now, they must change these unjust situations, and "rebuild our empire on a true foundation" after the war.[9]

In a subsequent column she more explicitly discussed her views on the morality of the war. It was "very hard to think clearly." The men who fought were heroes, she said. "Few of us are worthy of the sacrifices made for us." But as Nellie McClung had recently said, women found no glory in war and a victory " 'only means a battle-field strewn with other women's beloved dead.' " Atrocities perpetrated by the Germans, if the stories were true, did not justify war: indeed, a "host of trained murderers" was the natural outcome of militarism. "Better a martyred nation than a nation of militarists." The Canadian men who volunteered to fight were moved by "a feeling of unselfish patriotism ... I pray that when the war is over this great force will be directed into its true channels." But Gertrude found it obscene that fine young men like these should be slaughtered. And she found another obscenity behind recruiting advertisements she saw in English periodicals such as the *Daily Sketch*, which Fannie and John Livesey received. One showed a wounded soldier asking others to enlist.

Behind this young man are well-dressed, well-fed men of the "upper" classes, who are very evidently not going to the front. This boy, with his thin, suffering face, and whose brothers have been slain, typifies in his own great brave personality the horrible, cruel injustice of war. The class from which he is drawn, the working class, have been for far too long a time in every way, the victims of sacrifice that the life and prosperity of the leisured classes may remain intact. Oh yes, I know the heroism of the officers who are drawn from these classes, I know and honour it all, but even thus, war still means less to them than to the poor. Their women will not starve, the horror for the loved ones of these will thus be mitigated.

Bosses who refused to hire men so that they would be forced to enlist were beneath contempt, for the practice made a lie of the idea of the volunteer hero. In the postwar world, "We must force the power from the hands of men who make war" and build a world on "love and peace and kindness. Nations built on militarism are pagan though there be countless churches of the name of Jesus the Prince of Peace adorning their land." There was an alternative that must be brought about. "Let us pray for the triumph of Christian democracy, the over-throw of the whole social fabric which now needs armies of trained murderers to support it."[10]

Despite the war, a number of projects came to fruition. The Home Economics Society opened its Rest Room at the end of September, cel-ebrating with a substantial tea. One of the earliest in the province, the Swan River Rest Room consisted of a foyer, the main rest room equipped with couches and chairs, and a small library room. Various furnishings and other items were contributed by members, support-ers in the community, and local businesses. The library charged five cents circulation fee for borrowing books, but provided free reading in a warm and comfortable space. The group planned a series of fund-raising events to pay the rent; the next one was to be a "pork and bean" social. The Rest Room was more than a quiet and safe place for rural women to rest while in town; it also was planned as a social centre and "an agency for uplifting and interesting others." In the event, it became also a centre for Red Cross work.[11]

Women's activities now often had a new purpose. The suffrage group continued its sewing project; the Home Economics Society held a social (Gertrude and Robert did not attend) to which the fee for admission was a pair of grey Army socks (or their price), perhaps in response to the British War Office's request to the women of the Em-pire to produce 30,000 pairs. This group would be one of the most ac-tive locally, specialising in making "comforts" for soldiers and raising money for the Red Cross by holding various teas and other events.

The Daughters of the Empire sold flags in Dauphin, and asked for donations of clothing and medical supplies for the troops. Beneath the everyday activities, Gertrude was aware of "horror and woe and sorrow" and repelled by the image of an Empire whose soul was "calm and confident." Against this patriotic slogan, she counterposed a people whose "calmness became callousness, unthinking acquiescence in all these horrors" as men died for their sakes. At least in some parts of Canada there was a concerted effort to assure that families of soldiers did not go in want. But in the cities there was unemployment and no doubt the poor were suffering. Gertrude worried about these things while she and her friends enjoyed their comfortable life. She knew that they reaped the benefits of their own hard work; but she worried that they might also be reaping the benefits of the sacrifices of others such as the soldiers, and while she was outraged that the sacrifice was extracted, she equally feared unworthiness.[12]

By November 1914, the citizens of Swan River had founded a Patriotic Society, through which they would do Red Cross and other relief work. Gertrude found the relief aims laudable, but the patriotic trappings made her sick at heart. She reported that she could "not bear the blatant vulgarity that passes for patriotism." Much as she loved England she could not sing "God save the King," but rather sang silently the hymn, "When wilt Thou save the people – Oh, God of Mercy, when? Not thrones and crowns, but nations, Not kings and lords but MEN! God save the people, Thine they are, Thy children, as Thine angels fair, From vice, oppression and despair – God save the People." She prayed, "Thy Kingdom come," she said, whenever she heard "Rule Britannia." She still believed in the greatness of the Empire, and admired the courage and unity demonstrated in the face of the war. She was not willing to take the easy way out and blame male domination as the sole cause of the war; she believed that "militarism" was not only a male phenomenon. "In so far as we partake of the sin of national pride – in so far as we desire domination won by the sword – in so far as we approve the appeal to arms – we all, priest, woman or soldier are alike responsible." It galled her that those who sat in comfortable homes could speak of " 'sacrifice' – and boast of our 'confidence in the outcome.' " The virtues that blossomed out of the war were all very well, but at what cost and how contaminated? Would Jesus recognise Christianity as a religion of his teachings? It seemed to Gertrude more "a religion of 'Empire' with high sounding phrases that can nowhere be found in all the teachings of Christ." Although she had been bitterly disappointed by women's support of militarism, she still had hopes that women voters could bring about a better world. "That [woman suffrage] will be a factor for peace is shown very clearly by the fact that the great Imperialists (almost to a man) are opposed to it."[13]

Gertrude returned to the question of feminist support for the war near the end of 1914, when Mrs Pankhurst's militarist address in Leicester's De Montfort Hall was reproduced in the *Midland Free Press*; there could be no doubt now of the WSPU's official pro-war position (although not all members supported it). Gertrude believed incorrectly that the WSPU was the only suffrage group to support the war. In fact, Mrs Fawcett, head of the National Union of Women's Suffrage Societies (NUWSS), was pro-war (although not so fervently militarist as the WSPU leaders), as were a few others on her executive. However the bulk of the NUWSS officers and executive members were antiwar, and its membership, as had that of the Women's Freedom League, had split on the issue. Although historians do not agree on the numbers, a very substantial percentage had remained opposed to Mrs Fawcett's support for the war. Gertrude wrote, "Many are absolutely opposed to all war, others are working to help and relieve suffering and need, and taking no definite stand for or against." Internationally too, the feminist movement was split. Most members of the International Woman Suffrage Alliance (IWSA) supported their governments; but the internationalist faction of the IWSA leaders defied nationalism to try to keep up their sisterly connections. Their journal *Jus Suffragii*, edited during the war in England by IWSA secretary Mary Sheepshanks, published affirmations of international sisterly solidarity from women in the belligerent countries. Sheepshanks made an effort to obtain news from "enemy" countries, asking the neutrals to gather and send in material, and asking German and Austrian women to realise that poor coverage of their doings was not by design. Of course the "patriotic" contingent viewed this policy as despicable and traitorous.[14]

Gertrude read *Jus Suffragii* regularly. Other sources gave antiwar news. Although *Woman's Century* was adamantly prowar, until 1917 it contained occasional references to the women's peace movement. Until her departure in 1917 Francis Marion Beynon's column in the *Grain Growers' Guide* was a useful, consistently antiwar, information source; Violet McNaughton was more discreet, but she too published occasional information on peace activism. The Winnipeg *Voice* was another pacifist source. Sylvia Pankhurst, whose East London Federation of Suffragettes (ELFS) had split from Mrs Pankhurst and Christabel, mailed Gertrude copies of the ELFS newspaper, *The Woman's Dreadnought*. Gertrude knew about the strong opposition to the war by the Australian suffragists led by

Vida Goldstein (and Adela Pankhurst, who had emigrated) and was aware that their paper, *The Woman Voter,* had been raided and threatened by the authorities. Gertrude discussed various antiwar efforts in her Leicester columns, and, until she was excluded from its pages, in her columns in *Woman's Century.* Despite women's backsliding, Gertrude retained faith in her belief that women voters would still be a force for good. To illustrate this, she quoted Zoa Haight's address to the 1914 Grain Growers' convention in Regina that November: "Our women are always pre-eminently the home-makers, the devoted guardians of our children, the solace of all who suffer. None of these duties can be dissociated from politics. That thousands of our people die yearly from the dread tuberculosis and other preventable diseases is our business. It is women's business when the bar is placed as a temptation in the way of children. That our young men are perishing by the war is women's business. The bar must go and wars must cease, for nothing can ever repay a nation for the loss of its young men." Gertrude added, "This, I feel sure, is the heart belief of all true women."[15]

The Roaring River suffrage group grappled with the challenges to visions of womanhood presented by the ruptures in the women's movement. Womanliness and women's mission as mothers of the world had hitherto led everyone to presuppose that mothers would protect their children, and all children, against harm. War was stupid and harmful; solutions by force were antithetical to women's view of civilisation; women were opposed to war and brute force. Now, patriotic maternalism blessed women who sent their sons out to kill the sons of other women, in the name of civilised values. The suffrage group found it difficult to make such a switch. At their November 1914 meeting, they discussed "Christian versus Spartan womanhood" and agreed to participate in the day of prayer requested by the British Dominions Woman Suffrage Association (BDWSU) to take place on New Year's Eve day in all the overseas dominions. It was to be an occasion wherein women could seek guidance for their "true work" in the war and in the postwar reconstruction, to assure that women's views were taken into account and that "spiritual and permanent interests may prevail over those which are material and temporary." Gertrude had regularly been in touch with the BDWSU's honorary secretary, Harriet C. Newcomb, and had been invited to their July 1914 international conference in London. BDWSU events were often reported in *Woman's Century* – the BDWSU represented an Empire-wide suffrage connection of some importance, and in fact, some 1915 *Woman's Century* issues featured an endorsement by Newcomb on their front cover.[16]

Christmas festivities were much as usual that year, if a bit sub-dued: the Roaring River Sunday School Christmas party featured a mixture of patriotic and traditional recitations, songs, and the usual Santa Claus (who surprised Eliza Twilley with a stuffed and oven-ready turkey). On Christmas Day, the clan gathered as ever at Fan-nie's where they were joined by friends for tree trimming, feasting, and presents. No one had the heart for singing that year, but the chil-dren rushed about happily, unaware of reason to be gloomy. Gertrude and Fannie whispered in the kitchen about the war news, but in the parlour and dining room, all was festive. At this point Gertrude could still look ahead with hope to the postwar world and a time when life would return to normal and "true values." There would be great changes after the war: "We are going to put an end to war, to Kaiser-ism, to military domination, to aristocratic domination, to plutocratic domination, to domination of every kind. There is all the opportunity for altruism, for heroism, for 'manly virile virtues' (supposed to be exclusive military virtues at present) in our common sweet daily lives." Everyone must "rise to our duty ... and strive to destroy the evils in this world"; an ambitious agenda, but without her faith in the possibility of its achievement, Gertrude would have been lost, and for Christians this was the season of hope. Some of her suffrage col-leagues were particularly optimistic at this time, and thought that public support for woman suffrage was building so fast that women would have the vote very soon. A further campaign in every corner of the province might not be necessary after all. And when women got the vote, the first step would have been taken to shape public af-fairs to reflect the "true values" Gertrude spoke of.[17]

The war continued to overshadow Gertrude's usual activities and preoccupations in the new year. She was disgusted and alarmed by the increasing militarisation of everyday life, including religious life, and the glorification of so-called "spartan" values. She clung to her belief that women were on the whole against war and destruction. "This cruel war is not our work," she wrote in a column addressed to Leicester women. "It is comforting to remember that no woman of any nation had a hand in bringing it about ... I feel quite certain that if the women were consulted, there would not be war. Then the na-tions would have to find some other way out, and they would find it." On the face of it, "we women have not power – indeed, very few men have either – to prevent this and like calamities," yet she be-lieved that women had not done all they could to prevent it. "You know how half unconsciously we glorify the military life," she re-minded readers. "We associate war in our training with much that is fascinating and attractive to the boy's nature." Mothers often held up military examples of bravery to their little boys. But there were other examples that could be used. "How often do we tell of the heroic lifeboat men whose heroism is to save and never to kill?" What stories did women tell about the miners who unhesitatingly went into the burning pit to rescue trapped fellows? Gertrude had long been an enthusiast of the peace education theories of F.J. Gould, who advocated the use of nonmilitary examples of heroism for role models, and wrote about heroism among industrial workers, for example. Military heroism had long-lasting consequences, Gertrude pointed out: as a Winnipeg suffragist (whom she did not name) had recently put it, "A man who drives a bayonet through another man will never be quite the same again." Recognising that women had at least some degree of influence over their children, she urged women to make use of their power in their private lives, to sabotage the capacity of governments to make war.[18]

A welcome distraction offered itself that winter in the form of town meetings about a research project on community development. In the summer of 1914, concerned about falling church attendance and rural depopulation (in particular, young people's desire to head for the bright lights of the city), the departments of social service and evangelism of the Presbyterian and Methodist churches jointly undertook surveys of rural life in various parts of the province. The earlier rural surveys, based on the new techniques of social research, focused on churches and schools in older rural communities, but the survey of the Swan River Valley communities looked at a variety of institutions, and used six different research instruments to gather information. In three valley communities, including Swan River, questionnaires were also completed on all individual households, while in other areas random sampling of households was used. A special "town community study" was made of Swan River. The survey was intended to provide information about the resources that were available in a community for renewal and improvement of community life, and to make some recommendations about how some of them might be used for that purpose. The Swan River survey report consisted of five sections, which described the history, economic, social, educational, and religious conditions and institutions of the valley settlements; reports of the social service and evangelism committees and a bibliography of useful resources were appended. In accordance with the methodology of the rural surveys, after the publication of the report the researcher returned in January 1915 to hold a series of meetings and discuss his findings with the residents of the valley settlements. Gertrude attended the meeting in Swan River, which featured speeches by an agricultural college professor (who may have been

John Murchee, author of the report), a clergyman from the Social Service Council, and the local Methodist minister. Her report of the meeting referred to "splendid addresses" and "lively discussions," and she evidently enjoyed the occasion tremendously, not least because the war was hardly mentioned. Not coincidentally, many of the activities in which Gertrude and her friends were involved were precisely the sort recommended by the survey report to improve and strengthen community life (although their agenda was more sweeping than that of the provincial agricultural department's extension services).[19]

Early in 1915, Gertrude had received notice of the upcoming women's peace conference at The Hague, convened by the group of internationalists on the International Woman Suffrage Alliance executive (with the help of Dutch and other neutrals' feminists), who were outraged that the war had devastated the suffrage movement and placed barriers between women who wished to work across national boundaries. Although many of the records for 1915 have been lost, some survive, including early mailing lists. One which reveals something of the patterns of suffrage group networking that were used by the organisers shows three names for Manitoba: Mary Crawford (the physician who headed the PEL) and Genevieve Skinner (a suffragist newspaperwoman) in Winnipeg, and Gertrude in Swan River. Fellow suffragist Emily Murphy of Edmonton, convenor of the peace committee of the National Council of Women of Canada (NCWC), was also invited. Although she could not attend, she replied cordially and asked to be kept informed.[20]

Murphy was unusual among NCWC leaders in her sympathy for the Congress. She spoke positively of the provisional agenda, and wrote, "May I also, on behalf of the Canadian women, express our indebtedness to the women of Holland for their self-sacrificing work on behalf of the interests of peace." Murphy enclosed a copy of "Shall we Have Peace?" a piece she had contributed to a symposium published under the heading, "What Twelve Canadian Women Hope to see as the Outcome of the War," in the April issue of *Everywoman's World*, a Toronto magazine. Not surprisingly, the Congress organisers were delighted with Murphy's support, and someone has scribbled on the top of the letter, "I should like to read to you first the messages of the National Councils of Women of some of the" [*sic*], obviously as a script for the opening parts of the Congress. Murphy's friendliness was not a mere pleasantry; she made other attempts to find out about the Congress. For example, she wrote to Mrs Ryckman from the U.S., who had attended, to ask for an account of the event. Murphy had read a piece written by Julia Grace Wales, a Canadian from the

Eastern Townships who taught literature at the University of Wisconsin for many years, who was the originator of a mediation plan adopted by the Hague Congress. Murphy commented to Ryckman, "Canada seems to have gone war mad. This is one reason Miss Wales' article helped stiffen my rather limp spirit." Wales and Murphy corresponded; Murphy also continued to receive material from the International Committee of Women for Permanent Peace (ICWPP; the organization was founded at the 1915 Hague Congress, and renamed the Women's International League for Peace and Freedom in 1919), some sent via Women's Peace Party headquarters in Chicago which operated a forwarding service for some Canadian peace women. Whatever her views, to my knowledge Murphy did not take an open part in the antiwar movement. What she may have said in NCWC meetings is another matter, equally unknown.[21]

Most NCWC leaders (as was the case in all belligerent countries) were outspokenly opposed to the peace movement. The editorial in the April 1915 issue of *Woman's Century,* entitled "Women and peace," stated its disapproval of the planned Hague Congress; they (presumably the editor was speaking for the NCWC executive) did not object to the display of mutual friendship, one of the purposes set out in the Dutch women's invitation, but other items in the preliminary program were unacceptable. The Congress planned to ask the belligerents to state the terms upon which they would make peace. This was "an impossible demand to make of the Allies forced into this war by the lust of the Prussian militarists, with the Kaiser at their head, for world domination," said the editorial. "Prussian militarism must be crushed forever."[22]

However, other perspectives were represented in that issue: Christine Ross Barker, a Toronto suffragist involved in the pacifist circle within the Canadian Woman Suffrage Association, wrote a paragraph supporting the Hague meeting and pointing out that "the right of free speech is one of the fundamental British liberties," and it behooved Canadian women, who appeared willing to forego that liberty themselves, she said, to allow their sisters elsewhere to exercise it. "There is nothing really immoral or indecent in agitation for peace," she concluded. Barker herself had resigned from the Toronto business women's club she headed, over their prowar position. From the mainstream, Edith Lang, secretary of the National Union of Suffrage Societies of Canada and of its member federation the National Equal Franchise Union, announced the receipt of programs for the Hague meeting, and described the agenda in friendly tones. The Hague organisers had asked for delegates, but, "as the subjects to be discussed are highly controversial" and time was too short to canvass the member societies for their views, Lang had replied that they could not send delegates but would publish the information. She reported to Canadian readers, "We shall, however, watch with interest the results of a conference which, if successfully carried out, will prove the triumph of the unifying bond of a common cause over the divisions of nationality, and it will prove that at least one-half of the human race is capable of sinking national differences for the sake of the international good." The difference in tone between the NCWC viewpoint and that of the suffragists is marked, and the latters' apparent openness must have helped Gertrude maintain her sense that suffragists in general, as well as those she knew locally, had not abandoned internationalism.[23]

Gertrude became more critical of the British Empire as her preoccupation with militarism and issues of moral responsibility led her to scrutinise the underpinnings of civilisation and progress. Although in 1911 she had written matter-of-factly that only a few years before the whole of the Swan River Valley had been the domain of the aboriginal peoples, and commented approvingly on arrangements made for their support, by early 1915 she was developing a different view. She had written earlier about the death of the famous poet Pauline Johnson (Tekahionwake), a Métis of Mohawk and English origin whose fame was at its height around the turn of the century. Gertrude may have heard of Johnson before she migrated to Canada, for the poet made several visits to England and her work was reviewed in the English journals. In any event, Gertrude surely read a sympathetic 1912 article in the *Canadian Thresherman and Farmer*, and may have sent away for a book of Johnson's later poems and stories which was published as a fundraiser and memorial by her supporters in Vancouver, where Johnson died early in 1913. By 1915 Gertrude found meaning in other verses by Johnson, "speaking of her conquered race, and trying to explain their pain and suffering." As Johnson wrote, "They but forget we Indians owned the land / From ocean to ocean; that they stand / Upon a soil, that centuries agone / Was our sole Kingdom, and our right alone. / They never think how they would feel to-day / If some great nation came from far away, / Wresting their country from their hapless braves, /Giving what they gave us – but wars and graves … Though starved, crushed, plundered, lies our nation low … / Perhaps the 'White-Man's God' has willed it so." Although Gertrude did not name this poem or point out its historical setting, it is perhaps significant that its narrator was a woman seeing her husband off to fight the white invaders sent to put down the 1885 Rebellion. Gertrude wrote, "How much we have to repent of and to feel shame for" in the history of the Empire. "Do you not think we have need for repentance? Do you think we have room to criticise too strongly the actions of other nations?"[24]

The gloom was broken by a trip to Winnipeg in February 1915 for the convention of the Manitoba Political Equality League, which found Gertrude's political star ascending. The journey was more complicated than before the war, the direct train no longer being in service. Gertrude and Robert managed to attend a Presbyterian prayer meeting in Dauphin during a stopover, and heard an address by a medical missionary who was training surgeons for the front. Dr Scott opposed the war and urged Christians to do likewise, which Gertrude found heartening. In Winnipeg the Richardsons were bil-letted with the Hamples, a Christian Science family, and Gertrude was intrigued and impressed by their example of a "beautiful home life, where the spirit of Christian love" was so strongly in evidence. When Gertrude went to the Industrial Bureau to register for the convention, PEL president Mary Crawford asked Gertrude to join the deputation to Premier Roblin. The first afternoon's discussion centred on the PEL constitution; the evening session was a public meeting held at the posh Fort Garry hotel, featuring a suffrage play performed by PEL members. The visit to the premier took place the second morning. The delegation consisted of Mary Crawford, assigned to speak for Winnipeg women, Mrs Duff Smith for the WCTU, Gertrude to speak for Manitoba women in general, Mr Thorson of the Icelandic Equality League, and city councillor Richard Rigg of the Trades and Labour Council. Gertrude was convinced by Roblin's behaviour that he had been converted on the suffrage question; she noted that he sought reassurance from Mary Crawford that the PEL was non-partisan.[25]

However thrilling, the deputation was not the highlight of the convention; that came in the second afternoon session. In the midst of reports from the various presidents on the activities of their local suffrage societies, Gertrude was elected first vice-president of the provincial PEL, "the greatest honour of my life." She would be convenor for the committee in charge of organising groups in the province ("province" or "provincial" usually being a code word for "outside Winnipeg"). "I pray that God will give me strength for the great task, my appointed share in this, the greatest movement in the world," she wrote. At the close of the afternoon session, Mrs Hample held a tea and reception in her honour, a rather grand affair; the room was decorated with banners and cushions displaying the "Votes for Women" slogan, and each guest was given a bunch of violets tied in a yellow ribbon with a "Votes for Women" button attached. At the evening session that night, held again at the Fort Garry, Dr Sinclair of

St Andrew's Presbyterian Church chaired, and introduced the speakers: Miss Brown, the sole female school trustee in Manitoba, who was also an active suffragist and not afraid to make antiwar speeches in public, and Methodist social gospel leader Salem Bland. The big treat followed, a "splendid play, 'Women's Influence,' well conceived and delightfully acted." The final session of the convention was held Saturday afternoon, consisting of papers and discussions on various aspects of suffrage work. That evening Gertrude went with friends to an IODE reception whose entertainment was of a patriotic flavour; she enjoyed Sunday morning church-going more. They attended the Christian Science church with the Hamples and were "much impressed" by the large size of the congregation. The final afternoon and evening were spent visiting PEL and Presbyterian Synod friends and hearing the Reverend Dr Sinclair preach a peace sermon. All in all, a perfect time.[26]

The bloom was off the rose in relatively short order; although Gertrude had believed that Roblin was sincere in his claim that he intended to support woman suffrage, she wrote not long thereafter that "although he appeared to be touched at the time, he is trying to prevent anything being done." Attempts by the opposition to get a suffrage bill through the legislature were rebuffed. Gertrude asserted after these events, "We shall not allow our cause to be laid lightly aside, or to be dealt with as it had been dealt with in England ... We women are going to have our hands on the lever, that war and social evils may be crushed out of our world-life. And only bad men are afraid of it, and only indolent, careless selfish women are against it. I know that is saying a great deal. Nevertheless, it is true. We have suffered and wept too long. The time has come for us to take the place we should never have vacated, the place given to us by God."[27]

The convention had given her new energy, and a new authority. Her reaction is reminiscent of that of other antiwar feminists who became involved in women's peace movements in this period; for example, shortly after she joined the newly formed Woman's Peace Party, Boston feminist and Women's Trade Union League member Elizabeth Glendower Evans wrote to a friend, "Last summer I was like a person who had died and whom others had forgotten to bury. All the autumn I had been feeling like a corpse that was defiling those of the earth. It is unto that dead body that a new life has come." Her "whole soul" commitment to the Woman's Peace Party removed her "doubts and self disparagement" and she felt "so on fire that I can pass the flames along." Gertrude's columns after the PEL convention mark a new spirit of determination and optimism, which remained in evidence for much of 1915; the tone of despair and helplessness that permeated her earlier comments on the war no longer dominated. Not that she ceased to agonise and lament, but she was able again to see the seeds of the new world order in the decay and death of the old: as she wrote some weeks later, "I am so glad that in the blackest moment of the world's suffering I can yet realise the presence of something that seems like an embryonic promise of better ideals. Here and there it is manifest, and I am so thankful." After the PEL convention, she seems to have realised that she was in good company, and believed again that the suffragists would win. Locally, things were going well on the suffrage front. The Roaring River group held its annual meeting, and the executive reshuffled, Gertrude moving to the office of corresponding secretary. (Her mother remained honorary president.) At a Roaring River Grain Growers social, the chair said that when women got the vote, "The war-makers will have a hard time." In Winnipeg the PEL published antiwar news in its suffrage column in the *Voice*.[28]

Suffragists had long believed that women had special abilities needed for social change. Jessie Campbell MacIver, editor of the *Woman's Century*, whose extreme hostility to the Hague proposal Gertrude did not yet realise, wrote to Gertrude, "Oh, if we women only knew our power and wielded it in the right way! What could we not accomplish? What evils could we not crush?" Gertrude took this as support for women as peacemakers. Citing the opinion of a male speaker at a 1915 May Day rally that if women rose up against the war, "millions of men would stand behind us," Gertrude said, "So we are waiting for a leader. God give her to us soon." In Britain, Gertrude said, some government officials feared that if all women were given the vote, they would use it *en bloc* to vote the war to a halt. This insistence on women's pacifism against all evidence is easier to understand in the context of women reformers' information about scientific research on sex differences and human evolution. Suffragists who remained pacifists believed that scientific laws of human evolution linked women, peace, and human progress. As historian Jill Kerr Conway explains, the standard work by British authors Patrick Geddes and J. Arthur Thompson argued that males had a biological tendency to aggression, which caused a loss of energy, while females had an inborn tendency to "conserve energy and nurture life." Men were born to make war, women to make peace. Because these tendencies were biological and governed by the laws of nature, they were stronger than mere patriotism and military enthusiasm, both of which were socially rather than biologically produced. Thus, when they became involved with antiwar activities, women were acting in accordance with the laws of nature. If the laws of the universe supported

Progress, and cooperation constituted a fundamental part of the evolution of human society toward Progress, then women had reason to hope that they could stop the war, if they would only use their natural characteristics.[29]

That spring Gertrude found another source of comfort and inspiration in the natural world, and as she said, "As those with whom I come in contact become indifferent, I grieve more and more ... Oh! the glad, good world. Even as I write, the sun breaks forth, illuminating the brown earth and making bare branches beautiful. The cruelty of man only makes the tenderness and goodness of God more apparent to those who look for Him." This solace was present at Eastertime; as she had in her earliest period in Swan River, she returned to the theme of abundance, and of the reciprocal contract between God and humanity and nature. "God is always faithful to His promise of the harvest, and each year enough is garnered to supply the need of all the world. Withheld by the wickedness and greed of man from those for whom God gave it, held back by the military power, and directed into wrong channels, His little ones starve and die." But the evildoers would be punished in the end. "Materials for the building of homes God hath supplied in greatest abundance. The earth is rich in minerals of every kind, given for the need of man. Yet their wealth is diverted into evil uses, and the wisdom and ingenuity of man is made to serve the purposes of evil. What God gave to us all is taken without our consent by evil man, and formed into engines of destruction, directed against brothers of ours, made in the image of the same God." Yet there was abundant evidence in nature around her or God's kindness; the protective colouring of rabbits' coats according to the season, the ripening of flowers and fruits and grain, "infinite wisdom, tender love, fatherly provision is everywhere displayed." Gertrude turned to this display to refute the claims of those who argued that nature was bloody, based on creatures preying on each other, and thus it was natural law that humans do likewise. "God did not give us the law of the jungle, God gave us Jesus," she retorted. "God is the mother only of good, not of evil." How could anyone believe God was represented in battles? She saw Him in the nursing of the sick, "in the heroism which rescues, not that which destroys. Someone has asked us to 'imagine Christ in khaki thrusting a bayonet through a brother man' ... It is impossible ... He said 'Follow Me.'"[30]

Gertrude's columns in the Leicester paper referred from time to time to the activities of women in "enemy" countries; for some of her readers, this may have been a rare source of such news. The IWSA journal *Jus Suffragii* had published a Christmas letter from 100 British suffragists to German and Austrian women in its January 1915 issue;

the reply was published in March. This was not the first such exchange of greetings: in October 1914, Social Democratic British women had sent a "peace and solidarity manifesto" to their counterparts in the belligerent countries on both sides, using women's networks in the neutral countries to do so. Later that fall, Clara Zetkin sent greetings from the German Social Democratic Party (SDP) antiwar women, and a Swedish SDP women's congress held in Stockholm likewise sent out an antiwar declaration. In December, seven representatives of German women's suffrage groups sent a message hoping that suffragists' bonds would not be severed by the war. By January and February 1915, women from several neutral countries were pressing their governments to mediate; Lida Gustava Heymann, prominent Austrian suffragist, begged women to meet to work for peace, "as wives and mothers, as protectors of Humanity, and of true Culture." Individual women wrote open letters for publication (or sent smuggled letters via neutral travellers) to their sister suffragists in opposing countries, urging them to oppose the spirit of hatred and stick together. Some of these statements were reported in the suffrage or socialist press, others remained unpublished, but known of through the suffragist networks. Sylvia Pankhurst's paper also contained snippets of news from various neutral and belligerent countries. Although *Jus Suffragii* did not take sides in the war, it was outspokenly antiwar and an excellent source of antimilitarist articles and news. But news of this sort probably did not reach women who were not involved in one of the antiwar sectors of the suffrage movement, for the dailies were virtually all prowar.[31]

In June 1915 Gertrude wrote that she had read about German women's protest meetings and women's riots in Trieste. This affirmed her belief that true women everywhere opposed the war. She urged her readers to fight against the war. "The Government is well pleased to see you knitting, making shirts, nursing, toiling lovingly as women do toil for the brave, suffering ones. But while you work do not close your eyes. Are we to remove German militarism by the sacrifice of our bravest and best (for that is what we have been told) only to have a worse militarism forced upon us?" Gertrude believed that "nothing will end these horrors but a Christian democracy, where rulers are all done away with, and where an equal voice in Government is given to all persons of both sex. By Government I mean local, national, and international Government." Women had a different approach, she said, and a different perspective on issues than did men. "So again I ask all women readers not to be content with knitting and sewing. While we cannot help doing this, we are really helping in this hideous war, actually helping to carry it on, but God knows our hearts." Gertrude herself was struggling with the question of relief work: by sewing surgical shirts, operation stockings, and hot water bags as she did for the Home Economics Society, which met every Friday to do Red Cross work, was she not supporting the war effort? How was it possible to carry out humanitarian relief work without supporting the militarism she detested? But how could she leave wounded soldiers to suffer, when it was not their fault, and despite the fact that they would only be sent back to die once they had been nursed to health? Although she did not say so explicitly, it seems to me that the moral ambiguity of this and other relief work, and the conflict of conscience that produced, were eased when Gertrude (or other women) combined this work with vigorous opposition to the war. Thus the anti-war elements were strengthened and the meaning of the activity thereby clarified.[32]

In the spring of 1915 a scandal forced Roblin to resign and his government to fall; the Liberals formed a caretaker government and then swept the August 6 election. Toby Norris, the new premier, had promised women the vote if enough women signed a petition saying they wanted it. Gertrude predicted, "Then we will force bad men out of office and put in good ones, for women are independent thinkers and will be independent voters." The PEL stepped up its organising; they placed notices in local papers that supporters could affiliate to the provincial PEL in places where there were no local branches, and in the case of the Swan River area, since the town organisation (founded during the 1914 election campaign) was not currently active, the Roaring River group welcomed associate members. Petition forms were available; they would be brought for signatures upon request. In the midst of organising new branches in the valley, the Roaring River group took up the question of the terms upon which the franchise would be granted. The PEL feared that the final bill would contain a property qualification that appeared in a draft bill. The Grain Growers had passed a resolution at the 1912 convention that women should be given the vote on the same terms as men, and men did not have a property qualification to vote provincially, although municipal voters were subject to some property restrictions. The Roaring River suffrage group (which renamed itself the Political Equality League in 1915) protested to Norris: they were "most disappointed in the Premier's use of the words 'women entitled to the municipal franchise' in his reply to the recent delegation, and wish to emphasise the fact the it is for *the woman herself and not the property* that the vote is desired." Norris' reply was conciliatory but noncommittal.[33]

In addition to the suffrage group's regular summer activities, such as the annual picnic, Gertrude and her colleagues visited nearby towns to found PEL locals; in July she, Robert, and Margaret Martin set up a branch in nearby Oakhurst, twenty-four kilometres from Swan River. This meant leaving home early in the morning, holding the meeting in the afternoon, and setting out on the return journey in the evening. At the Oakhurst meeting Gertrude was heartened by expressions of antiwar sentiment. Shortly thereafter she went to found another group at Kenville, eighteen kilometres away at the opposite end of the valley. The suffragists in the valley carried the petition with them wherever they thought they might find sympathisers; Gertrude and her mother collected signatures at the Grain Growers picnic in Kenville. The Grain Growers often used their gatherings to promote woman suffrage. In late August she was appealing for women to carry the petition around to get signatures to meet the October 1 deadline. The completed forms would be counted and presented at the first session of the legislature. In September the Roaring River PEL, supported by the Oakhurst and Kenville groups, brought in Mrs Wright, the president of the Dauphin area WCTU, to speak in Minitonas and Swan River on the links between temperance and woman suffrage. Gertrude spoke at both meetings on "The Relation of the Women's Movement to the War."[34]

In the midst of this bustle of activity, the suffragists dreamed of what they would do after women got the vote; Gertrude wrote that they would form citizens' leagues to work for high standards of government, "and then we women will be able to show that we can be practical ... There is much to encourage and make us glad ... there is yet, as I have often said lately, a new spirit being born in the world. While we tread softly about our tasks, with bowed heads and tearful eyes, we are making resolutions, forming ideas, and striving for calm judgement." Hopes were high and plans ambitious, and Gertrude set out this list: "We are going to take the power that is our right into our own hands. We are going to drive from office all who are unworthy. We are going to break down barriers of sex, and raise womanhood from economic dependence that means slavery. And the next time a cruel war is sprung upon us, we shall be ready with our 'veto'; for the mother-half of the world is going to share the throne of dominion in the new day that is coming."[35]

Gertrude's hopes were further raised by the report she received about the women's peace congress held at the end of April 1915 at The Hague, which had founded the International Committee of Women for Permanent Peace (ICWPP). The reports were widely disseminated, and discussed or partially reproduced by several Canadian feminists. For example, Helena Gutteridge (who had been sent a Hague invitation), former militant suffragette and a Vancouver feminist and labour organiser since her arrival in British Columbia from England in 1911, wrote a lengthy article in the socialist Winnipeg *Voice* about the Congress, praising the resolutions and commenting on the abiding power of the maternal instinct in women. Gutteridge noted, however, that most women had traditionally expressed this instinct by succouring the men who fought, while the more progressive women put their maternal spirit to work trying to stop bloodshed and war. Edith Lang, secretary of the National Equal Franchise Union, wrote in the September 1915 issue of *Woman's Century* that she had received the official Hague report: "It is most interesting reading, and can be had on application." Gertrude also received a report on the Hague Congress from the British section of the ICWPP, which called itself the Women's International League (WIL), detailing the proceedings and resolutions of the Congress, the voyage of the Congress peace envoys, and post-Congress events in Britain. Gertrude noted that several names known to her from school days, the Boer War peace movement, and the suffrage movement were on the WIL general executive committee: Charlotte Despard of the Women's Freedom League, Sylvia Pankhurst of the East London Federation of Suffragettes, and Marion and Charlotte Ellis, Leicester Quakers and feminists. Gertrude knew the latter from Wyggeston Girls' School and Leicester suffrage activities (and she may have met Despard through Women's Freedom League campaigns), and had also worked with the Ellises and other Quakers in the antiwar movement during the Boer War.[36]

Gertrude continued to express optimism about the potential for suffragists to work effectively for peace, writing late that summer that "the world-wide Women Movement is the only international organisation the foundations of which are absolutely unshaken by the war," as compared, for example, to the international socialist movement. However she noted approvingly that socialist women from every country had issued antiwar manifestos; all this "gives us hope and courage to keep on with the struggle for the universal enfranchisement of womanhood, as a preliminary step in the enthronement of the Mother Spirit of our race." On the face of it, Gertrude's claims for unity seem ludicrous, considering the hostility of the prowar majority and their strong efforts to discredit the pacifist minority. She was not unaware of this, and indeed wrote of her receipt of the report from the Hague Congress, "These are being sent to representative women of the different countries, in order to counteract the evil effect of false and misleading Press reports – and we are asked to circulate the knowledge among all women with whom we come in contact." The National Committee of Women for Patriotic Service, composed of the presidents of national women's organisations in Canada, had circulated an anti-pacifist statement, "An open letter concerning peace," to counteract the Hague organising efforts in March and April 1915. Yet the Hague Congress and peace mission at that time still appeared to have a chance to succeed, and despite the fact that the women's peace movement represented a minority of organised women, it nonetheless existed and appeared to be growing. The argument could be made (and this likely was Gertrude's view) that it was the internationalist segment of the "world-wide Women Movement" that truly represented that movement, and thus it could be said to have been "absolutely unshaken" despite its abandonment by misguided pro-war women acting at national levels. Gertrude quoted an unidentified German woman who had written in *Jus Suffragii* that women must not keep silent in the face of the lie that true patriotism is that of the brute and killer, "No, they must raise their voices for a nobler love of country if they do not want to be accomplices in a hideous crime."[37]

Rare incidents of pacifist preaching gave her hope partly by contrast to the militarism she saw taking over institutional Christianity. Despite occasional laments by individual ministers about the pacific Jesus, and notwithstanding the peace witness of a few ministers, the Presbyterian Church as a body did not oppose the war, nor did the Methodists. When Presbyterian and Methodist ministers from Minitonas stopped for tea on their way home from a meeting of the interdenominational Ministerial Association (founded in 1914), Gertrude asked why Christian clergy were not antiwar. "They gave the usual evasive, ministerial answers (ministers rarely have led the world in any reform)." She opened her mail later that day and "found therein a terrible indictment in the form of a poem 'dedicated to all ministers who foster the war spirit.' It is by a young Canadian whose writings show him to have a good education, deep spiritual insight, and the noblest ideals. But it is too terrible to reproduce. The truth and the horror of it alike made me shudder. It ends thus: – 'As for us, our creed holds good, never fault or flaw, / We have struck "Thou shalt not kill" from the ancient law.'" Gertrude looked elsewhere for leadership and support. She had believed that "the Press will lead the world, and the Pulpit will take second place." W.T. Stead had thought that the press should provide a forum for ordinary people, and should pressure politicians to respond to the people's will; this as much as moral crusades was what Stead meant by "new journalism," and such was Gertrude's view, this interpretation no doubt solidified by shared Boer War experiences. A Christmas Day editorial in the Manitoba *Free Press* underscored her conviction that this must happen soon, as the clergy were not doing their job. The editorial read, "When the Christian churches really believe in [Peace on earth, goodwill to men], and live it, refusing to remain longer repositories for racial and national hatreds and prejudices, there will dawn a Christmas which will not find the nations either awaiting the signal for killing one another or actually engaged in the bloody business with the blessings of the priests upon their endeavours. Christ is the Prince of Peace, but when shall He come into His Kingdom?"[38]

Gertrude continued her discussion in subsequent columns. "I am so pained by the attitude of the ministers of the Gospel of Jesus who approve of war," she wrote, "I know there is no justification anywhere in the teachings of Christ from the beginning to the end of His recorded life for their attitude ... He distinctly forbade his followers to take the sword." Gertrude's religious beliefs did not include a God of war, she wrote in June 1915; "Indeed, I would never kneel to pray to one who demanded millions of human sacrifices. Such is not my God. I believe in and love the God of Love, not the god of War, and hatred, and lust, and rapine, and slaughter." Jesus had done his best to teach people the gospel of love, and if people refused to follow it, it was with the people, not the teaching, that the fault lay. Until people heeded the teachings, "these evil things will never cease from off the earth." Yet even in the darkest days, Gertrude believed, there was "an embryonic promise of better ideals." But she was disgusted by the nation-wide celebration that summer of Patriotic Sunday by the Presbyterian church. Although she found some "splendid" elements in some of the addresses, these were marred by the "spirit of war [they] breathed, a spirit for which there is no place in a Christian church." Reflecting on the Bible, she said, "Christ was a patriot. In present-day words 'He gave His life for His country.' Yet nowhere do we find him recruiting men for the Imperial army of Rome ... Nowhere does he uphold or exalt the military power to which God's chosen people had become vassal ... While the churches worship the war-god, the sword and the gun, let the children of Jesus wait with Him, and watch with Him in His lonely and darkened crucifixion." She had considered these issues during the Boer War and had dropped out of her evangelical Christian church, which had in other respects attempted to bring about the kingdom of Christ on earth, because of its militarist patriotism. She had found better Christians, as she had said, among the non-Christian socialists who opposed the war. Now she confronted similar apostasy, for she did not hesitate to name it so, among the Christian churches of her day. Reflecting further on the Patriotic Sunday, she later wrote, "I do not think we need to study what will be the outcome of obeying Christ. It will be now, as it always was, opposition to organised religion, that is used as a prop to strengthen Empire, just as in the days of Christ ... There is only one way for a Christian – the way of Christ ... Nothing will stop these terrible things, but the end of all tyranny, the coming of the Kingdom of Christ on earth ... If those who hear the name of Christ with one accord obeyed and followed Him we should arise one sweet morning to a new world – there could be no cruelty, no war, no oppression any more." After the depressing teatime visit with the Minitonas ministers she had written, "Oh, shame on the apostate ministers of Christ's Church. Such words as the above should come from them." Later that summer she read that an English bishop had advocated shooting slackers. No wonder atheism had grown so, she exclaimed. "It is painful to read of such things, to remember that 'bishops' are usually men who have their boots blacked for them, their meals prepared, and garments tended, that they may spend years in cultured ease, studying and 'preaching' – not alas! the Gospel of Jesus, but the gospel of force and militarism that, together with the hypocrisy of certain sycophant apostate Jews, was responsible for the crucifixion of the Gem of all Humanity."[39]

The Midland *Free Press* regularly published Gertrude's poems, and had done so for years, but her poem on the theme of apostasy, "The Justice of Jesus," which she "dedicated to all clergymen and ministers who preach war in the name of Christ," was not at all her usual devotional musing.

Ye have bidden them slay and slaughter, ye have bidden them go to die,
And here in grim heaps, untended, the sons of my suffering lie.
I came from my throne to save them, I suffered that they might live,
And gave you the message of mercy – the message of love – to give!

And yet from my holy temples, have bidden them forth, and blessed
The flags of the gathering cohorts, who on the battle pressed:
Behold them, the maimed and dying, the blinded and crushed and dead!
Ye sons of the men who slew me, and pressed with their thorns my head.

Not theirs is the guilt of slaughter: not theirs are the shame and sin,
For these are the sons of courage, who suffered their crowns to win:
Their souls shall by shining angels be gathered to love and light,
While ye who have falsely led them descend to the blackest night.

Go search through the holy record that gives to the world my word,
And mark how I loved the children, and cared for each flower and bird:
Then learn how I saved the dying, and see where I raised the dead,
And watched o'er the souls in anguish, and lifted the drooping head.

No message for all earth's children, but one commandment, "Love,"
The lesson I strove to teach you when I came from my throne above.
My children of every nation were bright with my blood out-poured;
Depart! ye accursed for ever, ye men who have called me "Lord."

When bore ye the bitter burden, when lay ye on battle-ground,
All wounded and maimed and bleeding, while the shrapnel burst around?
Ye have made but a huge Golgotha of my fair and flower-blest earth,
And stayed in your ease and culture, and laughed in securest mirth.

Ye cowards and murderous traitors, ye have borne my name in vain;
Mine, mine are the dead and dying, the wounded and worn and slain;
To my love in the Heavens eternal, all gathered for evermore,
But ye who have led them falsely shall be hurled from the Sacred Door.[40]

The timing of Gertrude's poetic condemnation of apostasy is worth considering. In the late summer and early fall of 1915 the Hague report was circulating among suffragists in various countries. It was clear that the wartime splits had not eradicated international sisterly solidarity, that militarist maternalism had not monolithically replaced earlier versions, and that large numbers of women still had the courage and the tenacity to persist in bringing about a new social order organised along womanly lines. The peace feminists were carrying out the laws of nature and God, they thought, serving the good of humanity and drawing on resources beyond their own to do so. Gertrude was clearly elated by the Hague report, and evidently was hopeful about the possibility that the ICWPP peace mission would lead to some form of the proposed "continuous mediation without armistice" and a conference called by the neutrals, which would eventually bring about a negotiated peace. It is important to remember that she was not alone in this hope, nor was it unfounded, although in the event it came to naught. The anti-apostasy poem appeared in the Leicester paper early in September; given wartime delays in communication, it seems likely that Gertrude sent it to them early in August. Of course it is possible she wrote it even earlier, but she often responded in poem as well as prose to events in her daily life, so it is likely she wrote it shortly before mailing it. During that period she was founding new suffrage groups, and hearing various antiwar comments from women and ministers; the petition campaign was going splendidly and the Liberals were swept to victory in the provincial election. The provincial suffragists (and indeed, Western feminists in general) had rejected the appeal to abandon "straight" suffrage work for war work, and continued to "work for the freedom of Canadian women," as Edith Lang's report explained in *Woman's Century*. During those golden late summer weeks Gertrude must have felt not only that she was on the right side, but that the right side was going to win, and soon.[41]

It was in this spirit of hope that she must have penned "The Coming of the Angel," excerpted below: [42]

We cannot hear her footsteps for the booming of the cannon;
We cannot see her beauty for the smoke that fills the air –
Yet I know that she is coming, for I feel her spirit's presence,
All its mystic inner radiance – tender, sacred as a prayer.

Very softly she is coming; and her feet are torn and bleeding,
For she treads the blood-stained pathways where our noble ones have
    died –
But her face is sweet and holy, and her eyes are full of pleading,
And her robes are white and snowy, like the garments of a bride.

We cannot hear her message to the wounded and the weeping.
We cannot tell the gladness that her coming will inspire –
She will light the lamps all darkened by the mocking clouds of battle,
She will lead to God in Heaven through the horror and the fire.

We cannot hear her footsteps, for our ears are full of battle.
We cannot see her glory for the smoke and stains of war –
But I know that she is coming, I can see her in the distance –
Glorious Peace, the Holy Angel, and her crown is like a star!

Although the war had brought a high demand for agricultural produce, 1915 was not a boom year in the Swan River area. Early promise had been changed by bad weather, with drought and frost at crucial points in the season. The fall of 1915 had a spell of glorious autumn weather, but it rained just often enough to make it difficult to get the crops in. There was a severe labour shortage and it was hard to find men to work on the crews. Because Gertrude and Robert stacked their wheat, storms did not make threshing impossible, but they were hurt in any case by low yields and low prices. "Much of the grain we thought saved is ruined. We shall have a 'very bad year' as it is called," she wrote. Even some garden crops and the wild fruits usually relied on for preserving were scarce and people had to buy food to preserve. Inflation had hit; sugar and tea prices had gone up. High prices for bought goods meant farmers could not hold back their grain for a better year: "We shall have to sell our sadly diminished supplies at a much lower price than we expected," Gertrude wrote in September 1915. They had still not threshed by late October, after the first snow. A week later the thresher had reached Fannie's place. When it finally reached Gertrude's, the separator broke after only two stacks. The next day it snowed heavily. Gertrude had spent days cooking; now threshing was put off indefinitely. They heard that only a quarter of the Alberta crop had been threshed, and a small proportion of the Saskatchewan harvest; their own would likely have to wait until spring.[43]

In the midst of worries about money and the harvest, the Twilleys celebrated Thanksgiving and Halloween, and Gertrude, her mother, and niece Connie went to see the Red Cross shipment before it was sent off to Winnipeg. It made a nice pile, and the ladies plied visitors with tea and goodies, for a price, – another fundraiser in the Home Economic Society Rest Rooms, where the sewing bees and other weekly work parties had been held all fall. Of course Gertrude had mixed feelings; although some said that women did Red Cross or other relief work just because it was fashionable now, she believed there was an unselfish spirit at work. For some she thought there was quiet heroism involved; she knew that a number of women doing relief work had already lost sons, and although "these may give no sign of their sufferings, that War has taken from them all that makes life worth while. Yet with steadfast courage they are going on doing all they can to mitigate the horror and woe."[44]

Gertrude found the fact that "the [Red Cross Society] officers are all women ... another manifestation of the awakened Mother-Spirit." But caring and compassion alone solved nothing: the wounds bound up would soon be torn open again. More was needed. "I am hoping and praying that soon the women of the whole world will rise and forbid all this slaughter." Gertrude believed that women who did not hate war did not possess "the soul of motherhood" which all true women had "from the time they play with their first dolls to the end of their lives." She had read that 200 German women had been killed in Berlin during an antiwar demonstration. "They are brave, are they not, to endure death in order to save their loved ones from the slaughter of war? Is it possible that these women – crushed down as we believe they are – are braver and nobler than are we of the British Empire?" she asked her Leicester readers. "Terrible as it may seem to think of them being killed in this way, it is a true picture of maternal love." One of her Winnipeg suffrage colleagues had written Gertrude a gloomy letter about the rise of the war spirit in women. "We women of the suffrage cause desire political power in order that we may help to lead the world out of this horror of barbarism," Gertrude commented, "and our hopes will be doomed to disappointment if women encourage and endure war."[45]

The suffrage petition campaign had culminated in September 1915 with ads in various newspapers (generally making use of the regular women's columns) to urge all women to sign. The Grain Growers, WCTU, and PEL circulated the forms through all their small local groups. Lillian Beynon Thomas wrote, "OUR MOTTO: MANITOBA FIRST." Did Manitoba women really want the vote, she asked, "Do Manitoba women want a legal claim to the clothes they wear – to the homes they have worked to make – to the children they have brought into the world?" Winona Flett Dixon wrote, "We believe in representative government, of the people, for the people, by the people – and WOMEN ARE PEOPLE ... Just government rests upon the consent of the governed ... Women should have an equal voice with men in the making of the laws they have to obey ... Taxation without representation is tyranny. Women are taxed, yet are not permitted to say how they wish this money spent." By this point all political parties had declared that they favoured suffrage; even the Conservatives had come out in favour just before the previous election – in a last-ditch (but ineffective) effort to win support, according to the cynical. But some politicians still implied that perhaps women did not really want to be enfranchised. Women must show they wanted it. Proof would consist of a designated number of signatures. So women all over the province circulated and signed petition forms, thirty names per form, and sent them to PEL headquarters in Winnipeg to be presented to the legislature. By mid-October "Lillian Laurie" reported that 40,000 women had signed the petition. The campaign had reached as far north as Norway House, and women of every ethnic community had signed. The magnitude of support and the achievements of the petition campaign were indeed cause for jubilation.[46]

The signatures were delivered to the government on 23 December 1915. In her Leicester column, Gertrude explained,

Most of the large Suffrage bodies in England on the outbreak of war dropped their active propaganda – militant or otherwise – and threw their best energies into the great task of alleviating the misery. This was noble and great and won the world's approval. Here in Manitoba, we continued our active struggle – which is about to be crowned with success. Our petition is in the hands of the Premier and the session is to open this week. Meanwhile, we, too, are quietly waiting, and busying ourselves with work to alleviate the sorrow and misery caused by the war. The Suffragists of Toronto and other eastern centres have formed a "Suffrage War Auxiliary" ... We of the west take different views. We desire political power that we may oppose more effectively the terrible onrush of militarism.

The bill moved through its stages of preparation. But at the last moment the Liberals apparently tried to pull a fast one. Lillian Beynon Thomas was given a peek at the draft bill, and she discovered to her horror that the bill did not provide for women to sit in the provincial legislature. Of course she asked the drafters to change it but they refused. She promptly phoned her PEL colleagues and sicced them on their MLAs, and she then called Francis Beynon, who was in Brandon for the Grain Growers convention. Francis Beynon threatened to mobilise the Grain Growers, if Norris did not change the bill. Norris changed the bill.[47]

The bill passed third reading 27 January 1916, with specially invited members of the PEL sitting in the chamber, and dozens of women sitting in the galleries as witnesses to the historic occasion. Then audience and members sang "For They are Jolly Good Fellows." With the lieutenant governor's assent the next day, Manitoba women were the first in the country to have the vote, two years to the day they had staged the male suffrage satire at the Walker Theatre. Gertrude rejoiced at the power this would give women to rid the world of war. The two went hand in hand. "The whole spirit of the women's movement is against the war," she proclaimed. Those who were militarist were contrary to the true spirit, she believed: "We are against war ... because we alone represent an unbroken international solidarity ... Our ideals are the highest known to the human race to-day; ideals of service, not domination – of love, not hatred – of mutual trust and understanding, not of armed suspicion. And it is because of our international character that we must oppose war. Ours is a women's movement knowing no frontiers, no boundaries. Wherever ... the voice of the world's womanhood is heard striving to express the divinity of the mother-spirit, the women's movement becomes a unifying force." The German women's antiwar uprisings "express for all time the soul of motherhood. And that soul is going to dominate the world – and cast out in God's own time the evil spirits that defile, destroy, and slay." In her report to the *Woman's Century*, Gertrude exulted, "Just a few weeks before the Political Equality League of Winnipeg was organized [in 1912], the Roaring River Woman Suffrage Association held its first gathering. The franchise looked a long way off then, when a handful of idealists honoured me by asking me to be their first President. It is now an accomplished fact!"[48]

The war drew closer to home for Gertrude in 1916: her brother Horace had become a leader in the Leicester antiwar movement, while her brother Fred had gone to England to enlist. Fred had discussed his views about the war with his fiancée Edith Watson and other members of his family. He had written to Edith in November

1914, "Awful thing, war. Hope something will be done after this to put a stop to it. It is out-of-date and belongs to the dark past when men knew no better." Nonetheless, by January 1915 he had more or less decided to sign up. Everyone was going, it sometimes seemed, although most of his own family were still antiwar. Fred himself had been on the antiwar side during the Boer War, and was not a kneejerk patriot, but was concerned about reports of German atrocities and believed this war was unavoidable and necessary. So did his older brother Wilfred, the Salvation Army officer then stationed in Korea. "If the innocent suffer and right is assailed by might, why, the right must fight too. That is Wilfred's idea of this war," he told Edith in June 1915. "He is strong for war against Germany." But Fred's younger brother, Horace, had his own wrestle with conscience and had come to an opposite conclusion. Horace was "for peace no matter what," Fred thought. "I guess Horace will be out of touch just now with everybody. Not much sympathy for pacifists in England just now I am afraid. Am sorry he holds views of that kind." That September Fred told Edith that he hoped Horace would keep his views to himself, because even level-headed men could get very upset at the "wicked atrocities the Huns have been and are yet guilty of." Fred recalled the hostility and mob violence directed against the "Pro-Boers" some fifteen years ago: "It is much worse now." Fred commented almost wistfully to Edith in November 1915, after he had made the decision to enlist, "I suppose you see many strange sights in Leicester during war time. It is a great experience for all who live in England now and something to tell their children about in the years to come. We see absolutely nothing here."[49]

Although Fred realised the war was a momentous experience for those who lived through it, he did not have glamorous illusions about the battlefield. He wrote early in 1916, about the prospect of going to the front lines, "So you do not think that I am suitable for fighting. Well, I am not, that's a fact. Nor are any or most of our fellows that are fighting now. It is a very unnatural thing to all but a very few and it will be grand when it is over." Nonetheless, Fred felt it was a question of duty: "I feel our family is neglecting its duty. My brother in Korea is the only one that is patriotic and even he is not willing for his eldest son to go." Horace would have agreed that fighting was unnatural, but he did not follow Fred's advice to keep his views to himself. He formed a local branch of the new antiwar group, the "No Conscription Fellowship." Horace found this a "brave" step to take, but Fred wrote in November 1915, "I think he is safe enough. I do not think compulsory service will ever be made law." Fred was a loyal brother but a poor prophet, as subsequent events would show.[50]

Fred and his mother left Swan River on the 17th of December, 1915, to go first to Boston, where they would visit cousins for the holidays, then on to England. It was not an easy trip in wartime, even with the Boston layover. The train journey was complicated and tiresome. Transatlantic shipping had been affected by the war, and virtually the only way for civilians to cross by then was via New York, 2300 miles and five days and nights from Swan River. There had been many farewell visits to friends. The Political Equality League had given Eliza Twilley (its honorary president since the founding meeting) a surprise farewell party, and presented her with a gold brooch shaped like a maple leaf as a remembrance. Eliza was a staunch pacifist who refused even indirect support for the war (such as the purchase of war savings certificates), but she apparently had accepted Fred's decision that he would enlist as soon as she was settled. He had wanted to escort his mother back to Leicester where she planned to live with Horace, and he could not obtain permission to enlist in Canada but delay reporting until he reached England. He had also worried for a time that the Canadian military might not accept him. A friend who seemed a prime specimen had tried to enlist at Dauphin, the nearest recruiting office. "We had a good send-off for him, the girls all weeping at the station and during the next day. He was a likely chap, much bigger than I, with good eyesight, good teeth etc. He was back in two days," Fred reported. "They have more applications than they want," he had speculated. "I guess that the English recruiting officers wouldn't be so particular."[51]

The remaining Twilleys celebrated Christmas as usual at the Liveseys' house, "sadly missing those dear to us, who are on their way to the Homeland." Gertrude's New Year letter to Leicester readers spoke of her hopes for the coming year, now that women would be voters, and reiterated the centrality of the antiwar spirit to the international women's movement. This spirit of the "soul of motherhood" would triumph, she said. Meanwhile, those who sorrowed and sent loved ones off to the war knew they were "sharing the universal burden." However painful it may have been for Gertrude to have a more personal involvement in the war, it strengthened her sense of being part of a community, especially a community of those who longed and worked for peace. Although the war drowned out the message of the angels of peace, Gertrude still could hear them that Christmas: "I am not alone, I know, in my thoughts and feelings," she wrote. "To you, dear friends, who read my little letters week by week, and understand and sympathise, I am increasingly grateful."[52]

The 1916 annual convention of the Political Equality League celebrated a turning point in Manitoba politics. As Francis Marion

Beynon commented, it was only four years since Lillian Beynon Thomas had invited a few friends to meet at her house to establish the Winnipeg PEL. "The first two years were hard sledding, while the mere machinery of the organization was being perfected." Having won the vote, the PEL disbanded and reconstituted itself as the Political Education League of Manitoba, to train women to make good use of their new power as voters. Now that the long struggle for suffrage was won, women could turn their minds to implementing long-sought reforms. Beynon listed "securing a minimum wage, improving the laws relating to women and children, compulsory education, prison reform and the friendly visiting of our new citizens." It seemed to Gertrude and her associates that women's influence was growing rapidly in the West. The Manitoba Grain Growers, staunch proponents of woman's full participation as citizens, had elected a woman to the executive. Grain Growers in other prairie provinces welcomed women's participation and often invited feminists to speak: Francis Marion Beynon addressed the Saskatchewan convention that February. Women won the vote in Alberta 1 March 1916 (the indomitable Nellie McClung had moved to Edmonton in the fall of 1914, which gave Emily Murphy's group a boost), and in Saskatchewan 14 March 1916. This cheering situation was paradoxical, because the impact of the war, and the hostility to those who spoke out against it, increased considerably in 1916. As Gertrude said, "Surely there was never a time when the maleness (if I may use the word) of the world-systems was never more apparent than this ... From Houses of Legislature, from pulpit, from platform, rostrum, and Press of every land, thunder forth to-day the gospel of dominance, of righteousness of force, the holiness of compulsion. Progress and retrogression go hand in hand." Despite the terrible times, it really did seem to her that the New Day was dawning, or at least a "hidden light" was there. The "new Child of Promise will be born – the Soul of Maternity. Strong, great and free, the divine Daughter of God. She is coming, not to serve but to wield the sceptre." Gertrude's own star continued to rise; she noted "From the editor of the 'Woman's Century' the other day, I received a letter saying, 'Can you not give us more? There is something magnetic in all you write.'"[53]

There were some happy moments in family life during 1916 that helped to offset the distress Gertrude felt over the war. One such occasion was the visit of her older brother Wilfred, his wife Eva, and their children, who arrived in late April for part of their six-month leave, and were disappointed to learn that Fred and Eliza had left for England. Gertrude had not seen them since they left England to go to Korea in 1909, although the family had written regularly, and the

Twilleys in England and Manitoba read of the couple's activities in the Salvation Army magazine *War Cry*. Gertrude was delighted to see them and found the children, especially the two smallest nieces, enchanting. There was a plague of mosquitoes (or perhaps no-see-ums) that summer and the children were badly bitten, but they nonetheless enjoyed the freedom of rural life, the chance to run wild and play with the farm animals. The second son, young Wilfred, did not have such a happy visit; he was not in sympathy with Gertrude's antiwar views and was marking time until he was old enough to join up. Wilfred and Eva gave talks in Swan River about their experiences as Salvation Army representatives in Japan and Korea, telling the Young People's Society about "Korean customs," and speaking on another occasion about missionary work. After some time in Swan River, the Twilleys went on a lecture circuit throughout the province, concluding with a series of appearances in Winnipeg. Mabel Sims (wife of the local Liberal MP) gave them a farewell reception, featuring fruit salad, ice cream, cakes, and tea, and a musical performance by Mrs Weir, whose husband was Gertrude's friend, the local editor. The highlight was Eva's rendition of "Nearer My God to Thee" in Korean. The two older boys did not accompany their family to England at the end of the visit. The oldest boy went on to the States, while young Wilfred worked in the local Commerce bank for a time, staying on in Swan River and keeping his distance from Gertrude. The Twilleys left in July for Montreal and thence to England for the rest of their furlough. Gertrude commented, "I am afraid ... that we have very little to teach 'heathen' nations at this time," and repeated a remark by a friend of hers, a "Christian lady" who had said " 'I do not know how a missionary can look a heathen in the face' " these days.[54]

Gertrude was pleased that her mother would be able to represent the Roaring River (and Manitoba) PEL at a June 1916 international suffrage conference in London, held by the British Dominions Woman Suffrage Union. For some years Gertrude had corresponded with the Union's secretary Harriet Newcomb, and had enjoyed hearing about BDWSU activities. This year was an especially good one for a Manitoba representative, since the provincial franchise had been gained, and suffragists saw the federal one practically within their grasp. Other Canadian groups were invited to participate or send papers: the National Equal Franchise Union (NEFU) appealed for members who might plan to be in London that July to represent them. The conference discussed such issues as women's loss of nationality through marriage, equal pay for equal work, legal inequality of women, crimes against women and children, special courts for women and children, and support of military dependants. Gertrude saw the organisation as a force for good, and wrote, "May it bind together the women of the great Empire, in this hour of rending and affliction, of stress and storm." Later that year she was sent a copy of the conference report by Dorothy Pethick (who had visited the Winnipeg PEL some years earlier). "Nothing could better demonstrate the world-wide vision of the great Woman's Movement,"she commented of the report. It came at a good time, as by the end of 1916 a number of discouraging events had occurred.[55]

The year had started with some optimism, at least on the suffrage front. Once Western women got the vote provincially they set about trying to exercise it federally. The provisions of the Dominion Election Act concerned with eligibility to vote in federal elections specified that the federal entitlement would be based on that of the provinces, with some exceptions (concerning Alberta, Saskatchewan, and the Yukon, the phrase "every male person" was used, and Indians were disqualified). In other words, under existing federal law, Manitoba women were eligible to vote federally, and if the government wished to prevent this, they had to change the legislation. Liberal MP William Pugsley in February 1916 moved that the federal act be amended to state explicitly that women who had the provincial vote could vote federally. After some embarrassment, the motion was scuttled by the Tories on the excuse that the federal franchise for women must be handled on a Dominion-wide basis, and careful thought was needed. Manitoba women protested to Borden and their Winnipeg MP, Robert Rogers (who had helped Borden scuttle the resolution). Rogers replied that "they did not understand," while Borden promised "the matter would receive consideration." Winona Flett Dixon, Winnipeg suffragist and pacifist whom Gertrude admired, wrote to NEFU's Edith Lang,

Personally I don't see how they can keep Manitoba women from voting at the forthcoming Dominion election. Of course, they may compile new lists, and permit only men to register, but look at the sentiment that will rouse up against them, it would be suicidal for the Manitoba members to attempt it, and I fancy Alberta women would give their representatives a strenuous fight. It would also give all the Liberal candidates such a powerful lever that it would react upon the Conservatives, and they would be mighty sorry they were so short-sighted. For myself, I love a good fight when there is some principle at stake, and wish they would do an unjust thin[g] like this so that we might show the entire Dominion that women are "persons" at last and will not submit to injustice. They need a lesson and now is a good time to give it to them.

She could not have foreseen that Borden and his associates would learn quite a different lesson from the situation she outlined, and would find a way to tame and coopt the Liberal opposition and eliminate their supporters, with no little help from a strategy urged by her "patriotic" sisters.[56]

The legal situation looked reasonably straightforward in 1916. Lillian Beynon Thomas wrote in August, "As I understand it, the only way we can be prevented from voting at a Dominion election is by an act passed by the Dominion parliament. I understand that the Hon. Arthur Meighen [minister of justice] has said that the women having the provincial franchise are automatically entitled to vote at a Dominion election, so long as the same voters lists are used." However, as Thomas pointed out the following week, the acid test would come when the new provincial voters lists were made up (the old ones being more than a year old, thus the federal government could update them for the federal election). "Every woman in Manitoba" who met the residency, age, and citizenship criteria and "who has time at all should go to the registration place and demand to be put on the lists." Manitoba tactics aside, she concluded, "It is a Dominion government matter, and with that government our fight for the franchise has just begun." In the summer of 1916 women from Manitoba joined with other enfranchised prairie women to organise a Dominion Suffrage Board, and sought representatives from all provinces, to try to get the federal franchise for all women. Louise Long of the Canadian Suffrage Association (CSA) reminded *Woman's Century* readers of Borden's words to a suffrage delegation on 23 December 1912. Asked by CSA president Margaret Gordon if women could be granted and could exercise the federal franchise before that of the provincial level, Borden replied in a manner apparently designed to deflect suffragist pressure away from Ottawa and redirect it to the provinces. He had said that the Dominion Election Act provided that the federal electors' lists were those of the provinces. Thus, he continued, if any provinces passed woman suffrage legislation, women eligible to vote provincially would automatically be eligible federally. It was really up to the provinces to give women the vote, he claimed, although he hinted that there might be ways the federal government could wriggle out of woman suffrage even with provincial enfranchisement. Specifically, he reminded the women of the delegation that Parliament could also repeal the old law in order to stop using the provincial lists, and compile federal lists.[57]

Four years later, Borden claimed that this last point was the significant component of his discussion with the suffrage delegation. The federal government would decide on Dominion-wide suffrage on a

Dominion-wide basis, as appropriate. Borden and Laurier had both admitted that women from Manitoba and British Columbia would be entitled to vote federally, having obtained the provincial franchise, and were it not for the "little joker" (as Francis Marion Beynon described it), the phrase "male voter" in the Saskatchewan and Alberta electoral qualifications, women from these two provinces too would be eligible. The Manitoba women's plan to get themselves on the new electoral lists had caused the intended update to be cancelled by Ottawa (who, Beynon said, had hoped that women would not notice the update).[58]

The government indeed seemed to be in a corner, without a legal or politically feasible way to prevent large numbers of women from voting in the next federal election, which Borden knew that the Liberals would not agree to postpone a second time and must be held in late 1917. The situation was complicated by the fact that by May 1917, Borden had promised the Imperial War Cabinet he would bring in conscription (although he had earlier pledged repeatedly to Canadians that he would stick to voluntary enlistment). In January 1916 Borden had announced that Canada's commitment should be increased to 500,000 men. By the end of the year it had been obvious that this would not be achieved voluntarily; in fact, enlistments had decreased throughout the year. Borden had gone on a cross-country recruiting tour in December 1916 without result. Meanwhile various groups had been urging him to introduce conscription. It would be difficult to bring in a conscription bill as a straight Tory issue. Accordingly Borden approached Liberal leader Laurier in late May and until early June 1917, attempted to persuade him to form a coalition government and bring in conscription. Laurier, a longtime anticonscriptionist, refused. Even if Borden had to contend only with the male electorate, Quebec and much of the West were traditionally Liberal strongholds, and sure to be strongly anticonscription. By early 1917, seven provinces had Liberal governments, and, for what it was worth, Laurier had promised that a Liberal government would bring in federal woman suffrage. In the worst case, from the Tory perspective, under present conditions the Tories would lose, conscription would lose, and the war effort would be gravely threatened. Giving the vote to women could only make things worse, especially since it was widely believed that "foreign" women (not of British origin) were more likely to exercise their right to vote than were their Canadian- or British-born sisters. Borden needed a way to ensure that any changes in the franchise would be to his party's advantage (which in this context meant Union government).

In a series of clever moves (thanks partly to strategic help from Meighen, and to strongly anti-Quebec prowar western Liberals like

John Dafoe, editor of the Winnipeg *Free Press*), Borden touted a Union government, and wooed enthusiastically prowar Eastern Liberals into its fold. The western Liberals were harder to persuade. Although the proconscriptionists were tempted, there was a strong anticonscription faction, and many who were prowar detested Borden. Liberals of both camps thought this might be their chance to form the government. Gertrude followed these events with great interest, and some hope. She wrote to her Leicester readers that although the western Liberal convention was supposed to dump Laurier, the opposite had happened. The four western premiers were pro-Laurier, as were a majority of delegates. Alberta delegates had gone so far as to bring a banner proclaiming "Laurier for the West" which so angered the Winnipeg Great War Veterans Association, a hooligan group of superpatriotic returned soldiers, that they attempted to invade the meeting and assault the offending delegates (a tactic they had routinely used with great success over the summer against anticonscription meetings). In this instance, they were thwarted by police guards. Although the convention supported the war, they emphatically defeated a proconscription motion. However, many Liberals had already effectively crossed over to the Union side by voting in favour of conscription during the debates on the conscription bill in July 1917. Borden wooed the holdouts by means of two brilliant bills passed in August and September 1917 that eliminated existing voters likely to support the Liberals and oppose conscription, and added new ones likely to vote Union and conscription. Since this eliminated Liberal supporters, the only way many western Liberals could hope to get back into office was as Unionist candidates. By the middle of October the deal was consummated.[59]

A key part of Borden's strategy was the selective enfranchisement of women who would be likely to support conscription and the Union government. Borden had announced his intention to bring in the federal franchise for women during the suffrage debate in the Commons in May 1917. He did this in two parts, in the bills passed in August and September 1917. The Military Voters Act gave the vote to British subjects who served in the Canadian forces (even those under twenty-one years of age): this included women nurses, ambulance drivers, and so on. The provision for the enfranchisement of women serving in the military attracted little attention during the debates, and affected relatively few women. However a useful feature of the bill was the section allowing the military vote to be distributed outside the electoral boundaries of the voters' home ridings; voters chose for or against the government rather than for a given candidate. But the *coup de grâce* was the thoroughly undemocratic Wartime Elections Act, which Meighen introduced and the government forced through in the face of bitter opposition. This act had three key clauses, the first two of which eliminated the right to vote to which certain troublesome groups of Canadian citizens were currently entitled: the disenfranchisement of (male) voters who were born in "enemy" countries (or in any other European country if their mother tongue was an "enemy" language), who had become naturalised Canadian citizens since 1902 (unless they had a son, grandson, or brother in the forces); disenfranchisement of all conscientious objectors (as a group, as well as on the basis of individual conscience, thus Mennonite and Doukhoubour men, for example, could not vote). Men who had enlisted (or had tried but were rejected as medically unfit) were exempted from these provisions. The third key clause gave the vote to women (who met age, residence and citizenship qualifications) who were the mothers, wives, widows, sisters, or daughters of living or dead members of the Canadian or British military (male or female) serving or who had served overseas during the war. Although this threefold reshuffling of the democratic rights of citizens was brilliant, neither Borden nor Meighen deserve sole credit for the third idea; a good part of the credit must go to the "patriotic" women of Canada who had orchestrated a campaign to persuade the government to award the suffrage to "British" women but not to the "foreign" women.[60]

By the fall of 1916 the country-wide campaign for the federal enfranchisement of women had gained momentum. It had also gained a reactionary tinge, in that a large proportion, which would eventually become the majority, of the leaders of national women's organisations had concluded that only those women who could be relied upon to vote prowar should be enfranchised. This position was directly contradictory to the traditional universalist tenets of the suffrage movement. That these were still central at the end of 1916 is evidenced by the fact that in December the National Equal Franchise Union reported it had sent a letter to provincial premiers asking them to support a federal bill to grant the vote to all women. The NEFU had also sent a resolution to that effect to Parliament, and it campaigned into the summer of 1917 for the acceptance of that universalist resolution. The government's options were seen as limited. Jessie MacIver wrote in December 1916 that the government had four choices: amend the law to (1) stop B.C. and Manitoba women from voting federally, (2) permit all provincially enfranchised women to vote, or (3) enfranchise all women, or it could leave the Dominion Election Act as it stood. "They are rather on the horns of a dilemma," she wrote complacently. The government would infuriate Alberta and Saskatchewan women if it refused to allow them to vote federally; it would infuriate eastern women if it permitted only their western sisters to vote; fewest would be infuriated if it gave all women the federal franchise.[61]

In January 1917 MP William Pugsley introduced a motion in the Commons that the government should either give the federal vote to all women who had it provincially or enfranchise all women. Women organised a "huge campaign of letter-writing … We are all sending personal letters to our Dominion members, asking their support of Mr Pugsley's bill for the granting of the Federal franchise to women," Gertrude reported. Nellie McClung wrote to *Woman's Century* that Alberta women could not afford the time and money to come to Ottawa to participate in a deputation for the support of the Pugsley motion. McClung believed it would succeed. "All the Liberals will vote for Mr Pugsley's bill, and so will all the Conservatives of those provinces whose women can vote Provincially, and so it should win at a walk." In the event it did not; the Tories stalled until Borden's return from England, and Pugsley's motion was displaced by a Tory member's blander motion that the government should deal with the federal franchise during the current session. That motion was debated on 16 May 1917; Borden stole the opposition's thunder by promising to enact federal legislation do just that.[62]

Yet at the same time, the selective faction had been gaining power, ironically with McClung's help, which she later recanted. One factor was their determination to support conscription; indeed, by November 1916 prowar women meeting in Winnipeg had sent a resolution to Borden urging him to bring in conscription. Although, as Gertrude commented, none of these were acting officially as such, suffragists were among the group. Most of the prowar women had rejected the notion that women would by definition vote antiwar; their own prowar views provided strong evidence that maternalism did not equal pacifism. However they seem to have been less certain about the long-denied claim that women would just repeat the votes of their menfolk. On the one hand, Jessie MacIver wrote about the U.S. election that women's votes from the western woman suffrage states had pushed Wilson to victory, and that where an analysis of female voting choices was possible, it showed that women voted for their own reasons, not duplicating their men's choices. Long the suffragists' claim, this was worth pondering. If this were the case, what would be the outcome of giving all women the vote? How patriotic were women in general and in particular? On the other hand what if they did follow their husbands' votes? How patriotic were male voters, especially those who had not enlisted?[63]

Nellie McClung's brief recruitment into the anti-universalist camp illustrates the rationale for the view that women should not be given the vote unless they could be trusted to use it for patriotic purposes. By now McClung had reluctantly moved to support the war, apparently in part because she believed media stories about atrocities and claims that the Germans had attacked the Lusitania without warning or provocation, but McClung was never a superpatriotic jingoist. By chance, she and Borden happened to be in Winnipeg at the same time, and McClung took the opportunity to do some lobbying. According to Cleverdon's account, she told Borden it was time he gave women the federal franchise without further stalling, as the women were too busy for an extensive campaign. And so they were; in the enfranchised provinces, women were preparing recommendations for legislative reform in a variety of areas, and many women worked long hours in relief organisations or wartime jobs. However, Cleverdon does not discuss the fact that McClung also told Borden that he should give the federal vote to British- and Canadian-born women only, as a wartime expedient. When challenged by Francis Marion Beynon, McClung explained her reasoning thus: the absence of the best type of men (who had enlisted) lowered the moral tone of the voters; "There are districts where almost all of the English speaking men have enlisted, leaving the Austrians and Germans in full numbers, and the indifferent ones of other nationalities." These men would vote against the war. How could this be countered? By giving only certain women the vote. McClung argued that "the German and Austrian women in these districts are entitled to the full franchise because they are responsible human beings, but their claim on the franchise is no greater (and no less) than it was before the war, but the right of the English speaking women whose men-folk have gone to fight, has become indisputable and imperative." She had told Borden, she said, that "as a war measure, and to offset this abnormal condition caused by the war" he must enfranchise the "Canadian and English" but not the foreign women. (She had added, she said, that since women in Manitoba and B.C. were already federally enfranchised, her suggestion applied only to the other provinces. How Borden was to do this without disenfranchising "foreign" women in Manitoba and B.C. was not clear from McClung's account.) I believe this conversation was of great significance in signalling to Borden that selective enfranchisement was a strategy whose price would not be prohibitive. To use Jessie MacIver's measuring stick, it would infuriate the fewest voters ("voters" being the key word here). Although McClung said she told Borden she was speaking as an individual, she was one of the most influential progressive women in the country, and if such as she would urge such a measure, Borden had a right to assume that it would be palatable to western suffragists who were not in the superpatriot camp.[64]

It was not. Francis Marion Beynon's Christmastime column revealed the depth of the dismay of many of McClung's comrades. Beynon argued that McClung should not have spoken up without consulting her colleagues, the majority of whom, Beynon thought, would oppose such a measure, since they had "fought and won the suffrage on the ground that democracy is right [and] still believe in democracy." If the English-speaking suffrage leaders wished democracy for themselves, they had to extend it to their fellows. "Having pointed out from the public platform time and time again the tyranny of unrepresentative government and the injustice of debarring any portion of the people from the franchise because of an accident of birth" it was unacceptable to support that same injustice in this case. "The foreign-born women ... will suffer just as great an injustice as we have done in the past, if their point of view does not find expression in the government of the country." McClung recanted, and in an open letter in Beynon's column, publicly withdrew her support from the selective franchise proposal on the ground that unity was crucial and her commitment to woman suffrage was paramount, and admitted that she might have been mistaken.[65]

Although the exchange was carried out in cordial tones with mutual expressions of regard, damage was done. Certainly various prairie suffragists were vocal in their condemnation of McClung's action. Gertrude admired McClung tremendously and must have been surprised and shocked at the change in her position. As a member of the PEL executive, she could not avoid getting caught up in the controversy. Gertrude reported in her *Woman's Century* column for February 1917 that the Manitoba PEL provincial executive had reaffirmed "the rights of the foreign woman in regard to voting." Shortly before, she had written in her Leicester column that Manitoba women were "registered in the provincial lists, and shall demand, en masse, that we be allowed to vote in case of an election." Her "we" included all Manitoba women voters. In her column in the monthly *Canadian Thresherman and Farmer,* Lillian Beynon Thomas took pains to emphasise McClung's tremendous contribution to the suffrage movement, and said that McClung had "thought only that it would be ... better to have some women voting than none." She reported that McClung had "withdrawn her request." Amidst her praise for McClung's previous insistence on "the widest possible interpretation of the word democracy" and unfailing work on behalf of all women, there was a clear warning that had McClung not backed down, the universalist suffragists would have fought her publicly, despite the fact that "it would have been desperately hard" to do so. Although McClung's retraction helped to repair some of the splits among the suffragists, her retraction probably made little impression on Borden.[66]

It was not only westerners who opposed such a suggestion. In August 1917, a group of patriotic women at a "Win-the-War" conference in Toronto were convened informally by the president of the National Equal Franchise Union to discuss the problem of assuring that only loyal women would vote. They sent out telegrams to various "outstanding women" asking them what they thought women's views were, and on the basis of the replies, the group decided that universal female enfranchisement would endanger the proconscription side. The group then sent Borden their conclusion: "Though the claim to the [general women's] franchise still stands," they told him, "it was waived in view of present exigencies." They suggested giving the vote to women kin of men fighting, or to provincially enfranchised women, stating that it was worth the continued disenfranchisement of women in non-enfranchised provinces to prevent Quebec women from voting. A group of women forming part of a Win-the-War delegation to Ottawa, including the presidents of the NCWC, NEFU, Jessie MacIver of *Woman's Century*, and "representatives" of the WCTU and other groups, were kept on after the delegation for tea and a chat, at which Borden discussed with them the problems entailed by various schemes to resolve the franchise issue. They settled on the scheme embodied in the government's two bills. Justifying this stand, *Woman's Century* said, "Once a German, always a German, and once imbued with the German principles of morality, such instances [as naturalised Canadians allegedly fighting for the enemy] prove that no Canadian ideals will rule, even though a Canadian freedom should be granted." Canadian women were "more than willing" to postpone the universal franchise "to do their part in making German ideals and German domination impossible in Canadian citizenship." But the Montreal Local Council of Women denounced the action, as did other locals, including a number from the west, and the NCWC had to back down, claiming that they, as an organisation, had not supported a limit on women's federal enfranchisement. The suffrage movement had long claimed the vote on the grounds of democracy; this argument did not disappear during the war, but rather was advanced only until it became inconvenient. In October 1916, Edith Lang had written that women did not have to claim their right to vote on grounds of their wartime service, that the "fundamental reason for the Franchise [was still] justice, and the logical applications to women of those democratic principles which, applied to men, have been the backbone of the Anglo Saxon race and its special genius." But as Francis Marion Beynon and others pointed out, expediency came to outweigh British principles.[67]

When the Wartime Election Act was passed, pacifist Margaret Gordon of the Canadian Suffrage Association (CSA) said, "It would have been more direct and at the same time more honest, if the bill simply stated that all who did not pledge themselves to vote Conservative would be disenfranchised." Gertrude was similarly dismayed. In a Leicester column, she attempted to explain the complexities of the Wartime Elections Act. "The vote is to be taken from 'alien enemies' (the conscriptionist term for the European settlers of enemy countries who were urged to come here under pledges of all rights enjoyed by native-born Canadians), 'conscientious objectors' (meaning Mennonites and Doukhobors whose religion forbids them to fight)." The Winnipeg papers had published names of prominent pro-conscription women who would not be eligible to vote under the terms of the law (because they did not have the requisite kin serving in the war), who were reputedly upset about their exclusion. Gertrude believed that nearly all of these were rich women who wanted to send "other women's sons, other women's husbands, other women's brothers and fathers … out to death." The Roaring River PEL protested to Borden "against the injustice of the War-time Election Act, and demand[ed] equality for all." This, despite the fact, Gertrude observed, that every member of the group was eligible to vote under the legislation. "We do not desire a vote that is not a vote – given to us on the assumption that we shall support conscription because our dear ones are soldiers," she wrote. " 'No indeed,' said one lady, 'we do not want to force others out; we want our own boys back.' "[68]

5 "My Soul Is Going Out from the 'Women's Movement' ": The Conscription Issue in Britain and Canada (1915–17)

Shortly after the war began, pacifists in England had begun to anticipate the possibility of conscription. Although there had never been conscription, various military-minded leaders had been suggesting since 1901 that it would be desirable. It sounded improbable to those who did not realise the extent to which military enthusiasm had permeated British society, and who thought that Britons would not accept compulsion. After August 1914, when war enthusiasm was high, the possibility seemed a good deal less remote. When Lilla Brockway's husband Fenner, a journalist active in the antiwar movement, pondered what steps to take if conscription should occur, she suggested he publish a letter to like-minded readers in the *Labour Leader*, the official paper of the Independent Labour Party, of which he had become editor in 1912. That letter was the beginning of the No-Conscription Fellowship (NCF), a remarkable organisation that helped conscientious objectors (COs) and their families deal with the consequences of refusing to be a part of the war. The letter appeared on 12 and again on 19 November 1914; Lilla handled the answers, and she soon found herself with virtually a full-time job responding to hundreds of replies. By February 1915 there were 350 members. Horace Twilley joined soon after that, and wrote to Gertrude and his mother about the new organisation. Horace helped organise the Leicester branch, of which he became the secretary.[1]

Early in 1915 the NCF had grown too large to operate out of the Brockways' house, and they opened a London office. The first NCF national conference was held in November 1915. Applications flooded in; staff had to be hired. The authorities had the organisation under surveillance by September 1915; blanket suppression was considered and then rejected in favour of picking off individual COs or supporters. Under wartime regulations, certain pacifist publicity was forbidden. Various people were arrested, fined or imprisoned under these regulations; for example, in March 1916 Nellie Best, of Sylvia Pankhurst's Federation was sent to prison for six months for "making statements prejudicial to recruiting," and in the summer of 1916, two young Quaker women were imprisoned for distributing antiwar leaflets. Fenner Brockway himself was arrested under those regulations and was in prison for a time in July 1916, but there was an excellent backup system of secret "shadow" appointees for each job in the NCF, so when the official person went to prison, the "shadow" could step in much like an understudy, and take over. Although many individuals kept the work going, the NCF's mainstay by the end of 1915 was the brilliant Catherine Marshall, a Quaker, socialist, and suffragist. Marshall was NCF leader Clifford Allen's "shadow." In 1916 she persuaded Bertrand Russell to act as co-chair; he made an excellent contribution until jailed late in the war (albeit she was the one who really had overall responsibility and did most of the day-to-day work).

The Quaker presence was strong in the NCF, and their practices pervasive, although the organisation was ecumenical. The NCF membership represented a range of beliefs, from traditional Christians to Christian Socialists to secular socialists to those of no particular affiliation or opinion save that it was wrong to kill one's "enemy." Most were socialists of one sort of another. The pacifism of some NCFers was allied to broad visions of social transformation; for others it was a single issue, and they were otherwise willing to take the world as it was, or with a bit of reform. However it is worth noting that the implications of pacifism could far reaching vis-à-vis such things as gender roles. For example, in the spring of 1915 a group of Quaker women meeting in Manchester sent the following message to Quaker men at the conference: "We ask you not to use force to defend us, where you would not use it for any other reason, but to trust God with us and for us. We did not feel we could lightly ask this of you until we had faced it for ourselves … We realize that trust in God is no passive looking-on, but an intensely active thing. It often seems to fall to a woman's lot to have to trust while she sees others suffer. It may be that our men have to share in this. And we realize that to ask you to be willing to do this is a very great thing to ask." This statement was later read at a national yearly meeting (annual general meeting) of the Quakers, and seems to have expressed a view widely held. This view, not restricted to Quakers, asked men to become more like women, in effect, as an expression of their peace witness. It is difficult not to wonder if CO rejection of masculinity (in this sense of characteristics and obligations) was a factor in the intensity of the outrage and scorn which often greeted them.[2]

Horace himself was a Congregationalist from childhood and much involved in the Wycliffe Congregational Church, a fashionable, intellectually up-to-date, culturally active and socially radical centre since its establishment in the 1870s. Minister Seaward Beddow was a pacifist who strongly supported the COs. Although for some years Horace had identified himself as a keen socialist, like Gertrude, he saw socialism as a necessary extension of his Christianity. He had written in one such discussion, "I am a Christian, an ardent, active Christian worker. I assert that Christianity implies Socialism, that the Bible and the ministry of Jesus, preached from beginning to end a deadly warfare against vested interests and monopoly." Although the records of the Leicester Quaker Meeting do not record his presence at services, he worked closely with them in the NCF, and it is evident that he found their spiritual and practical support helpful. It is worth remembering at this point that there was also strong labour and socialist support for COs, and that there was a good deal of overlap of membership and activities between ostensibly religious and ostensibly secular organisations.[3]

When the government announced the first conscription act, Leicester Friends were already involved in a variety of activities intended to help young men likely to be affected by the law. In April 1915 the Peace Committee had petitioned the prime minister to urge him to announce terms of settlement for the war. In January 1916 the local Friends helped to organise a meeting at the meeting house to give information and help to military-age men. Quaker William Appleton chaired this meeting, which had been planned with representatives from the Fellowship of Reconciliation (FOR) and the NCF. Since Horace was NCF secretary he was no doubt involved in planning these and other such meetings. Marian Ellis, by that time on the executive of the British branch of the ICWPP, spoke at the first FOR-NCF meeting on "The International Movement for Peace"; she had been one of the main peace activists in the Leicester Meeting during the Boer War. Shortly thereafter a Meeting committee explored other possibilities for helping COs. Granting them some form of associate membership was rejected, as any form of membership presupposed some previous connection, but any CO who needed support and advice was welcome, as were attenders at worship services.[4]

Support for COs and their families was not restricted to those with Quaker links. Quaker committees tried to think of specific ways that

Friends could help. Friends might consider talking to the members of the local military service tribunals to explain the CO position, for example. Friends could also contact the FOR and the NCF to volunteer. Individual Quakers attended the tribunals as observers, and some kept records of COs for the NCF. In March 1916 the Leicester Meeting wrote to other Quaker meetings about the unfairness of a tribunal decision against a local member, presumably as a warning. By May 1916 Leicester Friends were helping to provide some financial support to COs and their families. During 1916 the Quakers throughout England discussed and did their best to provide effective support for pacifists. Sometimes this meant delegations or letters to the authorities to try to get fair, or at least less brutal, treatment. Sometimes this meant breaking the law, paying fines (for themselves or for others), or serving prison sentences for illegal antiwar activities or as COs. Throughout the war, the Meeting as a whole and a number of individual members, especially, were involved in CO support.[5]

The arrests of COs started in April 1916, after the first conscription act for single men aged eighteen to forty-one went into effect in March. The authorities closed in on Horace in May 1916. This was not unexpected: Fred wrote to Edith on the nineteenth, "I wonder whether they have been after Horace yet? I quite expect that they will do so this week sometime. It is very trying and I wish for all concerned that this was over." The police did, and although they let him out for a few days on £20 bail, Horace was locked up by the military 1 June 1916, for refusing to join the military. The British government broadened the conscription act to include married men at the end of May 1916. Horace was liable for conscription under the first bill; that shadow had hung over the family near the end of January as Fred, Eliza, and Horace found a house for Horace and Eliza to live in while Fred went off to the army. The legislation automatically made every eligible man a member of the reserve, to be called up as needed. Since February, men had been receiving summonses to report; after two missed calls they legally became deserters and subject to arrest.[6]

Fred knew that Horace would be in trouble. He wrote to Edith on 1 June 1916, "Am very worried about Horace this morning as this is the day that he goes up and likely goes to prison or military detention. It is a great source of worry to mother. I don't know just how we shall do if he is taken." There would be difficulties with money; Fred inquired about a dependant's allowance from his military service. "I have spoken to the paymaster about that allowance matter and he says if Horace is placed so as not to be able to look after her, he will try and get it fixed up. Even if Horace gets off which is improbable, the notice his case is receiving will injure his business and make it bad for both him and his partner." Horace and two partners operated Vestry Street Mills, which produced Pixie Brand wool. Horace was in sales, and before the war had regularly travelled to Europe to get orders. In the event he was able to arrange that his share of money from the business be paid to his mother, but Fred thought it prudent to press on with his own arrangements, to assure some stable income for Eliza. A few days later, Fred wrote, "I have not heard anything more about Horace and expect that he will be having rather a rough time by now. I am very anxious to hear about him." By 9 June 1916, 1,001 COs had been arrested and handed over to the military. Anyone who wanted to claim exemption on grounds of conscience had to appear before a tribunal; many tribunal members were hostile to COs, did not accept the validity of or did not understand how to apply the somewhat narrow grounds of the legislation. There were provisions for noncombatant or alternative service, but these were still under the military and did not answer objections to military service. A CO who had not been exempted by a tribunal would be turned over to the local military, who would try to make him put on a uniform and submit to military discipline. If he refused, he was locked up for court martial.[7]

Horace was taken initially to Glen Parva barracks, about twelve kilometres from Leicester, and after several days of refusing to obey and being told by the Sergeant that they would "break [his] b[loody] spirit," he was sentenced to twenty-eight days "field punishment": two hours a day in irons " 'to tame me' as they put it," and repeated dragging to, and about, the parade ground where he refused to obey any orders. The dragging was literal and repeated. Horace refused to put on a uniform. Eventually the men "managed to get Horace dressed in khaki but he will not button up his coat," Fred heard. One of the corporals told Horace he wanted to be part of the "shooting party" when Horace was shot. Fred, by then settled at Shorncliffe with his unit, was quite worried about Horace. His mother had been to see Horace but the visit was not allowed. Fred wrote to Edith, "It appears that four of the fellows were knocking him about quite a bit and some other fellow objectors raised a protest so they fetched the doctor and he said that Horace was all right and could stand some more and the fellows that protested got the same dose. I know they do these things because down here we had a [CO] who had gone a bit out of his mind and he persisted in singing, so they pinned him down to the bed for two hours. It is an awful thing that men should be knocked about in that way and it makes me feel like throwing off the khaki myself."[8]

Since there seemed to be no effective way to stop ill treatment by appeals at Glen Parva, Fred decided to take steps himself. An NCF handbook urged friends and relatives of COs to "persistently demand … information," and if necessary go to the War Office; although it is not clear if Fred had NCF advice, that is exactly what he decided to do. "I have written to the War Office," he told Edith, "and to Mr [Ramsay] McDonald [*sic*] but I don't know if it will do any good. If I don't hear I shall go up to the 'War Office' and see if I can't do something." Fred did not agree with Horace's pacifist views, but he loved and respected his brother. Fred also was disgusted by the smug self-righteousness of the bullying. "I know that Horace is quite sincere and is no shirker or coward and he should be let alone. I think objectors are punished quite enough by public opinion and I am sure that it would be harder for me to have to face the ridicule of other than to face bullets." Horace would never give in, Fred knew. "If his health only holds up he will bear them out but I am afraid it won't." He wrote again, "Am so sorry that Horace is still where he is and hope that something will be done soon for mothers [*sic*] sake particularly. I have been before the colonel over it and the War Office have taken the matter up from him but expect that that is as far as it will go. I would gladly go to France tomorrow if Horace was free to look after mother. However we shall have to put up with it."[9]

Fred was not the only one who was concerned at Horace's mistreatment; family friends and fellow members of the Congregational Church, and their pacifist minister, had also apparently attempted to intervene, and a later comment of Gertrude's suggests that there may have been some mitigation. At the end of Horace's twenty-eight day sentence at Glen Parva barracks, he was sent to the jail cells at Richmond Castle in the north of England to await an official court martial. Fred's appeals came to naught, it seems; his first letter to the war office was sent back to his colonel, who chewed Fred out for not going through proper channels. The second one, sent via the colonel, did no good. Ramsay MacDonald referred Fred to someone else. MacDonald himself had come under attack from the ILP for a pro-recruiting letter, although he later denied that interpretation. Meanwhile, there was no fresh news about Horace. "I quite expected that he would soon be played out as he is not strong," Fred wrote to Edith. But Horace was stronger than he seemed. Nonetheless, his captivity and mistreatment continued to preoccupy Fred. Fred wrote about Horace's transfer to Richmond Castle early in July, "He is having a rough time … 'Tis a pity they have not something better to do."[10]

The NCF tried to keep track of COs (this work was carried out by the Conscientious Objector Information Bureau, or COIB, run by Catherine Marshall), whenever possible tried to arrange to have observers at their tribunals, and when the COs were convicted, have them seen by prison Visitors. Most of the Visitors were Quakers from the towns where COs were held in prison or military detention barracks, but some were from other denominations. Visitors had to be chosen by their meetings or congregations, then formally approved by the official in charge of the prison to which the Visitor would be assigned. By the end of 1916, about forty prisons had Visitors. Access to COs was controlled largely by the governor or commanding officer of the institution in question, who could make it easy or difficult for both parties. Quaker Mabel Horner Thompson's reports on her exchanges with the captain in charge of Richmond Castle in June and July 1916 illustrate some of the patterns. In June he quizzed her about her feelings about the Belgian women and children, whom the COs were, in his eyes, supposed to avenge. She replied to him, "I thought as always, when the men begin to fight the women begin to suffer, and for myself and the women of England I could not put my trust in Armed Force, but only in the protection of God." Previously reasonably welcoming, he was suspicious and hostile when she came on July 24, and wanted to know how she knew about prisoners who were not Quakers, and why she wanted to visit them. She explained that these men shared Quaker views on war, and the Quakers, in turn, "had a religious concern to visit them." The captain, she wrote, "said they were not worth my time and trouble ... I had to endure much conversation, chiefly about the absurdity of these boys' claim to have a religious conscience. Captain G said he wished I could go home and smash up the N.C.F which was merely a Labour organisation agitation." He cautioned her not to give the prisoners "seditious" literature. "I told him one of the books contained extremely seditious sayings from his point of view and he said he supposed that was the New Testament," she recounted. He told her he wouldn't even bother to shoot the COs, he would just put them in sacks and dump them in the river. Once she got past him and managed to see some of the prisoners, she found it was worth the trouble. One of them told her the "Nonconformist ministers have been nothing but recruiting sergeants," and he was glad to get some support.[11]

Mabel Thompson did manage to visit Horace on July 12, and her report sheds some light on how Horace was coping with imprisonment. She wrote, "I had an interesting conversation with Mr Twilling [sic], Secretary of the Leicester NCF who asked me to pass on the idea of the value of concentrated thought being directed towards our friends in prison at a certain time. He had felt a strange power at such times. For instance he knew that at eleven o'clock that morning Friends in Leicester were all thinking of and praying for him and the sense of power was unspeakable. 'In ordinary times' said Mr Twilling, 'we only think of our friends occasionally, we are too busy. But at a time like this much thought is coming our way constantly and it reaches us in our imprisonment.' " Glimpses of Horace's state during his imprisonment suggest that despite hardship and mistreatment his spirits remained high. Indeed, he seems to have found considerable spiritual strength. Horace was deeply religious, and the CO support networks were, at best, a closely knit spiritual as well as practical community.[12]

After his treatment at Glen Parva barracks, Richmond Castle was a reprieve. Horace wrote to Fred, "The worst is over now, I believe. I have had a fairly easy time here." He was grateful to Fred "for trying to get me out of here." Horace counselled patience, and a wait and see outlook: "I am afraid I must await developments. In any case do not worry. Everything may turn out all right in due course." At the time he wrote, he was "out of the cells now [and] quartered in a house with seven other COs" also awaiting court martial.[13] On July 15 Horace was sentenced to 112 days in prison, and after some days at the county jail in nearby Durham, he was briefly at Wormwood Scrubs (which would become notorious for harsh conditions and bad treatment of COs) for his formal tribunal hearing. The tribunal found that Horace was a genuine CO. Back at Durham, he was offered alternative service, which he refused, despite threats that he would be "treated with utmost rigour of military law" if he did not reconsider. His mother was allowed a twenty-minute visit in mid-September while Horace was supposed to be "reconsidering"; shortly thereafter he was moved to a military unit near Brampton. Horace had a break from prison in mid-October when he was allowed out for a day after completing a sentence. He spent the day in nearby Rotherham with his older brother Wilfred, who had arrived from Swan River, and their mother; for part of the day they visited their Flude cousins, the Bailey family. The next day it was back to business as usual: Horace refused to parade, was remanded for another court martial, and taken to Pontefract barracks. Duly sentenced at the end of October to one year with hard labour (commuted to six months without hard labour), he was taken under guard to London, thence to Wormwood Scrubs to spend the winter.[14]

Although Horace's comments are sparse, it is possible to get an idea of the experience from others there at the same time. Wormwood Scrubs has been called the "spiritual headquarters" of the NCF, because it had the largest number of COs. The Scrubs was a tough place (but not the worst) early in 1917; the cells were icy, the cots lumpy, the blankets thin and few. The food was scanty and of poor quality. Most COs were sentenced to hard labour in what was called the "third division": the harshest conditions. Initially such a prisoner had a month of solitary confinement sewing mailbags in his cell; the first two weeks he ate bread, porridge, and water only and slept on a bare plank. For the second month he could work with others (but not speak; prisoners were forced to keep silent most of the time), eat more diverse foods, and sleep on a regular prison cot. Usually a prisoner could keep some religious books in his cell, but no paper and pen. If he were good he could write one letter and have one twenty-minute visit after the second month. Although some prisoners managed to smuggle in pencil leads, and eventually several underground pencilled prison newsletters were developed, most prisoners were able to write only the restricted letters. A prisoner could gradually earn better conditions, more writing or visitor privileges, or time off his sentence. But because most COs served a series of 112-day or shorter sentences (longer ones were often shortened to avoid restrictions on treatment), they rarely got beyond the severely restricted conditions. They got forty-five minutes daily exercise. Corder Catchpool, a young Quaker CO whose term overlapped Horace's, wrote that although he entered in excellent form, within two weeks, "I could no more run above a couple of rounds than I could fly" in the small exercise yard. His biographer wrote that although Catchpool experienced the ubiquitous "listlessness, lack of energy and sleeplessness," it was the "loneliness and silence" that were the most difficult to endure.[15]

Two years of CO imprisonment under hard labour conditions was considered the most anyone could endure without permanent physical, psychological, or spiritual injury. It was also the maximum permitted by law. In fact the authorities used the Cat and Mouse Act (the 1913 Prisoners Temporarily Discharged for Ill Health Act of suffragette infamy) to circumvent restrictions on total time served, by allowing a day or so of liberty between the end of one sentence and picking up the CO to begin the process of court martial and another sentence. Some 816 COs served more than two years; Horace was one of these. Corder Catchpool tried to survive by using the long periods in his cell to read, to meditate, and pray. Some of these periods he recorded as "amongst the happiest, in a quite peaceful sense of the word, of my whole life." However even a devout Quaker used to long stretches of silent devotional exercise found it increasingly difficult to sustain these undertakings, as the harshness of CO prison life ate away at body, mind, and spirit. Indeed, few prisoners could stay in reasonable physical health, and medical care was infrequent and usually of poor quality, when it could be obtained. Some ten prisoners died in prison, about fifty-nine others died of prison-induced conditions after release, thirty-nine went insane, and others suffered chronic ailments for many years. NCF Chairman Clifford Allen, for example, nearly died, and was found to have developed TB.[16]

Under these circumstances, contacts with sympathetic Visitors (as opposed to hostile chaplains) and other prisoners were precious. In the early days at the Scrubs, sneaked glimpses or messages became vehicles for a "real exuberant, unquenchable joy, and the sense of fellowship held," despite everything. Horace noted on November 16, "Saw our great leader, Clifford Allen." Allen was brilliant, charismatic, and charming; even those who disagreed with him usually liked him enormously. A well-known pacifist, socialist, and labour writer and speaker who worked for the Labour Party newspaper, Allen had become a symbol of CO martyrdom; frail and in very poor health, he went to the Scrubs in August 1916. His presence boosted CO morale; word of his arrival was scribbled in smuggled pencil on the toilet wall. Around this time, the NCF also set up pickets outside the prison; one of their functions was to observe any COs coming or leaving to help the COIB keep track of them. The presence of the pickets also helped to lift the morale of the prisoners. Horace was allowed a visit from his mother and Wilfred on December 21; on Christmas Day 1916 he recorded: "A happy day; friends sang carols and songs outside prison walls."[17]

Gertrude had found the prospect of conscription one of the most horrific manifestations of militarism's growing violation of traditional British ideals. She had not believed it would come to pass in Canada; in late 1915 such suggestions had been "strongly repudiated" in the press, and Swan River editor Andrew Weir strongly opposed it and had claimed Canadians would never stand for it, they were too democratic. If conscription should occur, Gertrude had pointed out, then men would become "the property of the State ... This is the time the militarists are all busy. While the wonderful flame of patriotism is burning so brightly, while the heroism of our people is making our hearts throb and our eyes shine through our tears, the great men who control things are working to destroy us ... The Kaiser looks on women only as possible mothers of soldiers – and not only the Kaiser but all men with whom military domination is a passion. We must fight to the death against this insidious horror." In defending Belgium, the allies were stooping to the same methods as the attackers and becoming like them. "The evil of war will never be destroyed by war."[18]

Similar views had been expressed by feminists elsewhere who remained antiwar. In the neutral United States, where women quickly moved to organise the Women's Peace Party, the president of the

National American Woman's Suffrage Association, Anna Howard Shaw, had argued that women had a direct stake in the decisions leading to and consequences of war: " 'And when the question comes – who is the most deeply interested in war,' she asked, 'shall the very sex which furnished more than mere implements of war, shall that sex sit dumb in the face of outrage against them and that which deeply concerns them?' " Women had to be given a voice in these decisions because of their contributions as mothers. " 'And looking into the face of that one dead man we see two dead, the man and the life of the woman who gave him birth; the life she wrought into his life! And looking into his dead face someone asks a woman, what does a woman know about war? What, what, friends in the face of a crime like that, what does man know about war!' " Antiwar women did not accept the claim that men were property of the state to be disposed of as needed, without reference to those who produced those men.[19]

Gertrude had seen no precedent for conscription in Canada. Those who would support conscription "come from the class who have from time immemorial crushed down the poor." It was these people who owned the land that soldiers died to protect, and who were "investors in armaments from which huge profits are derived," and they supported conscription out of greed and blood lust. Those who objected to peace meetings being held in churches on the grounds that these were political, were hypocrites; churches were used for recruiting and for militarist sermons, equally political and certainly more reprehensible. She wrote an infuriated response to a suggestion from a titled woman that poor people could make delicious soup out of scraps. "Well, this soup may be very delicious, but I am not going to try it, our poor pigs might starve," retorted Gertrude. In a more serious vein, she demanded how much longer working people would put up with this sort of advice from "women who spend more on gloves than [the amount working class women] have to keep house on for all their growing families." Rich women thought that any scraps were good enough for poor people to eat but it was the workers who produced the food, and "the best that can be grown or produced is none too good for them – the producers and growers." Rich people were "also the class that uphold the war – support the churches that uphold the war – and worship the State and wave the flag." The war was destroying food, "the harvest fields, the homes, the mineral wealth, the clothing" and the people who produced all these riches were being told to feed themselves on "the husks that the swine did eat." Gertrude urged people to raise, not lower, their expectations, and to "demand good pure food, flowers, beauty, leisure, sanitary tasteful homes, yes, even now, while the war is raging." The war was revealing how little regard the "parasite class" had for the workers, and how easily the "oppressors" ordered workers to carry burdens and make sacrifices when they themselves had no intention of doing so.[20]

As the issue became more widely discussed in England, she noted that she feared a new age of militarism was developing. "The new religion, I suppose will be 'State Worship,'" she commented. "Let us beware all new 'freedoms' that are slaveries in disguise – all fake teaching and evil sophistry." Although her writings appeal to true women and true Christians to rise up and stop the war, and it is these groups she expected to remake the world at war's end, Gertrude at the same time saw economic self-interest of the ruling elites, and of the privileged classes who benefitted from their policies, as the driving force behind the war. Since these groups would not willingly forego their gains, she did not expect that many "slaveries in disguise" would evaporate after the war. "I believe that after this war the struggle between right and wrong will be fiercer than ever before in the history of the nations ... we have to fight all causes which tend to bring these battlefields into being ... It is certain that beneath all cruelty, all war, all oppression are economic causes. These we may all help to adjust, and in the meantime everyone who suffers, innocent or guilty (for we are not to judge) claims our love and tenderness and help."[21]

There were strong feelings on either side of the issue, in Swan River no less than elsewhere. By the spring of 1916, conscription no longer seemed unthinkable in Canada. Obviously those who were antiwar were also against conscription. In April 1916 the Twilleys' family friend Edward Minchen wrote a lengthy letter to the local paper arguing that it was unchristian to go to war. "The Christian is a citizen of a Heavenly Kingdom," and earthly citizenship was temporary. Christians were bound to each other through Jesus, he argued, and to kill another Christian was to kill Christ himself. (He did not say whether it was permissible to kill non-Christians.) These sentiments were close to Gertrude's own. But editor Andrew Weir put a disclaimer at the head of the piece: he had published it not out of sympathy but because the writer had insisted the paper's masthead motto ("Non-Partisan Politics") gave him that right. Weir invited responses from opposing viewpoints. Weir's own position on the war at this time is difficult to know. He was a staunch friend and admirer of Gertrude's, and if their friendship cooled because of her pacifist views, she does not discuss it. He was opposed to conscription; yet when readers failed to respond to Minchen's article, Weir wrote an antipacifist editorial suggesting that no one took such views seriously enough to bother about. Weir said that Jesus taught followers to seek the spirit rather than the letter; so much for Minchen's Bible verses. If Jesus defended a woman being stoned by a crowd, surely he would defend helpless Belgian women and children being ravished and tortured by cruel tyrants. Those who claimed Jesus would not fight to defend these were slandering Him. Those who made the terrible sacrifice to go fight were doing so in the belief that "they have the mind of Christ."[22] This may indicate a rift; if this is the case, it would have serious repercussions given an editor's standing in the community and Gertrude's view about journalism as a holy and influential calling. Weir in particular would be a sad loss, given their church links and the fact that he had also been close to Gertrude and Robert as their minister, when they courted and married. Gertrude may have been increasingly isolated in the community early in 1916.

Gertrude had written of her *Midland Free Press* poems, which she had published regularly since 1907, that her sole desire in life was "to help and strengthen and comfort." She herself continued to find comfort in her religious faith and in the early signs of spring and the promise of the convenant between God and humankind that the bounty of the earth would meet all needs. "God's faithfulness remains with us. He has given us so much. Nothing but the sin of man, the cruelty and inhumanity that are an offence to God and to all who know and love Him prevent this world from being a Paradise. God is love, abundant love, filled with a mother's tenderness, and a father's protecting and providing care. His great justice is only love, and only those who love can understand and approach him."[23] Gertrude's writings suggest that she alternated between grief and hope during this period. Rejoicing in the safe arrival of Wilfred's family in Swan River, she lamented Fred's military exile and Horace's uncertain future. Not surprisingly, and despite the demanding round of tasks of a farm woman (and she gave thanks for toil's capacity to occupy her thoughts), it was difficult for her to avoid thinking about the war. By April 1916 there had been large public meetings in Saskatoon and Winnipeg to demand conscription. "It is useless to protest against these things now," she wrote. Militarism was "growing even more in evidence." There would be "even greater conflicts between Christ and Caesar." Comments such as these suggest she felt helpless about prospects of change for the present. She still had hopes for the future. She looked to the postwar world, when "God grant we may look into each other's faces once again, each finding in the other's eyes new and great resolutions ... and may the greatest of all be that never, never more shall this carnage take place on the earth our Risen Christ redeemed."[24]

Although Gertrude said the aim of her poems was to bring comfort, she may have meant *only* her poems, because her columns generally contained upsetting information and distressing instructions to think about it and act upon it. Her letters were no better; she had written to Edith in December 1916 when their engagment was announced, "If [Fred] should be spared to the end of this cruel war, I suppose he will hope to bring you back with him," followed by a series of observations on the evils of war and Horace's suffering. Fred wrote to Edith, "Gertie's letter is not very cheering, but none of her letters are, and have not been since the war began. Her writings in the [Midland] Free Press are the same, so I do not care to read them on that account." Fred would not have enjoyed her other writings much more. In her May 1916 *Woman's Century* column, Gertrude urged women not to become calloused. "We may be brave, we may be patient, but until the horror touches us – do we CARE?" When men came back blinded and the rest of their lives would be blighted, women could not sit idle. "We have a work to do, greater work that anything we are doing, or have done. We have a work to do for humanity – a new world to build where our beautiful boys shall not be blinded, maimed or crushed or shattered more. We are far more responsible than we care to own – we are all responsible for the horror of this thing, and we are afraid to acknowledge this – and afraid to speak out our hatred of it all. God make us brave! Make us brave as the precious ones whose lives, hopes and happiness are all alike being poured out in sacrifice to the God of War." How could this be accomplished? She urged her Leicester readers to help "by thinking loving thoughts, by absolutely refusing to join in that chorus of hate and cruelty and vengeance" and by emulating Christ. "Loving deeds" should occupy the hours.[25]

God did not will the slaughter, she said. Any God that did would be a Moloch; Jesus had shown a God of love. Gertrude wrote that she was infuriated by "hypocritical self-righteousness and false ideals of Christianity" preaching militarism, and "broken-hearted" by ministerial claims that peace ideals were "namby-pamby, milk and water" ideas. Gertrude saw the struggle against conscription as a "fight between force and the human conscience"; an extension of the greater struggle for the use of peaceful means to resolve disputes, the struggle of women for rights of citizenship, and of social gospel efforts to remake the world. To decry peace as wishy washy nonsense was to side with force. The human conscience was, for her, that spark of the Divine in each person. Women's caring was an expression of that spark, and, if the conscience were properly engaged, women's caring would be the basis for implementing God's plan for the world. The plan was contained in the gospel of love; "May we have the grace to live out this gospel in our daily lives." Gertrude saw women's caring as a sharp and strong tool for change. But it was a double-edged blade, for it cut the user. Although she had long advocated that women care as if their own kin were involved in the war, and had demonstrated her own capacity to do that, now that Fred was in uniform it was a bit more personal. She kept expecting Fred to walk in the door filled with news, she said, and she longed to see him. Millions of other women must feel the same; "Let us hold each other up with loving prayer," she wrote.[26]

Although she sometimes may have felt helpless as an individual, she still believed that women working together in peace groups had the capacity to accomplish something. Her spirits were lifted when she heard news of ICWPP doings. About June 1916 she received a "call ... for the development of a 'Women's International League.'" The British branch of the ICWPP had sent out a "Call to the women of the British Dominions Overseas," expressing appreciation for their loyalty, and sisterly solidarity in the grief and sacrifice caused by the war. The British women asked others to stand with them to "save future generations from war" and to take part in a planned ICWPP international women's meeting. They urged women's groups in the Dominions to select representatives to go to the international conference, and to otherwise work to carry out the aims of the Hague Congress. This sounded like some progress was being made. In fact, although Gertrude does not mention this, in May 1916 all the British peace groups had organised a joint petition campaign for peace by negotiation, and at peace rallies all over the country they got 200,000 signatures, and endorsements from trade unions and other groups with 750,000 members. In the summer of 1916, there was a good deal of hope that this demonstration of broad public support for a negotiated peace would push the government to accept some sort of mediation. If Gertrude knew about this (and it is hard to imagine she did not, given her obvious access to WIL and NCF news), she had reason for hope. Gertrude may also by then have received material from Laura Hughes and Elsie Charlton in Toronto, who were working to set up pacifist study circles as precursors to a Canadian branch of the ICWPP. Since Gertrude's *Woman's Century* articles made clear her pacifist convictions, they if nothing else would have led Hughes to contact her. Hughes and Charlton sent out a circular letter and copies of the Hague Resolutions to possible peace sympathisers in 1916. Hughes had published a substantial article in the March 1916 number of the WCTU's *White Ribbon Bulletin* about the origins and events of the Hague Congress, the resolutions, and the envoys. Gertrude was a

WCTU supporter and had close WCTU associates from suffrage campaigns. The publication was widely read; Gertrude may have seen it.[27]

Gertrude had a number of opportunities to put herself in regular contact with ICWPP information about national or international activities. The ICWPP monthly newsletter, *Internationaal*, reported in the 1 January 1916 number (its first issue) that the Toronto group had sent out fifty copies of the Hague resolutions with a circular letter, for study circles to discuss. Laura Hughes wrote a later update about the promotion of study circles: "I have a number of names of women from all over Canada who are pacifists and who are willing to join our Ass." The *Internationaal* also reprinted a clipping Hughes sent of the Edmonton *Leader*'s report on the recent WCTU convention, excerpting Peace superintendent Mary Chesley's presentation, which had urged WCTU members to support the work of the ICWPP. Gertrude was probably an *Internationaal* reader by early 1916; the newsletter was useful for networking across Canada's vast distances, and internationally. By late October 1916, Laura Hughes wrote, the Canadian ICWPP had members working in every province except B.C. Gertrude's Roaring River suffrage group was among that number. Through her British connections, such as her correspondence with the BDWSU, Sylvia Pankhurst, and others, Gertrude had additional access to antiwar news. Pacifists could also glean scraps of news from the *Woman's Century*, which by mid-1916 still tolerated some information about peace activism. The July issue featured an article about Julia Grace Wales, her widely endorsed plan for "continuous mediation without armistice" that had been adopted at the Hague Congress, which could be obtained from an address given in the article (it was that of the Women's Peace Party in the U.S., which acted as a conduit to send ICWPP material to Canadian women), and information about subsequent efforts to initiate some sort of mechanism for peace mediation by neutrals. These continuing efforts probably helped Gertrude believe during 1916 that something could be done about the war. It was not until that December that the few Asquith Cabinet ministers who were willing to consider negotiation were ousted and the new Lloyd George coalition government's beat-them-to-their-knees war policy came into effect. As long as the U.S. stayed neutral, it was still possible to hope that mediation by neutrals could happen, and that the endeavours of the ICWPP and its sympathisers would accomplish something.[28]

The harvest time was usually a time of rejoicing and hope for Gertrude. As it happened, the fall 1916 harvest was marred by awkward weather, and there was as much to worry about as hope for, but

Gertrude still found comfort in the seasonal lessons. She wrote poems to prisoners of conscience expressing a certainty that their sacrifice would win "a great, glad world, renewed, re-born," and, revealingly, "You, from dark despairing grief, these hearts of ours shall save!" God would give them courage, the example of Jesus would sustain them, rich blessings would come to them. "Freedom calls for heroes now," who would "stand in steadfast faithfulness." This poem was probably written after Horace's ordeal at Glen Parva barracks and transfer to Richmond Castle for his first court martial. Despite Gertrude's worry about him, his steadfastness sustained her faith in the promise of her religious beliefs about the part that she and other followers must play in helping the universal plan to unfold. A month later she wrote "Harvest gold," excerpted below, a poem that illustrates how, in her hopeful moments, she saw this working.

> They are bringing in the harvest, cutting down the waving grain,
> Grain that tells once more the story of the triumph over pain,
> Tells how "corns of wheat" were buried, how they died to bring forth life,
> Giving grandeur, exultation, to our sorrow and our strife.
>
> Tenderly the sun is shinging o'er the glad sweet harvest days,
> Tenderly our hearts are lifted in a sweet, sweet song of praise
> (Yet our tears are ever falling for the crimson harvest plains,
> Where the sons of men are gathered – and we cannot know their pains!)
>
> For the harvest yet is coming, harvest of the Kingdom fair;
> We can bring it by our toiling, by our faith and by our prayer;
> We must sow our seed 'in weeping,' yet we, too, shall reap in joy!
> Joy that shall not end for ever – joy divine that cannot cloy.
>
> And at night the stars, unfolding o'er the countless sheaves of grain,
> Tell of One Great Star of wonder shining over Judah's plain,
> Tell the new and blessed story of the wonder of His life,
> Of the harvest after sowing, of the peace that follows strife.[29]

The harvest was more than a metaphor of hope; the event itself brought Gertrude evidence to support her theories. Because of bad weather, the threshing gang did not reach Gertrude's until late October or early November. The usual difficulties of getting someone in to help were made worse by the war, so Gertrude had to do the food preparation and service on her own, although Fannie did manage to help her for part of the time. The threshing crew included five "Austrians" that year, so the "Canadians," Gertrude said, tried to avoid discussing the war. In the midst of the threshing, Gertrude heard the news that Australian voters had just defeated conscription in a referendum. That may have started things, but in any case the conversation turned to the forbidden topic. Gertrude told the men about Horace. One self-professed keen Christian seemed to think Horace deserved it, but the rest were amazed and indignant. " 'We are brothers and sisters; God made us to love, not to kill each other,' I said, and I shall never forget the quick flash of gratitude that passed across the face of one of these men." It must be hard for them to live as "enemies," she wrote; their children would be "Canadians." This moment of closeness and sympathy (and the Australian news) cheered her greatly. "People are all good at heart. How terrible when they have false leaders!" Gertrude's heart went out to the misguided as well as the steadfast: "How I pray for the dear, brave soldiers, and for all the sufferers in this war; and for everyone who is fighting against war and its terrors for Christ's sake."[30]

Spreading Horace's story was one important early form of Gertrude's antiwar activism. However, many were hostile to her message. Her November 1916 column in *Woman's Century* detailed Horace's story, and spoke of thousands more of these "true followers of Jesus" and of her own pain and faith. The editors had begun to add a disclaimer to Gertrude's column: "The Editors do not hold themselves responsible for the sentiments expressed above, but beg to remind the readers that Woman's Century is open to all thinking women as a medium through which to express their views." But the year ended on a hopeful note. Her Christmas card contained a "vision" story of Jesus healing and lifting up all the war's sufferers, angel choirs celebrating, and heavenly joy. The "war-makers, the oppressors, the false preachers ... the hypocrites and the extortioners, the proud and self-righteous and cruel," who had tried to sneak into the blessed circle, were told "Depart ye cursed." Justice would prevail.[31]

The 1916 Christmas season had held some promise: Woodrow Wilson had been re-elected on a neutrality platform; in early December the German government sent out peace feelers, and shortly thereafter Wilson did likewise, suggesting a peace conference convened by neutrals and asking the belligerents to publish their war aims. In January 1917 Wilson gave a pro-mediation speech to the U.S. Congress. Some ICWPP members thought there might finally be a negotiated peace, now that Wilson, the nearly unanimous choice for convenor, seemed to be ready to act. During 1916, the ICWPP leaders had attempted to schedule their own international meeting to plan the next step and give some thought to their involvement in the peace settlement, whenever that might come. The first date had been rescheduled due to Jane Addams' illness, and the second attempt had been cancelled when various delegates could not get passports to travel to Copenhagen. Some members had objected to the cancellation: the Hungarian women said that just as suffrage demonstrations did some good even when the demonstrators knew there was no hope of being heard, the public efforts of women to attend the meeting would have had value. "So the attempts to get passports for international meetings even if unsuccessful, would be a success of the idea of Internationalism during the war," they wrote. The spectacle of refused passports would have made the nature of military government clear, some believed; the cancellation had been a mistake. The ICWPP leaders tried again in December 1916 to schedule the conference for summer 1917, but it would never be held. By late 1916 the ICWPP had turned to national conferences (held easily in the neutral countries, and only with great difficulty elsewhere) to promote its ideals.[32]

Behind the scenes things were getting worse, not better. Within two weeks of Wilson's pro-mediation speech, the Germans escalated to unrestricted submarine warfare, as they had planned all along (to try to destroy the food blockade behind which civilians were starving), and in February 1917 the U.S. broke off diplomatic relations. This shift in the U.S. position was due partly to a scandal arising from a telegram (known as the "Zimmerman telegram") from the German government to its representative in Mexico, intercepted and decoded by the British and passed on to the U.S., saying Germany planned unrestricted submarine warfare as of 1 February, and instructing the German representative to offer Mexico an alliance with Germany (and asking Mexico to bring in Japan), in the event of U.S. entry into the war. The Germans further suggested a Mexican invasion of the southwestern U.S. to retake territory that had been seized from Mexico in the nineteenth century; Mexico would be given permanent title as part of the peace settlement. Although the Mexicans were unhappy about recent U.S. armed incursions into their territory, and had good reason to fear that U.S. hawks wanted in any event to use the war as an excuse to invade, their government did not take up the German offer. After much uproar, the German official who had sent it admitted the telegram was authentic, and U.S. public sentiment shifted dramatically away from neutrality. A couple of U.S. ships were sunk. By the end of March, the whole Cabinet, most of the Congress, and a large proportion of the populace were prowar. The Women's Peace Party and various other groups had mounted a huge campaign to avoid entering the war, but they were outmatched by superior forces supported by the military, expansionists, and a variety of patriotic manufacturers, who had mounted an increasingly successful campaign for many months to bring the U.S. into the war. The Zimmerman telegram and unrestricted German submarine warfare were the last straw. The ICWPP's work had come to naught; there would be no mediation by neutrals.[33]

In Canada things had been getting worse quite openly. National registration was implemented, although not made compulsory. Some labour groups, especially in the west, protested, seeing this correctly as the beginning of conscription. Borden's May 1917 announcement that there would indeed be conscription was no great surprise. Various forms of resistance (such as a general strike) had been debated in anticipation of this eventuality, but in the end, no direct action was agreed upon. Various labour and socialist groups joined to form branches of the Independent Labour Party, based more or less on the British model. This activity was concentrated in Ontario; ICWPP activist Laura Hughes was on the founding executive of the provincial ILP. The formation of the ILP strengthened existing overlaps beween labour, socialist, and women's antiwar activism. To what extent this touched Gertrude's daily life is uncertain, but as the conscription issue further polarised her feminist and community networks, she drew closer to Winnipeg socialist circles, where most of the anticonscription movement was concentrated. By now she had lost her main source of information about Leicester, the Radical, populist, and nonpartisan socialist newspaper *Midland Free Press*, which became a casualty of wartime materials and personnel shortages and ceased publication with its 31 March 1917 issue. This represented a severe blow, I believe; she had been writing for them for more than ten years, and had become one of their star features. The *Free Press* connection represented continuity, respectability, and recognition as a writer, spiritual comforter, and political thinker. It had also been the means for continued participation in the life of her home city, which she very much prized. Her Winnipeg connections must have helped fill the void to some extent. By this time she must have been reading the *Voice* regularly, as it was the best regular source of information about their activities. Whatever her source, her columns make it clear that she knew about Winnipeg antiwar events.[34]

The Roaring River Political Education League continued regular discussions of peace issues in early 1917, as it grappled with the difficult splits within the Manitoba women's movement over the war, and the attempts by prowar women to restrict the federal franchise to proconscription women. As requested by the British branch of the ICWPP, the PEL discussed the Women's International League at their monthly meeting during the holiday season. Gertrude maintained close contact with the antiwar leaders of the Winnipeg PEL, who still held control of the executive. The active membership, too, appear to have supported their executive, at least on the matter of universal woman suffrage federally. As the *Grain Growers' Guide* reported, the PEL annual convention "went on record as being absolutely opposed to limiting the franchise to Canadian and British women." In addition to Francis Marion Beynon and Lillian Beynon Thomas, such PEL activists as Winona Flett Dixon, her sister Lynn Flett, and Mrs Luther Holling worked closely with socialist and social gospel groups on such ventures as the People's Forum, set up by J.S. Woodsworth and Lillian Beynon's husband Vernon Thomas. (Winona's husband Fred Dixon and Vernon Thomas were themselves in hot water for their antiwar views early in 1917. In January Dixon, an MLA, had made an anticonscription speech in the legislature. Thomas, covering it for the *Free Press*, went to shake Dixon's hand; for that he was fired. The Thomases left Winnipeg for New York and did not return to Canada until the 1920s.) Gertrude's Winnipeg suffrage colleagues were active in antiwar circles. When conscription was announced, the conflicts between prowar and antiwar factions intensified. Gertrude followed these events, probably through the *Voice*. Through her personal contacts, which branched out beyond the original suffrage circles about this time, she expanded her own peace networking. Gertrude discovered Horace Westwood, minister of All Souls' Unitarian Church, who regularly preached peace sermons and since 1914 had been giving antiwar talks in such venues as the People's Forum. Westwood was a stalwart on labour issues, and came out for such groups as the Woolworth's clerks when they went on strike in June 1917. Gertrude also became more directly involved with the Social Democratic Party.[35]

Gertrude's closer ties with Winnipeg activists came at a particularly lively time. Western labour organisations had been at odds over the registration issue with both their eastern counterparts and their high national officials. When Borden announced he would bring in conscription, several western cities became centres of revolt. The Vancouver Trades and Labour Council voted almost unanimously to resist strenuously, and the B.C. Federation of Labour initiated a province-wide referendum on a general strike if conscription were passed. The strike vote passed by a 5 to 1 majority, but the provincial convention delegates decided to delay a strike in favour of political action. Similar reactions took place in parts of Alberta and Manitoba. A Calgary Unitarian women's group passed a resolution calling for a general strike. Elsewhere, many labour groups were unwilling to accept conscription of men without parallel measures to conscript wealth, measures ranging from nationalisation to stiff income taxes.

Although many labour groups were willing to support the war, they were fed up with profiteering, worsening health and safety conditions, a falling standard of living due to inflation, and the restriction of workers' rights. For some, conscription as it was proposed (without some provisions to distribute hardship fairly) was the last straw. Various anticonscription coalitions were formed.[36]

In Winnipeg, representatives from socialist and labour groups formed an Anti-Conscription League to coordinate a campaign against the proposed legislation. League members included religious and secular pacifists, anticompulsion liberals, and diverse socialists, some of whom might not have been opposed to the war *per se*, and others who were vehemently antiwar. Proconscriptionists were outraged by the League's formation, and patriotic extremists responded by attempting to intimidate opponents. The Winnipeg *Tribune* published a thinly veiled invitation to the pros to beat up antis at a rumoured meeting at the Labour Temple. Trades and Labour Council secretary Richard Rigg wrote letters of protest to the mayor and the attorney general, complaining about "illegal and Prussianized methods of robbing the people of the right to discuss a measure" being debated in Parliament. Such methods were greatly in evidence at subsequent meetings. The Anti-Conscription League (ACL) had planned a meeting for June 3 at the Labour Temple, but the authorities persuaded the building managers to refuse to rent it without an expensive bond posted to pay damages; the venue was moved at the last minute to the Grand Opera House. It was set up in the usual way; a platform of speakers, all very respectable. City Councillor John Queen chaired, and the ACL speakers were joined on the platform by three military representatives who asked the several hundred hostile vets (among a crowd of about 2,000), to allow speakers to be heard. After two speakers were shouted down, the chair adjourned the meeting. When most of the audience had cleared out, several soldiers approached Fred Dixon and tried to start a fight. Dixon refused and walked outside; they followed and hit him. He reentered the building, chased by ten or twelve men who roughed him up. When the attack was eventually broken up by bystanders, Dixon was taken away by car, suffering from undetermined injuries (which proved to be minor). Several others were roughed up, apparently more or less at random.[37]

The ACL next scheduled a meeting for June 17, to be held outdoors at the Market Square (a traditional site for speakers). The organising committee met with the police about security arrangements. The police commissioner had been informed that bully boy extremists would cause bloodshed if the meeting were held, and he proposed to ban all such meetings, even though he agreed they were perfectly legal. The committee agreed to cancel for safety reasons. Huge crowds showed up despite the cancellation. Because press reports on the anticonscriptionists were usually wildly inaccurate, a large number of antis concluded that the meeting really had not been cancelled and arrived anyway. So did hundreds of proconscription bully boys, ready to assault the antis. However, they were all dispersed without serious incident. Despite the fact that large-scale violence was averted, an ugly situation had developed in Winnipeg. Civilians were being terrorised by squads of out-of-control military men, whose superiors apparently were unable or unwilling to exercise their authority. Anticonscriptionists pointed to this situation as an indication of what might be expected if the military had even more power after a conscription law were passed. The cancellation of the Market Square meeting marked the beginning of a "free speech" campaign in Winnipeg. The ACL protested the loss of citizens' democratic rights, and circulated petitions to their MPs, but it did little good.[38] Francis Marion Beynon was one of Gertrude's suffrage colleagues who was involved in the ACL. She wrote scathingly about the refusal of "patriots," who claimed to be defending cherished British principles against undemocratic prussianism, to allow democratic rights to "antis." She pointed out, "The real test of liberty is whether the minority opinion is allowed to find expression when there is strong opposition to it." When proconscriptionists felt free to hold a public meeting and threaten harm to any anti who attended, while at the same time say that no anticonscription meetings would be allowed, "it gives the lie to the theory that the Union Jack stands for personal liberty and freedom of speech, as opposed to the Prussian ideal of the subjection of the rights of the individual to those of the state." That was Beynon's last column for the *Grain Growers' Guide*. Shortly after that she fled to the States to join her sister and brother-in-law in New York. She may have received death threats or been roughed up by the patriots at anticonscription meetings. In novel she published after the war the heroine, a feminist journalist, dies of injuries received in similar circumstances. The Beynons and Thomas had been key figures in the Winnipeg peace, suffrage, and socialist movements, and their departure left a big gap.[39]

In June 1917 Gertrude began to publish articles and poems in the Social Democratic Party (SDP) newspaper *Canadian Forward*, with a circulation of about 30,000, published in Toronto by editor Isaac Bainbridge, who had already been in trouble with the authorities for publishing "seditious" material (mostly from British Christian pacifists). The paper reported on labour and socialist activities and views, and published material from feminist socialists and peace activists, including accounts of Canadian Quakers' public discussion meetings and official policy statements on peace issues. Although Gertrude does not say how she became involved with the newspaper, there are a number of possible connections. Harriet Dunlop Prenter, one of the Toronto ICWPP group, wrote regularly for the *Forward* and her work appeared in the *White Ribbon Bulletin* and *Woman's Century.* Gertrude surely knew Prenter's name, and may have contacted her, or vice versa. Gertrude was also in touch with Laura Hughes, who with her mother, educational reformer Ada Marean Hughes, was involved in various SDP activities. Or Gertrude may have been given copies of the journal by her feminist or social gospel anticonscription friends in Winnipeg.[40]

Her first article was an excerpt from Horace's diary outlining his imprisonment and mistreatment. Her next few pieces gave further details. She warned her readers that similar abuses would take place in Canada under conscription. Gertrude had previously lamented, warned, and exhorted her readers to take note of various examples of women's antiwar actions. Now she went beyond general admonitions to take heed, and sent "a call to Canada's women" to act. "Are we going to endure this here?" she wrote. Some women had not. "Three times the women of Germany, massed in the thousands, have stoned the palace of the Hohenzollerns, demanding that the slaughter of the men shall cease. Bayoneted, sabred, shot – they are for all time the example to all true motherhood. Women of Canada, shall we arise and save our men? From my little farm home where I weep and pray and suffer, I call to you women with mother-hearts. If you will help, write to me, enclosing a stamped, addressed envelope; and let us form our plans to resist this accursed slavery." Letters poured in from all across Canada, and from the U.S., where her articles had been reprinted, she said.[41]

Sometime in early July 1917, the Women's Peace Crusade took shape. By then Gertrude had made explicit connections between the women's, peace, and socialist movements. As in the Boer War, she found her place as a true follower of Christ here. In her 10 July 1917 piece, Gertrude wrote asking all members of the Crusade "to take a braver stand in the cause of Peace and Freedom" by writing letters to Ottawa to protest Bainbridge's imprisonment. She announced that William Ivens, a Winnipeg social gospel minister, had lost his pulpit for his antiwar views. She spoke of women's mission to work for a "new day" when such injustice as political imprisonment would not occur. Her future Women's Crusade pieces would follow a similar format, giving details about abuses of justice, prisoners of conscience, efforts to improve their treatment, hopes for better world, and the part that women could play in bringing about the new world. To those who wrote in, she sent the Crusade flyer, containing a "resolution-pledge" (as she described it to the ICWPP office). This manifesto was probably composed in June or July of 1917; it has Gertrude's characteristic flavour, but it is possible that she modified an early draft in consultation with her respondents (who wrote after the first *Canadian Forward* piece). The manifesto appeared in several versions, none dated, so it is difficult to be sure of the order in which they were developed. The text reproduced below is probably a version from August or September 1917. The standard "pledge" of the first three paragraphs, the heart of the Crusade, seems to have been from the early period. (There were slight variations in versions; in her 24 August 1917 *Canadian Forward* piece, the word "equality" was substituted for "purity" in the third paragraph. The second section, "Save the boys," probably was added later, given its references to members.)[42]

THE WOMEN'S CRUSADE
(International)

We, members of the Women's Crusade, believing that the men and women of all nations are the brotherhood and sisterhood of the great Family of Humanity, assert our opposition to all war, conscription and slavery.

We pledge ourselves to support, by our influence and voting power, only those who will work for freedom and peace, and the suppression of militarism under all forms.

We desire social and political purity, the world for the workers (to whom it belongs), the true religion, which is the fulfilment of the Golden Rule, the creation of a safe and happy world for the unborn.

SAVE THE BOYS.

Sister Women,

The forces of Militarism – the evil fruit of war – are let loose upon the world. We women, who love our kind – who care more for our dear ones than for "separation allowances" – are banding together in a great effort to combat these forces of unutterable darkness. In our Crusade we do not recognize frontiers, and already women from Great Britain and the United States are enrolled with us in Canada. The forces of love and goodwill are gathering power. The world is war-weary; many hearts are broken; many fear and dread the news the day may bring.

Mangled, torn, blinded, maddened, slain, are the victims of this inhuman strife. Europe is a vast charnel house, yet still the Molochs of War cry out: "More men; more of the flower of earth's manhood," and still the monster is insatiate.

Vainly have we looked to the servants of the Prince of Peace to lead the way out of the horror.

False apostles, they have "bowed the knee to Baal," and have joined in the mad orgie [sic] of blood and lust in the name of righteousness.

There is nothing left – no hope, save the pent-up forces of the world's motherheart. Sister women, we can end the war; we can destroy Militarism. Will you help? If you will, read carefully the above pledge and send your name and address signed below, with 25 cents membership fee, by return mail to the address below.

Name ....

Address ....

"Dreamer of dreams," we take the taunt with gladness,

Knowing that God, beyond the jeers we see,

Hath wrought the dreams that count with men for madness,

Into the substance of the life-to-be.

(Mrs) GERTRUDE RICHARDSON,

Swan River, Manitoba,

Canada.

The inspiration for the Crusade may have come from several British sources: the Peace Crusade organised by W.T. Stead to support the Czar's peace proposals, just before the Boer War; the Christian Peace Crusade organised during the First World War by Wilfred Wellock, and the Women's Peace Crusade that began in the summer of 1916, fizzled that winter, and revived and spread like wildfire across England and Scotland beginning in the summer of 1917. (Wilfred Wellock was a socialist Methodist minister from a Lancashire textile worker family. In 1916 he published a newsletter, *The New Crusader*, concerned primarily with opposition to conscription. He refused to take advantage of his clergy conscription exemption and served several prison terms as a CO. He was later active in pacifist groups, a follower of Gandhi, an ILP MP, and involved in various social reconstruction schemes in the thirties and forties.)[43]

The Women's Peace Crusade started in Glasgow, where there were commonly overlaps between different varieties of suffrage, peace, labour, and socialist groups. It was founded by about 200 women from sixteen organisations, at a meeting organised by local socialist suffragists who had founded a branch of WIL but wanted to do antiwar work in a more militant and explicitly socialist context. The group held a series of open air meetings around Glasgow and Edinburgh, concluding with a WPC demonstration 23 July 1916 that attracted 5,000 people. Children's writer Theodora Wilson Wilson, a Quaker radical and suffragist from Cumbria who had been on the Hague

Congress Planning Committee and had hoped to get the Congress to endorse a resolution for an immediate cease-fire, was among the speakers at that July meeting. It was she who took over coordinating the Christian Peace Crusade when Wilfred Wellock went to prison. Sylvia Pankhurst's *Dreadnought* carried news of WPC events and ideas in the summer of 1916, so Gertrude could have read about them. The ILP's *Labour Leader*, Fenner Brockway's paper (which Gertrude read until it was later outlawed in Canada) assiduously reported WPC events, and acted as a sort of clearing house to help WPC organising. The mainstream press did not report on most of the anti-war activities of the WIL and other groups, especially the successful ones. Helena Swanwick, active in a whole alphabet soup of acronyms of peace groups, said in her memoirs that WIL held thousands of public meetings, indoors and outside, between 1915 and 1918 and most of these were not covered, except perhaps by the publications of the groups involved. However, personal and organisational networks could have helped Gertrude to keep up with the news, especially after her mother had returned to Leicester.[44]

Although little was done in Scotland by the WPC over the winter (possibly because a number of the key organisers were too busy with other antiwar campaigns), the Crusade began again with a large meeting in Glasgow 1 June 1917. Within weeks it had spread to dozens of other cities and was drawing thousands of women out for antiwar demonstrations. Although these huge public meetings were dangerous in the cities, where prowar opponents, usually men, threatened and sometimes attacked the women speakers and spectators, in smaller centres or country districts the WPC was able to hold successful meetings and demonstrations that attracted unprecedented numbers of supporters. The membership was broad, and drawn largely from working class women. Gertrude's columns for the late summer and fall of 1917 and thereafter show that she was in touch with the British WPC. Some of her old Boer War peace activists, her school chums, and her suffrage comrades and acquaintances from Leicester days, as well as her mother, were almost certainly involved.[45]

The lines were drawn more firmly in Canada between the prowar and anticonscription or antiwar elements by the late summer of 1917. As the conscription legislation was passed and various turf wars were fought over terms and alignments for the upcoming election, what little tolerance had existed within the *Woman's Century* circles virtually evaporated. The depth and finality of the antipacifist stand was evident in a harsh statement presumably written by MacIver. The statement was prompted by a report that "prominent suffragists" Laura Hughes and Harriet Dunlop Prenter had attempted to claim some connection between suffrage and pacifism in Ontario, in a letter to New York Women's Peace Party members. *Woman's Century* wrote that the "National Union and the Ontario Equal Franchise Association have again and again expressed themselves as repudiating utterly any question of premature peace. Any pacifist literature which has been received from the Hague and elsewhere has been consigned by those societies to the waste-paper basket. *Woman's Century* again wishes very definitely to repudiate all utterances ... or any pacifist propaganda, and to reiterate once again that it stands for a Union Government, Conscription, and Winning the War."[46]

Gertrude's column, "The West," ceased to appear. Gertrude's serial novel, *The Motherhood of Nyria: A Story of the Roman Empire*, begun in the March 1916 issue, halted in mid-story after the December 1916 installment. Mysterious gaps appeared between the publication of the latter portions of the novel, as the story line became concerned with the persecution and imprisonment of Christians and the heartlessness and bloodthirstiness of pro-establishment women "in the days of Rome's degradation." The reasons are not hard to find, given that the entire story is about the refusal of Christians to bow, even at the cost of their lives, to the cruel and evil practices required by the state. The last chapter eulogised Nyria's beliefs, and such lines as "every child was sacred to her because of her own" were catch phrases of the pacifist maternalist position. The story's epilogue commented, "To become a Christian meant, of course, to refuse to arm to slay a fellow-creature, and in later times many young men sealed this article of faith with blood." The publication schedule, and certain awkward spots in the story, suggest that there may have been attempts to force Gertrude to rewrite certain sections under threat that they would otherwise be unpublished; however, in the absence of her original manuscript, or her correspondence with Jessie MacIver, it is impossible to tell whether such threats or rewriting occurred. It is also possible that Gertrude may have attempted to cut the novel short, as she became disgusted enough with MacIver's increasing militarism that she did not want to be associated with it any longer. However, if that were the case, Gertrude would likely not have continued to write her column – unless MacIver persuaded Gertrude to stay on a bit longer in order to obtain the remaining instalments of the story. Whether Gertude quit or MacIver dismissed her, it is certain that Gertrude did have a falling out with MacIver and the magazine, as Gertrude wrote to fellow columnist Violet McNaughton: "I cannot support that paper now as it has become so reactionary. It was a real grief to me how Mrs MacIver treated me so very strangely, pretending to be sympathetic with my ideals, yet outwardly repudiating them all."[47]

In August 1917 Gertrude began publishing in the Leicester *Pioneer* in place of the defunct *Free Press*. The *Pioneer* was the local ILP paper, and tolerated antiwar views although for the most part it took a prowar position. By the fall of 1917, then, she had three main outlets: the SDP's *Canadian Forward* which was unabashedly antiwar (wartime Director of Security C.H. Cahan would later characterise it and the SDP as "effective agents of German propaganda in this country"); the largely antiwar Winnipeg *Voice*, and the *Pioneer* – prowar but tolerant. (The Swan River *Star* now took only the occasional poem.) She used all three as vehicles to organise and operate her Women's Peace Crusade. There were few active peace groups in Canada at this time, and difficulties of geography as well as immense public hostility and growing official intolerance made a "mail order" group attractive. Gertrude continued to pass on news about British and Canadian peace activism to her readers in the other countries.[48]

Gertrude's first piece for the *Pioneer* attempted to summarise the reactions of Canadian women to the war. This discussion is noteworthy for its coherent explanation of complex events, but also striking for what it reveals about how her views had changed in the last few months. When she had written in the new year about the well-attended public meeting of women in Winnipeg who had pressed the government to bring in conscription, she had hastened to add that no suffrage organisations as such were represented. Now she wrote, "The women of the suffrage movement, promised the federal franchise by Sir Robert Borden, have in very large numbers gone over to conscription," and would likely vote for the government in the upcoming election. "As a Suffragist of many years, I always believed that the coming of women into electoral life would be the end of wars. I am saddened beyond measure to find that, here at least, such is not the case." Such women seemed hardened, calloused, to her, "neither manly nor womanly ... scarcely human." But some women have "hearts that are full of the mother-love that true women all the world over are looking to, to heal the wounds of the rent and broken world, when this crimson storm of war is past."[49]

Gertrude described to Leicester readers her newly established Women's Peace Crusade and her networking through the *Canadian Forward* which had brought letters from SDPers who wanted to support the Crusade. Although it was indeed a women's crusade, and her appeals would continue to focus on it as such, Gertrude's political, and indeed cultural and spiritual orientation, and her centre of loyalty, had changed. All her adult life she had been a feminist, and had believed in women's mission to redeem and transform the world. No longer. "And so my soul is going out from the 'Women's Move-

ment' out into the great new world that is being born from this horror
of strife and I have awakened to find myself one with the great soul
of the New Humanity. I have discovered that not only women, but
men, have great, tender hearts, strong courageous souls, beautiful
minds." Men who suffered for their ideals, be they soldiers or COs,
set a new example of courage, and made militarist women look bad
by comparison. She charitably concluded that women were "passing
through a phase of evolution." Meanwhile, when they counted the
votes in the federal election, she wouldn't be "looking for the miracle
I once hoped would come 'when women voted.' Instead, I shall hope
to be counted worthy to cast my vote as one of the brotherhood and
sisterhood of the New Humanity."[50]

The "new humanity" were working hard in Winnipeg. The anticonscription campaign had developed into a Workers Council, the
title of which at least owed some debt to the Russian Revolution,
which most socialists involved in the antiwar movement in Canada
(and in Britain and the U.S.) greeted with great enthusiasm as a symbol of hope and the great potential of the human spirit to seek liberty
and democracy. Accounts of its founding and activities are scant, but
the *Voice* reported that the Workers Council was founded by representatives from the labour groups in the city, in September 1917, inspired by models of representative government they saw in the
workers councils of the Russian Revolution that spring. Its platform
emphasised the importance of freedom of speech, thought, and action
as fundamental to liberty and democratic society, and set out the
Council's primary purpose as the defence and promotion of democratic liberties. The Council included group and individual memberships. Its platform demanded repeal of conscription, equal male and
female suffrage, freedom of speech, press, and assembly, and the right
to discuss international issues with those of other countries, and no
industrial conscription. They intended to further their objectives by
discussion, dissemination of literature, and public meetings. Thus, although the anticonscription campaigners had experienced great difficulty in speaking about their views, they had not been silenced. They
could see that the obstacles they had encountered were a taste of
worse to come, and they wanted to do what they could to ensure
their rights as citizens. As Council activist S.J. Farmer wrote, the suppression of free speech was not a minor problem that would affect
only the short term, but an issue that had implications for the postwar world. Undemocratic foreign policy had helped to get the world
into the current mess. It was important to assure that terms of peace
would be democratically determined as well as democratic in content. "The right of free speech and free assemblage, nationally and

internationally, is not to be insisted upon merely as an academic proposition, but as a vital prerequisite to securing those principles for which the peoples are making the appalling sacrifice of this war."[51]

Gertrude followed these events with interest, and wrote some weeks later about the activities of the council. "I think the promoters of the Council are men and women of the highest ideals," she wrote. The group intended to run anticonscriptionist independent candidates in the upcoming election; S.J. Farmer was one of those who stood. Gertrude compared the Workers Council to the People's Council for Democracy and Terms of Peace (PC) in the U.S., which also took its inspiration from the events in Russia. The idea for the People's Council came from Rebecca Shelly, Emily Balch, and Crystal Eastman, feminist peace activists playing key roles in various U.S. campaigns. The People's Council's aims were peace with justice at home and a negotiated settlement of the war. Its foundation was approved in principle at a large conference in New York in May 1917, but the conference was cut short by the authorities, so the nuts and bolts planning for the PC's establishment before and after its Chicago constituent assembly (also shut down early) was done by committees which considerably watered down the women's early vision. If the group were too radical, the commitees argued, it would not be able to attract any support, and it would be repressed by the authorities; these were realistic fears, given the systematic persecution of dissenters in the U.S. by then. Laura Hughes was involved in the U.S. group, first as a keynote speaker, and later, after her December 1917 marriage to Erling Lunde and move to Chicago, as a member. Isaac Bainbridge also attended Council meetings.[52]

In September 1917 Gertrude went to Winnipeg for a few days to pick up Eric, a seven-month-old "war baby" she and Robert were adopting. The arrangements had probably been made through the Methodist or Presbyterian church. Eric's mother, Maggie Carr, was a teenaged Scottish domestic who had only been fifteen when the baby was born in February; his father was a soldier. He was baptised Edward (Maggie's choice) Horace (Gertrude's) Eric (Robert's) Richardson by the Reverend Dr MacLean, a Methodist minister. Gertrude had gone down by herself to finish the legal arrangements; Robert was probably too busy with the harvest to get away. Eric was a healthy, intelligent, beautiful, and happy baby, to all accounts, and Gertrude and Robert adored him. Although this was a momentous event in anyone's life, and particularly to Gertrude who had longed for a baby for so many years, she wrote not one word about the adoption in her newspaper columns. The personal may have been political, but some things were private. Her discussion of the visit to Winnipeg is concerned with glimpses of the city in wartime and the radicals she was able to meet.[53]

There was lots to say; the Wartime Elections Act had passed and was awaiting royal assent; the conscription act was in place and men were anticipating being called up. With the large-scale defection to the prowar side of many of her former suffrage acquaintances, and the loss of the Beynon sisters and A.V. Thomas, Gertrude's former social circles in Winnipeg were somewhat diminished, but she quickly made a place for herself among the antiwar activists. Gertrude was at last able to meet in person some of the men and women she had known only through their political ties. At Winona and Fred Dixon's house (she compared him to Ramsay MacDonald, also the target of a petition campaign for his antiwar views), she met various activists "whose ideals are those I call the ideals of the New Humanity." Although she did have antiwar comrades at home in her Roaring River PEL and Grain Growers circles, and a growing support network through her socialist correspondents from across Canada and the U.S., it was important to her to feel a part of Winnipeg antiwar circles.[54]

Gertrude's spirits were noticeably higher in the fall of 1917, as her Women's Peace Crusade organising bore fruit and her mail was full of letters from supporters. She did reply personally to those who enclosed stamped addressed envelopes, and used her *Canadian Forward, Voice*, and to a lesser extent, Leicester *Pioneer* columns to reply to the rest. In October 1917 she wrote to *Forward* readers, "Take courage … there is so much to encourage us as we hear what the women of other lands are doing to-day. The movement among women is increasing every day." She wrote in a similar vein in the *Voice*: "In Belfast, Glasgow, London, Melbourne, Johannesburg, New York, Seattle and many other places large bands of women are bravely fighting war with Christ's bloodless weapons of love and faith. In Canada we are forming a Women's Crusade. Will you join us, you sister women who read these lines?" It was a peculiar oganisation, existing primarily as a network of socialist women bound by shared determination and connected by letters of information and encouragement. "We are not an organization in the ordinary sense," she wrote. "Just a few women bound together by sympathy, working each in the way we find best against the hideous evil. We are just trying to stand bavely for love instead of hatred, for internationalism against the false 'patriotism' and unworthy nationalism of today, for truth against the hideous lie of war." Some of the actions suggested seem unremarkable, but others take breath away. "I have two suggestions to-day that I give for your consideration: First, that we boycott all capitalist jingo newspapers. (That suggestion came from a lady in the U.S.) Second, that we rise and quietly leave every religious service where war is preached in the name of Christ, as a protest against the blasphemy." It is hard to understand today what an outrageous act this would have been. Such a suggestion has little resonance to our secular peacetime society, but for small town church communities in this period, to propose walking out of a service in this manner is shockingly courageous.[55]

But women were taking public risks everywhere. Gertrude got many letters from U.S. women who reported on the lively antiwar movement there. Despite an increasngly repressive climate, a number of the prewar groups had continued their activity after April 1917, and new groups were formed. Her correspondent told her that peace women in Los Angeles had founded a new group, "Women's League for the Extermination of War," which was rapidly spreading to other West Coast cities. She wrote in her columns that women in Australia, Canada, and Britain were active and growing bolder in peace groups. True, repression was also growing (and indeed, that winter would see the imposition of a new series of controls beyond anything she imagined at the time), but "suppression of a great and true cause has here led to growth and development" of resistance.[56]

Gertrude was also heartened in the fall of 1917 by a letter from Horace, who had used one of his rare mail allocations to write to her. "The power to compel does not exist, and a State or a society which endeavors to suppress the determination of an honorable man, though it lend to the purpose every available material resource, must inevitably yield before the unquestionable supremacy of the individual soul. Moreover, and this is a comforting reflection, the one who feels this sense of power – this ascendancy within himself – can regard his immediate circumstances with perfect equanimity and can await further developments with the utmost confidence, and his material 'deliverance' with a patience absolutely tireless."[57] Horace was bearing up well under difficult conditions. In February 1917 he had been taken with sixty-odd COs from Scrubs to Wandsworth prison. In early February he was allowed a visit from his mother, and Mr Dilks, one of his partners, who appears to have been supportive. A month later, his mother took Catherine Gittins to visit; they found him "fairly well," Fred reported. Catherine Gittins (1840–1930), a highly respected retired art teacher, from a prominent Unitarian family, was a mainstay in various philanthropic organisations, and had become involved in suffragist, socialist, and pacifist groups early in the century. The Twilleys had known her from Boer War peace movement days.[58]

Horace's second court martial sentence ended 27 March 1917. Fred wrote, "I suppose it will be the same thing again, another court-martial and sentence." This time, however, Horace was out for a week between sentences. On 29 March he recorded, "Met at Leicester by friends; dinner at cafe with mother and friends; taken to unit; allowed to stay right at home (joy unspeakable)." The next day Horace went through the usual routine: he was taken to Glen Parva barracks (where he had been tortured in June 1916): "Refused all orders; charged before captain and remanded for D.C.M.; placed under observation; conversation with captain; billetted at home; being released on word of honour to appear at stated times." Horace spent the evening at an NCF meeting. For the next few days he enjoyed the novelty of seeing family, friends, and peace comrades. On the Sunday he spoke to the Sunday School students (Horace had been active in managing the Sunday School) and attended evening services at the Wycliffe Congregational Church, where the pacifist minister, the Reverend Seaward Beddow, gave him communion. Fred wrote, "The change will do him heaps of good, even though he gets sentenced again. I would like to see him but he is not free [to travel] … I wonder how much he will get this time." Horace got eighteen months at his third court martial on 6 April; Fred told Edith, "Evidently they mean to keep him locked up." At least this time Horace was imprisoned at Leicester prison on Welford Road, close to home and friends.[59]

By mid-April 1917, the NCF's Conscientious Objector Information Bureau reported 1,422 COs in civil (as opposed to military) custody; Horace was among the 536 of these who had faced two or more courts martial. Prison conditions generally had worsened early in 1917; that winter had been unusually cold, and an alleged blanket shortage had resulted in the failure in some prisons to provide the officially required three thin blankets. Rations were cut in the spring of 1917, due to food shortages and the government's refusal to institute food rationing for the general population. The prison diet was harsh and skimpy at best, as it was based on the minimum calories necessary for sustenance. Although there were medical regulations that supposedly safeguarded against severe weight loss, that did not offer COs much protection because the "normal" weight of record was that when they had begun their current sentence. Since COs virtually always lost weight on the low calorie prison diet even if they were given all they were entitled to and it were edible, and many repeaters had grown very thin during previous sentences, they could fall to dangerous levels without any medical intervention. Horace was not robust to begin with, but he seems to have been in reasonable physical shape, and his spirits remained high. He was able to enjoy the comfort of regular visits by his own minister, Seaward Beddow, who was the designated CO Visitor locally. Although the prison's governor had at one time told Quaker Visitor William Appleton that he "was of the opinion that all COs should be lined up against a wall and shot," at least nothing could be done to Horace without someone finding out about it. He also had continuing reminders that many people cared about him and considered that he was serving a good cause. Local supporters formed a choir to serenade the COs; Eliza Twilley was a member. They sang "'Abide with me,' 'Lead kindly light,' and 'The Red Flag,' and other hymns and Socialist songs," Gertrude reported in her *Canadian Forward* column. Things seem to have gone reasonably well for the first few months, as Fred wrote, "I have not Horace to worry about now. I think that he is alright [sic]. Am glad that he is not bothering himself, for if a person takes it hard they would not survive it long, I am thinking."[60]

Gertrude passed on news of the activities of a growing British antiwar movement to her Canadian readers. Although there were various groups carrying out actions, she was most familiar with the Women's International League, the NCF, and the Women's Peace Crusade. By the fall of 1917 the *Labour Leader* was proscribed, and she probably was no longer able to obtain copies. She had the ICWPP newsletter, although it came out irregularly; she probably read the NCF *Tribunal*, as she sent it news, and presumably she read the *Dreadnought* and *Jus Suffragii*, but other overseas publications that covered antiwar news were harder to come by. She did get news from her correspondents, some of whom were deeply involved in these activities. Not surprisingly, given that she was developing her own Crusade, she wrote mainly of Women's Peace Crusade events such as a demonstration in the Market Square in Leicester attended by 3,000 sympathisers. After the women speakers concluded, they led their listeners in singing hymns, notably "The Red Flag," which was, a speaker said, "'the emblem of the blood of martyrs who had died for their faith.' And so they sing it in their hundreds, the mothers of men facing death sing it with tear-stained faces and trembling voices. My mother is among them, and her voice rings with passion as she joins the chorus, the same which she joins at the gates of the prison where her boy is incarcerated because he will not join in the multiplicity of murders called war. And as they sing, the men stand by, hats raised in reverence. Sister women, the day is dawning." At other WPC events, men did not stand in reverence, they assaulted the pacifists, but Gertrude focused here on the good news.[61]

She also wrote about London vigils in front of Parliament: banners said "We want our sons back" and "I want my daddy." The defeat of the 1917 conscription referendum in Australia was another cause for cheer. Despite the awful war news and the mounting toll of deaths (over one and a quarter million men had died by the end of 1916, and between August and November 1917 at Passchendaele alone more than 450,000 British and German troops were killed; 380,000 Germans civilians, mostly children and old people, died of starvation by the end of 1917), Gertrude was able to say that fall, "The movement among women is increasing every day ... From all parts of Australia, Great Britain, and Canada the news continues to be very gladdening." Surely so much bravery and witness must produce some good, in the end, she thought. Of the COs as a symbol of courage and hope, she wrote, "Yes, Christ is there, where sons of men / Rise to be sons of God; / And so to-day our brothers tread / The way a Saviour trod."[62]

As Gertrude began to work more closely with SDP women, she developed a friendship with Helen Armstrong, a key figure in the Winnipeg left. Helen and her husband George Armstrong had arrived in Winnipeg by 1906, and by 1914, when her children ranged in age from nineteen to seven, Helen had become immersed in labour organising and politics (and later joined Gertrude's Crusade). In March 1917 Helen and several other socialist and labour women founded the Women's Labour League (WLL), the aims of which were to support women workers, facilitate cooperative action, carry out research, educate the public, and instigate legislative reform on women's (and children's) wages and working conditions. The WLL was open to women workers, women kin of male trade unionists, and supporters of labour. Under its auspices or individually, Helen Armstrong was "the leading figure in women's labour activism in that period," helping to found unions and organising or supporting several labour disputes, such as the Woolworth's clerks' strike. Although Gertrude appreciated Armstrong's labour activism, what really drew her admiration was Armstrong's peace activism. During the anticonscription meetings in the summer of 1917, Armstrong "was the only woman on the open-air platform ... She was most brutally handled by soldiers, on one occasion being bruised severely from head to foot. Often she stood alone between the soldiers and the anti-conscription men, and refused to move." Armstrong argued that there were alternatives to conscription. One way to increase voluntary enlistments would be to give good allowances and pensions to dependants; the Anti-Conscription League had agitated for $100 month. Armstrong also had the courage to go with fellow activist Mrs Queen, who had lost three brothers to the war and had a fourth called up, to a mass meeting of proconscription women held in August 1917. The two women spoke against conscription, and attempted to insert the phrase "some of the women" in the proposed prowar resolution beginning "We the women of Winnipeg in mass meeting here assembled." They set off quite off an uproar.[63]

Gertrude had been corresponding with Laura Hughes, whom she may originally have "met" through Hughes' and Elsie Charlton's ICWPP circular letter sometime in 1915 or 1916 (although they may have known of each other through *Woman's Century* or the WCTU *White Ribbon Bulletin*, and Gertrude would have read Hughes' reports in the *Internationaal*). Hughes had been sympathetic about Horace's imprisonment. The CO issue had become more personal for Hughes by the summer of 1917, when she had become engaged to Erling Lunde, a Chicago CO who was later jailed. Winnipeg radicals had expected Hughes to visit the city on a western speaking tour late in 1917; she was widely known as an excellent and logical speaker, well equipped with persuasive statistics, "an ardent Pacifist, very fearless and outspoken." Her uncle, Sir Sam Hughes, was minister of militia, which no doubt heartened or scandalised those who followed her labour and peace movement activities. It also probably helped protect her; although she was under surveillance, she was never arrested. Gertrude hoped to meet Hughes in person during the speaking tour, although it is not clear whether she entertained any hope of getting Hughes to Swan River. In the event the tour never came off; after Hughes and Lunde married in December 1917, her activities focused mainly in the Chicago area. However, Gertrude and her Roaring River group had assiduously followed the steps Hughes and Charlton set out in their ICWPP letter. The group had sent away for peace material and had studied it over two winters. The winter of 1917–18 their studies included the booklet *Militarism versus Feminism*, which Gertrude called *Feminism versus Militarism*.[64]

Militarism versus Feminism, one of the classic feminist-pacifist tracts of the First World War, illustrates the ideas of this group of pacifists, and others involved in the British women's peace movement. Jo Vellacott and Margaret Kamester traced the history of the pamphlet, first published by Allen and Unwin in the spring of 1915. It was composed of bits by two authors, which had previously appeared in two magazines. The major author was Charles Kay Ogden (1889–1957), a Cambridge academic, freethinker, and editor of *Cambridge Magazine*, who supported feminism, unionism, educational reform, birth control, and the peace movement. During the war, his magazine regularly published a survey of the overseas press (on both sides), and took an antimilitarist position. His contributions to the pamphlet (which were the major part) originally appeared the March 1915 issue of *Cambridge Magazine* as part of a series on changes in women's status due to the war, published under the pseudonym Adelyne More (he wrote under other pseudonyms too); and in the February and March 1915 issues of the NUWSS suffrage journal *Common Cause* (his own name was on these segments). The second author was Mary Sargant Florence (1857–1954), an artist and suffrage and peace activist. Before the war she was involved in a suffragist tax resistance group which refused to pay taxes since they were not allowed full citizenship; twice she had property seized and sold for taxes. She was on the general executive of the WIL, along with other of Gertrude's earlier acquaintances. Sargent Florence and Ogden jointly wrote other sections of the pamphlet; these appeared in the January and March 1915 issue of the IWSA's *Jus Suffragii* (as jointly authored). There may have been other contributing authors; the records are ambiguous and Vellacott and Kamester were not able to determine the details.[65]

The pamphlet itself is subtitled, "An enquiry and a policy demonstrating that militarism involves the subjection of women." By militarism, the authors mean all institutionalised forms of violence and suppression. They say in their introduction, "Violence at home, violence abroad; violence between individuals, between classes, between nations, between religions; violence between men and women: this it is which, more than all other influences, has prevented the voice of woman being heard in public affairs until almost yesterday." These forms of violence add up to "war, militarism, imperialism," which are antithetical to women's position and interests. Societies which are not permeated by militaristic values and practices are much better for women; the authors give various examples. They are careful to explain that their "indictment is against militarism" not against individuals; that decent individuals can nonetheless be forced to act contrary to their decent beliefs, when they are caught up in and directed by militarist systems, most obviously in wartime. The pamphlet reads well today; it is instructive to compare it to modern studies of the impact of militarism on women, such as the work of U.S. political scientist Cynthia Enloe, and to such studies as Maria Mies' history of imperialism's effects on women in colonised and colonising countries. Gertrude's ideas were close to those of the authors, including her pessimistic predictions about the postwar world. That this school of thought is not better known, and taken more seriously, is a loss. Relatively little attention has been paid to the ideas of peace activists by Canadian historians, despite a few happy exceptions. This is ironic, given the urgent threat of nuclear extinction during the 1980s, its still-present potential in the 1990s, and the lives under a virtual state of seige of many women globally. Numerous studies in our own time show that militarism indirectly and directly is a clear threat to the lives of women and children (to say nothing of men) today. Sargent Florence and Ogden's comments should give us pause too: "War, militarism, imperialism: in every form they have proved her undoing, and yet women hesitate today on which side to throw their influence! Over and over again the greatest statesmen have said that peace was utopian only because public opinion was not ready for it ... But who is to create the new public opinion? Have women no better answer than hatred or despair? ... Militarism will not change in the future ... In each single nation, taken for itself, men will be able to make a really good case for militarism, if the movement to educate public opinion does not become international ... Here at last it is clear that the higher ideals and aspirations of women coincide with the future welfare of the whole of humanity. In them is the hope of man."[66]

As the December 1917 election neared, Gertrude's Women's Peace Crusade organising was occupying much of her time. In addition to the usual demanding workday of a farm wife, she now had the baby to care for. She could not keep up with the mail that flooded in. She distributed leaflets; Crusade supporters filled out the coupon attached to the bottom and returned them to her. Her contacts with U.S. women were fruitful; many sent poems, pamphlets, and news about women's peace activities, CO work, and repression of civil liberties. "I am so thankful to find so many women on the side of humanity," she said. She wrote about the British counterparts, the Women's Peace Crusade originating in Glasgow and now spread all over Scotland and England, and the Christian Peace Crusade, by then coordinated by Theodora Wilson Wilson. The two crusades often worked together, Gertrude reported. "Will you please help me?" she wrote. "There is no head of our crusade. We are all sisters, equal in responsibility, trying to help each other. May God give us strength and courage ... Let us not be afraid. May we at least have the courage of the brave men in the trenches. And if they call us 'traitors,' well, it may be hard but what matters seeing that it is false? We are the truest patriots, living for our country and the world. Please help to spread the gospel of humanity."[67]

Gertrude's ideas about womanhood and its connection to motherhood had undergone some change during the war, not surprisingly. She had been shocked that some mothers were eager to send their sons off to kill and be killed. She had abandoned the women's movement as the carrier of women's traditional values of peace and nurture to the world, lost her hope that when women got the vote, evil would beat a hasty retreat. Although she now pinned her hopes on the brotherhood and sisterhood of the new humanity, she had relied on the pacifist remnants of her years of suffrage sisterhood one more time, in reaching out through socialist circles for support for her Women's Peace Crusade. She headed many of her appeals, "Sister Women." Gertrude still believed in motherhood, but not as a female universal; at least not the kind of motherhood she believed in. Her "new world motherhood" as she would soon come to call it, was very much akin to what feminist antimilitarist thinker Sara Ruddick today calls "preservative love": something women are more likely to be trained to do, but not only the province of women. Gertrude wrote late in 1917, "This war has proved ... that the Motherhood that is to save is something other than physical motherhood, something possessed by many who are not physical mothers at all." This was not new; she had written much earlier that motherhood was a capacity as much as it was an actual state of affairs; women who did not bear and rear children could also have mother hearts. "It is a deep, spiritual possession, a love for humanity, a glorious, self-giving longing to protect, conserve and guard and save." Unfortunately, not all women, even those who had children, exercised this unselfish love. It was based on unselfish love above all. "We who love each other are finding each other one all over the world." This commitment to "the Motherhood that is to save" was fundamental to any hopes for a humane world, now and postwar, she believed. "We, who deplore the endless sacrifice of the innocent, both in peace and war, and getting down to first causes, we find the universal enemy of humanity to be the strong power of Gold wedded to Cruelty, this awful cruelty of the exploiter and oppressor. War ... is merely the symptom of the greater evil, the strongly entrenched foe that we must fight with our bloodless weapons until we have overcome." She wrote, of the women who signed up for the crusade, "The women with tender hearts are responding – these are the ones we want." Tender hearts must be put to practical ends: she organised a mail-in lobbying campaign. Crusade members were supposed to "send our pledges to every candidate for Parliament." The pledge, reprinted earlier in this chapter as the first three paragraphs of the Women's Peace Crusade flyer, was "to vote only for those who will work for freedom and peace and the suppression of militarism under all forms."[68]

During the election campaign, Francis Marion Beynon had been entreated to come home and fight; she had decided to remain in New York and do what she could by mail. In a *Canadian Forward* letter published under the title "Democracy," Beynon called the election a threefold betrayal: of the citizenry's faith that their democratic right to vote was secure from tampering; of immigrants who were lured to Canada to build the country, so that now "no foreign born citizen of any nationality will ever again set any real value on the naturalization papers issued at Ottawa"; and finally of the soldiers who had died fighting for "a free and honorable Canada, while the politicians and the financiers stayed at home and made it into a little Germany." Referring to the fact that Quebec was virtually solidly opposed to conscription (and vilified for it), she wrote, the Wartime Elections Act was a "monstrous act of injustice that has already roused bitter race hatreds which will endure for generations. It has in it the seeds of un-told national disaster." She reiterated her faith in the "abiding princi-ple of decency in the Canadian people" and her hope that they would refuse to elect the Unionist government that was eager to carry forth its program at whatever cost to democracy and principle. She pro-claimed that "the people will win, even against such great odds, for democracy is always right." Although several of Beynon's gloomier statements have been partially or wholly borne out by subsequent events, her belief that democracy would triumph was not well founded.[69]

The long-awaited election took place 17 December 1917. But in the Swan River Valley, voting was postponed. Gertrude wrote to Leices-ter readers the evening of December 25, "We have not voted here at all. There were many against the Unionists here, therefore the election for Swan Valley was mysteriously 'deferred.'" It was a crooked elec-tion in any case, she believed. "Had justice had even a chance, the powers holding the sceptre to-day would not have held it." Was this accurate? Guessing "might have beens" is a dangerous occupation for the historian, but there is evidence that such a view was not en-tirely without foundation. Although the final outcome was Unionists 153, Liberals eighty-two (and a sprinkling of other oppositionists), the Unionists got only 100,000 civilian votes more than the opposi-tion. The military vote of 200,000 was crucial, even after the efforts to disenfranchise anticonscription and pro-Liberal male voters, deny the federal franchise to women who could not be counted upon to vote pro-Union, and give it to those women who most assuredly would.[70]

Christmas was not very jolly that year. The young man who usu-ally played Santa Claus at the Roaring River Sunday School Christ-mas party had been killed overseas. He was the first of the Roaring River soldiers to die at the front; he had been a member of the suf-frage society, active in the Roaring River Sunday School, "big and strong; finely built, as are many Canadian boys." Gertrude felt "sick at heart" that none of the women beyond his immediate family and neighbourhood circle seemed deeply touched by his death. A Swan River friend barely skipped a beat in her cheerful chat about other things, when Gertrude asked if she had heard. "Are the women cal-lous there?" she asked Leicester readers, "content that boys in the very dawn of life shall in their thousands pour out their blood while they live on. Why should they die that we may live? Why are things all wrong? If we were true women, women with mother hearts, merely natural women, we would infinitely rather die to save them (if dying to save be truly necessary) than allow them to die for us. I look in amazement when I hear some women speak. I wonder what can have happened to them. Surely all the mass of the world's womanhood cannot be like that! Oh surely not!"[71]

There was little in her immediate surroundings to reassure her that season that things would all come out right. Her family, always a mainstay whatever their differing views, was split up. Eliza was away in England; Fred was in British uniform and could be sent to France; Horace was in jail enduring cold and hunger because he would not kill anyone. Robert was ill, and Gertrude "felt troubled and anxious" about all these things. It was bitterly cold, the coldest she had ever seen in Swan River. But John Livesey drove her and young Eric over to Fannie's for dinner, to salvage what happiness they could for the occasion. "It is my baby's first Christmas, and though we had no Christmas tree as we have had other years, we sat round and gave each other our little gifts, thinking all the time, with tears, of the loved ones for whom we long." It was a sad contrast for John, Fannie, Connie, and Gertrude, to the usual house full of family and friends. But Eric was too little to be gloomy. "The gifts of love made Horace Eric wild with delight, and the dear little one's happiness made us laugh with him in spite of all. He has a motor-car, and a horse and waggon [sic], and a drum, and numerous other things dear to the heart of babyhood. So sweet, so innocent, so loving, when I look at him I can understand the meaning of the words: 'A little child shall lead them.'"[72]

Behind this welcome moment of happiness lay the pervasive misery over the election and what it indicated about the human heart. "What troubles me most is the women's vote," Gertrude wrote. "Wealthy women, who desired conscription and are enriched by the war, have won over the great majority of the mothers and other women relatives of soldiers, telling them that conscription would end the war, and bring home their boys sooner, and so the priceless mother-love has been diverted to wrong ends." She clung nevertheless to the hope that a truer kind of motherhood would prevail. "It is only for a time; yes, only for a time, thank God!" She quoted Theodora Wilson: "'I have heard the voices of the women also. Not the women – the revengeful, insane women – who cheer while the blood of youth drips under the guillotine, not the mad laughter of the chaffing girls, who cheer their brothers and lovers to deeds they hate. No, I have heard the voices of the other women, the women who see and do not fear. I have heard the voices of the Motherhood of the World!' Thank God. Thank God for the New Motherhood, the World-Motherhood, born of this terrible war. I have a drawer full of precious letters, treasured documents they are, full of love and tenderest anxiety, letters from world mothers. One is from a little girl, a world-mother too. 'Send me some leaflets, please,' she writes. 'I want to do something to end this terrible war.' That letter filled my eyes with tears and my heart with joy.' "[73]

6 Comrades of the New Womanhood: Canada's Women's Peace Crusade Versus "The Reign of Force" (1918–19)

" 'They are slaves who fear to speak
For the fallen and the weak.
They are slaves who will not choose
Hatred, scoffing and abuse,
Rather than in silence shrink
From the truth they needs must think.
They are slaves who dare not be
In the right with two or three.' "

NCF vigillers sang this verse outside the Welford Road prison in Leicester where Gertrude's brother Horace and other COs were confined. Nineteen eighteen promised to be a grim year in Britain. Prison conditions had worsened for British COs; bread rations had been cut and it was dreadfully cold that winter. In Canada, the last vestiges of hope for a negotiated settlement had disappeared with the announcement of the December 1917 election results. The conscription act was now being implemented. Gertrude began to hear dreadful stories from her friends and correspondents, whose sons were dragged away by the military authorities. A Winnipeg acquaintance of Gertrude's wrote to her:

An army of soldiers appeared at our door. My husband opened the door; they forced their way in, right through the hall, dining-room, and scanned the sitting-room. My husband said they were conscientious objectors. They threatened to take him too. They brushed me on one side, and the officer ordered a dozen lads in khaki to take my Frank out; then my other boy, Cecil, who has scarcely recovered from his illness, gave himself up to go with Frank. Oh, dear friend, will you pray for me? My dear boys; I would sooner be mourning them in their graves than that they should go and help to kill a brother man. I feel just as though my reason will go.

Gertrude would have worse to tell, as the Canadian conscription regulations were implemented.[1]

Canada's provision in the conscription law for conscientious objection was muddled; for example it exempted some Mennonites from the Military Service Act (MSA) entirely, some partially (from combatant service only), and some not at all. Conscription tribunals did not respond uniformly; some gave *de facto* temporary exemptions to the Mennonites, despite the technicalities of the law. Doukhoubours were generally exempt from the MSA altogether. Other religious groups were not exempted *en bloc*; members of religious organisations whose doctrines prohibited them from combatant service could apply as individuals for exemption on religious grounds. In the earliest months, it was often easier for COs to get exemptions as agricultural workers or on some other grounds than go through the arcane CO procedures. In April 1918 all other grounds were cancelled, because over 90 percent of men called up had claimed some exemption. The cancellation infuriated some farmers who had supported conscription on the understanding their sons would not have to go. In July 1918 an appeal court ruled that Seventh Day Adventists, Quakers, Christadelphians, Tunkers, Dunkards, and Mennonites were all religious groups whose members could qualify for exemption from combatant service. However if an individual CO from one of these groups refused some form of alternative service, which was usually under military discipline, he risked a prison sentence. Members of other religious groups not recognised as pacifist (such as Jehovah's Witnesses, known then as International Bible Students, or Pentecostals, Church of Christ, Plymouth Brethren, or, say, Baptists or Methodists) did not satisfy the CO requirements, and if they refused to join up, they faced military detention. Military commanders were supposed to find out if a CO's religious opposition was sincerely held. If it was, he was to be put into a noncombatant unit; but if he were a secular CO, or refused noncombatant service, or if the officer decided he was a fraudulent CO, he was likely to be sent to prison.[2]

If the opposition had won the election, conscription might not have gone forward; hope had been faint, but there nonetheless. Gertrude was beyond sadness about the election. "The forces of reaction have won a seeming triumph," she wrote. "So they did when Jesus of

Nazareth was murdered as a felon by the executioner's methods of those days ... It is only a seeming triumph for the scaffold. I wait the future, and though evil is indeed upon the throne, the throne itself will totter and fall." She had given up expecting anything decent from organised religion. "I believe that true Socialism ... is Christianity. The 'official' Church of that name bears no more resemblance to its Master than the Jewish nation of Christ's day did to the ideals given by Moses." She had concluded that political affairs were so far gone that revolutionary change was needed, and inevitable. Knowing that there was considerable opposition to militarism in Britain, she thought that, postwar, returned soldiers would "come back to help fight it." After the war, she wrote, "The Church that has become degraded to be the hand-maid of militaristic statesmen must be overthrown, there will be no place for such in the new world order." The prowar sermons she heard were "reptilian." For her, "A Father God and a Human Family dedicated to service by love must be our new religion – yet it is as old as Creation, for it is Eternal Truth. Away with the lie of war, with its cruel unnameable horrors – and as for those who have taken away our Freedom in Freedom's name let them be deposed in shame for the betrayal of the people's trust." As for the election, "The election does not in any way represent the people of Canada; it was won by corruption and lies, and I would rather be on the losing side with a man like Laurier than sell my soul for pence or popularity as many are doing everywhere to-day."[3]

The loss of British liberties became more pronounced in Canada. Authorities banned more publications Gertrude relied upon for news of antiwar activities, including the socialist *Seattle Daily Call*. She had been startled by the conviction "by a jury of working men" of *Canadian Forward* editor Isaac Bainbridge on a sedition charge arising from the publication of several antiwar leaflets and a couple of letters by socialist women. Gertrude said that she had read the letters several times and could not find anything seditious in them; they were "full of a very beautiful, very ardent faith in Social Democracy ... Their passionate love of their ideals reminds me of the faith of the Early Christians." If the charges of sedition were fallacious, why did the authorities persecute those who made such utterances? "The truth is fast becoming apparent to me that the authorities do not fear pacifists nearly as much as they fear the spread of the doctrine of the social revolution – no, not even in this time of war."[4]

Gertrude's networks by then were largely socialist, as mainstream journals including the local paper would not print her antiwar material. As Gertrude's Peace Crusade organising letters reached ever larger numbers of readers in Canada and the States, they sent her

clippings, copies of pamphlets, newsletters, and an array of information about economic and social inequality and its relation to the war,
civil liberties and human rights abuses, and various forms of resistance to these. Lillian Beynon Thomas, her old Manitoba suffrage
comrade, was one of the U.S. women who joined the Crusade and
sent Gertrude information about conditions there. Thomas had still
been relatively optimistic before the December 1917 election: "The
dawn is certainly breaking, and hatred and bitterness are passing
away," she had written Gertrude. But other events seemed to give no
cause for such hope. In a case that Gertrude found outrageous, Seattle
anarchist Louise Olivereau had been sentenced to ten years in prison
for violations of the U.S. conscription legislation. In 1917 she had
written a pamphlet circulated by the IWW, urging men to resist conscription. Her defence statement seemed to Gertrude like "the defence of St Paul. It is so beautiful, yet so logical and convincing. How
could men be found to hurl such a woman to prison to-day, in this
world of ours?" Gertrude had great faith in the ability of ordinary
people to find the truth and act in decency, but that faith was being
put to a test. "I used to wonder why they crucified Jesus when I was a
child. I wondered how they could possibly get anyone to put the nails
in His hands and feet. I wonder no more for those who are suffering
the modern crucifixion are those who have His spirit, people who
love the poor and oppressed, who hate and loathe with the loathing
of Jesus those who as wolves indeed batten on the lives – the very
blood of the innocent." The more Gertrude read about war profits,
the more she was convinced that the elites had pulled the wool over
peoples' eyes and conned them into tolerating unprecedented abuses.
"Here those who would be free are treated with brutal severity," she
wrote of Canada. "In the United States their treatment is worse." She
looked to England to "lead the way out. I wish you to stand true,
workers and idealists, till England becomes (as Miss Olivereau, the
poor imprisoned lady had dreamed that the United States should be)
not the Fatherland, not the Motherland, but the 'Brotherland of the
Free.'" But she questioned her belief not long after writing those
words, after reading that the British Parliament disfranchised COs,
not only during but also after the war. "I do not understand how the
British love of fair play can tolerate such things for one moment, and
I wonder sometimes what has hypnotised the British people."[5]

Gertrude's information about persecution of dissidents in the U.S.
was derived from her Crusade members and from her reading of various U.S. socialist newspapers and magazines (these are hard to trace
as she virtually never mentioned titles). Canadian wartime censorship gradually cut her off from radical publications, but she could

still count on her Crusade network for news. Her network seems to have been primarily western, although her correspondents sent news from all over, which she often passed on in her Leicester columns. One name she mentioned to her Leicester readers was Upton Sinclair, who accepted the war as necessary but argued for a just peace. He sent her a copy of his new magazine featuring an exposé of terrible prison treatment of COs in Los Angeles; Gertrude appreciated his dedication to a new international order but wrote that she intended to write to him for an explanation of why he had been "swept ... from his moorings" and tolerated the war. She also received details of the Christian Peace Crusade established in the fall of 1917 in California by pacifist ministers from fourteen denominations. Its initial meeting produced a statement of principles signed by 100 ministers. Its second, larger meeting was prohibited but eventually held anyway, and three ministers were arrested, convicted, and sentenced to six months in prison and fined $1200. The Christian Peace Crusade exemplified for Gertrude what Christian ministers of the gospel should be doing about the war. Gertrude commented,[6]

If the Christians had all been true to their Christ, if the Socialists had all believed in their international solidarity, if the women had all been true to their womanhood, this war would not have been; and if it had commenced would, long ago, have come to an end. Is it not sad? Women have been good, of course, and very, very brave; but if their courage had only gone in the way of saving as well as of enduring! But it is of no use to wring our hands and weep. We have to win back our freedom, our world-wide freedom, and there is only one way, the way of brotherhood. God grant we may yet learn to tread that way!

In January 1918 Gertrude's husband was a delegate to the annual Grain Growers convention in Brandon. On the train on the way to Brandon he saw conscripts being escorted by a constable, taken to the military authorities. He also inadvertently became privy to one of the best-kept secrets of the war. He told Gertrude, who passed this information on to her Leicester readers, that during his time in Brandon, "a train passed through Brandon station filled with Chinese on their way to work behind the trenches in France. When the train stopped it was guarded by men with loaded rifles lest one of the poor fellows should escape." Farfetched as this might have sounded, it was quite true; Britain and France had signed a secret contract with China to import Chinese labourers across the Pacific by CPR steamship and across Canada by train, hence across the Atlantic (the Panama Canal could not be used because the U.S. was not then well enough organised militarily to handle the shipments) to work as labourers in France and Belgium. To my knowledge, no one else published any information about it at the time. Gertrude found this situation still more disgusting given that Prime Minister Lloyd George had led an outcry against Boer use of Chinese labourers in the Rand mines after the Boer War, under the rallying cry opposing "Slavery under the British flag." Robert had other information about wartime responses among the farm movement. At the convention, there was lots of talk about patriotic hog raising, with reminders that there was "money in it" for farmers. "So they were willing to give their sons to be murdered and to slay, but they must have plenty of money for their 'hogs!'" Gertrude wrote. "Is it not terrible?" In fact at that point many farmers were willing to give other peoples' sons on the condition that their own would not have to go.[7]

Still, her husband returned with "some very cheering reports" about a current of dissent underlying the cheerful talk of high prices and profits to be made from the war. Two women speakers gave peace talks. Robert had a long conversation with one of these, Saskatchewan's Violet McNaughton, then president of the provincial Women Grain Growers' Association. Gertrude had read McNaughton's columns; McNaughton told Robert that she too "had known [Gertrude] through her writings to 'Woman's Century' and other Canadian periodicals." McNaughton joined the Women's Peace Crusade, bought a subscription to *Canadian Forward* (which Robert was flogging on Gertrude's behalf) and cheered Gertrude up greatly with her messages and news. McNaughton asked Robert to pass on the information that in her travels she found "a strong under-current throughout all Canada, a revulsion of feeling against the seemingly endless slaughter of men, and the curtailing of liberty, and the persecution everywhere." This was timely, given that so many people in Canada and Britain seemed to support the current situation. The Australians had just defeated a second conscription referendum; "a light in the darkness and a new vindication of the cause of Labour!" Why couldn't Canadians respond in this way? Despite Gertrude's conviction that the conscription election of December 1917 had been rigged, she also noted the general jingoism of Canadians.[8]

Gertrude wrote a long letter to McNaughton shortly after Robert's return, that illustrates the extent of her peace contacts and activities by early 1918. She said that as a result of her newspaper columns, she had "correspondents from all over the world now. Yesterday a [Women's Peace Crusade] leaflet came in signed by a lady in England," who had learned of the Crusade through Gertrude's column in the Leicester *Pioneer*. Gertrude told McNaughton about the British

Christian Peace Crusade whose founder was then in jail as a CO; the Women's Peace Crusade of Scotland and England; the Women's Peace Army of Australia which had played a part in the campaign that led to the defeat of the Australian conscription referenda. She also mentioned Canadian contacts: the Beynon sisters now in New York, Laura Hughes and other socialist women in Toronto and Vancouver. She realised she was part of a larger movement, and she appreciated being in touch with other "crusaders." However, she was isolated, living where she did. "Here, I have often felt alone … we are all so far apart … there must be very many more – if only I could find them." She was not the only one who felt alone and discouraged that year; the indefatigable Mary Chesley of Nova Scotia, convenor of the peace and arbitration department of the WCTU, commented in her report, "In concluding this meagre and discouraging report I may say that I am very uncertain as to the utility of trying to conduct this department under present adverse and difficult circumstances."[9]

Gertrude subsequently had cause to revise her belief that dissenters were treated better in Canada than the U.S. In the latter country, the law allowed COs to spend up to two weeks chained to the walls for eight hours daily and kept on bread and water diets. Further torture was illegal but not uncommon; some COs were hosed with ice water and beaten. But the situation in Canada was bad too. Stories hit the Winnipeg press in late January 1918 of torture of COs in Canadian military barracks. In one instance, three men (two International Bible Students and one Pentecostal) had been stripped and held under ice cold showers by soldiers at the Minto Street barracks in Winnipeg in an attempt to make them agree to follow orders. Robert Clegg testified at the subsequent inquiry that he was taken out of the shower, "lashed dry," dragged up and down stairs by military police, and sent to his cell. Later that day he was put back in the cold showers after which he was set on a cold stone slab. Semi-conscious, he was then dressed, dragged across a concrete floor, up a set of stairs, across another floor, and dumped into the detention quarters. He was by then unconscious. The first shower torture had been supervised by a non-commissioned officer, the second by a returned soldier. Other soldiers protested against the treatment after the fact, and one testifed at the inquiry, and although it seems clear that only a few soldiers approved of or initiated torture, the officers in charge did nothing to stop it, and under military discipline the soldiers could do nothing to prevent the officers from tolerating or ordering this. Eventually Clegg was sent to hospital, where he recovered, and his sworn affidavit was published in the Winnipeg papers. Mistreatment, casual or deliberate to the point of systematic abuse, was commonplace, and to a degree accepted as either inconsequential or deserved, but this incident went beyond the usual limits. The mainstream press had called the normal abuse "horseplay," and military authorities had dismissed it as "tomfoolery," before the details of the Clegg case were revealed, but public outcry forced investigation and cessation of the worst abuses. Gertrude's associates were involved in the protests: her husband introduced a motion passed by the Roaring River Grain Growers that they protest to the minister of militia "against the treatment meted out to the Conscienous [sic] Objectors recently at Minto St barracks Winnipeg, and further object to German Frightfulness methods being used in Canada." Borden's office sent a note to the minister of militia about the adverse publicity over the incident; the reply was that it had all been investigated and that no doubt "the case has been greatly exaggerated." Those responsible for the water torture were never disciplined for their actions. Although one of the officers involved was court martialled, the charge was dismissed and he was acquitted.[10]

The fuss was just beginning to die down from that incident when another sensational case hit the papers. Embarrassing questions were asked about treatment that led to the death of another CO, David Wells. Wells had been a burly young teamster when he went to Stony Mountain prison 22 January 1918 to serve a two-year term for refusing to fight. Something happened to Wells during three weeks in jail to cause him to go mad and refuse to speak or eat. The authorities transferred him to the Selkirk Mental Hospital where he died shortly after arrival. The authorities initially claimed he had not been ill-treated, and went mad simply because he was in prison. There was an enquiry of sorts; Methodist minister William Ivens wrote to Ottawa, and the minister of justice was asked to look into the matter. The resulting memorandum said that by the end of Wells' first week, the medical officer found him showing signs of disturbance, diagnosed as "manic depressive insanity," and less than two weeks later his condition was "very serious" and he was sent to Selkirk. The only explanation the medical officer could offer, according to this memo, was that Wells was "overcome with shame and that this preyed upon his mind until finally he broke down." The warden said that Wells "was never punished in any way." Wells had agreed to do Red Cross work, and arrangements were in train to transfer him, when he became ill. This report satisfied the government, but not Winnipeg pacifists and radicals. As Ivens had said in his letter, "His treatment must have been out of the ordinary for his death to occur from collapse within a matter of three or four weeks." Their questions were never answered.[11]

The revelations about torture of COs had prompted many people to speak out against this extreme abuse. Fred Dixon had protested in the Manitoba Legislature, saying the authorities might just as well shoot them. However, Gertrude wrote, many other "good people are silent from fear." Winona Flett Dixon told Gertrude "that many are afraid to speak out because if their opinions were known they would be dismissed from their employment; 'And you know,' she went on, 'What can one say when men have families looking to them for bread and all they need? How can we be true to ourselves, dear? If the suffering only means for ourselves, how gladly we can all bear up – but for our loved ones, and our children – oh what can we do? That is how I feel regarding many people. I know they are afraid for others' sake, not their own.'" Intimidation was a problem, when most working people were economically vulnerable and feelings ran high against those who criticised the war. Francis Marion Beynon had made a similar comment to Violet McNaughton about the results of the 1917 election: "It seems there was such a spirit of terrorism abroad that everybody was afraid to come straight out and say where they stood."[12]

William Ivens spoke out about CO mistreatment; he demanded that all be released, claimed himself to be a CO, wrote to Ottawa about an investigation, and raised the issue repeatedly in the press. When the Methodist paper *Christian Guardian* published an editorial entitled "The Vice of Pacifism," Ivens responded with a rebuttal entitled "The Ministry of Murder." He argued that murder was contrary to Christ's (and the church's) teaching, that war was murder organised by the state, and that when the state demanded war and the teaching of the church commanded peace, Christians had to choose between them. He believed that eventually the church would see it had been in error to support war, just as it had eventually seen its defence of slavery to be in error. "Then we shall see that a passionate patriotism has been mistaken for a Christ-like Christianity ... Until that day, if I must choose between ... the destroyer and Jesus the Saviour, I shall choose Jesus and say: 'Lord, what wouldst thou have me do?'"[13]

Ivens had been in touch with Gertrude since the previous year; in March 1918, a week after David Wells' death, Ivens sent Gertrude a petition to circulate, asking that the act be amended "to apply equally to all bona fide Conscientious Objectors." The complex provisions of the Military Service Act designating a variety of categories of exemptions and exceptions available to members of certain religious groups were to be replaced by a single all-inclusive provision for anyone who objected on grounds of conscience. Gertrude seems to have had help circulating the petition locally but it is not clear who was involved. Robert probably took it to his Grain Grower associates, and some signed; presumably the Minchens, Alice Cox, and a few other suffragists were still antiwar, but beyond that, I do not know the identities of her sympathisers. Gertrude wrote that she found it hard to get signatures in the valley: "The preachers have preached war here and howled for blood till the poor people are hypnotised – but we have had some signatures that have greatly encouraged and surprised us. In the City of Winnipeg amazingly large numbers have signed." Ivens was in trouble himself. His congregation was split over his socialist and pacifist views. He wrote Gertrude, "You will likely hear within the next two months that I have been forced out of the church. My days are numbered. June will see the end – at the latest. Let me congratulate you for having a brother in prison in England for this cause. It will not be in vain." Ivens was removed from his post by the Methodist Church, despite a petition signed by 1,000 socialists who testified they had been attracted to his services by his "brotherly Christian personality." Ivens was offered another local church but he refused, saying that he thought his pacifism would cause trouble there, too; he requested and was granted a year without a posting. He had wanted for some time to start a labour church; the Methodist committee apparently did not object to his plans.[14]

Ivens preached a spectacular farewell sermon to a packed church in late June, entitled "What is True Patriotism?" "I got my call to preach not from any church board but from the Mighty God of Heaven and until He takes His hands off my head I intend to keep on preaching," he said. "I can quit this pulpit but I can't quit my convictions – and I won't." He argued that civilisation was doomed unless some better methods were found to conduct international relations. "Shall we be loyal to humanity as a whole or to the little section that we call our country?" The state should express the will of the nation, but "too often it is used for the purpose of crushing the soul of the nation." It was used for wrong and "sordid ends. Consequently true patriotism becomes loyalty to the nation as a nation, and may or may not be loyalty to the state." The soul of the nation is international, based on enjoying the cultural and intellectual riches of all nations. "The realities of the nation are letters and learning, morality and religion, etc., but the realities of the state are … political, commercial, military and dynastic, or imperial [interests]. These interests are accompanied by such sentiments as honor, prestige, national dignity, etc. It is out of these state interests that wars arise." Loyalty to the state was not a legitimate demand when the state pursued ends that were disloyal to the best interests of its citizenry, he concluded. Hereafter, Ivens' preaching would take place in other settings: the following week he spoke on "The Basis of Peace" at the Labour Temple.[15]

There were other reverberations for pacifist ministers whom Gertrude admired. J.S. Woodsworth resigned from the ministry over pacifist issues. Jesus' teachings were antithetical to war, Woodsworth said, and as a Christian, he could not participate in war, or persuade others to do so. The churches were joining the state in the use of "so-called Prussian morality that might makes right, and that the end justifies the means." Horace Westwood was luckier; his Unitarian church tolerated his pacifism. William Irvine was removed from his Calgary Unitarian congregation by the denomination's headquarters in Boston, after members complained about his anticonscription views in the fall of 1917. Gertrude wrote about some of these events under the heading "The seed of the church": from the seeds planted by individual martyrdom, suffering, and courage, a new church would rise, true to the teachings of Jesus, which would help to bring about a better world. "There is going to be a new church for a new Humanity – a church beneath whose holy roof all men of every race shall gather, where the love of God and of each other shall be one love finding expression in pure and lofty service." Later that summer Gertrude gave her Leicester readers more information about the new "Labour Church," or "Creedless Church," as Ivens called it. It would be democratic in administration and in creed, as Ivens said in an address at the Labour Temple, and would not be dominated by one person, "whether he be alive or dead." Gertrude was delighted. "Personally I have long felt ... that the ... churches with which we are familiar are doomed. They no longer attract the thinking people, and many are merely servile, contemptible cringers to the State. There are good people in them all, but they are wondering and doubting and questioning more and more – as is well." These "good people" would presumably gravitate to the new church (as did a number of Horace Westwood's members), which opened in June 1918, with over 200 enthusiastic attenders at its Labour Temple service. Religious activity was very much a part of Winnipeg socialist and labour circles, as witnessed in the People's Forums, begun in 1910, which J.S. Woodsworth had called a kind of People's Church.[16]

In March 1918 and again in June, the military authorities sent Canadian COs to England along with the other Canadian soldiers; COs were sent to military camps and beaten by British soldiers to try to force them to submit to military discipline. The Winnipeg COs in the first draft were "told that they would be sent 'straight to the front,'" and had been held incommunicado in barracks for five days before leaving, "so as to have no opportunity of saying 'good-bye' to their loved ones," Gertrude wrote. Relatives of some Winnipeg COs sent telegrams to Borden asking him to stay the proceedings; Borden's office enquired and was told by the minister of militia's office that this was routine procedure; no stay was granted. A friend in Winnipeg who had seen the draftees shipped off wrote to Gertrude, "Heart-rending scenes at the Union Depot, this time the poor lads were not willing to go," although the papers reported only good cheer. The men who had been tortured at Minto Barracks were sent over with the first shipment. Gertrude had written to the Bible Students office to express her sympathy with their members' mistreatment. They wrote back saying that their members appreciated her support and " 'have been enabled not only to endure these hardships as good soldiers of the Cross, but are very happy in the thought that they have thus been deemed worthy to partake in some way in the sufferings of Christ.' " Later, Gertrude wrote she had heard that "singing hymns, [Bible Students] marched down the main street of Winnipeg, joyfully enduring the modern crucifixion. Thank God! oh thank God! for souls that refuse to be enslaved." Other COs had been "taken to the station in ambulance waggons, in handcuffs and irons, [to be] shipped over with the draft," Gertrude reported.[17]

Subsequent investigation into the treatment of Ontario CO O.K. Pimlott in the British camp revealed that he and his companions had been daily subjected to several hours of pummelling by groups of men wearing boxing gloves, ostensibly trying to force the COs to "box," generally beaten up and threatened with worse. Pimlott had been dragged by the feet over rough ground, beaten on the head, and kicked into unconsciousness. He had to be sent to hospital for an x-ray to be sure he did not have a skull fracture. Others were similarly assaulted and threatened with shooting; Robert Clegg had a rib broken by a gun butt. At the end of this treatment, the Bible Students in the group were sent to Wandsworth Prison, where they and other court martialled Canadian COs were subjected to the normal harsh treatment. This meant rotating punishment; a period of the harshest treatment (bread and water, mattress removed in the morning, empty cell, complete isolation), followed by a respite in which they got to keep their beds, and were given more than bread and water (but a diet still inadequate in quantity and composition). After a few days of improvement, they went back to the harsher stage. Some men were kept on this cycle of punishment for one hundred days and began to break down, according to a report that another CO managed to get out to the NCF.[18]

By spring 1918, as conscription abuses occupied an increasingly large proportion of the socialist press' attention, Gertrude's writing became angrier and angrier, and she appears to have become more determined to fight. Her language became furiously intemperate (for her, that is; Eric recalled that if someone said "darn," she would "practically run for the soap" to wash out the filthy mouth). This was typical of her outraged comments: " 'This war is for righteousness and human liberty,' say the ministerial worshippers of the butcher-god, with pious upward looks. They say it from their hearts doubtless, their black, blasphemous hearts, with all due solemnity. The statement is echoed by the servile press (unspeakably servile in Canada to-day). 'This war is to make the world safe for democracy,' complacently assert those who do not expect to have to take any part in the fighting. Oh! the sickening horror of it! Meanwhile, we are becoming more and more enslaved." The news that the tortured men had been sent overseas seems to have been a last straw for Gertrude and some of her associates. "It has filled us with rage against the hideous, loathsome power that is destroying everything – every priceless treasure, every holy thing, every sacred belief and hope. Our churches, the shrines to many of us of our holiest beliefs and faith, have been handed over to the devilish horror worshipped to-day as God. Oh! the blasphemy, the awfulness of it all, the mountains of dead, the armies of maimed, the dark hosts of blinded, the crowds of mad, in the name of righteousness!" She expressed this rage and disgust in a bitter poem excerpted below, "Modern Idols":

> "The heathen, in his blindness, Bows down to wood and stone."
> – Missionary Hymns.
> We do not kneel to the ancient gods, We are wiser and greater now!
> We have made us idols of tempered steel And to these to-day we bow.
> The iron monsters that belch forth death Are the gods to whom we pray,
> And in these we trust with a mighty faith In this "enlightened" day.
>
> And apart, afar, stands the murdered Christ, All crowned with His wreath
> of thorn,
> And if men see Him they turn away – Still turn, with a look of scorn;
> While those who tread in His holy steps Are bound in our prison-hells;
> And still in the name of the murdered Christ We are ringing the sweet
> church bells!
>
> Have we learned from the "heathen" juggernaut? From the Moloch of
> ancient fame?
> With the added skill of our modern day We have put such gods to shame.
> We crush out lives with our idol tanks, Our machine-gun gods are great;
> We have cast down Christ from His Throne of Love, Enthroning the
> Moloch-State!

Then was it a dream that the angels sang In that beautiful long ago?
That cherished tune that we love to sing When the earth is wrapped in
  snow?
Oh, only a dream that a Saviour died That a precious race might live?
Look down once more, come back again Dear patient Christ – forgive![19]

Mounting protests against sending Canadian COs overseas (and
the fact that they were also considered dangerous centres of propaganda who might influence other soldiers), led the Canadian government to reconsider its action and no more were sent. Near the end of
1918 the Canadian COs were all brought back home.[20]

The bad prison conditions of COs in England had brought increased protests from prominent Britons. In the summer of 1917, Margaret Hobhouse, a prowar Tory whose son Stephen was an absolutist
CO, published a pamphlet (which had actually been ghostwritten by
NCF co-chair Bertrand Russell) entitled "I Appeal Unto Caesar," and
helped to organise a public campaign by leading citizens to pressure
the government to lessen mistreatment and harsh sentences for COs.
Thanks in part to these efforts, anti-CO hostility diminished somewhat, and the authorities were shamed into a compromise policy that
"medically unfit" COs would be released; technically, released into
the military reserves, but in fact allowed to go home. However, many
who were medically unfit were not released, and most COs were not
sufficiently ill to fall into that category in any case, according to the
official definitions. Judging from who was released, only those who
might otherwise die in prison were sufficiently unfit. Although in
theory COs were permitted to ask for a re-hearing of their cases, in
practice this did them little good. Probably the most useful change
was a series of improvements in the daily conditions of those who
had served more than twelve months. They were allowed to receive
and write letters every two weeks instead of monthly (but the letters
were shorter), they could have monthly visits in private (if there were
private rooms), they could talk to each other during their daily two
brief exercise periods (but not at other times), and they could have
their own books (as long as they were not on current events).[21]

Gertrude reported to Canadian readers that a petition signed by
1,231 clergy asking for the release of British COs had been given to
Parliament; she took this as a hopeful sign. Noting that various con-
cessions had been made in prison conditions, she saw "powerful …
influences ranging on the side of those who are truly fighting militarism by refusing to submit to it." But it did not mean that the COs
were "giving in and becoming more reasonable," as had been reported in some Canadian papers. "Please do not believe that, it is

untrue. They are stronger, braver, firmer than ever," she wrote. Her intense pride in Horace's "faithfulness in this dark hour to the ideals of Christianity and Humanity" was an important source of strength for her. She wrote that she received letters from all over Britain, Canada and the States, asking about him and the CO cause. Horace had passed his second Christmas in prison, the day made happier by carollers singing outside the walls. The singers had come faithfully every Sunday since April 1917; Leicester had one of the longest-standing NCF choirs in the country. One of its members wrote to urge other NCF locals to sing weekly, not just at holidays, as it made such a difference to CO morale, and was also a very effective propaganda method. "Providing one is able to stand within hearing distance of the ugly walls, it does not take many voices to send a 'volley' of music 'over the top,'" he wrote, and the group had selected "hymns and tunes having best carrying power for open-air singing."[22]

Horace was released briefly from prison in February 1918 after he completed his third court martial sentence (eighteen months, commuted to twelve). During Horace's cat-and-mouse break between his third and fourth courts martial, he wrote to Gertrude, "All the military and civil authorities can do is make me conscious of a power within which is easily supreme over all un-toward circumstances that surround me." Horace sent Gertrude a special gold bracelet in the shape of a chain and padlock. His fourth court martial sentenced him to two years at hard labour. "He is unconquered and unconquerable," Gertrude wrote proudly. But heroic responses to evil did not mitigate it. "I used to think this a very beautiful world. Now there are times when I wonder why it was all created." The mother of another CO serving a two-year sentence at Stony Mountain prison wrote to Gertrude, "I sometimes feel so bitter … It is all so cruel." Gertrude concluded it was still better to be Pilate's prisoner than Pilate, the one who suffered than the one who caused suffering, better to be an outcast from this kind of a world than "to share in its blood-stained honours." She wrote about the certainty of justice (and perhaps an element of retribution), "Let it comfort us to know that the world-rulers of to-day … are to stand at the judgement-bar of History with Pilate and Judas."[23]

Although there were various individual and group actions of resistance within British prisons, such as work stoppages, hunger strikes, or refusal to abide by the silence rule, I have found no evidence that they occurred at Leicester prison or that Horace was involved in them. However, in March 1918 Fred wrote that Horace was refusing to eat meat. Was it a sudden addition of meat to the prison diet that gave Horace the occasion to refuse? Not likely: meat (albeit in extremely limited quantities) had been there all along. A "special war diet" was introduced in the spring of 1917 for all prisoners. Breakfast was three ounces of bread with a bit of margarine and a pint of oatmeal; supper was a pint of cocoa, three ounces of bread with marge, and an ounce of cheese. Dinners varied, but little meat appeared: Monday, two ounces of fat bacon, Wednesday and Saturday, ten ounces of suet pudding; Thursday, five ounces of boiled boneless meat in a cup of its broth; Sunday dinner featured five ounces of tinned bully beef. There may have been symbolic (political) elements at work in Horace's refusal. Some COs believed that they should reject improvements in their conditions, as acceptance would imply complicity in various thin-edge-of-the-wedge situations designed to persuade COs to accept government proposals that were technically or symbolically a form of cooperating or giving in to alternative service. Perhaps the authorities offered more meat and Horace refused all, to make a point. It could also well be that Horace had been previously inclined to vegetarianism. Horace's replacement as Leicester NCF secretary (and future wife) was Ella Stevens, according to a 1917 list of contacts, and her address was given as "c/o Cafe Vegetaria." I asked family members if they recalled anything about this question. Horace's great nephew Keith Twilley wrote that he was "sure that Horace and Ella were vegetarians." Whatever the case, in 1918 Fred wrote, "He never did have much liking for [meat], but under the circumstances he needs all the nourishment he can get." At this point, Fred said, he was more worried about his mother than about Horace, who had shown he could take care of himself. Fred had tried again to get Horace released, this time on the grounds of Eliza's ill health, but his commanding officer had not forwarded Fred's letter to the war office. Fred did not know whether he had just been too busy or had forgotten, what with the man's impending marriage, or if he had been unwilling to send it. "There is not much use in trying to get any grievance adjusted" when soldiers had to write via their commanders, he told Edith.[24]

In late March 1918 the Women's Labour League invited Gertrude to Winnipeg to speak at the Labour Temple on "The New World Motherhood." This was the "first public meeting" of the Crusade; Gertrude found the labour affiliations particularly appropriate, she wrote. She stayed with Helen and George Armstrong, who filled her in on the latest news and antiwar doings. Gertrude wrote one Leicester column from Winnipeg, the morning of her Labour Temple talk. She described a cartoon and poem shown her by the Armstrongs that had been printed in the Australian socialist paper from Victoria, *The Messenger*, which had featured largely in the anticonscription campaign for the second Australian conscription referendum; conscription had just been defeated by an even larger margin. The poem portrayed a mother's horror when God's voice told her that her "yes" vote had meant a "grim death-warrant of doom." The mother asks her little son to pray for her soul "that the scarlet stain may be white again / In God's great judgement roll." Just Gertrude's cup of tea: she asked her women readers to "read it and read it till the truth of the message is burned into your souls. If we are silent and acquiescent, we are equally guilty." Helen Armstrong told Gertrude that "the women here who voted for 'Union Government and Conscription' are now horrified at what they have done. But it is too late."[25]

The theme of general responsibility for the horrors of the war was not restricted to Gertrude's set; near the end of 1917, some Presbyterians who had supported the war, conscription, and Union government, seem to have had second thoughts. Their report, *The War and the Christian Church*, echoed Gertrude's point that it was mainstream middle-class people who were responsible for the war, in that they had benefited from social and economic and political systems that caused it, and they did not rise up and stop it. This report apparently had little effect. Religious, or for that matter, secular antiwar rhetoric seems to have touched the already converted and been shrugged off by others. Yet the antiwar activists kept trying, as witness this event.[26]

By now Gertrude was moving in the most elevated of antiwar circles; also on the same bill at the Labour Temple were William Ivens and Fred Dixon. Gertrude's speech was a big success, and she got many signatures on her Women's Peace Crusade leaflets. "We organized for active work," she wrote. The trip was important for personal contacts and support. Gertrude met other activists; the evening before her talk, she had supper with the family of a Women's Labour League member whose two oldest boys had been taken away by military police. The day after her talk, the Armstrongs were "besieged with telephone messages asking to see me, and until my return home I hardly had a free moment." William Ivens visited, as did Horace Westwood, "who has sympathised from the first in my great grief for my brother. He is a very scholarly man of most attractive personality." She had lunch with the Dixons, and Sunday dinner at the home of Arthur Puttee, editor of the *Voice* and member of Horace Westwood's Unitarian congregation. Sunday evening Helen Armstrong had a reception for Gertrude, where she heard more stories about boys hauled away and resistance activities. She left "full of faith," greatly buoyed up by the knowledge that there was an active Crusade group nearby.[27]

Gertrude continued to issue appeals for Crusade support in her *Voice* and *Canadian Forward* columns. To *Forward* readers she wrote of

Horace's two-year sentence after his fourth court martial, David Wells' death, and the certainty that "many other boys are being imprisoned. Many more will be." Beyond COs, "How little we are doing to preserve the ideal of liberty and freedom of conscience." She knew it was not easy to make the commitment to act. "Once more I appeal to the mother-hearts. Please come forward and help; there is so much to do. If you are afraid – and I know the obstacles, just be brave and arise in the strength of loving womanhood and the way will all be clear. Not only is that my experience, but it is the experience of all who follow the inward light." This sounds a bit blithe to a modern reader, but it is useful to remember that it was just a few years since Gertrude had first dared to wear her "votes for women" button in public, in an atmosphere generally supportive of the suffrage movement, when that button expressed the majority opinion. The obstacles were greater now, and more strength needed to speak out. But the stakes were higher too: "The poor suffering boys in the trenches, in the ambulance wagons, in the hospitals, and lying untended on the field of woe and death, cry to you – the boys in the prisons, brutally treated, starved, insulted, chained – cry to you; the poor boys in the asylums, driven mad by war, cry to you. Will you not answer? In the holy name of motherhood, I appeal!"[28]

Her poem "The Call" ("Dedicated to the Women's Crusade"), published in *Voice* early in April 1918, further explored this theme:

> They are calling from the trenches, where the war god's ghastly breath
> Scorches youth and hope and beauty, changing all life's joy to death:
> Mothers! will you heed the pleading – will you listen to the call?
> Will you rise and save your children from the war god's deadly thrall.
>
> They are crying in their anguish, they are bleeding as they lie.
> Were they made for hate and slaughter, born in agony to die?
> Were they given in their beauty – yea, in God's own image – all,
> That in life's fair, hallowed dawning they should fight, and fighting fall?
>
> By the sunny hair of childhood, by the baby smiles and tears,
> By the angel-like caresses, by the touching baby fears;
> By the joy God gave you with them, by the memories sweet and fair,
> Will you yield them to destruction, in that awful "Over There?"
>
> Some are hurled to court and prison, some are doomed for Christ to die,
> If they dare to front the Moloch in the name of liberty;
> Shall we serve the crimson war god, with his hands defiled with blood?
> Mothers! let us bow in reverence at the throne of Christ, the good.

They are calling, they are calling, from the dungeon and the field,
We will rise and march to save them, we will never, never yield!
By the sacred name of Mother, by the love we bear them all
Let us answer "We are coming, children, we have heard the call."[29]

Gertrude saw her special constituency as the motherhood of the new humanity (the broader motherhood having let her down), and it was on that basis that she usually wrote. She sought to convert the undecided, heat up the lukewarm, and to move her readers to action by bringing new information about injuries to her readers and to others, in both cases requiring a response. In March 1918 she wrote to "mothers of Canada" about the dangers of the militarisation of the school curriculum. In England, a teacher had been fired for refusing to use Navy League materials for her lessons. Cadet Corps were widespread for fourteen- or fifteen-year-old boys: a sort of pre-enlistment military program to do some early recruiting and training. The Leicester school board had issued a compulsory military education handbook, arguing that the skills needed in warfare could be taught under traditional educational rubrics: mapreading as geography, practical training with bombs, guns, grenades as a form of applied science. Bayonet drill should be regularly taught as part of physical education, and trench drill: jump into a trench, approach a sack representing the enemy, use your bayonet to stab him in the throat. Gertrude reminded readers that many people argued for military training in Canadian schools; she thought mothers would find this abhorrent, as she did. The prowar side claimed this would be the last war, but this training would make it impossible to teach boys the "ideals of humanity and brotherhood." Such training would lay the groundwork for a world of "universal hatred." Gertrude recalled that at the beginning of the war, much had been made of the horrible "militarisation of German children" as an example of the wickedness of Prussianism and a reason why Germany must be beaten down. "To-day our enemy stands revealed," she wrote. "The enemy is neither Germany nor Austria, the enemy is the spirit of cruelty and conquest developing in the conditions of war and militarism, the oppression of the mother and of all weak and unprotected persons – the institution of slavery in every form." The seeds of militarism could be planted by the schools if this were not prevented. "We are enfranchised women and have power to-day to make our demands for righteousness," she reminded readers.[30]

Not all news from Britain was discouraging. Discontent had increased to a degree alarming to the government. There had been demonstrations and strikes about food shortages and high prices, including some rent strikes, some of which were led by WPC women, and although the authorities blamed the food problem on German submarines, profiteering was the more popular explanation. There was increasing support for a negotiated peace, and not just with the radicals or working classes. The newly ensconced Bolsheviks had published secret agreements about postwar division of the world among the allies, which gave credibility to antiwar groups' arguments that Britain was not an innocent defender of the good and the right in this war, but a nasty imperialist like the enemy. The government planned to conscript engineers and to raise the general conscription age to fifty-one, a potential last straw from which a general strike might result, uniting antiwar and labour groups. This fear was treated seriously by the government, who took pains to appeal to various shades of opinion. Lloyd George had campaigned on promises he would extract reparations from Germany; that was attractive to those who wanted revenge or money. In January 1918 his government had cleverly published a statement on war aims that echoed that of the Labour Party and sounded quite reasonable compared to the previous aim of total conquest; this took some of the wind out of the sails of the antiwar groups. Key politicians also managed to keep Labour in the coalition government and helped keep the lid on within the Labour Party. The introduction of food rationing in March 1918 also lessened the likelihood that discontent would spill over into something more threatening to the government.[31]

Nonetheless there were still possibilities not only for a negotiated peace but for much more radical social change, or so thought hopeful activists of the various and overlapping peace groups. Gertrude wrote for Canadian readers of the large turnouts at British Women's Peace Crusade meetings, part of the multi-group campaign for a negotiated peace. Several prominent peace women with socialist, suffrage, and labour backgrounds were working virtually full time on the Peace Crusade campaign. At Leeds, 4500 women passed a resolution for negotiation, after a speech by Theodora Wilson Wilson; Charlotte Despard (whose brother was a leading general) and Ethel Snowden were on the road organising and speaking, and a huge demonstration was being planned for July in London to conclude the campaign. In the event the demonstration was banned by the authorities, and by summer 1918 the war situation had changed in ways that supported pro-rather than antiwar sentiments in Britain. The March 1918 Treaty of Brest-Litovsk allowed Germany to concentrate all her efforts on the Western Front, and British war losses increased still more. This fuelled the desire for revenge or at least some definite victory. Bertrand Russell had concluded by this time, as he entered prison to serve his six-month sentence for violating the Defence of the Realm Act (DORA) regulations in an article he wrote in the NCF *Tribunal* that the public mood had changed sufficiently that there was no longer any use in the NCF trying to overthrow militarism and end the war. However, that the already-appalling war losses, the possibility that the Allies could not gain a clear victory, and the unsettled economic and political situation still left room for some support for a negotiated settlement was encouraging to peace activists.[32]

There were hopeful signs in other countries; an international women's conference planned to take place at Berne, the peace agitation of women in France (who were accused of causing French soldiers' mutinies at the front late in 1917), the continued antiwar efforts of German socialist women such as Clara Zetkin and Rosa Luxembourg. German women were involved in a huge munitions workers strike in late January 1918, demanding peace without reparations, and workers' participation in peace negotiations. Gertrude's source of information about these events included the *Canadian Forward* which reprinted in July 1918 a German Socialist Women's antimilitarist manifesto that had been circulated in their own country just before the new year. It castigated the kaiser and the war party for not publishing the details of secret treaties and the Bolshevik peace initiative, and called for a negotiated peace and the withdrawal of German troops from Russian, Belgian, and French territory.[33]

Gertrude's views on the degradation of morality caused by the war differed from those of mainstream feminist writers, who tended to condemn soldiers for licentiousness, blame loose women for causing temptation, or blame soldiers for ruining the virtue of naive young women. The April 1918 issue of *Woman's Century* featured several stories on lowered moral standards. Germany was claimed to have millions of illegitimate births, France was licensing and regulating prostitution to lessen venereal disease. But Gertrude pointed out that there had been "strenuous opposition" in these countries to such assaults upon womanly ideals by "leading women" who had "recognised, as we do, that war and militarism are the bitterest of all foes of womanhood, wifehood, motherhood, and the home." It was not surprising that womanly ideals should also be war casualties, she said. As long as most people supported war, "what is the use of complaining about what is merely one of its results?" And why were women not also protesting the sacrilege against the "bodies of men, made in God's image" of the murders on the battlefield? "Shall we who drive them to the hell of war condemn their departure from our standard of morals? Ours is the responsibility, not only for the blighted purity, but for the maimed forms, the shattered brains, the sightless eyes." Next to this, protest against soldiers' temptations was indecent, especially "from men and women who uphold conscription of men for murder, by which they are hurled into forced commission of every crime beneath the sun." Gertrude had no patience for condemnation of the victims, male or female, as if they were the cause of the purity crimes that pious militarists inveighed against: "As for me I hold the nations themselves as entirely responsible for all the evils they condemn, for the brutalising of the human mind and spirit, for the callousness that looks unappalled on the spectacles of millions and millions of murdered and maimed; yes, and for the very horror over which they raise up hypocritical hands of dismay. What we have sown we must reap. It is the eternal law."[34]

Gertrude cheered from the sidelines during the Winnipeg workers' strikes in May of 1918. She described the situation to Leicester readers: the country was full of "seething discontent," farmers furious about broken conscription promises, Quebec rebellious, and labour fed up with inflation and profiteering. The firefighters went out first, then the telephone operators; other unions went out in sympathy. Some hoped that their general strike would spread across the whole country. The well-off citizenry were aghast, and the daily papers echoed their outrage; strikers were called traitors. Some suggested that striking firefighters should be rounded up for military service since their exemptions were based on their essential jobs; if they were refusing to perform their duties, they no longer should be exempted. Middle class ladies' organisations made use of the 600-strong Women's Volunteer Reserve to scab as telephone operators, and provide other forms of antistrike support. This was not new; the Local Council of Women had opposed women's strikes the previous year, and had called the police to arrest picketers during the Woolworth clerks' strike in June 1917. The ladies of the Next-of-Kin Association had Helen Armstrong arrested for distributing "rubbish" – a pamphlet by constitutional expert John Ewart. Gertrude was, of course, solidly on the side of the strikers. "Workers ... are certainly all over the world to-day beginning to understand their enormous power," she wrote. "'Patriotism,' so sacred, so grand and so holy, is to-day like 'Liberty,' in the days of the French Revolution, made the excuse of the vilest crimes, the most cruel and shameful suppression. The economic cause of war is ever becoming more and more apparent to me. I do not think I ever understood it till it was revealed by this war ... We shall emerge from this 'war for freedom' in abject slavery – yet, no! we shall not all." Some still fought.[35]

Gertrude had by now lost much of her earlier optimism that women's internationalism could survive the war. She "felt great disappointment" that the majority of "women of the world have so ardently supported this cruel war." Many of the problems of the day, such as " 'Food Conservation' [which] is fashionable now," could be solved "if the Red Cross energy and the knitting energy and all the other energy wasted to-day to help along the cause of destruction could only be turned into the right channels." But the opposite seemed to be happening. Both governments and militarist women's groups worked to prevent international contact. A patriotic German women's group (Order of the Fatherland) had recently sent the kaiser a petition against peace negotiations. Their Canadian counterpart, the Imperial Order of the Daughters of the Empire (IODE), had passed a resolution threatening to pull out of the National Council of Women of Canada if the latter did not "repudiate all connection with women of the enemy countries, not only until after the war," Gertrude reported to Leicester readers, "but 'until in the judgment of right-thinking people it is wise or safe to resume connection.' "[36]

If Gertrude had known details of behind-the-scenes discussions in NCWC executive meetings about the resolution embodying the IODE ultimatum to the NCWC, she would have been even more upset. The original wording of the IODE resolution had been too harsh for the NCWC executive, beginning "Whereas the object of the National Council of Women is the furtherance of the Golden Rule to Society, custom and law, and whereas the German nation has repeatedly broken the Golden Rule and has expressed no repentance." The NCWC had been staunchly prowar from the beginning and was not about to consort with the enemy, but that preamble was unseemly. The eventual compromise wording of the preamble referred to wanting to set straight misunderstandings about contact with enemy women through the ICW. The resolution reiterated that there had been no contact, and said there would be no postwar contact with enemy women through the International Council because it would then be made up of National Councils from allied and neutral countries only. If not, the NCWC "would not remain in federation with the International Council." This version of the resolution was discussed at the annual meeting, and the point was made that the issue was moot in any case, because the German NCW had resigned from the International Council of Women when the war began, and the ICW was more or less in abeyance during the war. The annual meeting eventually passed a resolution that the NCWC would act postwar in concert with the other NCWs of the Empire. As Henrietta Muir Edwards explained, the NCWC decided it should wait until the Empire decided its postwar policy, not decide "now independent of the rest of the women of the Empire, what they shall or shall not do after the war."

The IODE withdrew; it remained one of the more rabid groups until well into the next decade. Incidents such as these made Gertrude treasure all the more news that the Austrian suffragists sent congratulations to British women when the latter obtained a partial enfranchisement, and said they looked "forward to the time when they could 'once more work together for the healing of humanity.' "[37]

By the summer of 1918 Gertrude's suggestions for women's action had become more drastic than walking out of blasphemous religious services. She wrote in her Leicester column that after the cancellation of farm sons' exemptions from conscription in the spring of 1918, fifty local young men had been sent off from the Swan River station. "Fifty boys, every one of whom is more than needed here, apart from the wickedness and cruelty of sending boys to be massacred to save lives that are far less valuable. I have come to the conclusion that if this is to go on it is time the women demanded to go right to the trenches, for women are not worth the name if they wish men to die for them. I should think that everyone, of every age, and of either sex, would wish to be there if it be true that all this horror is necessary." On the one hand this was a case of chickens coming home to roost, for she had seen farmers support conscription on the condition that their sons would not be affected: "Hurried notices were printed everywhere, in all agricultural papers of every class, and wherever there were farmers, to the effect that no farmer or farmer's son working on the farm would be conscripted, so the alarm was allayed and the Union Government swept itself into power." (Farmers belatedly protested, 5,000 of them marching on Parliament Hill in mid-May 1918, but to no avail.) On the other hand, some Quaker women in England had made a similar declaration: they did not wish men to defend them; whatever happened, women and men would face it together, trusting in God. Gertrude had written before of her worry that women would not be worthy of the sacrifice made by the soldiers in combat. And although she found the war repugnant, it was logical to conclude that if it was right and necessary for anyone to die, all should take that risk. (Francis Marion Beynon had written about a similar, albeit more limited, proposal: there should be a referendum on a proposed war, and if it passed, any man who voted yes should go and fight.) Gertrude's conclusion was consistent with her belief that motherhood's purpose was to preserve and protect: it was mothers who should face harm, precisely in order that their children should not. Some of her visions were daunting, but presumably symbolic: for example she wrote in June 1918, "I saw a vision as the armies met / A woman stood with calm and fearless eyes, / Like the Madonna of the ancient art, / Gentle and strong, and in her loving, wise; / Yes, as the armies met she stood between / A vision of sublimest womanhood – / and looking down the future, Hope returned. / I was not dreaming – I had understood. / For so shall women stand / Command Peace! / And all Earth's strife and cruel war / Shall cease."[38]

Later that summer, Gertrude heard of an attempt by British peace women to persuade the authorities to release COs who had served long terms, and allow women to go to prison in their place. Gertrude had written on several occasions that women should be prepared to protect their children, rather than send them off to be injured or killed, or to harm other women's children. Her poem, "A Call to Women," expressed this view.

> Will you stand with me at the portal now, As the Dawn o'er spreads the sky
> For light, and for love and for liberty Prepared for your faith to die?
> Will you stand with me neath the Standard White That gathers beneath its shade
> The men and women of every realm In God's own image made?
>
> Will you stand with me, though the tempests lower? We shall hear the "Peace be still"
> Of the Loving One who was done to death On the brow of a cursed hill.
> We may bear like Him the cruel scorn Of a blood-mad angry crowd
> Will you stand with me for Humanity While the war-cry rages loud?
>
> Will you stand with me for the babes unborn? I plead from my breaking heart,
> Our boys are crushed neath the Juggernaut In anguish we bear our part –
> Shall we rise from grief with our faces calm To build a sad world anew?
> Will you stand with me for a world at peace? My sisters, I call to you.
>
> Will you stand with me neath the Flag of Hope Emblazoned with Love and Joy?
> Will you stand with me, though your heart be torn For your loved and dying boy?
> Will you stand with me. Must I stand alone While the battle rages high,
> Oh: come to the help of a war-torn world Prepared for Truth to die.

This note followed the poem: "A petition is being prepared to be presented to the Imperial Parliament by women desiring to go to prison as substitutes for conscientious objectors. Many Canadian boys are now in prison in England. Will any desiring to sign petition please write to me at once."[39]

Gertrude meant her ideas about maternal caring to be taken literally, that is, if there were opportunities for women to carry out some concrete action, albeit a risky one, she expected that they should be willing to do so. This was a chance for women to put their protestations of motherly protectiveness into practice. This petition to the British Parliament cited as their precedent a Quaker offer of 1659 to substitute for prisoners of conscience. The petitioners pointed out that it was merely an accident of sex or age which had kept them out of prison. Gertrude explained to Canadian readers that she had been sent a copy because the originators thought that Canadian women might like to have the chance to be included as substitutes for Canadian COs. The Canadian response was scant; women did not queue up to go to prison in place of COs. To be fair, their prison conditions were not well known, most of them had only been in prison for a few months at this point, and it may have seemed too far-fetched a scheme to take seriously. Francis Marion Beynon was among those who offered to go; most of the women who sent their names in were from the States. Gertrude knew, she said, that "some ... cannot go to prison, but others can" and everyone could attempt to fight militarism. She urged her readers to further efforts.[40]

In a more practical vein, Gertrude's columns suggest that she tried to encourage support like that of the NCF for prisoners of conscience. She wrote that Women's Crusade member Minnie Hardin, whose son the Reverend Lloyd Hardin was one of the clergy imprisoned for starting the Christian Peace Crusade in California, was caring for Lloyd's child and visiting and taking food to him in prison. Gertrude tried to initiate similar efforts on behalf of western Canadian COs; she wrote to the governor of Stony Mountain prison to obtain permission to send them books or "comforts," but this was refused. She had publicised the details of the trials and prison sentences of *Canadian Forward* editor Isaac Bainbridge, who like many imprisoned radicals had been shocked by prison conditions. Gertrude passed on his request that Canadians protest not only on behalf of prisoners of conscience, but for "all our unfortunate brothers and sisters in the prisons of Canada."[41]

On 2 August 1918 the new *Western Labor News*, edited by William Ivens, took over the place formerly filled by Arthur Puttee's *Voice*. Puttee had regularly printed social gospellers' views and news. Since Winnipeg was a veritable social gospel think-tank, and religiously based perspectives were prominent in local socialist and labour activities, these had occupied many column inches. Puttee's paper had remained the labour and socialist voice until the civic workers' and general sympathetic strike of May 1918. Puttee had been sympathetic to the workers and had been involved in negotiating a settlement with the firefighters that would have avoided the strike, but this had been sabotaged by antilabour Winnipeg City Councillors. Puttee had criticised the decision to strike as IWW tactics; he thought they should have tried arbitration first, mainly for strategic reasons. This had infuriated some leading radicals in the trades council, who had grudges against Puttee from earlier days, related to factional struggles over the efficacy of using political action such as electoral politics for social change. Old enemies from the SPC had persuaded the trades council to get Ivens to edit a strike paper called *Labor News*, saying Puttee's was not a true labour paper. Soon after the strike the trades council fired Puttee and set up Ivens as editor of its new paper *Western Labor News* (*WLN*). Although accounts of these events do not identify other current grievances against Puttee, these may have existed. Isaac Bainbridge thought that Puttee had not taken a strong enough antiwar line, for example. He wrote to Gertrude, "I feel sure that Mr Ivens' valuable services in the position of Editor will do much to strengthen the militarist opposition in contradiction to the war policy of the 'Voice.'" Ivens' editorial approach was representative of the Winnipeg SDP antiwar group, a mix including radical Social Gospellers, maternalist feminist socialist pacifists, labour, and international socialists. An early issue of the new paper featured an article by Francis Marion Beynon on "The New Womanhood," written at Ivens' request.[42]

There is a gap in Gertrude's published writings in the fall of 1918, for reasons varying by publication. The Leicester *Pioneer* changed hands at the end of August 1918; the new editor referred to a certain ambiguity in the previous editor's position on the war, and said this would not appear in the new *Pioneer*, although he claimed not to be wholly prowar and supported a negotiated peace. He printed not one word of Gertrude's. No doubt she continued to correspond with those numerous Leicester readers from the *Pioneer* and the *Midland Free Press* who had written to her over the years, but she no longer had an English forum for her views. In the case of the two Canadian papers in which she published, the last date for her articles in the *Western Labor News* is 28 September 1918, and her last *Canadian Forward* article appeared in the 24 August 1918 issue. The likeliest explanation for this gap is the stepped-up suppression of dissent brought about by a series of Orders in Council under the War Measures Act, issued in the fall of 1918.[43]

Although the government had been greatly concerned by the vehemence and popularity of labour and socialist criticism of conscription and of the war in general, it had stuck to harassment of individuals and refrained from any wholesale repression until after the December 1917 election put the Union government officially in power. Ross McCormack points out that the Press Censor had wanted to shut down the BC *Federationist* and the *Western Clarion*, but had contented himself with raiding the B.C. SDP's *Victoria Messenger* in July 1917, due to fears of "disastrous" reactions. The spring 1918 Orders in Council that had established political censorship and prohibited "sedition," or virtually any criticism of the war effort, had been supplemented in September and October by others such as PC2384 outlawing fourteen radical groups including the SDP, to which most of the antiwar radicals of Gertrude's acquaintance belonged. It is not clear whether the Order was really intended to apply to the SDP. Correspondence in the Borden papers indicates that while the Order itself included the SDP, Senator Gideon Robertson said the SDP was not meant to be among the banned groups. Privy Council president Newton Rowell, who had been out of town when the Order was passed, and agriculture minister Thomas Crerar protested the inclusion and suggested the Order be modified. They (and various editors) pointed out that the SDP was a legitimate political party, similar to the Labour Party of Great Britain which was represented in the Mother Country's coalition government. Indeed, much of the SDP's platform was taken directly from the British Labour Party. Nevertheless the ban was not immediately lifted. Public Safety Director C.H. Cahan, an extreme reds-under-the-beds fanatic who had been commissioned by Borden in May 1918 to produce a report on radicalism and then appointed in September 1918 to put his recommendations into practice, successfully led the campaign against the SDP, whom he considered "the chief exponents of German propaganda throughout Canada." Soon after the Order, the authorities raided and smashed the Winnipeg SDP office, part of a series of raids of offices and homes of targeted radicals. The last issue of the *Canadian Forward* was published 24 September 1918; it was declared prohibited on 5 October. Although the Toronto SDP disbanded the party and got rid of seditious literature in its possession, forty-four Toronto socialists, including Bainbridge, were arrested in raids on 20 October 1918.[44]

Gertrude had written some of the articles that Cahan and others thought too dangerous to be allowed. Cahan quoted from one of Gertrude's *Canadian Forward* pieces in a memo arguing it was imperative to retain the ban the against the SDP and the *Forward*. His choice is surprising as it was one of her milder pieces. This was the excerpt as Cahan quoted it (he omitted some phrases which I have added in square brackets): "The election has passed. The forces of reaction have won a seeming triumph. So they did when Jesus of Nazareth was murdered as a felon by the executioner's methods of those days. So did they [they did in Spain] when Ferer was shot at dawn; and in America when John Brown died for the slaves. It is only a seeming triumph for the scaffold. [I wait the future, and though evil is indeed on the throne, the throne itself will totter and fall.]"[45]

Although a number of Gertrude's pieces were overtly socialist and some could justifiably be considered revolutionary by the authorities, even those expressing the mildest socialism, when combined with strong pacifism, would have been considered a threat to the war effort, and violated various of the War Measures Act Orders in Council. Indeed it is worth remembering that a reprint of British NCF co-founder Fenner Brockway's speech, explaining his reasons for conscientious objection, was one of the seditious publications that earned Isaac Bainbridge prison sentences. The *Western Labor News* fared a bit better, in that it was not shut down. The Press Censor warned Ivens that if he continued to publish pacifist or revolutionary articles his paper would be prohibited. Ivens complied with these restrictions, but the authorities were not satisfied. There was considerable pressure for the Press Censor to outlaw the paper, but the government was afraid of the consequences if it attacked the Winnipeg Trades Council (whose official paper the WLN was) and did not take the next step. Nevertheless for Gertrude's purposes, it may as well have. She was effectively silenced by the end of September 1918.[46]

Because Gertrude's columns were suppressed and her personal papers did not survive, it is difficult to know how she responded to and was involved in some of the remarkable events of late 1918 and 1919. The flu epidemic hit the Swan River Valley by October and killed at least one of her Roaring River neighbours. The end of hostilities was announced on 11 November 1918; various accounts of people's reactions say that "relief" dominated. The Winnipeg labour movement, like other antiwar activists, had expected that repressive wartime measures would be lifted after the armistice, but they were not. In some respects they became more severe, and in response, various labour and socialist groups became more outspoken and radical. Gertrude would have sympathised entirely with her comrades' frustration and determination to restore (or more accurately, to achieve) democracy, in the events that led up to the general strike of 1919, which her son Eric told me she had enthusiastically supported.[47]

Other issues, too, would have captured her interest. Alberta feminists led an unsuccessful campaign to get a woman appointed as a member of the Canadian peace delegation to negotiate the Treaty of Versailles. They suggested Louise McKinney, Nellie McClung, or Rose Henderson. Not all women's organisations were in favour. For example the Winnipeg Local Council of Women prowar leaders objected, saying that they did not think there were any qualified women in the country; Christina Murray wrote to Violet McNaughton (who helped to organise the Saskatchewan campaign) asking disapprovingly, "Are the women of each country to ask for representation – surely that would be impossible." Women's groups from Alberta to Nova Scotia sent telegrams to Ottawa in support of the request, upon which Borden did not act. There was also a campaign led by militarist and conservative eastern feminists to establish a Women's Party, which the westerners rejected out of hand. The westerners were opposed to gender separatism, but there were much deeper points of disagreement than the utility of a separate political party for women. Sisterhood was a sham, after the wartime splits, but there were other differences. These eastern women were reactionary on labour issues: as James Naylor points out, they believed that restraint and discipline at work were reasonable and necessary, and did not infringe upon British liberty. Certainly workers should enjoy freedom, but during their leisure time. Their priorities included "ensuring the maintenance of patriotic zeal in the postwar period." They were, Naylor says, "little more than a 'Conservative annex.' "[48]

The surviving written evidence relates to Gertrude's connection to the British No-Conscription Fellowship. The NCF had barely struggled through the last months of the war; many NCFers were exhausted and discouraged, as it seemed the war would never end, and COs were especially ripe for death from flu and pneumonia. The bravery and hard work seemed not to have been for any useful purpose. Lloyd George easily won the December 1918 election. He said he would not retain conscription, but his government did not release the 2,000 COs who were still in prison despite petitions signed by eighty MPs in one instance and 130,000 citizens in another. Not until April 1919 did the gradual release of COs begin, starting with those who had served more than two years; the last ones were not freed until the end of July. The NCF set up a reception and rehabilitation service (many COs were in precarious health, and very few jobs were available in any case) and a relief fund and tried to help ease the COs back into normal life.

There were varying views among the membership about what the NCF should do next. It was eventually decided to hold a convention in London in late November 1919 to decide a future course of action and celebrate their achievements: a "Festival of Fellowship" was planned. Horace Twilley was among the 400 delegates, representing about 4,000 members, down from 10,000 in 1916. He had been one of the longest-serving COs, with four courts martial to his credit. The

NCF did celebrate their achievements, but were less sure about a future role for the organisation. For my purposes, the rivetting feature of the final convention was the reading of greetings from supporters all over the world. "Mrs Gertrude Richardson, Secretary, Canadian Women's Peace Crusade," was one of these. Gertrude had been in touch with the NCF from the middle of 1916, although the exact nature of her connection remains unclear. The British government had forbidden *The Tribunal* to be mailed to overseas subscribers, but she could have been sent some issues by her mother or by friends. It seems likely that this happened, from the timing of some of her discussions of CO issues. What is much clearer, however, is that she wrote to the NCF and periodically sent them material. *The Tribunal* contains several references to "our correspondent" and quotes some of her columns from the *Canadian Forward*.[49]

The courage and suffering of Horace and the other COs helped Gertrude enormously. If they and their supporters in the NCF did not succumb entirely to despair, how could she permit herself to do so? She had done her best to duplicate the work of the British Women's Peace Crusade, founding a counterpart organised to take into account the geographical circumstances that constrained her ability to carry out a peace campaign. She tried also to carry out the propaganda and direct prison support work of the NCF. She was able to reach readers in Leicester and Canada, to give them information about wartime repression and resistance that they might otherwise not have, to urge them to join in, and to provide a network of support for their efforts and perhaps help them to get through difficult times when they felt alone and a bit crazy for persisting in their "antipatriotic" ideas. That is considerable accomplishment for the times, and for a woman in Gertrude's situation. She could feel that she was part of a brotherhood and sisterhood of the new humanity, even if it seemed at times that they were vastly outnumbered by the barbarians and their deluded supporters. What would the postwar world bring? Pessimism and optimism vied to answer this question for those who had been against the war. In their optimistic moments, most would have agreed that after all the horrors of the war years, surely the future must be brighter.

7 Despair, Illness, Endurance, Loss, Death – No Happy Endings Here (1920–46)

Lovest Thou Me?

I can hear the cry of anguish, little children weep for bread
Wistful eyes are raised in wonder, mothers moan beside the dead.
I can see the shrunken bodies, I can hear the sound of woe,
And it pierces God's high Heaven, rising from the world below.

And I think how, on a hill-side, Christ's kind hands broke bread for all.
(How His gentle heart is grieving o'er the sorrows that appal!)
Once again I hear Him saying: "If you love me, feed My sheep."
But the world is cold and heedless, and His people are asleep!

Oh! a million little children die to-day in want and pain,
Crime of crimes, in Heaven recorded, Christ's own innocents are slain!
"Feed My lambs," he whispers gently, "They are dying in the cold,
Everyone is dear and precious, gather all within the fold."

He shall come at last to judgement, He who sits upon the Throne –
From the world that waits before Him, He shall call and choose His own –
"I was hungry, and ye fed Me, and ye clothed My shivering form,
And ye sheltered Me so kindly, when I fainted in the storm."

"Sick and weary and in prison – outcast – scorned – and left to die,
"Ye, who sought Me out and loved Me did not dream that it was I.
"Come, ye blessed of My Father, share My blest Eternity,
"Ye have comforted My children, ye have done it unto Me."

"I have written the above lines in the hope of touching some mother-heart with the sad story of the suffering little ones of Europe," Gertrude wrote in the Swan River paper in February 1920. "Conditions are appalling beyond words, in all the war-devastated area. A million young children have no milk, in the hospitals there is nothing but paper in which to wrap the emaciated new-born babies of starving mothers. Will any who read this make a little garment in the care of Him who said: 'In as much, etc'?"[1]

Although by this time she had no outlets for her writing (save for politically tame and ostensibly devotional poems, which the local paper would print), it seems likely that Gertrude also wrote to her wartime peace network urging members to respond to the suffering in the former enemy countries. The famine was not new, and Gertrude had known about it for some time. As early as August 1918, the Canadian Food Controller had written in *Woman's Century* scolding Canadians for whining about wartime food restrictions: "Europe starves while we talk of sacrifice," he had reminded them. He had estimated that "tens of thousands" would starve in Europe, "do what we will." Canadian food priorities were to feed the troops, the Motherland, and the nearest allies. Nothing, the Controller had made clear, could be done about the others. He had estimated that 4,750,000 Europeans had starved to date, mostly women and children. (He had predicted that an even greater number would starve during the coming winter, with Russia especially hard hit.) Ironically, given later government policy toward "enemy" starvation, he had appealed to Canadian women's "just plain decency" to shift their consumption to perishables and leave the preservable essentials (beef, bacon, fats, sugar, and wheat) for the overseas hungry. "If those hungry babies of Europe were right at our own doorsteps ... every Canadian woman would open her door to them. She would take them in and feed them. She could do no less. But because they are three thousand miles away ... there is nothing but our own conscience to shame us when we waste food that might mean life to another human being."[2]

Gertrude read the WILPF (the ICWPP took WILPF as its new name after the war) bulletin the *Internationaal*, which reported on food shortages, malnutrition and starvation, and various attempts by WILPF members after the armistice to get the Allied governments to lift the food blockade. One such attempt was the petition by the British WIL to the Lloyd George government early in December 1918, "To Alleviate the Food Situation in Central Europe." Early in 1919 the newsletter carried a letter from the French section of the organisation to German women, in response to appeals by the latter (which had never been published in the French daily press) that French women pressure their government to lift the blockade and relieve the widespread starvation of children. The French WIL appealed to President Wilson, saying that precisely because they knew the suffering of French women and children in the areas occupied by Germany during the war, they begged him to end the policy of responding to evil with like. Swedish feminist Ellen Key initiated an international appeal to women of the victorious countries, an appeal echoed by various national sections of the WILPF, to urge their governments to lift the blockade, to allow the relief of starving German women and children. British WIL members sent a million rubber nipples to Germany; mothers were too starved to produce breast milk for their babies, and there was no way to feed babies what little milk was sent in. In April 1919 there was a protest in London against the food blockade, attended by 10,000, and in May, English feminist peace activists were involved in founding Save the Children, of which Gertrude was an early member. Details about her particular contacts with the founders are not known, but there were a number of ways to learn about the group: personal contacts, the WILPF newsletter, and other peace and humanitarian publications. Gertrude sewed assiduously for the organisation, and sent over huge bundles of clothing and quilts.[3]

The blockade had been a major issue at the International Congress of the Women's International League for Peace and Freedom held in Zurich in May 1919. The original plan had been to hold the Congress in the same place as the peace negotiations, but because not all members would have been allowed to go to Paris, the locale was shifted to a neutral country. Even so, some were unable to get there. The draft of the Versailles treaty had been released and the Congress, dismayed at many of its provisions, predicted that these would lead to another war. The Congress was a moving and energising experience for most, but there were painful moments. Perhaps the most personally upsetting was to see the effects of malnutrition and starvation in those of their comrades who had been in the affected areas. In addition, during the Congress a trainload of 800 refugee children arrived from Vienna, brought in by the railway workers' union; spindly limbed and fragile, these were the healthy ones. Nearly twice that number had been left behind because they could not survive the journey. Delegates knew that not all the suffering was the result of a deliberate blockade; nonetheless, it was an important factor if only because it was something that could be changed by a decision of the governments involved. WILPF delegates from the unaffected areas were horrified and outraged. The Congress called the famine "a disgrace to civilisation," and demanded that the blockade be lifted, and if necessary, that all transportation be reserved for relief shipments and all countries institute rationing until relief was adequate. Only thus could "permanent reconciliation and union" of humanity be brought about. The Congress sent envoys to convey its official resolution to the officials at Versailles. None of the men agreed to comply, despite the fact that there was no denial of widespread starvation among women and children. Indeed, even after the treaty was signed, the Allies continued to refuse permission to send in food relief to certain areas. Widely circulated Red Cross reports spoke of many thousands of infant and child deaths not only from hunger, but from cold and disease to which malnutrition made them vulnerable. A February 1919 Red Cross report on conditions in Budapest (which the WILPF reprinted in a July 1919 newsletter and to which Gertrude seems to refer in the note to readers following her poem at the head of this chapter) described appalling scenes of suffering. There were virtually no soap, cleaning materials, bed linens, blankets, diapers. WILPF International Secretary Emily Balch commented in July, "No supplies of any kind are allowed to be sent into Hungary, a rigid blockade being still in force. It is not now a question of securing money or supplies, but of securing permission from the Allied Powers to send help – at the very least to send condensed milk for the babies and medical and hospital supplies."[4]

Following the Congress, WILPF moved its headquarters to Geneva and appointed economist Emily Greene Balch, a U.S. Quaker feminist who had been fired by Wellesley College for her peace activities, as their secretary. She coordinated the mailout of the Congress reports, and various of their campaigns. At the beginning of October 1919 WILPF carried out a survey of milk supplies and distribution in various regions of Europe in order to present a report to an international conference on the economy held in London by the Fight the Famine Council (several of whose founders were WILPF and other women's peace group leaders). In May 1920 WILPF published a special supplement to its new journal *Pax et Libertas* on the economic situation. This supplement featured a discussion of the economic consequences of the war, the history of the famine, an analysis of the policies and circumstances that exacerbated and perpetuated it, and information about WILPF. Early in 1920 Emily Balch sent Gertrude two copies of *Pax et Libertas* and the report of the Zurich Congress. Gertrude wrote back that although she had subscribed to the *Internationaal* and was "in absolute sympathy with all the splendid work" of WILPF, she could not afford to pay a subscription that year "because I am giving everything for the little suffering children of Europe. I have no private income, and subscriptions to papers must give way before the greater need." Balch replied that Gertrude need not pay for her subscription: "The object is not to increase our income but to spread our ideas, as of course you know." Balch suggested Gertrude get in touch with Harriet Prenter in Toronto; it is not clear whether she did. Gertrude's May 1920 letter was written on Women's Crusade International letterhead, and she enclosed a copy of her poem "The Call." Gertrude had previously sent WILPF headquarters a letter (which they received 12 October 1917) containing information about her wartime activities, the founding of the Women's Peace Crusade and its pledge; the January-February-March 1918 issue of the *Internationaal* had reproduced this letter. Some readers had presumably contacted Gertrude as a result; however the WILPF papers do not contain a copy of this letter, and Emily Balch appears to have been unaware of Gertrude's Crusade activities, as she asked for more information.[5]

The Canadian WIL was in poor shape, organisationally. It had been weakened by Laura Hughes' departure for Chicago in late 1917; although she stayed in touch by mail and continued to visit her mother and friends in Toronto, the Toronto group was tiny, wracked by differences about how to proceed (and possibly by personality clashes and power struggles), and in any case was too beleaguered to have any impact. Hughes responded in August 1919 to a request from Emily Balch to help organise an official Canada-wide Canadian branch, but Hughes could not identify anyone suitable to take on the task. Gertrude was her first choice: "a steadfast pacifist but she lives in such a small place. It is hard for her to do big work." Hughes may have written to Gertrude about this; lacking Gertrude's personal papers or published account, it is impossible to be sure. It is unclear what information Hughes had about the extent of Gertrude's Women's Peace Crusade network, which might have been a useful starting point for this task. On the other hand, Gertrude's effectiveness as a WILPF organiser might have been weakened by her outspokenness during the war. But in any case, her biggest handicap was her isolation. There were limits to what could be done by mail, and with little money and a small child, she could not travel extensively. The Toronto chapter was by this time in the hands of Harriet Dunlap Prenter, active in Labour politics and the SDP; she had regularly contributed to *Canadian Forward* and would have known of Gertrude's activities through that paper; I do not know whether she and Gertrude corresponded or if Prenter became a Crusade member. Although WILPF did slowly become established in various parts of Canada in the 1920s, and it is quite possible that Gertrude read about these activities, for a variety of reasons it does not seem likely that Gertrude was involved in them.[6]

As the poem at the beginning of this chapter suggests, Gertrude had made child relief a priority by 1920, and was directing every spare bit of money and energy toward that cause. She did not have much cash to send, but she did have her superb sewing skills to put to use: she made clothes to send to the children. Eric was very small then (he was born in February 1917) but still remembers Gertrude sewing, hour after hour, at her portable machine on the cherrywood kitchen table that Robert's parents had brought out from Ontario. Eric played with the deep wooden cover which sat on the floor (probably left there for that purpose) while she sewed. One time he fell in and hurt his head, he remembers; she rocked him until he was comforted, then went back to her machine. Her health was not good, but she pushed herself to exhaustion quite regularly. She was entering menopause at age forty-five, and her menstrual periods had become irregular. She suffered from neuritis, with sometimes severe headaches and back and leg pains, and often, serious insomnia. Her doctor said it was just menopause, and it would pass; there was not much he could do about it. It seems likely that the root cause of these difficulties was an underactive thyroid gland, which in turn may have been affected adversely by her meningitis more than twenty years earlier. But this was apparently not diagnosed; endocrinology was not well developed, and the ordinary family physician was unlikely to suspect such a possibility. Too, late in the war she had suffered from a lengthy bout of kidney trouble, with agonising back pains and frequent urination at night, according to Robert's later discussion with another doctor. Although this particular episode seems to have cleared up (or at least her kidney troubles shifted from acute to chronic in nature), it could not have made her subsequent health problems any easier. She became ill during the summer of 1920; she probably made her condition worse by refusing to rest and take care of herself. Recalling this period, Robert reported that Gertrude had been dreadfully upset about the situation in Europe, worried to the point of obsession about the suffering of children, and was haunted by images of the scenes described in the reports she read. "She became almost stuporous" from worry and overwork at times, a doctor later recorded in his notes of a conversation with Robert. There are few details available about her activities during this period. She published a few poems in the local paper, and these suggest that her distress over people's indifference to the famine in Europe did not diminish. Her poem, "The Children's Cry," suggests that various facets of her daily routine confirmed her sense that the callousness she found so repugnant in wartime had become entrenched in the postwar community:[7]

'Twas in the Church at eventide, I heard the children's cry
The music and the song were hushed – a cloud passed o'er the sky.
A woman's voice was sweetly raised, "My peace I give to thee"
"Let not your heart be troubled, O! believe, believe in me."

As in a dream I heard the cry, the myriad-throated moan
Of drooping, dying children sweet – and woeful was the tone:
Ah! would that Christ would break once more the loaves the children need
He whispers, "Give ye them to eat" and yet we do not heed!

They die, those little suffering ones, for bread our hands with-hold!
God scorns our praise and worship, and loathes our tainted gold!
His little ones are dying, oh! their cry is full of pain
Their little hands are lifted up, and lifted up in vain!

Yet would that they who succour these might see my glorious dream:
The King of Kings in judgment set, above the rain-bow gleam,
The tender voice, so matchless sweet, the smile divinely bright,
The face of one once crowned with thorns, lit now with dazzling light.

"Not all who call Me 'Lord' " He says "but those who love and care"
"For those for whom I lived and died My priceless joy shall share"
He turns away unheeding, while the song and prayer rise high
And weeps again, in anguish deep, while little children die.

The apostate church had disgusted her during the war; the complacent church of 1920 was little better. Some 10,000,000 soldiers had died, another 20,000,000 wounded, and no one knew how many millions of civilians. In the nearby valley village of Minitonas alone, 155 had enlisted, twenty-four were killed, others severely wounded. Few came home unscathed. Bystanders were still dying and in that sense the war had not ended, it had simply shifted its targets. Under those circumstances, what was the meaning of Christianity in the immediate postwar period? How was the message of the gospel to be expressed, what was required of Christians? In another poem published in July, Gertrude wrote of some of these concerns. Jesus was not far away, he was near enough to touch, she wrote. But the nearness revealed his wounds; his "throne is set where human need is greatest" and his "reign in hearts that love." Anyone who wanted to serve Him should start by living lovingly. The praise that Jesus wanted to hear was not that of "holy songs of love." He said, she wrote, " 'If you would praise Me, lift the weak and dying / And lead the lost above.' " Those who wanted to see the Saviour could see His "gaze reflected / In pure and loving eyes," and "Behold me in the forms of toiling millions / Broken and sorrow-worn." Gertrude was describing a religion of service and transformation, akin to the social gospel, but did not find fellow followers of this form of Christianity among her neighbours and friends in Swan River. Perhaps they were there, but if so she did not see them; what she could see was people's complacency and their lack of concern for those who suffered.[8]

There were times when she could still believe that the hopes for a better world would yet be realised. The following month she wrote of the time when that would come to pass: "Bye-and-Bye," excerpted below.

I will not linger where the sounds of strife
And war and blood-shed fill the startled air,
My feet shall journey where the song of life
Grows ever purer, sweeter and more rare,
For all earth's weapons shall be laid aside –
And Peace herself shall be God's children's guide.
        Bye-and-bye.

I would not tread the rosy, sunlit way
When other feet must feel the piercing thorn,
Yet I will greet the coming of the day
With eyes uplifted to the light of dawn.
For all the darkness and the dread shall flee
And all the world a Paradise shall be.
        Bye-and-bye.

I do not understand the pain of Earth
    The wailing cry, the long and bitter groan,
Yet in the travail of some wondrous birth
    The whole creation makes her heavy moan:
The sun shall rise, and over all the land
    A fairer, sweeter, gladder life shall spring,
When love shall pour, with kind and bounteous hand
    Her countless blessings on each living thing –
Oh! I shall know the meaning of the pain,
For I shall dream my golden dreams again.
        Bye-and-bye.[9]

By the fall of 1920 she had begun to feel somewhat better physically. She had been seeing a new doctor, probably Dr Cameron in Minitonas, and whatever his treatment, it seemed to be helping. Perhaps it was just a question of time, as her body recovered, and perhaps he was sympathetic, and that helped too. Perhaps during the summer when she knew that at least children were not freezing now that winter had passed, she had felt able to leave her sewing machine from time to time. Whatever the reason, by October Gertrude was able to return to some of the activities she had let go earlier that year. She wrote a long-overdue reply to Emily Balch in October 1920, which reveals something of the bleakness of this period, despite her attempts to cling to hope ("I would not tread the rosy, sunlit way / When other feet must feel the piercing thorn, / Yet I will greet the coming of the day / With eyes uplifted to the light of dawn," as she had written in that August 1920 poem). The anguish of the war had receded, but her frustration at being unable to influence events for the better is still very much in evidence in this letter. Gertrude wrote that she greatly valued the Zurich report; she needed to be informed, but her letter makes clear that still more, she needed to be connected to the peace movement. "I wish that there might be better ways of corresponding with women of other countries so that we might listen to each others' views and learn from one another … I have often thought how much I would love to write to Lida Gustava Heymann, and some of the other women, but not knowing them I hesitate." These sorts of contacts seemed particularly important to Gertrude at this time. "I must confess that I am disappointed because women (here, at any rate) seem to have forgotten the war and very few see any need of banding together for peace. It is disappointing and very grievous. But it may not be so in other places." Although Gertrude did not find like-minded women nearby, she did still have contact with those she had come to know through the Women's Peace Crusade "from many parts of the world." With these she had shared disappointment that many peace women had not persisted when the U.S. entered the war, "when the real test came." Jane Addams, for example, had made compromises of which Gertrude disapproved, and "did not measure up to the ideal which we had expected." Gertrude and her radical correspondents had expected more: "We ought to be ready to endure all things for our faith – at least the *leaders* among us." (Perhaps Gertrude had expected too much: Fannie said of her not long after, that she "has always been most decided and strong willed and has a habit of idealising people and forming opinions rather hastily. When she finds out that her ideals are shattered, she feels very bitter.") However comforting those ties that Gertrude had retained from her wartime peace group, they were long distance, and left something to be desired. "How I wish I might meet some of these women and get help and courage in this lonely spot where through all the years of war I stood almost alone against it."[10]

Balch's reply accompanied the current bulletin and reflected her hope that Gertrude would become active in WILPF. Balch discussed several upcoming international meetings to which she invited Gertrude, suggested Gertrude's Women's Crusade International might become affiliated to WILPF through the Toronto branch, urged her to write to Heymann, and discussed Addams' position. Addams "says herself she had never bowed the knee to Mars, so much so that when she was to speak at a Canadian University [Toronto] recently, the Canadian authorities objected and would not allow her to come. I think if you knew all the circumstances you would revise your impression." Balch encouraged Gertrude to provide names of anyone to whom she would like material sent, or who might be interested in attending the planned 1921 congress in Austria and the following summer school in Salzburg.[11]

Gertrude could at that point have tried to reestablish connections with women like Violet McNaughton, or closer still, Winona Dixon, Lynn Flett, and some of the other Winnipeg SDPers and suffragists who had been antiwar – those who remained, at any rate. (Francis Marion Beynon, Lillian Beynon Thomas, and her husband were still in New York; Beynon never returned, and the Thomases did not quite yet. Helen and George Armstrong were soon to leave Winnipeg to go to California, partly to recover their health after years of struggle.) Gertrude could have written to Harriet Prenter and asked for names of western women who wanted to develop a peacetime peace movement. A few eastern women from the old pacifist suffrage group were becoming involved in absolutist pacifist organisations founded with U.S. feminist pacifists; there was the Fellowship of Reconciliation, there were other groups, and she almost certainly knew some of the individuals involved. She could have followed her wartime patterns of networking, operating by mail and personal contacts. Indeed, she may have done some of these things. She had family support; her mother had returned with Fred and his wife Edith (they had married in 1918); Fannie and John were still there, Robert and Eric were well and happy, and although many farmers were badly hit by the depression in farm prices, there is no evidence that the Richardsons were desperately hard up. But times had changed; it was one thing to struggle on somehow in wartime, and pin hopes on change for the better when the war ended. It was quite another to find that the peace was not peaceful (the Allies were still at war in Siberia, and many European countries were torn by civil strife and revolution), it was not just (wartime repression had scarcely diminished, and Winnipeg labour was decimated by fear and disunity after the strike), it was not compassionate, and in many ways the world in 1919 and 1920 was no better than it had been during the war. Gertrude's illness in the summer of 1920 was probably as much dis-ease of the spirit as it was of the body, if the experiences of other peace activists were typical. The wartime era did not end with the war; persecution of radicals and hostility to peace activists lingered, and wounds took months or years to heal (depending on the issues, the setting, and the individuals). Some had managed to make the transition to peacetime activism or just back to their "normal lives," but others did not fare so well.[12]

Many had relied on their hope that good would come at the end of the war, to keep themselves going during the war, when it seemed everything else they cared about had been destroyed. Englishwoman Vera Brittain had been nursing at the front. She wrote of the first few months of 1919, "But when it came in, it appeared to an enchanted world as divine normality, the spring of life after a winter of death, the stepping-stone to a new era, the gateway to an infinite future – a future not without its dreads and discomforts, but one in whose promise we had to believe, since it was all that some of us had left to believe in."[13]

A grimmer view soon set in for some. Helena Swanwick's comment about the Armistice could well be applied to a lengthier period: although the shooting had stopped, the hatred had not, and in the face of that, "I seemed still to be crying all the time inside and I had to hold myself tight." For many of those who had been pacifists, I suspect from my own limited experience that antiwar work added the extra burdens of guilt and despair at being unable to stop something sickeningly wrong to the exhaustion and sorrow that most people felt by the latter part of the war. Frances Early's research on the experiences of feminists doing civil liberties and peace work in the U.S. found that feelings of "isolation and estrangement from the larger society" were common, but they mostly got through the war period. What some could not survive intact was the U.S. postwar climate of antifeminist backlash and reactionary extremism; "burnout" and "temporary physical or emotional trauma" were admitted by several leaders (the men activists generally did not admit to this if they did experience it, Early found, and since antifeminist backlash was part of the problem for feminist activists, the men may have had less difficulty). She also found that a number of women "needed time not only to recover from the incessant demands of wartime activism but also to gather energy and inspiration for future work in a hostile milieu."[14]

Some peace workers fared better at the end of the war, seemingly due to a combination of circumstance and outlook. Catherine Marshall, who with Bertrand Russell had coordinated the NCF, had experienced a nervous and physical breakdown in 1917, due to despair and overwork. This had forced her to rest, and she was nearly recovered when the Armistice came. She was able to re-involve herself in constructive activity, and was a key figure in postwar peace politics. It probably also helped that she was a Quaker and could find solidarity and continuity in her religious community. It was easier to make the transition when the person was part of a strong and sizeable community of dissent, religious or not, as was the case for the British pacifist feminists. Laura Hughes was fortunate in her personal circumstances; her father-in-law was a stalwart comrade in the CO support work she had done in 1918–20, her CO husband was released from prison in the fall of 1920, and she had her hands full with their new baby. Chicago was a WILPF stronghold, which helped. But she had also the advantage of expecting the worst. As she had written in 1916, "If this is to be the last war, as so many of us hope it will be, it is going to take every ounce of pacifist strength to make it so. The reactionary forces of the world are always stronger after a war. The militarists have more power than ever. And after this war the international armament trust, which is largely in control of the manufacture of munitions on both sides, will have control of most of the money of the world, and therefore be very powerful; and it won't allow its market to be destroyed if it can help it." She had all along been thinking in the long term, about restructuring the machinery of government. Her expectations for the postwar world had apparently been met. If her 1916 prediction reflected her outlook accurately, then she did not have to cope with the loss of a hope she never had.[15]

Bertrand Russell pointed up one of the consequences of dissent, for those who were not similarly situated (or had not the taste for political activism as a regular activity in the long run). Writing of his decision to retire from the NCF as of the beginning of 1918, he had said, "I think very good things will happen after the war (not so much in this country) but I have no longer any wish to have a part in them ... Public resistance to one's community seems somehow to sever one's roots, so that one gradually perishes." This feeling of alienation, and of perishing, seems to describe Gertrude's experience.[16] Another lingering aftertaste for many was bitterness, intensified by a sense of failure. Bertrand Russell thought it was all futile: "When the war was over, I saw that all I had done had been totally useless except to myself. I had not saved a single life or shortened the war by a minute. I had not succeeded in doing anything to diminish the bitterness which caused the Treaty of Versailles." But some COs did not feel that it had all been in vain: as Clifford Allen said in his address to the closing convention of the NCF, for these, their imprisonment had been a testimony to the kinship (or brotherhood, as they called it) of humanity. Although they were free, they saw the world still in chains. "It can be released by the spirit of unconquerable love ... We acclaim the new hope of human liberty now challenging ancient tyrannies in industry, within the State and between the nations, and dedicate the liberty we have regained to such service as shall contribute to the healing of the wounds inflicted by war, and to the building of a world rooted in freedom and enriched by labour that is shared by all. It is in this spirit that we go forth to meet new tasks, confident that through its long and bitter suffering mankind must yet come into the way of love."[17]

Could this have been a source of comfort for Gertrude? She almost certainly read the issue of *The Tribunal* containing Allen's remarks, and would doubtless have agreed with that conclusion, and probably as well with most of the comments quoted here, contradictory though they may be. I suspect that she felt all these things after the war; exhaustion, bitterness, futility, despair, and hope. Although this is sheer speculation, I wonder if she did not also lose her belief that people were basically good and caring, if only the false leaders (and the class system) would get out of the way. She also must have wavered in her believe in God's promise of the harvest, or at least her hope that it would ever be fairly shared out. Most people simply did not want to know, or to care, about unfairness, or about their complicity in benefiting from the suffering of others. As J.S. Woodsworth said in another context, the general public objected to being inconvenienced. "The general public has not been innocent ... It has been guilty of the greatest sin – the sin of indifference." Because of her isolation in a sea of indifference and complacency, her attempts to retain her grasp upon the spirit of unconquerable love were by necessity solitary. This does not work well for most people; peace activism is best as a shared activity. It seems to me that it was not just changes in her own feelings and beliefs, her neighbours' indifference to leftovers from the war, and the lack of a base for a peace movement, that she found so wounding. Her place in the community had changed. During the war when few wanted to study peace issues, she could attribute their disinterest to the war; but when few wished to involve themselves in study and the sort of commitment to reform that she valued, and that had been so much a part of her prewar experience in the suffrage movement and in the Roaring River and Swan River communities, a crucial part of her life was cut off. The community had changed and she was no longer a leader; nor even much of a participant. She would have been welcome in, say, the Grain Growers (other Roaring River women, Fannie for example, participated in the main and the women's organisation). In the end, she could not break out of her isolation, not because it was impossible, but because she was incapacitated by a return of her summer illness, which became more acute and finally overwhelmed her.[18]

Although Gertrude had felt better through the fall and winter of 1920–21, she was still not in generally good health. This was probably due in part to residual effects of her kidney flareup and to hormonal imbalances related to menopause, but it seems likely that the crucial factor was hypothyroidism. Medical records from subsequent months and years show that her thyroid had not been functioning properly for some time; the symptoms that plagued her in the spring of 1921 suggest a worsening hypothyroid condition. In March or April 1921, Gertrude's neuritis started to bother her again. Her menstrual periods had stopped, and although her doctor had thought that her earlier symptoms would diminish, they worsened. By early May her neuritis came back with a vengeance and she was nearly incapacitated with severe neck, back and leg pains. Her headaches got worse. Sometimes her legs got very weak; once the pain was so bad that the doctor gave her morphine, but he could do nothing to eliminate the cause of the pain. He was mystified, but attributed it to menopause. Her improvement since the previous summer might just as well never have happened. Weeks dragged on, and the pains and lack of proper sleep wore her down. She refused to lie down and give in to her headaches; she tried to carry on with her daily routines. Her outlook became increasingly gloomy, and her thoughts centred on failure and disappointment. Robert later tried to describe Gertrude's feelings at this point in her life. He said that she had "always [been] easily worried and upset, but not easily depressed" before then. She had been very active in community and political affairs, but he thought that she was "disappointed in the results" of the woman suffrage movement. She had always been "very ambitious, energetic and a good housekeeper, a very hard worker for various charities during and after the War," but now this gave her little satisfaction. She had often taken the world's troubles onto herself, always had a tendency to think of others' upset or pain, and, it seems to me (and to some family members) to empathise to the point where she could hardly bear to enjoy anything. Her nieces told me in 1986 that they remembered their father Fred Twilley saying that when the Richardson dog had been injured and was in pain, Gertie and Robert had thought of the poor wounded soldiers and felt twice as bad. Always so earnest, they would bring up subjects of wrongdoing and suffering at family gatherings, and this was clearly a normal part of their daily talk and preoccupations. But now Gertie had gone much farther; she felt responsible for others' suffering, according to her and her family's statements recorded in her medical records. It sounds as if she felt that if she could take that suffering upon herself and suffer, that might make it get better, might give some meaning to it, might redeem it somehow. If there was evil, then she had to suffer it too; otherwise, she was part of the cause of the evil. Better Jesus than Pilate. If it was utterly wrong to be calloused and complacent, then she was becoming increasingly utterly right. Robert told the doctor that there had been a blizzard on 12 May "and she has never been right since then." Robert attributed it to overwork, a last straw that compounded her physical ailments and pushed Gertrude over the edge.[19]

And she did go over the edge at about that time, if the records can be believed. "She imagined she had to bear all the sins of the world. She had delusions of an accusatory nature. Everywhere she looked was misery and gloom." She had "very vivid auditory hallucinations. She heard voices calling and weeping and she heard sound that must have come from souls in torment. She did not recognise any of the voices except that of her adopted son who seemed to be calling her … She also had visual hallucinations. She has seen herself in the midst of the sea with a great number of war ships rushing toward her. She was surrounded by flames." Shell shocked soldiers also experienced such visions (and not infrequently, a sense that the slaughter and suffering were their responsibility). Although doctors initially thought that only inferior soldiers could be shell shocked, by mid-war "they had come to agree that the real cause of shell shock was the emotional disturbance produced by warfare itself, by chronic conditions of fear, tension, horror, disgust, and grief," as Elaine Showalter explains. Although soldiers at the front must have found it easier to have horrific nightmares, given their closer acquaintance with the subject, any peace activist with any imagination at all might have had similar nightmares at times. But for Gertrude, as her physical health further deteriorated, these "variable and intermittent" images appeared when she was awake. Before, she had been able to write about them or escape them somehow. Being able to do something, trying to arouse people to stop the suffering and evil of the war and its consequences, finding kindred spirits, hoping it would eventually be over, and feeling she was doing her part to bring that about must have helped to maintain her sense of purpose and worth. But no one can carry on forever, and even if her spirit had still been willing, her system was no longer able to cope. By June she had yet more severe ailments; her headaches and insomnia got worse, she lost what was left of her appetite, and began to retain fluid, her ankles puffing alarmingly. She feared she had blood poisoning. About 7 June, she told Robert she felt something coming on, she felt "unnatural … that she was another person walking about." One night she gulped down a double dose of her sleeping draught and went to lie down, but this quantity was no more effective than the normal amount, and she remained sleepless. Eventually she got up and went for a walk. Robert went looking for her and found her standing knee deep in the rapids. He carried her home, wrapped her up, gave her a hot drink. He talked it over with someone whose name is blanked out in the records, presumably Dr Cameron in Minitonas or Dr Bruce in Swan River, who advised taking her to Winnipeg to the Psychopathic Hospital, which had opened in 1919. This modern institution had been developed under the direction of the new Provincial Psychiatrist Alvin Mathers as part of the Norris government's reform of mental health services in the province; the new facility's development had been prompted by a sharply critical report on the existing two facilities at Brandon and Selkirk, by the recently established Canadian National Committee for Metal Hygiene (the study was requested by the Manitoba Public Welfare Commission). Robert and Fannie took her down on the train on 14 June 1921.[20]

I read these details for the first time in a shabby motel room in Swan River on a hot July day in 1991, thrilled that after more than seven years of research, Gertrude's thick hospital file might finally fill in gaps and solve puzzles. The medical file was a treasure of information; it included several lengthy autobiographical letters full of details about her family, childhood, education, first marriage, and daily life. It took nearly three hours to skim the file. That afternoon I periodically jumped up and down and shouted with glee (in a muffled sort of way; the door was open and there were other people about) and talked to myself, excited as I found answers for so many of these questions. But by the time I finished reading, I had shed tears over the waste of her talents, her undeserved pain, her punishment of herself for what was certainly not her fault, if it was anybody's. She had driven me to tears before, to my embarrassment; I had sniffled my way through her antiwar writings in the microfilm room of the library at the University of Saskatchewan in 1984 as I looked up the material in *Canadian Forward* that Linda Kealey had spotted during her research on socialist women of the period. (In 1984 we thought we were going to die in a nuclear attack any minute, and a feminist foremother's passionate antiwar writings hit a nerve.)

However, that afternoon marked a turning point in my feelings about researching Gertrude. Before, research about her life after 1920 had been a sort of game, and the excitement of finding more had outweighed the content of my discoveries, although I liked and admired her a great deal. But those autobiographical letters from Gertrude may as well have been written to me; she talked to me then, and I felt desolated that I could do nothing to help her, that no one had helped her, or been able to. I came close to giving up this book that afternoon, because her final defeat was so painful to encounter that it seemed to overshadow her earlier accomplishments. I guess I still expected things would usually turn out right, that it was normal to be more or less healthy and happy, and that goodness and courage were usually rewarded. Not a thoughtful or dispassionate response by a trained historian, by any means. Neither was the resolution I reached. I decided that if I could do nothing to help her then, at least I could tell her story now. She would not have wanted this part told then, but if she could come back now, I think she might say, "Tell it all." We have so many taboos against revealing ourselves when we are sick or vulnerable. These periods are made less taboo if they become part of a story of struggle with adversity that ended in triumph. But Gertie's story did not end in triumph, it ended in defeat. "They done her in," as Eliza Doolittle says in *Pygmalion*: her time and place, her passion for justice, her years of bravery, her despair and burnout, her fundamentalist indoctrination into sin and guilt, her oversensitivity (oh so appropriate for a Victorian lady), her body, maybe her chemistry if the hypothyroid (or for that matter, other) biochemical explanations for depression are accurate. Most women's history and biographies are about the women who triumphed. Most of us probably triumph in many parts of our lives, too, but not all of us, and certainly not in all parts of our lives. We often castigate ourselves, in those times when we go down to defeat. We have too few stories of heroic women who were defeated in the end and, like commercials for perfect skinny bodies that give us false ideas of what we should look like, stories of winners can mislead us about how to regard "losers." Gertie was a loser in the end. This is what it was like to be defeated. Maybe this will comfort someone else who gets defeated. The rest of this chapter is very hard to write; like trying to speak honestly about parts of my own life that I feel shame about, even though it is not my life and I know that shame is undeserved. If I ever wanted to believe in heaven and going to Jesus, it would be to know that Gertie is up there rejoicing. The most painful thing, perhaps, is that today she might not have had to suffer through those years; seeing her suffering is like watching a beloved friend sicken and die of something that five years later could have been cured. But this book is the best I can do for her. Back to the story: in June 1921 Gertie was taken to the Winnipeg Psychopathic Hospital.

It was a dreadful experience for her. Looking back on this period several years later, she said that she had thought her life was over.

She had felt as if something awful were going to happen but she did not know what it would be; gradually she had became "so depressed that she felt she wanted to die to escape this dreadful calamity that was hanging over her." She would get a feeling "sweeping over her ... she wasn't afraid of [seeing] God but at that time was more afraid of being alive." Considering what she was experiencing at the time, it is easy to see why death might look appealing. Ordinary events could become terrifying. During the train trip, Gertrude had fantasies that the train destroyed everything it passed, and that every town she, Robert, and Fannie passed through was set on fire. When they got to the hospital, she had been afraid people would kill her. Her spatial perception was distorted: she had said she felt tiny and insignificant in a setting that seemed to her full of very large people. A nurse who Gertrude later realised was quite a small person seemed to her at the time to be huge. Gertrude was by then seriously ill, quite stiff and having difficulty moving. Robert later described her as being more or less unconscious for about five hours after admission. Within a week, her health was improved, and she was able to tell more about how she felt.[21]

Gertrude's comments were recorded with evident sympathy by the unnamed physician who talked to her then. He describes her as a quiet, small, middle-aged woman with an English accent who spoke very clearly and precisely. As she told him about her family and personal history, he recorded his impression of her as a "courageous conscientious" person who had been keenly interested in current affairs and "the serious interests of life generally," an avid reader who was fond of history and literature. "In her time she has taken a keen interest in matters pertaining to women's rights etc." She told him she had been "a regular church attendant but now feels that she will never be able to go to church again." Gertrude told him she thought that "her mental and physical health were permanently destroyed and that the future is absolutely hopeless." The doctor's summary continues, "She feels she is a terrible burden on her husband and accuses herself of not having told him of her previous mental trouble. She is sure she will never get to the place where she would occupy her former position in the community. For all this she is willing to believe she herself is to blame." He added that she did not realise how much she had improved in the short time she had been there. She was no longer having the regular hallucinations – voices calling, warships and fires threatening her – that had been so frightening earlier. Now what little remained of these was relegated to the world of nightmares. But, he said, she still felt "hopeless ... that there is no future for her ... a constant feeling of anxiety and dread. A feeling of guilt." In describing her earliest years, in the midst of a discussion of infant illnesses she told him she wished that her mother had let her die, saying it wasn't worthwhile. Her father was such a good man, she said: "I am just the opposite." She still was utterly convinced of "her own inferiority and sinfulness ... and absolute helplessness mentally," the doctor commented. "At times she weeps over what she is sure is a hopeless future." Indeed, it may well have been close to hopeless, diagnostically speaking, for whatever the physical cause of her psychiatric illness, according to the psychiatric wisdom of the early twentieth century, manic-depression (as she was diagnosed) was considered a progressively degenerative condition. If I am correct in my view that this manic-depression was caused by her progressively worsening hypothyroidism, then the doctors were not far off the mark in their gloomy prognosis. (Although they noted her bodily ailments, they not surprisingly concentrated on her as a psychiatric patient.) But leaving aside for the moment the physical factors, ideas about mental illness were changing, due in no small part to the experience of dealing with numbers of shell shocked soldiers. The "shell shock" phenomenon showed that healthy, normal, and indeed, intelligent, well-bred, noble, and brave people could break down mentally under severe stress and exhaustion. (The fact that there were four times as many cases among English officers as enlisted men must have hastened the demise of victim blaming.) Many could also recover, eventually, and go back to productive normal lives. Maybe gloom was misplaced. Gertrude had recovered completely from her breakdown, years before, so why not this time? On the other hand, now she was older, and her condition was complicated by other factors (such as the hormonal changes of menopause, deterioration in kidney function that can accompany aging, and, crucially, a thyroid ailment, to say nothing of the cumulative effects of years of severe stress) about which, given the current state of medical knowledge, little could be done. The medical personnel had to do what they could to help her rally her own powers of recuperation.[22]

She slowly got better over the summer. By fall she seemed well enough to go home. On 21 November, she left with Fannie. The doctors were not convinced she was ready, and they made Fannie sign the usual form that said she knew she was taking Gertrude home against doctors' advice (meaning they were not ready to pronounce her cured), but home she went. She stayed with Fannie in Swan River (the Liveseys had moved into town by then) for three weeks, but wanted to go home to Eric and Robert, which she did on 6 December. She managed "fairly well both physically and mentally," as Fred wrote later that winter, but she did not recover completely. She was sometimes depressed and forgetful, and would lose track of what she was doing, having to ask Robert what to do next. She was often fatigued, was not really able to do much at home, and Robert took over most of the work around the house.[23]

She sometimes had headaches in the mornings and felt "stupid and strange," sometimes worse. "One day she pulled her face into all shapes and [gave] a terrible scream," Robert said. The hallucinations came back toward the end of February. "During these fits she would [see] millions of demons. She thought they had actually taken possession of her when she made the faces. A week later [she] had another attack but was not so bad, then a week after that again she had a third which was worse than the first," Robert reported. The attacks became intermittent. Her spirits sank lower; although she had for a period been sleeping soundly (despite occasional nights when she could not sleep at all), she now began to sleep badly, and she found this new pattern worrying. She lost her appetite and could not digest her food properly. Her soul sank into the bottomless pit again, as it seemed to her, and she became suicidal. She hid pieces of cord, then tied them around her neck. One time she took a cord to bed and tried to strangle herself beneath the covers; Eric found her and ran to get Robert. (Eric does not remember this incident but it is recorded in her file.)[24]

Robert spent most of his time taking care of her when she had these bad spells. They got more frequent. About a week after the first bad attack, the family had decided she had better go back to the hospital. As Fred put it, by the end of February she had become "unmanageable." Robert sent his brother Jim in to town to talk to the local magistrate about getting her back into the hospital. The magistrate conferred with the doctor, and they decided "that under the circumstances, it would avoid local excitement for Mrs Richardson, if you or some friends took her direct to Brandon, say, and commence all proceedings there" to have her committed. But Fred was worried that something might go wrong with that arrangement. It was such a long train journey to undertake without some certainty that she would be received at the other end. After a flurry of letters, Fred contacted Dr Mathers, head of the Winnipeg Psychopathic Hospital, who arranged for her admission to the Hospital for Mental Diseases at Brandon. Gertrude was a bit better for part of March, but not enough to reassure her family it was anything but temporary. Seeding time was approaching, and Robert had to be out in the fields. Robert took Gertrude to Brandon on the first of April. She weighed only eighty-five and a half pounds. Even though she was a small person, that was much too thin.[25]

Gertrude was acutely ill most of the summer, suicidal at times, wretchedly unhappy, certain she would never recover. Fannie and

Robert wrote regularly to inquire about her condition. By fall she was a bit better and was writing to Robert. What she said in the letters was discouraging, focusing on her wickedness, illness, and lack of hope for recovery, but at least she was showing an interest in "outside affairs. The fact that she writes shows that she is more like her old self, as she was always a good correspondent," he wrote hopefully to her doctor. But she stopped writing in October, and Dr Baragar reported that "she is very depressed and constantly asks that she be given something to put her out of the way. She believes that she cannot recover." Robert decided he should not try to visit her until she felt better. She was able to enjoy a game of cards at Christmas, and had some days that were less unhappy, but did not get much better. Robert missed her. In March 1923 he wrote to Dr Baragar that he had not heard from her for a long time. "When you said that it might take a year I felt that I could not face such a long wait, but it looks as though there would be a lot more of it." He visited her and she did write to him again that spring, but by July it had been more than two months since her last letter. Dr Baragar responded to Robert's inquiry, there was no great change. "She is of course still depressed and feels that she cannot get better." Such would be the tenor of their correspondence for the next couple of years.[26]

There are real problems of evidence for this period of Gertrude's life. Most information about Gertrude's experience and condition at this time is second-hand, described or recorded by others, and much of it is shaped by the conventions of the case record. By 1920 taking a detailed case history was standard practice, and this document was an important tool for the medical staff conferences in which diagnoses were made. Dorothy Smith has discussed the ways that an individual's experiences and decisions get packaged as a "case" in the creation of records in psychiatric (and other) settings, and the distortion that accompanies this process. Gertrude's file is rich in correspondence and her doctors' accounts (often purportedly verbatim) of interviews with her, Fannie, Fannie's husband John, and Robert. These accounts are largely sympathetic and present Gertrude as having been a competent and admirable person. But once she became a patient, that status became the central organising device for what went into her case file. Nevertheless, whatever its distortions and limitations, the case file is the major if not the sole source for most of the period after 1920, when Gertrude's own writings were no longer published.[27]

Although it too is shaped by the fact of Gertrude's illness and her hospitalisation, there is some direct autobiographical material in the case file. These several letters written by Gertrude herself are a rare first-hand source. The first of these was written to her doctor, 27 August 1923. She spoke of Robert's loneliness and of her utter misery and hopelessness.[28]

People tell me I shall get well but *I know* there is no hope – though I can see and feel and hear, and go on existing – while all those who have loved me so are suffering so terribly on my account. Do you think there is anything that can be done to bring me back, and remove this horror – this [illeg] from me? There is our little boy, whom we adopted, in order that we might love and care for him, and give him a happy home – and now, what will happen to him?

It is so cruelly hard for my dear husband, who has always been so gentle and kind and does not know what to do. Of course, I have only one desire – that I may die, since I cannot recover. I am full of unutterable misery, since I love what is good and beautiful and must now go down into shame and misery irretrievable.

Please try to do something to restore me if you can, will you not?

She was also shocked and frightened by some of her reactions to attempts at treatment. Late in July the doctors had started giving her "ovarian extract," which seemed to have no effect after a week, and early in August they put her on twelve grains of thyroid extract daily; hormone extracts (especially the thyroid) sometimes helped with depression. She did respond to the thyroid, although not as well as the doctors had hoped. Not surprisingly with such a hefty dose, her temperature went up, her pulse raced at 120, and she felt ravenously hungry all the time, an "unnatural appetite … I have developed into a kind of a monster." She had always been a "tiny eater," and this drastic difference horrified her. A week after writing this letter, she made a half-hearted gesture at suicide. But she had begun to perk up, according to a friend who had visited early in August. Did the thyroid help? The records make clear neither the dosage nor duration of the administration of extract. But something had changed. Gertrude wrote several relatively cheering letters home, and the ward notes sound hopeful for a change. She told one of her doctors late in September that she wanted to do something to help herself, but was not sure what to do. He reported, she "feels depressed, but the last few days she has felt that if she could only get something to lift her out of her depression she would be alright. She fully realizes that it is the depression that has made it so that she is unable to do anything. She says that she feels she wants to do it; and that she is strong enough to do it; yet she cannot." His own impression, he said, was that "she is very much better, and that she is beginning to feel that there is some hope ... and that she is reaching out for something to hang on to, to help her ... She has got a fairly good hold on herself." Unfortunately, she could not sustain her recovery and slid back into her previous condition later that autumn.[29]

Over the winter of 1924–25, Gertrude had small ups and downs but little changed in the long run. Robert continued to write anxious letters to the medical superintendent, asking for reports on her conditions and seizing hopefully on small signs. But these were few. Gertrude had trouble sleeping (it is not clear if she was still on thyroid extract), and was troubled by wartime flashback nightmares again. She said she "saw a field of blood and it was all babies' blood. They had been murdered by a number of men that were all standing there. They said it was her fault; that she was responsible for the death of all those children." Of course she was "terrified" to go to sleep again. Robert was able to get down to visit her in March 1925, and about that time she was a bit less dragged down. The doctor noted she was up "sewing baby clothes," probably for her beloved niece Connie who had married in June 1923 and was expecting her first child, Donald, born 2 August 1925. (Gertrude had made some of Connie's clothes when she was young, usually with lots of frills, which she thought suitable for a little girl.)[30]

A lengthy letter from Gertrude to one of her doctors, written in May 1925, provides some insight into her thoughts at that time.[31] It discussed in some detail her early health, physical and sexual development, the circumstances of her first and second marriages. She apparently had been scrutinising her past to seek an explanation for her present illness. This may have been a personal undertaking rather than prescribed therapeutic activity. Although there was encouragement for patients to consider their experiences, circumstances, and reactions to these, in hopes that this would help recovery, this was not a main emphasis. Treatment relied largely on baths, cold packs, seclusion, and useful activity, such as needlework or farm work, rather than psychotherapeutic conversations. In any case, Gertrude's self-flagellation would not have been encouraged, but rather considered part of her illness, a feature of which was her deeply rooted conviction that she was sinful and tainted. But she had not, apparently, previously said what on her part had brought this about, save that wartime and postwar suffering was somehow her fault. She now offered a more concrete and specific explanation, in her habit as a newly menstruating seventeen-year-old of masturbating to relieve cramps, done in all innocence until she read with "intense horror" in a book given her by her beloved father on her twenty-first birthday that this was a pernicious act. Although she immediately stopped, had never told anyone, and had eventually forgotten it and married "as a pure maiden" and gone on with her life, she now concluded that it was this terrible sin that lay at the root of the punishment she was now undergoing. She believed that she was ruined forever by this act. Masturbation as a cause of mental illness was still a commonly held (but no longer scientifically acceptable) belief; but eternal ruination was a bit extreme. Nonetheless, this was her conclusion.[32]

On the basis of this new insight, she concluded that her former happiness had been illegitimate. After she and Robert had married in 1912, she wrote,

We went home, and lived very happily, except that the war grieved and troubled me so much, as I did not believe in war. I believed that God was love, and I could not think people were made to kill each other. I was disappointed that we had no children but felt happy when we adopted Eric, who was known as a war baby. But *now* I know that I had no right to my husband, to my home, to my life in Canada, at all. And I cannot bear the dreadful shame and misery. I know Mr Richardson loved me dearly – and until my illness came, when I could do my duties, we were happy – but *now* I have brought shame and misery and horror upon him and upon us all. What am I to do? I know my body is corrupted beyond all remedy – but will my telling you all this give any clue to a remedy? *Now* I suffer horribly, and in my corrupted womanhood there is no hope. The shame is all, the awful, awful shame. I have been a Pharisee and a hypocrite and betrayed *all* my loved ones. I cannot bear the dreadful shame and misery because the other side is there, the side of me that *loathes* and *loathes* all evil. I cannot write to my mother, so good and so unselfish. I know that I deserve death – and yet I am fearfully afraid of it. There were so many – oh! so many, who looked to me for guidance. I cannot tell you how I loathe all I have wrought.

I do not want to move from the bed, or ever to see *anyone* again. I am so sorry. I do wish I might die and be out of all existence for evermore. Please consult with the other doctors and decide upon the immediate and private poisoning or other *absolute* destruction of my body, as I cannot live and endure this. I am in less pain, I ask not to go out, or to get up. I ask as a special privilege the great boon of death. You know it is terrible. I have no need to tell you, have I!

She signed herself, "Very deeply praying for this, Gertrude Richardson."[33]

It is not clear what she means by "do her duties." My first reading of this was, her sexual duty. However, she may mean more general duties: the domestic and farm tasks, the interpersonal relations between husband and wife (and child), and between the farm wife and the larger community. In any case, it is clear that in her analysis her failure to perform adequately has brought disaster upon her and her loved ones; she is not only a failure and a disgrace, but a danger to the community. Moreover her inability to perform properly did not exempt her from blame, because she caused her incapacity, she argued, by her unnatural adolescent licentiousness.

This poses interesting theological contradictions. Gertrude had insisted that she believed in a God of love, and a world where forgiveness and redemption were possible if repentance existed. People could commit grievous sins out of ignorance or misguided intentions, but not be condemned if their motives were good (self sacrificial, for example). Soldiers who murdered their fellow men were not to be condemned, but rather their courage and selflessness were to be appreciated; they erred, but out of love and innocence. She had urged women not to condemn the sinners who fell from grace (wartime immorality) but rather to uphold their own high standards in a loving and charitable way. The sole suggestion of a vengeful God was her oft-repeated assertion that the apostates, warmongers, and greedy politicians and elites would be judged and barred from heaven for their misdeeds. But now her God was an Old Testament hellfire and damnation version. Without placing too much emphasis on ahistorical intrapsychic interpretations, it is fairly obvious that her visions of devils (Eric told me that these were devils with pitchforks and tails and fire like the Gaderine swine, old-fashioned fire and brimstone fundamentalist devils) were a part of the punitive religion of her childhood environment, which formed part (not the whole) of her early experience.

There is also no mistaking the element of crucifixion here. It seems pervasive and unending; there are paradoxical elements. She had written often that the followers of Jesus must be willing to risk suffering his fate, at least to some extent, and she had also suggested that the battlefield carnage represented a continuing crucifixion of Jesus. So, presumably, did the famine deaths in postwar Europe. And ironically, her suffering the tortures of the damned without release or redemption goes one better the crucifixion of Jesus; at least he eventually died and went to heaven. Yet he could still be crucified repeatedly, while at the same time he sat at the Heavenly Throne. And Gertrude asked repeatedly for her suffering to end in death. She did not want it to go on without end. Whether she thought she would be admitted into heaven is not clear, but I rather doubt she did.

These themes are discussed in a letter that Gertrude wrote to her husband in August 1924; Robert had told Dr Baragar that he had not had a letter from her for a year (although he had news of her from replies to his inquiries, and from Fannie, who had recently visited Gertrude), and suggested she might be reminded to write. She did so. "My dear Bob," she wrote, "I cannot believe it is possible that I have not written for a year ... I have been trying to write but I did not want to write any unhappy things to make all worse than ever." She continued,

I did not dream that our marriage was wrong – was sinful – and unblessed. I was so happy in our little home, so peaceful and full of love – or so it always seemed. Certainly I never dreamed, till the curse fell on me, that all was evil, and that I must bring the awful, unthinkable curse upon everybody ... I thought I was one of God's children, that, failing our own, he gave Evil [sic; Eric] to complete our happiness – and that together we were guiding him on the way to Heaven. No one knows the unutterable anguish I am suffering, now that my eyes are opened to the terrible, terrible thing that has happened. I wish I could make your life happy, as I believed I was going to throughout this life and the next. I wish, now that I am a curse and not a blessing, that God would *annihilate* me – because that is the only thing that could ever make anything right. The thought of Eternity – the destruction of all – of body and soul and mind and hope and love and truth and faith it is all so terrible. I wish I had never been born. [a line and a half are blanked out] curse is upon the whole world, and I have brought it on, and everything I ever believed *is a lie*. Yet I hate and loathe all evil, and all war and all cruelty and all however – and I do not understand why God made this terrible world, where under the surface, there is nothing at all but suffering, misery and death, no eternal life, no Heaven, none of the things I had always believed when I looked at the starry sky, and all other things that seemed so very wonderful. Now, I can only, for evermore, bow my head in a shame unspeakable. I wish I could be to you what I thought I was. Poor little Eric, the lovely little boy God gave us – I thought that we would save him. Oh what shall I do – what can I say. My reason has not left me – I am accursed for ever. It is too terrible. I cannot pray as I used to. Nothing can help me. I cannot bear to dwell on you and what you must suffer, and my gentle mother, and Horace, who loved and trusted in me. I thought we would all persevere until the end, and be in perfect happiness for all eternity. If God would only give me back what has gone for evermore. Oh I cannot write any more. If only I might somehow, somewhere along [sic] and be what I believed I was. xxxxxxxxxx Your love and forever doome[d] wife, Gertie[34]

Although Gertrude's religious tradition is not one I share and perhaps do not adequately understand, her suffering and pain are impossible to deny. The trials of the flesh were also a plague. She had periodic physical illnesses; some were passing flu or colds, but in the summer of 1924, she had chronic diarrhoea, and, given her childhood history, the doctors feared she had developed tubercular enteritis. She continued to have abdominal pain, and although that gradually improved, she had recurring diarrhoea as late as December 1924. Doctors rejected the TB diagnosis, but were not able to find another cause.[35]

Luckily these bad times were punctuated by periods when Gertrude was happier, distracted, or getting better. In October she had begun to perk up in the afternoons and had starting going to occupational therapy sessions. She had intestinal problems in November and lost some ground, but later that month her previous improvement resumed. This continued in December, and although she felt unwell in the mornings she generally was up and more cheerful by afternoon. Her physical health remained better, too, save for chronic gastrointestinal problems. By early January 1925 she was relatively cheerful, lucid in interviews. She told one of the doctors that the idea of suicide seemed impossible to her now. She knew she was not totally well yet, but she was certainly much better that she had been for the previous two years, she said. She was now able to resist her negative thoughts. She felt lonely and apathetic in the hospital, and wanted to go home. Robert had been to visit her while he was in Brandon for the United Farmers convention early in January 1925; this had made her feel "ever so much better." She said that if she were in her own home, had a bit of housework to do, she could begin to find other interests, things that would occupy her thoughts and keep her from bad feelings. She would start out slowly, and gradually take up her normal life, she said. She really wanted to go home; she thought she was ready. The doctor who had the most frequent contact with her was sceptical. He noted that she had never showed any interest in doing work around the hospital, never showed signs of adjustment, never tried to help. "No ambition, no ability to make an effort, would not get up for breakfast even." However, the superintendent thought she could safely go home, so she left with Robert (who had to sign the release form that he knew he was taking her out against doctors' advice) 11 January 1925.[36]

Any notions about puttering around her beloved little farmhouse were soon dispersed. Robert, his brother Jim, and Eric had been batching it for more than two years and the place was a dirty jumble. Fannie came in twice a week, and did washing and cooking, but keeping the house in order would have been a full-time job. According to Fannie and Fred, it was not just a question of the state of the house. They both thought the setting of the farm was gloomy and depressing, and that Robert and Jim, "though both good natured and well intentioned, were very depressing people to live with." Whatever the reason, after three weeks at home Gertrude "became so low spirited that she had to give up the idea of running the household," and she went to stay with Fannie in Swan River, where she spent most of 1925. She managed fairly well there; although she stayed in bed in the mornings, she was livelier in the afternoons and evenings. At least she stayed on a more or less even keel. She went back home in December, perhaps because Fannie was going away and there would be no one to take care of her, and there she took up what she could manage of her normal routine.[37]

She had her ups and downs through the next few years at home with Robert, Jim, and Eric. Fannie continued to visit periodically when Gertie needed help – to clean, cook, and do the baking, or nurse Eric if he were sick; although it must have been harder to do this now the Liveseys lived in town. The families celebrated the holidays together; Christmas at Fannie's, New Year's Day at Gertie's, or at Fred's while Gertie was away. Robert and Fred shared a threshing machine. Robert, Fred, John and Fannie were mainstays of the local Grain Growers (later United Farmers of Manitoba). Eric did well, and his memories of childhood are mainly happy ones. Sometimes things were strange at home. Eric's friend Elmer, two years older, remembered that about 1927, when Eric was ten and Elmer twelve, sometimes when they would ride home after school on their bikes they would find Gertie still in her dressing gown with her hair down and behaving oddly. But there were good periods, too, when things were normal. Eliza Twilley wrote to her sister Charlotte Flude's daughter Lottie Bailey in December 1927, "Gertie seems much better the last two weeks, it is so nice when I phone her up, to be able to have a nice chat together. I hope she will be able to keep it up, it will be an effort but will be worth it."[38]

On the whole the twenties were good times in the valley. The Richardson family fortunes rose and fell somewhat (as farmers' do) according to the weather and the markets. Robert and Gertie had a model T Ford (but Eric remembers that sometimes money for gas was short if a summer frost damaged the crops) so outings were not difficult to arrange. Gertie sometimes went into town with Robert to shop or visit Fannie. During the winter, they used horses; Swan Valley Museum director John Dubreuil told me about encountering Robert and Gertie coming into town one snowy day late in 1926, and helping Robert with makeshift repairs to the harness so they could get the rest of the way in. Gertie was bundled up, and did not greet him. She had written years before about how she loved winter sleigh travel, despite the discomfort. Robert continued to superintend the Bible class, and

Eric always went with him to Sunday School. Gertie sometimes went, too, but Eric did not recall how often. Gertie's name does not appear in the Grain Growers minute books, and my sense is that she probably stayed close to home, her sense of humiliation keeping her there if nothing else. She had been a community leader for years before her breakdown, and having it widely known that she had been in "the Mental," given the tremendous stigma of being committed, would have been painful for her.[39]

In 1928 Gertie went through a six-month period of having "spells" that lasted about two minutes. These were irregular, "she might have none for some weeks, on the other hand she might have two in ten minutes." She would fall down, become stiff, and her fingers would twitch. But she did not exhibit other signs of epilepsy, and that diagnosis was eliminated. The cause remained unclear; Fannie and Fred were not sure whether Gertie became completely unconscious, or if she had any control over these spells. (It sounds as if they thought she might, from a later report.) She became depressed again, and it became somewhat more difficult for her to be at home. Still, she had good periods. But early in 1930 it all started to unravel again. Eric showed me a snapshot of him and his cousin Jackie Twilley, Fred and Edith's son, dated New Year's Day 1921; Fred had been taking New Year's Day family photos. Gertrude may have intended to send it to someone; on the back she had written, obviously in 1930, "I have been ill nine years terribly." In February 1930 she had insomnia, got very worried about having contracted venereal disease, blood poisoning, or goitre, and talked incessantly. In a phone conversation in March, Fannie found she "could not get a word in edgewise." The following week Gertie visited Fannie, seemed very excited, talked without pause, and was edgy and irritable. Shortly thereafter she decided she wanted to go and live with Fannie and John again. She feared that Robert and his brother James wanted to murder her, she told Dr Bruce in Swan River, and later that day she smashed a window at home to underscore her dismay at Robert's misdeeds. (No one seems to have taken these accusations seriously; Robert was notoriously gentle, kind, and continued to be devoted to Gertrude through these years.) Fannie could not cope with having care of Gertie, and neither could Robert (although he wanted to), even if she were willing to return home. Gertie wanted to live with Fred and Edith, but they had small children and an infant and feared it might not be safe. By mid-April the family decided they had to take her back to Brandon. Robert was reluctant, "He [does] not like the idea of her going away again but ... begins to realise that she must have attention." The humiliating visits to the local doctor and magistrate produced the required documents, and Fannie, John, and Robert took Gertie down on the train on 23 April 1930.[40]

Gertrude was indeed very ill; in addition to her severe disturbance and various minor physical ailments, she had symptoms of a severely worsened form of her chronic thyroid problem. Clearly her fears of goitre were not so unrealistic as they sounded to her kin. Her records show she by then had myxedema, a dangerous and, if unchecked, potentially fatal condition of hypothyroidism. There is no indication of how long she had taken the thyroid extract prescribed for her in the mid-1920s, but if she had been taking it all this time, it obviously was not working. By now the brilliant young psychiatrist Ewen Cameron (who would later conduct brainwashing experiments on his patients in Montreal for the CIA) had been recruited by Provincial Psychiatrist Alvin Mathers to join the staff at Brandon (he was there from 1929 to 1936). He was responsible for admissions; he interviewed patients and their accompanying relatives and friends, and sorted patients into acute (where he worked) or chronic sections of the hospital. Cameron was known for trying innovative treatments; he wanted to heal patients, not warehouse them. However, Gertrude was diagnosed as manic-depressive, and there were few treatments available even by the 1930s. Thyroid therapy had seemed to help sometimes, and other hormonal extracts had been tried less successfully. But most of Cameron's innovations were aimed at other illnesses than Gertrude's. However badly the doctors wanted to cure people, about all they could do for her was try to fatten her up a bit, improve her general health, fill her time when she was able to function, wrap her in cold cloths or keep her in prolonged hot baths to calm her when she became overexcited, and failing that, sedate her.[41]

Gertrude had a difficult summer; her weight dropped to seventy-seven and a quarter pounds, skeletal even on her tiny frame. The doctors tried various sedatives and other medication, to little effect. Finally at the end of September she began to put on a bit of weight, and calmed down enough to enjoy occupational therapy and tell jokes. But this hopeful trend lasted only a few weeks, and by mid-November she was launched into a pattern that would characterise her reports for some time to come. She had brief periods of relative calm wherein she participated with some enjoyment in activities (walks, needlework, reading, chats, letter writing, concerts) and was reasonably lucid and beginning to be herself; then she fell into confusion, excitement, incessant and disconnected talking, hostile and disruptive behaviour. Robert and Fannie wrote regularly, hoping for progress. They (and Fred) visited now and then. But Gertrude was angry at both of them; she blamed Fannie for putting her back in the hospital (although it had been a joint decision, she never seemed to blame Fred as much, perhaps because he had not accompanied them on the trip), and she accused Robert of all sorts of unlikely things. Occasionally she wrote abusive letters; the hospital gave her back one such letter in October 1930, which infuriated her. However, when Robert visited during a United Farmers convention in November 1931, she was mean to him at first, but then enjoyed his visits, and was much calmer and slept better for a period thereafter, according to the records. Reports from her doctor that fall were guardedly optimistic; he told Robert that he feared it would be a "long drawn-out case, but I hope that the improvement will continue." Nonetheless she was hostile toward Robert more often than not; she refused to wear slippers he sent. In January 1931 she wrote out her will, leaving everything to Eric, with her brothers as trustees. Robert's name is not mentioned. However at other times she wrote to him; she also wrote to Eric (she sent him embroidered handkerchiefs) and periodically to other family members, letters which were sometimes normal, other times mixed. Fannie and Robert wrote regularly but Fannie wondered if there was any point; when Gertie was badly disturbed could she read and enjoy letters?[42]

Gertrude often could manage visits. "She holds herself fairly well in hand and her conversation is fair but rambling," her case notes reported. Eric recalls that Robert took him to see her when they went to the Brandon Fair when he was about fourteen; she recognised him and was glad to see him and she spoke more or less normally (although he found the surroundings and the other patients frightening). Naturally enough, after a good visit her visitors thought she was getting better and their hopes were raised. Fannie wrote to one of her doctors in July 1931, "We seem so far away from her and it is impossible for us to visit often but she is always in our thoughts and it seems terrible for her to be there in that condition. If there is the slightest chance that home treatment would be helpful at any time will you please let us know and I will do my best to look after her." But these hopes were dashed when subsequent enquiries brought reports that she was still (or again) very disturbed and her behaviour was often extremely disruptive, abusive, or erratic.[43]

During her bad periods, Gertrude behaved in ways that were indescribably different from her healthy norms: filthy talk, screamed abuse, grossly neglected hygiene. Despite her small size, at times the staff found "it seems almost impossible to keep her under control with drugs, except with heavy doses." The doctors tried to increase her physical exercise (assigning her to participate in a walking group) but nothing seemed to help. It was difficult to know what to do.

Doctor Goulden wrote to Fannie in response to her July 1931 letter, "I agree with you that these cases are very sad and it is very hard to feel one is so helpless when we see people whom we have known in health so afflicted. I can assure you that everything that it is possible to do for Mrs Richardson will be done. I am unable to suggest anything that you might do to help at present. There will be a time which I hope won't be long when she is more able to co-operate and we shall be able to do more for her than in her present uncontrollable condition. It is quite right for you to continue writing letters, she can read them and understand them but of course her overactivity both of mind and body prevent her reacting normally to them." The next month Dr Goulden wrote to Robert that he hoped for a "considerable improvement within the next few months. As you know, she just swings from excitement to depression with short periods during which she approaches normal ... I regret that we can offer very little hope of permanent recovery, but we can look forward to a period when she will be much happier than she is at the present time." Despite this pattern, it is clear from letters in the file that Fannie and Robert continued to hope she would improve enough to go home. She did not. She had good days, or even longer periods, but in the long run, there was little real change. This exhausting and painful state of affairs went on for years and years.[44]

Such a cruel situation wears on devotion and faith. Fannie wrote in the fall of 1933 just after a visit that she had "found her more rational than any time since her return to the Hospital. I expect she does have these good periods, she was able to carry on quite a rational conversation ... each day I found her improved, it made it hard to leave as she keenly feels being in a mental hospital and feels we were cruel and wicked to let her go ... She said the time was long, she could not read and said she was lonely [when she was in a private room as a calming measure during disturbed periods] ... She is, I know, only one of hundreds of patients under your charge, but to us she is Sister and if there is anything I can do to help please let me know because I know she is lonely and sad. I wondered when there, whether there could be a God or whether the Creation of the World was any use after all, but must live on and try to believe."[45]

There were other stresses in the lives of Gertrude's family. Robert was hit by the Depression. The valley was not droughted out, luckily, but there was hardly any point growing crops, prices for agricultural produce were so low. There was pressure from debts; Robert had bought a tractor and other farm equipment in 1928 and 1929. It had seemed like a good opportunity, now that Eric was older and able to take on more work on the farm, for the family to work some of the unbroken land. So Robert had opened the land and put in 200 acres of wheat, but it sold for only 17¢ bushel. Storage charges and other costs ate up the money. Robert was getting older and life was not going well. He continued to be active in the farm movement and in progressive politics. Eric said that the twenties had been a relatively quiet time in the valley for political involvement, but in the early thirties there was a great deal of activity. Eric, who was by then becoming a young man for a father to be proud of, often accompanied Robert to meetings (and had done so since childhood). Robert continued to be active in Sunday School. But in the fall of 1933, this pattern changed. Robert too had a "nervous and physical breakdown." He wrote that he had recovered from it, but it sounds from family memories as if he were not unscathed. He had always been a very calm, deliberate and slow-moving type of person, but now he became more so. He wrote poetry (some of which was published in the local paper) about happier days. Some of his verse was set to music. Eric showed me "Sweet Are the Memories":

> Sweet are the memories of days gone by,
> When our hearts were happy and our hopes were high;
> Memories that cannot fade and never will die;
> Memories of long ago.
> >Chorus:
> >Memories of happy days when you and I
> >Strolled through the meadows and the woods near by,
> >While gladness sparkled in your clear blue eye
> >Beaming with love for me:
> Such are the memories of days gone by,
> Sweet as the perfume of roses on the breeze.
> Memories hold dear though they make us sigh,
> Memories, memories.

(Gertrude, according to the hospital records, had brown eyes.)[46]

Robert and his brother Jim were not really able to manage the farm after his breakdown; Robert lived in a world of poetry much of the time. In January 1934 Eric dropped out of grade eleven to keep the farm going. Robert remained attached to Gertrude throughout, it seems, although he could not visit often. He and Fannie, John, and Fred visited, wrote, and kept each other posted on Gertrude's condition. By now they had more or less accepted that she would not get better but they still hoped from time to time that she might recover enough to come home to be cared for there. Gertrude had some good periods, more bad ones. A letter to Eric survives in her file, apparently to thank him for a box of candy he had sent for her sixtieth birthday in January 1935. The letter reads as if she were watching two movies at once and interpolating their plots: she thanked him warmly for the sweets, then told him, "The boy I adopted (named the same as you – Edward Horace Eric) died in an Australian gaol last Christmas day, 1933, murdered by the god-damned devil, who has employed you as a 'hired' trick-man, so I heard from someone named Livesey, she came to see me. I thought she was Fannie but she was a better woman – a lady, and I imagine a Christian, who could certainly not consign her sister to a lunatic criminal asylum for life … Eddie H.E. died fighting militarism, and he was my adopted son … xxxxxxx I feel much better, will write again soon, take care, Mother."[47] Her file suggests that this was a troubled period. There are various mentions of her appreciation for the kindness of staff, or of her enjoyment of various hospital activities, but these are interspersed with comments about her resentment at being committed and kept there (at "Dr Goulden's god-damned lunatic asylum" or "Cameron's Hospital Murder Home," as she called it in her thank you letter to Eric, for example). Garbled letters such as the above were small comfort to the recipient, yet lucid letters raised hopes. Robert wrote in late March 1935 that Gertrude's last letter to Eric seemed "better composed … Does this mean that her condition is improving?" What greater lucidity typically meant was a slight improvement; in this case she was well enough to go to a movie shown in the hospital, but these better times often were swiftly followed by another period of excessive ups or downs.[48]

Today Gertrude's illness would probably be called bi-polar disorder, and it would be treatable. But today she probably would not have had a full-blown breakdown in the first place. Growing up in England, she would not have had tubercular adenitis, with its long-standing damage to her adrenal system; her meningitis could probably have been nipped in the bud, if she ever got it. Today in Manitoba her kidney disorder could have been treated, her thyroid imbalance compensated, and so on. The whole range of underlying endocrinological stresses she experienced could have been avoided or ameliorated. Although there are no guarantees, there are various options now at every corner that simply did not exist in her day. Early attempts at hormone therapy explored endocrinological solutions, but not enough was known about the neurological and biochemical systems involved to make progress in treatment when hypothyroid (for example) illness was as far advanced as hers. In the late thirties and early forties, experimental treatments with insulin shock and electroshock were used, and reportedly showed some benefit for some forms of manic-depression, but not until the seventies and later were antidepressant drugs or other substances available that attempted to correct or counteract problems caused by biochemical imbalances, which were by then generally thought to cause manic-depressive disorders. This does not rule out a situational explanation; stress of whatever kind can cause changes in body chemistry. But whatever the cause of Gertrude's illness, there is no question that it was painful. The fact that a belief is deluded does not eliminate its pain.

In 1936 a series of events took place which would lead to drastic changes in Gertrude's family. Eric's birth mother Maggie Carr (and her daughter, two years younger than Eric), came to visit her boy. Such visits were permitted in the adoption agreement but she had not come before, and it appears that she had not been in touch with the Richardsons. (However, she may have received reports on Eric's wellbeing through the church or from Gertrude and Robert.) Gertrude had met her when the adoption formalities were concluded in Winnipeg in 1917, but Robert had not accompanied Gertrude on that trip, nor met Maggie elsewhere, as far as I know. Maggie's reasons for visiting, her knowledge of the family circumstances, and her own circumstances are unclear. However her presence could have been a godsend if she had been willing to "do" for the household of Robert, Jim, and Eric, which was no doubt in a dreadful state after years of batching, despite Fannie's efforts. She did stay. She was young (not yet forty), vigorous, headstrong, and probably was able to improve the household's comfort considerably in short order. (Not that they all got along happily all the time, for there were disagreements sometimes, but it was not an easy situation.) Still, that was all to the good.[49]

Things got complicated when Robert became attracted to her and decided they should marry. In order for him to marry Maggie, he had to do something about the status of his marriage to Gertrude. Robert consulted local lawyer S.R. Wright. There had been some discussion of her first marriage to John Leonard Dexter in Leicester in 1899 and the validity of a proposed second marriage in 1912, if Gertrude's recollection of the events was accurate. Whatever the legal particulars, some termination of the present marriage would be necessary. In the summer of 1936 the lawyer initiated inquiries in England about the date of Gertrude's first marriage, as a first step in determining how to deal with Robert's desired remarriage. Gertrude's family got wind of this; they may already have been upset about Maggie's presence in Gertrude's home. Having someone there who would take over domestic responsibilities was a boon; Fannie had pitched in over the years but she was getting older and in any case there were limits to how much she could do to keep Gertrude's household afloat. But having another woman take over Gertrude's husband was quite another matter. The precise sequence of events is not clear, but the situation caused the previously close relationship between the Richardson household and the Twilley-Livesey households to erupt into hard feelings and mistrust all round.[50]

Robert wrote to the Medical Superintendent in December 1936, "Please ask Mrs Richardson how old she was at the time of her first marriage." Dr Pincock replied the record said thirty-six years old, referring to the 1912 marriage. Robert wrote again, "If Mrs Richardson is well enough, there is no reason she should not give you the answer, either her age at the time of her marriage to Leonard Dexter, or the year. Her relations have been spreading slanderous reports about me and my lawyer tells me that it is necessary to get the information that I am asking for at once. Under the circumstances we cannot go to them to find out what we want. It means a great deal to me so if you can help me I shall be very grateful. It takes too long to get a reply from England." Once the information was received, Wright obtained the details from England. It seemed that the first marriage had never been annulled, and despite the fact that it had never been consummated and would automatically have been annulled upon application, until such an application was made, the marriage remained a fact of law. Thus, Gertrude had not been free to marry Robert. Their marriage had been bigamous. The advice they received in 1912 had not been sound. Why had their advisors given them the wrong information?[51]

The issue is more complicated than it would at first appear. There was a distinction in English law between a void marriage and a voidable one; a void marriage never had existed in law and could be ignored, while a voidable one had to be declared null and void, even if such a declaration would be automatically forthcoming upon application. A void marriage, for example, could involve an invalid ceremony (fake clergy, no paperwork), parties ineligible to marry each other (too closely related, underage, married to someone else), or lack of consent (duress, unsound mind). A voidable marriage could involve inability to consummate (consistent refusal could be taken as a form of inability under some circumstances), or unsoundness of mind, for example. The situation has been ambiguous; sometimes it could be hard to distinguish void from voidable, and it may have been thought that his inability to consummate or her insanity were both indications that this was a void marriage. In the twentieth century the trend has been a move from void to voidable (which is another confusing factor, since theoretically a marriage could be void at one point in time, then have become voidable purely due to the passage of time and evolution of legal practice). The absolutely safe course was probably to go through the court process and get a declaration of nullity. But under the circumstances, it is easy to see why that was not done; it was expensive and may have seemed unnecessary. However incorrect the advice given in 1912, it is not difficult to understand how Gertrude and Robert might have come to the conclusions they did.[52]

Not only had Gertrude's first husband been alive at the time Gertrude and Robert married, Wright learned, he had not died until 1934. That was all Robert needed to know, but I wanted to find out more. I learned that Dexter had also remarried, in March 1920 to a twenty-three-year-old nurse (he was then forty-six) who bore twin boys that July. According to the marriage licence (and the record shows that it was he who provided the information), he was a widower, employed as a political agent (an employee of a political party; I was unable to find out which one). His wife came from a wealthy area in the countryside, the daughter of a farm bailiff (farm manager) for one of the estates. I do not know what he did between 1901 and 1920, but at the time of his marriage he was living in Loughborough at the same house (called Rose Cottage) that his family had occupied since 1899.[53]

During the early 1920s Dexter worked as a cabinetmaker, entering the Loughborough union local at the end of May 1920, according to union records. Cabinetmakers' earnings could vary widely depending on their level of skill and the circumstances of their employment, but the union rate in 1921 (after a two penny an hour wage cut) was nearly £21 a week. The pound was worth about $5 then, so in Canadian terms this was a very good wage indeed. This would not be enough to buy a house but it was certainly enough to support a family respectably and comfortably, assuming full hours. I lost sight of the family until Dexter's death at age sixty in December 1934; at that time they were living in Sutton, Bonnington, Leake BD, in Nottinghamshire. He likely had been ill before his death (as there was no postmortem) from "cerebral haemorrhage" and "hyperiesis" [sic; hyperpiesis]. I did not trace his children or second wife.[54]

Robert was angry when he saw the documents from England, probably some time in January 1936. Eric told me he had not paid much attention at the time (and of course it was not the sort of thing that Robert and Maggie would discuss in detail in Eric's presence), but he thinks Robert was particularly upset that he had not been fully informed during their courtship about the details of Gertrude's first marriage. Eric described it as an issue of full disclosure. Robert belonged, Eric said, to an era when someone's personal word was as good as a signed contract and personal honour depended upon fair dealing. Robert thought the family had not dealt fairly with him in respect of full disclosure. It is not clear to me what crucial piece of information Robert felt had been withheld. According to Gertrude's accounts (discussed in chapter three), Robert knew the marriage was unconsummated. I presume he knew that there had been no formal annulment (although it is conceivable that this was never baldly stated). Robert had talked to a lawyer and their minister, and they too, and possibly the minister who performed the ceremony or the city clerk who issued the licence, knew the pertinent facts, if I have correctly interpreted what Gertrude wrote about those events. Had Robert assumed Gertrude was a widow (Fred told John Dubreuil in 1972 when he donated Gertrude's poetry manuscripts to the local museum that the first husband had died during the Great War) and Robert was horrified to learn he had been alive all these years? Or perhaps the family had used the "seven years missing and presumed dead" rule of thumb for Dexter, on the basis of which Robert (and they?) assumed Gertrude was a widow? Eric wondered if Robert thought that Gertrude had concealed her inability to have children; however her account of the circumstances of the remarriage suggests that she had no such knowledge to conceal. She had hoped she could still have children, she said. (Besides, no one had ever established which was the infertile partner, as far as I have been able to determine; everyone assumed it was Gertrude.) However, it is impossible to reconstruct who told (or did not tell) what to whom about this first marriage. Whatever the case, Robert now had grounds for an annulment. Eric has the impression that Robert was going about this quietly; public arguments were not his style. It is not clear what contact Maggie had with Gertrude's family or with Swan River residents, what she may have said about the situation, which by that point was explosive.[55]

The family split became total. Fred was as upset as Robert, possibly (Eric thinks) because the family name was besmirched again, or would be if Robert's annulment and remarriage exposed Gertrude as a bigamist. Fred had a temper; whether or not as the result of a confrontation with Robert, he took action. Fred went to Robert's house and removed Gertrude's personal things: her wooden writing desk, her sewing machine, a chest of drawers where she kept her papers, various items that Wilfred and Eva had brought or sent from Japan and Korea, and other treasures. If Gertrude wasn't a Richardson any longer, then Fred had the right to collect her belongings, which had no place in that house, he told his daughters. Fannie wrote to the hospital enquiring how Gertrude was faring, saying "I used to get the information from Mr Richardson, but now he has living at the farm the mother and sister of the adopted son and there is talk of him trying to divorce my sister ... Under these circumstances I have no communication with him." Robert wrote in June 1937, "These will probably be the last articles that I will be providing, so please send requests for clothing direct to Mrs J. Livesey in future. I sent her the last one but she returned it though the mail. You will be surprised to learn that I have discovered that the marriage between Mrs Richardson and me was not legal and a former husband was living up until two and a half years ago. I have positive proof of this, and am applying for an annulment which I expect will be granted as I have legal advice from three different places. I am taking this step not because she is where she is, but to get out of an intolerable situation. Some of her relations here have spread lies about me and a lady friend, and you would not blame me if you knew all the circumstances." Fannie later wrote in response to the hospital's query about her willingness to supply clothing and other necessaries, "I have bought all her clothing since she has been in the hospital until the last order and my husband was unwilling for me to do this whilst another woman was living in [Gertie's] home."[56]

The records are unclear as to whether Gertrude knew any of this. Robert or his lawyer could have written to her; Fannie or Fred could have told her. There are comments in an autobiographical letter she wrote to her doctor in 1939 that could indicate she knew what Robert had learned and intended to do, however these are ambiguous. There is also her behaviour late that summer. She went through a very bad spell in August of 1937; she had been overexcited for months, but in August for several days she "would stand at the windows screaming," and had to be transferred to an area where she would not disturb her wardmates. However she had gone through similar periods before, and this may be coincidence. Even if she had been told, she regularly accused herself of so much wrongdoing and experienced pain from imaginary tragedies, that this real one might have been just one more. There is no trace of any further contact with Robert. Fannie continued to write and visit, supply necessities, and do what she could to make Gertrude's life more pleasant. Fannie sent parcels of sweets sometimes, and Gertrude enjoyed these. The doctor had said in September 1937, "I think she will appreciate some little attentions of this kind. We are anxious that she might be given as much individual care as possible. She has been quite difficult lately and still remains in a rather sad state of excitement ... but is looking well physically." At the suggestion of the doctor, Fannie regularly sent small amounts of money to be credited to an account with which Gertrude could purchase fresh fruit or other treats to supplement the monotonous (and inadequate) hospital diet. Fannie still hoped for some miracle that would allow Gertrude to get well enough to go to Fannie's to be cared for there. Gertrude spent her days reading (especially enjoying a weekly newspaper sent her for many years by a friend in England), listening to the radio, and attending hospital entertainments. Her niece Connie, and once Connie's daughter Peggy, visited at various times in the late 1930s, and found Gertrude to be seemingly just fine, rational and able to enjoy a visit. The nurse told Peggy it was a good day. Retired nurse Jean Findley McGregor recalled that during good periods, Gertrude sat in the day room and talked – and talked and talked, at times to no one in particular.[57]

Robert died suddenly of a stroke in November 1938 at the age of sixty-two. The annulment proceedings had not been set in motion; Eric told me that all the necessary documents had not yet arrived from England. Robert's obituary made no mention of Gertrude, saying "he had no family [wife] and Eric is an adopted son." The doctors decided not to tell Gertrude he had died. Robert left no will; at that time the estate (up to $10,000) automatically went to the surviving spouse. It is not clear that Gertrude was still legally his spouse (she was listed as such on the death certificate) or if the estate went to Eric, but in any case there was not much of an estate. The farm was saddled by debt, as so many were during the Depression. Robert had bought another piece of land just south of his quarter section; the loan had been guaranteed by some cousins and the original homestead used as security. When Robert could not pay off the loan, the Manitoba Farm Debt Adjustment Act allowed Robert, Jim, and Eric to farm and keep the machinery, paying a third of the grain crop toward the debt, to the company from whom they had borrowed. After Robert's death, the cousins took over title. Eric, then twenty-one, rented the farm from them for a couple of years; he and Jim farmed and Maggie and Eric's sister lived with them. Maggie did not want to lose her boy to a daughter-in-law and discouraged Eric's contact with young women. His cousin Jackie, Eric's closest friend from babyhood, who sounds like a delightful scamp (and who unfortunately died young, leaving a widow and small children), tried a bit of matchmaking from time to time; Eric was a well-brought up, intelligent, and handsome young man, and an accomplished banjo player who occasionally played for social events. But Jackie and Eric never quite managed to pull it off, and Maggie was determined when necessary. (I heard stories about this from an old-timer who I promised would remain nameless; Maggie insisting at community dances that Eric dance only with her, Maggie making a scene when she caught Jackie and Eric talking to girls.) Eric never married. In 1941 he had gone to a relatively nearby wooded area of Saskatchewan and cut timber; he subsequently built a two-storey house into which they moved into in 1953. At some point around then, Eric's sister moved into town where she still lived in 1991. Jim had left in the 1940s; he and Maggie did not get along. He died in a nursing home in The Pas in 1959, aged seventy-seven, and is buried in the family plot in Dauphin. Maggie Carr died in the 1970s. Eric still lives in the house he built for them; he is retired, still plays the banjo once in awhile, is an enthusiastic gardener, an absolutely dreadful housekeeper (batching it), an intelligent and well-informed conversationalist. (He was very kind to me. I still have two pink flowering houseplants he gave me, grown from cuttings from the daughter-in-law of one of Gertrude's old suffrage colleagues.)[58]

"It is dawning on me that I may not live to see my boy or my beloved Homeland," Gertrude wrote to her doctor late in 1939. Indeed, she did not. She spent the rest of her life in that "terrible place" as she called it sometimes. Perhaps she could have gone home for brief periods; as her doctor wrote to Fannie, in her good periods "she goes along quite happily most of the time," talking, hearing voices from the past, writing letters, going to movies and concerts. I had assumed before reading her file that the main obstacle to her return home after 1936 was the fact that another woman was living with her husband and it was known that he was divorcing Gertrude (or worse, that she was a bigamist). In such a small community that left Gertrude no place to be comfortable. Because she seemed so rational during visits and her letters often were quite normal, her family thought that she could have been home, at least for some periods. (Today, no doubt, she could have been, or she might have recovered entirely.) I no longer think that. Perhaps by the 1940s she could have gone home for visits during her good times. But even then she was very easily upset and could become extremely irritable and then very noisy. She was much less upset than formerly, and no longer needed heavy sedation, baths, or cold packs to calm down, but she still spent much of her time in isolation to keep her agitation to a manageable level. Fannie asked in 1942 if there was any chance she could go home, but Gertrude needed more nursing care than Fannie could provide, and the doctor did not think it would be good for either of them. Gertrude had for several years been eating and sleeping well; earlier concerns about her weight had vanished and by 1944 she weighed a plump 130 pounds. "She is a likeable person when she is well," an attendant noted, "cheerful, courteous." Gertrude seems to have resigned herself to being in the hospital by then; a case file note from April 1945, when Gertrude was seventy, described her cheerfulness, and said, "She is always putting bread crumbs on the window sills for the birds. She enjoys all hospital entertainment and helps with the ward work." But she still talked incessantly and often incoherently, saying, for example, that "she was the devil's only daughter."[59]

A letter to Connie written in February 1946 was perfectly rational, discussing family news, birthday gifts and messages, and describing a surprise birthday party she had enjoyed. There were several different types of cake (including one sent by Edith Watson Twilley), cookies, grapes, and a box of birthday chocolates (all rare delicacies during wartime rationing), "so there really was a feast." Another undated letter contains a lively description of an impromptu tea, combining goodies Connie had brought with hot cross buns baked by another visitor; her wardmates and the nurses shared the goodies. Gertrude does refer to a recent bad day, and parts of her discussion of Swan Valley people seem less coherent (on the other hand, they were also less legible and I didn't know the people or the events to which they referred). Nonetheless, she had some enjoyable times and was able to remain involved with her family. It was not all suffering and misery. But she was far from well. Eliza Twilley had died in England in 1942; they had not told Gertrude. However when Connie's nineteen-year-old-son Donald was killed overseas in the spring of 1945, Fannie thought they had to tell her; she always asked for news of him and "it is hard to have to deceive her." Gertrude had been doing well, but later that summer she was so agitated for a brief period that she had to be physically restrained. The old pattern of ups and downs still was in place. When Fannie visited Gertie in February 1946, she was "so perfectly rational when we were there that we wonder if there is a chance of her being alright again or a possibility of her coming home." The doctor replied, "Mentally, there is no change and I think you would find her very confused and restless should she be discharged. We would advise strongly against this move."[60]

Gertrude's physical health worsened; she had arteriosclerosis and degenerative heart disease. She was weak, confined to bed, and when Fannie visited her in August she found Gertrude "had failed considerably since I was there six weeks earlier." Should she come again, Fannie asked? "I want to help her if there is anything I can do." But they had said good-bye. Gertrude died of heart failure the fifth of September 1946. Family members left to mourn her, according to her obituary, were her sister Fannie and her brothers Fred, Frank, and Horace Twilley; Eric was not named. Some months later, the hospital sent Fannie her sister's personal effects; along with the book, locket, wedding band, garnet and diamond ring, and silver brooch was the gold bracelet with padlock that Horace had sent her in 1917, to celebrate their love for and pride in each other's stand for conscience's sake. Horace was never defeated by that war, by his years of imprisonment, or by life. Gertrude was. Given her bent for martyrdom, she probably would have agreed to undergo her twenty-five years of suffering as a prisoner of another sort, if God had sat her down and made her an offer, if she thought her suffering would bring about any sort of redemption for the world. Or for anyone. But I don't think it did. I don't think she thought so, either.[61]

Epilogue:
"These Things Were
Worth Doing"

A Dream of Mine

I did but dream, for still I hear The cruel sounds of strife;
And woe and misery and fear O'erhang all human life.
And yet I dreamed, dreamed that the day, Had dawned for earth again,
That love, encrowned, held royal sway And triumphed over pain.

I dreamed that toilers toiled no more As goaded oxen do,
But that the whole world's garner store Belonged them as their due;
That books and songs, and all things sweet And beautiful and fair
Were poured as treasures at their feet Till life grew like a prayer.

I dreamed that children played in glee, That men were proud and brave;
That Life was Love and Liberty, That all men sought to save;
That "hero" meant no more the man Who drew a warrior sword,
But one who loved the nobler plan Of Jesus Christ, the Lord.

I dreamed that gardens bloomed anew With tenderer, lovelier flowers,
All touched with early morning dew; That on the golden hours
Each day sped by – but now, alas! The sounds of war I hear –
Oh may the hideous discord pass And joy and peace draw near!

I did but dream, I did but dream – I did but dream I knew,
But I will toil until I die To make the dream come true.[1]

Gertrude wrote that poem around the time she set up the Women's Peace Crusade near the end of 1917, with conscription looming as the near-inevitable outcome of a rigged election. It seems remarkable to me that she was able to draw on this vision of a peaceful world, to keep working toward hope. She would begin to lose that capacity for renewal in the next few years, not so much because of depressing changes in the world around her (although these were plentiful), but because her health breakdown blocked her access to her source of vision and hope.

Discovering that Gertrude had experienced mental illness in 1901 and again later in her life had raised questions for me about telling women's stories: What is worth talking about? What is properly the subject of historical or biographical writing? The stories of ordinary women's struggles and tribulations are rarely told, little is known about the experiences of working class women, and the history of war and peace is heavily slanted toward the prowar side. Little is known about antiwar movements, and especially about the lives of women activists. Aside from scholarly issues, we know from our own experience that it is frightening and sometimes dangerous to make waves, and the more we can learn about what difficulties our foremothers faced and how they overcame them, the more we can be heartened or forewarned. But the emphasis in such inspirational history as does exist is usually on overcoming obstacles, rather than on the times that someone was overcome by them. People do get overcome. Illness overcame Gertrude in 1901.

The details of a debilitating illness pose problems for a biographer. Does talking about being overcome not make Gertrude seem like a victim? Are only victims overcome? In fact, Gertrude recovered from that first illness. But even if her story had ended there, she still would have contributed an important part to our legacy of remarkable, brave, caring women, and her story would be no less meaningful. An illness that cuts short a life and a woman's contributions is still worth exploring; at the least, it sets a life in context. Dissent can have painful consequences. If we believe that we benefit from the bravery and courage of a woman like Gertrude who worked for peace and justice in the past, and I think we do, then we benefit from her having risked these painful consequences. That conclusion was much easier to come to when I knew Gertrude had recovered and gone on to contribute so greatly to the feminist, socialist, and pacifist traditions, and before I learned how she had spent the last twenty-five years of her life.

What can the historian (or anyone, for that matter) conclude about the meaning of a life, when it followed the patterns of Gertrude's? When a productive and admirable life turns to incapacitating illness, to madness, when the person herself is unable to look back in the ripeness of her years, trace her own paths, and assess her destination, how can an outsider presume to step in and do so in her stead? Even before postmodernism, that would create an untenable subject position. My world and world-view differ so from Gertrude's, I am not sure I grasp adequately what I hear her saying to me. But some things are pretty clear. Gertrude came from a world where duty was fundamentally important; inexorable, freely chosen, binding, loving, joyous, liberating, paradoxical duty of a life of Christian service. Like many evangelicals or others of profound passion and commitment, she was accustomed to rely upon prayer, meditation, and deep searching to discern the form that her service was meant to take. Many devout seekers found paths different from hers; during the wars, to take an obvious example, most people felt called to a duty that put them into direct opposition to Gertrude and her comrades.

For Gertrude, the way to discernment was to put Christ into the picture. Whatever would be the right thing to do in response to his actual living presence in a particular setting (in a situation of poverty, cruelty, ineqality, injustice, war), that would be the right choice for her. Conversely, if it would be wrong to do it to him, then it was wrong to do it to anyone. Everyone was as important as he; everyone deserved as much as he. He had left instructions: feed my lambs; whatever you do to someone, you do it to me; love one another. She took these literally.

Gertrude had known from the time she was a girl that she wanted to spend her life in service to her fellows. The details of her plans changed according to circumstances; and the methods, no doubt, and certainly too the strategies she came to see as necessary to accomplish her aims, as she carried out her calling. Gertrude believed with certainty that there was a Creator at work in the world, summoning humanity to live lovingly and courageously and thus grow toward its ultimate purpose. She apparently knew what that was; I don't understand, but I know she believed it. She cherished "womanly" qualities as those which all people needed to cultivate in order to help humanity achieve its purpose. As she said about what she called callousness, that is, the ability to forget painful things and get on with everyday life, "Tenderness for human suffering, increased sympathy for the wrongs and sorrows of others, have ever tended to a higher refinement of the individual, as of the race." Tenderness and sympathy were not very comfortable for those who felt them, those who might otherwise feel themselves immune or lucky in their escape from pain, but without tenderness and sympathy people closed themselves off from each other. It was only through being open to each other, by admitting to our connection, living in a spirit of community, that individuals could be fully human. "Let us make the world a small place; let us bridge the gulfs, enlarge our borders, stretch the hand of brotherhood across the chasms." Any pontificating politician could say that; Gertrude tried to live it.[2]

Gertrude had a taste for sacrifice; as she said of herself in December 1914, thinking about the war in Europe, "I possess a nature that suffers with others, so that unless I pray to grow more selfish, I cannot be happy while men are dying – and homes are being desolated." But sacrifice is not the same as suffering. Sacrifice is redemptive; some good comes from it. Some lesson is learned, some path chosen. Some happy ending, further on down the line. Her images of sacrifice were those of Christ, of women bearing children and caring for others, of men refusing to kill others, of women refusing to urge them to, and of soldiers suffering and dying for high (if mistaken) ideals.[3]

As No-Conscription Fellowship leader Clifford Allen said retrospectively of the paradoxical situation created by the war, bitterness and hatred internationally had been counterbalanced by "the most wonderful exhibition of self-sacrifice and unselfish heroism ... [whilst people] were held by ... the spell of the military machine ... [and] believed it their duty to bow before that machine."[4] Gertrude believed it was her duty was to oppose the machine, but she recognised other heroisms. She and her comrades were diverse in beliefs, but they were united in their conviction that each person was sacred (or whatever the equivalent term); each one expressing some essential value and worth, which could never justifiably be assaulted. How ironic that in the latter part of her life she lost her certainty of a Creation formed in love and goodness, and felt herself to be cast out from any community, human or divine. How ironic that in the last decades of her own life the motif was not redemption, but struggle against the inexorable deterioration of her body, her intelligence, her spirit, and her dignity. How dreadful that her essential person was confounded, her inner voice silenced, the line out of service except for periods when the static was so heavy she could not decipher the message. Except in a few moments of extreme pessimism and illness, Gertrude would never have foreseen that outcome for her life. While she was in health, she could draw on faith and hope. Despair was a feature of her illness, not a byproduct of foresight.

I do not share Gertrude's religious beliefs, her temperament, or her taste for sacrifice. I cannot find any good in her years of illness; they remind me more of waste, of travesty, of the cruel tricks of time and place. It is difficult not to succumb to the historian's sweetest temptation: to think "if only" things had not turned out as they did, if only she had recovered. And yet, Gertrude is not diminished by my inability to walk her whole path in her shoes. When I "met" Gertrude, I wanted to know how women like her managed to do peace work, where they drew their strength and found their courage, what they accomplished, and how they sustained each other. Knowing the horrible details now, I see that there is no easy path, there is no blueprint. Feminist theologian Sharon Welch could be talking about Gertrude, as she discusses an ethic of seemingly hopeless struggle. Welch calls this an "ethic of risk." Such an ethic "begins with the recognition that we cannot guarantee decisive changes in the near future or even in our lifetime," she writes. It is "propelled by the equally vital recognition that to stop resistance, even when success is unimaginable, is to die. The death that accompanies acquiescence to overwhelming problems is multidimensional: the threat of physical death, the death of the imagination, the death of the ability to care."[5]

Gertrude risked caring; she risked applying literally the ultimate Christian principles and practice to daily life and to social organisation. She looked to see what that would be like, and she risked telling what she saw. As Dorothy Smith points out in connection with the disruptive potential of women's truthtelling, "The story she would tell, if taken seriously, if heard fully and properly, and particularly if heard and taken up as a basis for making change, would disrupt the locally established order of home and family." For starters.[6]

The title of this epilogue comes from the farewell column by the editor of the No-Conscription Fellowship weekly newsletter *The Tribunal*, published between 1916 and 1920 in England. The newsletter and its publishers were under surveillance, and, in the latter part of the war, underground. Joan Beauchamp, the official (legally responsible) publisher of the newsletter, and Bertrand Russell, the co-chair of the NCF, both spent time in prison for material they published in the newsletter. Thousands of men went to prison as COs. Again and again, by nearly any measure, the NCF and their ilk were on the losing side. They did not prevent conscription, eliminate militarism, or shorten the war. Yet Ernest E. Hunter's farewell editorial was quietly triumphant. As he saw it, *The Tribunal* had accomplished three things: exposed military tyranny, helped to create a network of support for prisoners of conscience, and "won a noteworthy victory for liberty of opinion and the freedom of the press." He believed "these things were worth doing" for their own sake, and better still, to inspire supporters to carry over into other parts of life the spirit that had animated the endeavours of *The Tribunal*.[7]

Gertrude's life work was worth doing for the impact she had on her own time, in her own terms. Certainly she made an important contribution to the suffrage movement, to community building, and to the antiwar movement. But there were, and remain, other more fundamental standards by which to judge her life. In those terms the real question was not efficacy but faithfulness to the way of unconquerable love. In those terms, her life was glorious and triumphant. The worth of her life in our time, in terms other than those of the social gospel or Christian radical, depends almost entirely on us: on what lessons we learn from her and how we apply them. Certainly there are great courage, strong conviction, and loving service to be found; an eye for beauty, for berries in the woods, veggies in the garden, and wonderful food on the table. When I drive in the changing seasons between Edmonton and Athabasca, I see valleys crystallised with hoarfrost, or fields of green so lush I wish I ate grass; I see huge skies of impossible blueness, or of black cloud pierced by white and gold columns of light. I think of Gertrude then, of her faith in the earth's goodness and her joy in the beauty of the prairie landscape. Gertrude was not afraid to stand up for right; or, rather, Gertrude sometimes was afraid but she stood up anyway. I have been living with her for more than ten years now, off and on; spying on her, following her, eavesdropping, reading her letters, listening in on her conversations, gossiping about her with anyone who knew her or her comrades. I have learned a lot about her, but I think I have learned more *from* her.

Solving the mystery of Gertrude's life: the historian as detective. Is that a biographer's conceit? What is there to learn from such investigations? I read mysteries; a lot of historians do. Reading mysteries is reassuring recreation, but there are also important insights below the easy surface. Mystery writer David McCullough's fictional snoop Naomi's comment at the end of an adventure gave me pause: "The thing about mysteries is that they are never really solved. It's all a matter of memory and forgetfulness and secrets that best stay that way. That's why detectives in novels are such fools. They actually seem to think they know what happened. There are always the bits and pieces we can never really know."[8]

During the despairing days of 1918, Gertrude wrote to Violet McNaughton, "There must be others, if only I could find them." She and her comrades find people like us, across time. Like the fictional detectives I have quoted in the beginning and end of this biography of Gertrude, this nonfictional historian knows that I really cannot be sure "what happened" (nor can anyone else; historian or not). Looking back on my reconstruction of Gertrude's life, I cannot be sure who has created which piece of her story. I wanted to help her tell it; she could not speak to you by herself. I guess I did not turn out to be the simple mouthpiece I anticipated, as I seem to be speaking my words, not just hers. Yet I have had to allow myself to be changed by her words, in order to write my own. Although I know that I cannot ever get her story quite right, I still want to tell it to you. She dreamed of a world of love and justice, and she worked as long as she could to make that dream come true. I hope that her story will inspire and sustain others who work for that dream.

Notes

INTRODUCTION

1 Gertrude Richardson to Violet McNaughton, 12 January 1918, McNaughton Papers, VM A1 E52, Saskatchewan Archives Board.
2 There is a voluminous literature on feminist peace research and activism: on Canada, see for example the two special volumes of *Atlantis* that I guest edited with Micheline de Sève, vol. 12, nos. 1 and 2, autumn 1986 and spring 1987 respectively. See also Williamson and Gorham, *Up and Doing*. On Ursula Franklin, see *The Real World of Technology*, the CBC Massey Lectures she gave in 1990.
3 Roberts, "No Safe Place," and "The Death of Machothink."
4 Roberts, "Why do Women do Nothing to Stop the War?"
5 Roberts, "Women's Peace Activism in Canada."
6 "Nothing Like the Freedom" is from *Prairie Spirits*, Karen Howe, Deborah Romeyn, and Barbara Spence, songwriters, Winnipeg, Grannyfone Records, 1986.
7 I am indebted to historian Michael Owen, then Assistant to the Vice President Academic, Athabasca University (now Director of Research Services, University of Saskatchewan), for his support and help with the SSHRC grant application, and to CRIAW, Athabasca University, and SSHRC for their research support.
8 Linda McKenna's expertise made it possible to enter into Gertrude's world with a rapidity that would have otherwise been impossible. Linda had agreed to co-author the Leicester section of the book, but her work schedule later made it impossible. I am grateful for her help.

9 Creighton, *John A. Macdonald. The Young Politician* and *John A. Macdonald. The Old Chieftan*. For my critique, inspired by a conversation with Jack Bumsted, see Roberts, "They Drove Him to Drink." Colegate, *Deceits of Time*, 122–3.

10 Stanley with Morley, *The Life and Death of Emily Wilding Davison*.

11 Trofimenkoff, "Feminist Biography," and Cook, "Biographer and Subject." On religion, women, and social change see Eck and Jain, *Speaking of Faith*. I found the writings of Carter Heyward very helpful for understanding Gertrude's perspective. I also appreciated the Amenicida Collective's *Revolutionary Forgiveness*, Welch's *Communities of Resistance and Solidarity* and *A Feminist Ethic of Risk*, and Ruddick's *Maternal Thinking*.

12 Grant, *Blind Trust*, 252.

13 Grant, *Blind Trust*, 252. Smith, *The Conceptual Practices of Power*, 155–60. Valverde, "As if Subjects Existed," and see also her *The Age of Light, Soap and Water*.

CHAPTER ONE

1 See Osterud, "Gender Divisions and the Organization of Work in the Leicester Hosiery Industry." On public health improvement, summer diarrhoea continued to kill hundreds of infants annually until after the turn of the century, despite improved water supply and sewer and sanitary systems: Simmons, *Leicester Past and Present*, 2–25, 151. Hosgood, "Shopkeepers and Society," 4–8. On the earlier history of Leicester, see Patterson, *Radical Leicester*. Chartism was a working class reform movement regarded by the Tory upper classes as revolutionary. Its People's Charter of 1837 (hence the name) included six demands: universal manhood suffrage, vote by ballot, abolition of property qualifications for suffrage, salaries for MPs, equal electoral districts, and annually held parliaments. See Thompson, *The Chartists*.

2 Information on William Twilley and Matilda Cox, interview with Fannie Twilley Livesey dated 15 June 1921, found in medical records from Gertrude's file at the Brandon Hospital, 18 ff., cited hereafter as Brandon file, obtained courtesy of Dorothy Twilley Shewfelt, July 1991. Marriage of William Twilley and Matilda Cox, 28 July 1834, St Nicholas Marriage Register; marriage of James William Twilley and Eliza Richardson, certificate in the possession of Keith Twilley, Leicester. I am grateful to Keith and Jean Twilley for their kindness in recalling family history and going over family records with me and Linda McKenna, January 1991. Keith is the grandson of Gertrude's brother Frank. For information on the Twilley children, and for the Flude branch of the family, I am grateful to Charlotte Flude Bailey's daughters, Margaret Bailey and Olive Burrell, whose grandmother Elizabeth Richardson Flude was the sister of Gertrude's mother Eliza Richard-

son Twilley. I visited them in January 1991 in Scarborough. I am also grateful for their warm hospitality and delicious meals.

3 Information on Eliza's family from interviews with Dorothy Twilley Shewfelt and the late Joan Twilley Wallcraft, and Fannie's daughter Connie MacDonald, Brandon, Manitoba, September 1986 and on subsequent occasions. Connie has generously given me access to photographs and family mementos of her mother's and answered innumerable questions during several visits and subsequent correspondence between 1986 and 1992. I have also had help from her daughters Myra Carter-Squire and Peggy Neufield. Information on the children's births also draws on listings in the 1881 and 1891 censuses, on a family tree drawn up by Margaret Bailey and Olive Burrell, and on records held by Keith and Jean Twilley.

4 Elastic webs were an essential part of the Victorian boot, for example to ensure fit over the arch of the foot. See Leavitt, *Victorians Unbuttoned* on elastic webs, 41–7, and on webs in footwear, 156–7. On elastic web weavers, Lancaster, "Towards a Socialist Commonwealth?" 48–66. See also Martin, "Elastic Web Manufacture," 326–7, and V.W. Hogg, "Footwear Manufacture," 314–26, in McKinley, *A History of the County of Leicester.*

5 Information on James Twilley's business is based on city directories, the 1881 and 1891 censuses, and interviews with Fred's daughters Dorothy Twilley Shewfelt and the late Joan Twilley Wallcraft, in LaRivière, Manitoba, in September 1986. Dorothy has been very helpful with Fred's material, and before her sudden death in September 1987, Joan spent many hours organising Fred's collection of Gertrude's newspaper clippings, which Dorothy's son Grant Shewfelt kindly photocopied for me. Without their help, and especially Dorothy's, I am sure I could not have done this book. I am grateful for their sustained interest, hospitality, and kindnesses over the years. Dorothy Shewfelt's mother-in-law's pink poppies now grow in my garden, as a reminder of Dorothy's generosity.

6 James Twilley could have been a union member even after he ceased factory work. Leicester boot and shoe outworkers were usually also in the union; there were special agents to liaise with those beyond the shops. Nineteen-year-old daughter Florrie worked as a shoe machinist, and fourteen-year-old Fannie as a shoe fitter, according to the 1891 census.

7 Gertrude recalled her mother as not in very good health and subject to nervous illnesses, but that is at variance with Fannie's and Fred's recollections. On the other hand, "normal" health for many working class women, especially those who were overworked and responsible for the care of large families on small budgets, was not very good. Fannie's and Gertrude's descriptions of Eliza are from the Brandon file, interviews 15 June 1921, 18, and 5 April 1922, 25. Other information about the family is drawn largely from family records and interview sources in Canada and England cited above.

8 Gertrude described her father as having a "nervous, irritable temperament … subject to neuralgia … delicate and frail physically," but Gertrude's descriptions of family health tended to point up nervousness and
   illness far more than Fannie's; this probably reflects the temperaments of
   the two daughters as much as the health of the family. Parts of descriptions of James Twilley are from the Brandon file, interviews 15 June 1921,
   18, and 5 April 1922, 25. Other information is from interviews with Joan
   Wallcraft, Dorothy Shewfelt, Eric Richardson, Keith Twilley, Margaret
   Bailey, Olive Burrell. Fred's recollection is from a letter to his later wife,
   Edith Watson, 11 April 1913. Edith kept his (and a few other) letters and
   brought them to Canada with her in 1918; Joan's widower Bob Wallcraft
   and I unearthed them in Fred's little museum building on the Wallcraft
   farm in LaRivière one evening in July 1991. I am indebted to Nancy Kariel
   for hours spent photocopying them. On the Friars Lane school, Gertrude's
   recollections in a letter in the Brandon file, 6 October [1939], 224–31, and
   an interview with Connie MacDonald, September 1986. Subject to the consent of the family, they, and nearly all of the other material cited in these
   notes, will be donated to the Provincial Archives of Manitoba as the
   Gertrude Twilley Richardson collection.
9 In the newer Victorian housing, the outdoor privy was atop sewer lines,
   but older areas used a form of septic tank or honeywagons, as they were
   called, went around to collect the contents of the toilet pails. On Leicester's development and on housing in the Highfields area, see Pritchard,
   Housing and the Spatial Structure of the City. Linda McKenna and I were
   able to trace the better part of the Twilleys' housing history; we found addresses for the Twilleys in the city directories for various years, supplemented by birth and marriage certificates and the like, obtained from the
   registry office on Pocklington Walk, the Leicester local history collection,
   and other materials in the Leicestershire record office or from family
   members. We drew on Linda's knowledge of renovated Highfields terrace
   housing (she was living in one of the more comfortable examples at the
   time) for the probable layout of the Twilley dwellings. In January 1991 we
   did a walkabout to see what still stood. I am grateful to Celia Harrison
   and Lindsay Manship from the Registry Office for their help in hours of
   searching, and in interpretation of the material we found (or its absence).
10 Information on the parents and early family life from interviews with
   Connie MacDonald, Joan Wallcraft, and Dorothy Shewfelt, September
   1986 and on subsequent occasions. Also comments from interviews with
   Fannie and Gertrude, 14 June 1921, 14; 15 June 1921, 15; and 5 April 1922,
   25, and an autobiographical letter from Gertrude, 6 October 19[39],
   224–31, Brandon file. On Chinese footbinding and noble characters,
   an apparently autobiographical sketch "A True Woman: Her Life and
   Labour," *Canadian Forward*, 10 September 1917. On the London Road

church and the Carnall family, Richardson, "Housekeeping in Canada," *Midland Free Press* (hereafter *MFP*), 4 July 1914, and James, "Centenary of London Road Congregational Church, 1857–1957," pamphlet in the Leicestershire Record Office, and city directories. About the theatre, Gertrude's brother Fred later wrote, "I don't blame my parents at all for not letting me go when young." By then Fred had concluded that "high class theatre is both elevating and instructive," but he thought that young people would gravitate to the cheap thrills; better to avoid it altogether: Fred Twilley to Edith Watson (hereafter Fred to Edith), comments about the theatre, 2 April 1913, 18 May 1913, 19 February 1917, and 25 December 1917, and on early church memories, 7 March 1913 and 3 August 1917.

11 On the Friars Lane elementary school, interview with Fannie's daughter Connie MacDonald, September 1986. On Wyggeston Girls School, Isabel C. Ellis, *Records of Nineteenth Century Leicester*, 232–4. The Admission Registers for the early years were still held at the school when Linda McKenna and I saw them in January 1991. They record Gertrude Twilley's attendance from 13 April 1887 to 18 April 1889, as an exhibitionist (scholarship student). Information on pupils' ages and fees is taken from Wright's city directory for 1887–88.

12 Issues of the *Wyggeston Girls' Gazette* are held at the Leicestershire Record Office. Issues for the years that Gertrude was a pupil contained discussions of such topics as socialism, life at various universities and training colleges for women students, social science articles on poverty, social welfare issues, wages, women's trade unions, visits to cultural and industrial sites, various local examinations and matriculation exams and their results, social events around the school, contests in translation, sewing, essay and poem writing … and so on. There was a distinct feminist slant, and while it was definitely a middle class outlook that was expressed, there was much sympathy for working class and socialist reformism. In fact, many of the prominent Leicester citizens involved in the ILP were among the school's parents, and Wyggeston girls went on to be prominent in socialist, pacifist, and feminist circles. For girls' education ideas of the time see Dyhouse, *Girls Growing Up*, and Gorham, *The Victorian Girl*.

13 After reading several items written by Gertie's older sister Florrie, we wondered if she had also been to Wyggeston, since she obviously had a good education, but there is no trace of her in the school's records. Given the strength of Leicester working class intellectual and cultural life in this period, it is quite possible Florrie was largely self-taught. Bill Lancaster mentions the importance of the auto-didact in Leicester working class culture, and the high importance placed on self-education by hosiery workers is also likely significant as another source of encouragement in Florrie's milieu: Bill Lancaster, *Radicalism, Cooperation and Socialism*, 58–62,

and photograph of the education room of the Leicester Hosiery Cooperative, between pages 42 and 43.

14 Information on Gertrude's cousins is from the Wyggeston Admission
Registers. On pupil-teachers and girls' and women's access to further education, Purvis, *Hard Lessons*, 35–41, 175–81. Charlotte Flude's daughters
Margaret Bailey and Olive Burrell showed me her application for a teaching job around 1924, that contained information about her training and
credentials. Charlotte was Fannie's age, two years younger than Gertie,
and was at Wyggeston from September 1888 to December 1891. Charlotte
left Wyggeston after two years to enter the pupil-teacher program in January 1892, completing the certificate training course in 1899, and along the
way obtaining passes, honours, prizes, and certificates in assorted subjects. She continued her education after some years' experience, obtaining
technical institute certificates in dressmaking and needlework in 1909. On
access to universities, see Turner, *Equality for some*, 167–9, and Vicinus,
Independent Women, 163–77.

15 Vicinus, *Independent Women*, especially chapters 4 and 5.

16 On James Twilley's sacrifice, Gertrude's girlhood recollections in a letter
in the Brandon file, 1 May 1924, 102. On Rodhouse, Richardson,
"Militarism in Canada," *Leicester Pioneer*, 9 November 1917, and information in Leicester city directories. On feminist reformers and working class
women, see Mappen, "Strategists for Change."

17 On her school years and illness, interview with Gertrude and Fannie,
14 June 1921, 14–18, interview with Robert Richardson, 1 April 1922, 23–4,
interview with Gertrude 5 April 1922, 25, letter from Gertrude 1 May
1924, 102, all from the Brandon file. Marriott was honorary surgeon to
various local groups such as the Blind Society.

18 Gertrude described her occupation as "costumier" on her marriage certificate. On dressmaking as an occupation, see Walkley, *The Ghost in the Looking Glass*.

19 Mrs Conquest measured a teacher, then drafted, cut, and pinned a bodice for her, and did the basic draping on a foundation skirt to her measure on a dummy, all in a short period of time. Mrs Kate Conquest is
listed in the city directory for 1887–88 as manageress for the association,
but it is not clear whether the association's offices included a training institution. Her home address appears to coincide with that of a stained
glass artist of some renown, but the relationship is not clear; however,
she was definitely a very respectable type. The technical school listing
mentions "Scientific Dressmaking" in 1900, so it sounds like Mrs Conquest's method represented the approved standard by then. On Gertrude's training, interview with Gertrude and Fannie, 14 June 1921, 14–
18, interview with Gertrude 5 April 1922, 25, letter from Gertrude 1 May
1924, 102, Brandon file. One third of the students at the Working Men's

College in Leicester were women students by the 1890s; see Purvis, *Hard lessons*, 175, 181.

20 Information on her further study and collapse, "A True Woman: Her Life and Labour," *Canadian Forward*, 10 September 1917, and interview with Gertrude, 14 June 1921, 14, and 8 January 1925, 21, Brandon file. I have been unable to find out anything about her parents' education, but Vincent, *Bread, Knowledge and Freedom*, provides information about some self-education strategies of working men in this period.

21 Gertrude's income is impossible to estimate, but a self-trained Liverpool dressmaker who did ordinary sewing in 1887 charged three shillings for a plain servant's dress, seven shillings for more complicated or voluminous styles, and ten shillings for a stylish dress. She estimated that on average she made ten shillings a week for full-time work. Slop workers, who were sweated outworkers who sewed at home, could make as little as sixpence for three days' work. See Jarvis, *Liverpool Fashion*, charges and income data, 18–20; I am grateful to history of costume expert Anne Lambert for this source and for her generous help with information on the history of dressmaking and other aspects of Gertrude's milieu. Fred to Edith, 22 January 1913. Fannie's birthday book, the *Album Scripture Text Book*, London, Ernest Nister, nd, is in her daughter Connie's possession.

22 Family members in Canada told me the boys had worked in the business, but they were unaware that Fannie and Florrie had also done so, at least for a time. The photograph album Florrie gave to Charlie in 1897 is inscribed, "To Charlie with fondest affection from Florrie, 23 August 1897." Florrie's time in the States and information about the Boston cousins are discussed by Fred in letters to Edith, 31 May 1914 and 24 December 1915. Florrie discusses the U.S. in her antiwar letter "Liberalism and imperialism," *MFP* 31 March 1900. Information on Florrie at the time of her marriage is from the marriage certificate at the Leicestershire Registry Office, dated 11 September 1897. On Florrie's interest in religious and political questions, for example, Fred wrote 7 March 1913 to Edith Watson that Florrie had attempted unsuccessfully to get in to a lecture by visiting U.S. preacher Dr Morgan while she was visiting in London. Also on Florrie, see Richardson, "My Canadian letter," *MFP*, 5 December 1914, and Davie, "Let the Capitalists Fight," letter to the editor, *Morning Leader*, 20 September 1899.

23 Information on Fannie's marriage is from Charlotte Flude's daughters Olive Burrell and Margaret Bailey, who were able to provide the details for a family tree of the Flude line and of the Eliza Richardson and James Twilley family, and Connie MacDonald. On outwork at Cooper and Corah, this firm was considered a good employer; they used the most advanced technology and machines. They gave their regular workers paid holidays, but outwork was still badly paid: see Leavitt, *Victorians*

Unbuttoned, 126–30. For several persons I think Fred was referring to the mid-1890s period in his scribbled note on the factory's picture: he only mentioned Gertrude and Eliza, and since Florrie and Fannie probably would have helped if still at home, they likely had left already (unless Florrie was in the States and Fannie still in school); the presence of a lodger suggests hard times; Gertie's and Fred's schedules and time away from home also put it before 1900. On hosiery outwork, see Osterud, "Gender Divisions," 51–2, 61–4.

24 Fred's comments on the Salvation Army are in Fred to Edith, 7 December 1914 and 4 April 1915.

25 Influenced by Lyman Moody's 1873 revival, Meyer had been a minister in a Leicester Baptist church from 1874 to 1878, at which point he decided to leave his appointment to devote his energies to mission work and social evangelism. A group of his followers persuaded him to hold services in the museum building. He also preached at huge outdoor meetings in Victoria Park and opened a mission room in Oxford Street that summer; mission rooms in other districts soon followed. He and seventy-seven founders built a substantial chapel in Highfields in 1880, and the congregation and its activities grew rapidly. On Melbourne Hall, Ernest Kendall, *Doing and Daring*.

26 Gertrude's and John Leonard Dexter's memberships are recorded in the Melbourne Hall Roll Book, 1893–1913, and Committee Minute books, 1896–1901, held by the Melbourne Hall solicitor who generously allowed access to Linda McKenna in February 1991.

27 On Victorian girlhood, see Deborah Gorham, *The Victorian Girl*, especially her chapter on managing puberty, and 88–92.

28 For Gertrude's accounts of these issues, see her letters, 1 May 1924, 102, and 6 October [1939], 224–31, Brandon file.

29 A second book was by Henry Varley, a popular and conservative evangelical writer. He published sex education for boys, among his other works, such as *Private Address to Boys and Youths on an Important Subject*. Gertrude was a good deal more radical than Varley on theological and social matters, although she may not have been at the time her father gave her Varley's book. For example Varley criticised the new theology; Gertrude admired and adopted it. Varley, *The New Theology*.

30 Stead's father and brother were Congregational ministers. F. Herbert Stead was at Leicester's Gallowtree Gate Congregational Church from 1884 to 1890: "Leicester Congregationalism 1800–1900: A Souvenir of the Leicester United Congregational Bazaar 1900," np nd, pamphlet held at the Leicestershire Record Office in the Congregational Church records. Walkowitz, *City of Dreadful Delight*, contains two excellent chapters on "Maiden Tribute" and its cultural consequences, 81–134; thanks to Deborah Gorham for this source. On W.T. Stead, the Sally Ann, and the age of

consent campaign, see Sandall, *The History of the Salvation Army, vol. 3*, 105–12. Stead's articles were published in the daily issues of 6 July–10 July 1885 of the *Pall Mall Gazette*. Also on Stead's campaign, see Raymond L. Schults, *Crusader in Babylon*, 128–92, and Frederic Whyte, *Life of W.T. Stead, vol. 1*, 159–86. Also see "W.T. Stead Memorial Number," *Review of Reviews*, London, May 1912, in the "Collection" compiled by W.H. Fairbarns. Gertrude wrote an obituary poem to Stead and the other Titanic men victims: "Requiem," *MFP*, 8 June 1912.

31 On Josephine Butler, for a brief overview see the chapter in Forster, *Significant Sisters*, 169–204. The Contagious Diseases Acts were passed in 1864, 1866, and 1869, and repealed in 1886. For a later comment by Gertrude on Butler, see Richardson, "Communication," Swan River *Star*, 6 June 1913.

32 Gertrude's underlining. See Gertrude's letters, 1 May 1924, 102, and 6 October [1939], 224–31, Brandon file. Although she reportedly had meningitis in 1893 or 1896, she recovered.

33 I saw the Dexter family house in Loughborough in January 1991. Information about occupants of Gimson's Cottages comes from city directories and burgess (voter's) lists. Gertrude's later account of the marriage: her letter to [illeg] 6 October [1939], 224–31, Brandon file. Information is from the marriage certificate obtained from the Leicester Registry Office and other Dexter family documents obtained from the Loughborough Registry Office. I am grateful to staff at both offices for their enthusiastic help in successful searches and wild goose chases in January 1986 and January 1991. On Gimson's cottages, see Elliott, *Victorian Leicester*, 30. Although the cottages are no longer standing, the immediate neighbourhood is now industrial. I thought this sounded rather grubby, but Leicester historian Malcolm Elliott said not: he got out the architectural drawings at the Leicestershire Record Office and went over them with me. The plans are listed as "Vulcan Street plans 4–1–78, 12596" in City of Leicester records. Malcolm Elliott was a marvellous resource person for diverse aspects of Leicester's past; he facilitated my access to several record collections and helpful informants, and was always ready to chew over questions. I am grateful to him and Jenny Elliott for their warm hospitality. For information on the Gimsons and Vulcan Works, see Walker, "Engineers and Secularists: Some Aspects of the Lives of Josiah and Sidney Gimson." Linda McKenna's expertise in local history was invaluable as she turned up various clues in the voters lists and interpreted items from the Leicestershire Record Office.

34 Underlining in the original: Gertrude to [illeg] 6 October [1939], 224–31, Brandon file. On the tentative VD diagnosis, aside from his use of a common euphemism for VD, his recorded cause of death at age 60 is consistent with syphilis. Here I benefited from conversations with my father, the late Paul Roberts, MD. I have also relied on advice from medical historian

Janice Dickin McGinnis, as well as many hours of reading gory details of the course of the disease in modern and contemporary medical textbooks. "A good many of the strokes leading to sudden death in middle life are probably cases of neurosyphilis, although often set down as early arteriosclerosis of a nonsyphilitic nature," note Stokes et al. *Modern Clinical Syphilology*, 987.

35 Hinton, *Protests and Visions*, 1–12; Rempel, "British Quakers and the South African War," 75–95; Summers, "Militarism in Britain," 102–23; Jones, *The Christian Socialist Revival*, 198–205. Methodist estimate given in Marks, *The Churches and the South African War*, 25; Alfred Marks was honorary treasurer of the Stop-The-War Committee. On the Baptist antiwar position, Halevy points out that despite the official position, some Baptists were imperialists: *Imperialism and the Rise of Labour*, 94–9, 104–10.

36 Hinton, *Protests and Visions*, 3.

37 On the Quaker response in Leicester, Minutes of Leicester Monthly Meeting, 10 October 1899, Leicestershire Record Office. Thanks to Malcolm and Jenny Elliott, co-clerks of Leicester Quaker Meeting, for permission to use this material. Countrywide, see Hewison, *Hedge of Wild Almonds*, 79–84; on the peaceful settlement petition, "National Memorial," *Morning Leader*, 9 October 1899. On working men's clubs see Price, *An Imperial War*, 15–6, 68–83.

38 Stead publicised the STWC in his *Review of Reviews*, see for example the November 1899 issue, "To all Friends of Peace," 473; the magazine is a good source of antiwar activities. On the roots of the Leicester Peace Society, see Rogers, "The Leicester Peace Society." Liddington, *The Long Road to Greenham*, discusses women's nineteenth century peace activism and the timidity of the Peace Society, 13–45. Apparently it was still intimidated by the hostility generated by its efforts during the Crimean War. The British Peace Society had concluded in its annual report for 1861, "It now seems accepted as a maxim which it is almost disloyalty to call into question that whenever England has become involved in a quarrel in any part of the world, the justice or injustice of the quarrel is a matter of no moment compared with the assertion of British supremacy and the maintenance of our military prestige." See Beales, *The History of Peace*, 102, 242. Controversies over Hugh Price Hughes' stand and descriptions of Peace Society activities are in the *Morning Leader*, for example, "Peace From the Pulpit," 14 December 1899, a series of outraged letters about Hughes, 28 and 29 December 1899, "The 'Peace' Society," 6 May 1901, a letter to the editor critiquing the inactivity of the local branch from "Pro-Boer" in Liverpool, 8 May 1901, and a defence of the record of the society and a call for Hughes' removal from Thomas Wright, 11 May 1901. Stead's newsletter *War Against War in South Africa* ran for thirty issues from 20 October 1899 to 10 August 1900. He published a long article against Hugh Price

Hughes' jingoist stand, "The Rev. Hugh Price Hughes: A Study in Super-natural Gifts," in the 2 January 1990 issue.

39 The wrap-up meeting was postponed. The International Peace Crusade is described in the issues of *War Against War: A Chronicle of the International Crusade for Peace*, published from 13 January 1899 to 31 March 1899. The *Review of Reviews*, "Topics of the Month (1) The International Crusade of Peace," January 1899, 34–6, outlines the beginnings. See also Whyte, *The Life of W.T. Stead, vol. 2*, 134–65. On Stead's attempt to promote a national women's committee, "Where are the Women?" *War Against War*, 10 February 1899. The Women's Liberal Federation (WLF) resolution and activities are described in the WLF 1899 annual report section on "Resolutions as Carried by the Council 1899," 99–100; the report noted that WLF executive members were on the committee of the Crusade. Robinson was a Quaker socialist, and key figure in Priscilla Peckover's network of Local Peace Associations; she spoke thousands of times on peace all across the country, from the 1890s until her death in 1912. On her talk in Leicester, see the announcement in *Peace and Goodwill* ("A Sequel to the Olive Leaf. A Quarterly Periodical and Organ of Local Peace Associations"), January 1899. On Leicester and the Peace Crusade, see Stead, "The International Crusade of Peace," *ILP News*, February 1899; "Leicester Town Meeting," *War Against War*, 10 February 1899.

40 Stead reported Peace Crusade activities in *Review of Reviews*; see for example the map of Crusade meetings, March 1899, 253. "The International Women's Demonstration" in the June 1899 issue, 449–50, reported on a planned 15 May demonstration to be held simultaneously in several countries in support of the peace congress. "The John Bright League" is on page 448, ibid. On women peace activists, see Cooper, "The Work of Women," 11–28. Douglas J. Newton, *British Labour*, outlines the British labour and socialist reactions to the tsar's proposals, 63–70.

41 Gertrude's claim to being the first woman, "A True Woman – Her Life and Labour," *Leicester Pioneer*, 26 October 1917; this biographical article was probably written by Gertrude herself.

42 On setting up the networks and Gertrude's involvement, see Stead, "Stop the War! An Appeal for Helpers," *WAWSA*, 17 November 1899, and "Stop the War Memorials: List of Collectors," *WAWSA*, 5 January 1900. The Leicester *Midland Free Press* published Stead's "The War. Proposed Memorial to the Queen," 25 November 1899, informing supporters where to obtain petitions and leaflets. Gertrude probably responded to this notice. I am indebted to Joseph Baylen for help in interpreting clues about Gertrude's STWC activities.

43 The *Leicester Daily Mercury* was owned by Francis Hewitt, president of the Liberal Association, who followed the moderate Liberal line. He printed occasional antiwar letters but did not strongly oppose the war until farm

burnings became an issue and Campbell-Bannerman spoke out in 1901. See Phillips, "A Study of Attitudes." *Midland Free Press* editor Edwin Crew was the father of Gertrude's Wyggeston schoolmate Ethel. On Gertrude's links with the editor, see Fred Twilley to Edith Watson, 15 December 1912. Crew's views, "To Stop the War," *MFP*, 20 January 1900.

44 The WLF was founded by seventeen local Women's Liberal Associations in 1886; within ten years it had grown to 470 local branches. Hirshfield, "Liberal Women's Organizations." An example is given in "Women to the Fore," *WAWSA*, 10 November 1899, describing the annual meeting of the Union of Women's Liberal and Radical Associations in the Metropolitan Counties held 8 November at the National Liberal Club in London, at which an antiwar resolution was passed. The antiwar petition signing and subsequent activities are recorded in the WLF 1900 Annual Report, 19–20. On Gittins and the WLF, see *Summary of Federation News* No. 82 (June 1900), 5; the material is held at Bristol University Library Special Collections.

45 Wicks information from *MFP* obituary articles: "Death of Mr William Wicks" 8 June 1901; Stanton, "The Late William Wicks," "The Late Mr Wicks: Funeral," 15 June 1901; "Leicester Temperance Society," "George Newell and William Wicks," 22 June 1901. See also the eulogy by Gould in "Local Comments," *The Leicester Reasoner*, July 1901. Wicks' letters on the war include: "The Transvaal War," 4 November 1899 and 18 November 1899; "What Shall we Gain?" 13 January 1900; "The Leicester Peace Movement," 10 March 1900; "The Stop the War Meeting," 24 March 1900; "Military Glory," 31 March 1900; "The War Meeting," 7 April 1900. Wicks, "And the Devil Laughed!" *MFP*, 18 November 1899. On the WLF, Hirschfield, "Liberal Women's Organisations," 35–9.

46 Edwin Crew reprinted James' sermons in the *Free Press*, for example, "The Church and the War," 4 November 1899, and "War and God's Providence," 2 December 1899. On James' offer to resign, see Minute Books of the Wycliffe Congregational Church, James to Mr Cox, 9 November 1900, Church Committee meeting minutes, 12 November 1900, special meeting minutes, 21 November 1900, adjourned meeting minutes, 28 November 1900, and James to Cox, 28 November 1900. Thanks to church secretary Mr Howard Rees for access to the Wycliffe records; the church moved in 1952 to suburban Evington.

47 For similarities of Gertrude's and J.E. James' views, see, for example, his sermon, "War and God's Providence," *MFP*, 2 December 1899; Gertrude's later antiwar writings during the First World War consistently echoed the points in this sermon. On Christian atheists and hate mail, "A True Woman," *Leicester Pioneer*, 26 October 1917. One of the founding members of Melbourne Chapel had been a Miss Annie Vice; a woman by that name was a Christian Socialist active in the STWC. On Annie Vice, see, for ex-

ample, "Promotion of Peace," *MFP*, 29 December 1900, and the list of original Melbourne Chapel members, Hunt, *Doing and Daring*, 19–20. The Leicestershire Record Office holds bound volumes of Fullerton's sermons. Miss Vice may have switched to the Wycliffe Church; a Miss Vice is mentioned in committee minutes in connection with a bazaar, 21 January 1903; Archibald Gorrie, peace society member who was active in labour and socialist groups, was also a Wycliffe member. His name appears in the Church Committee records, passim, until the end of the First World War period: Wycliffe Church Minute Books, Wycliffe Church papers.

48 The definitive history of the LSS is Nash, *Secularism, Art and Freedom*. I am indebted to him for his generosity with his research material, his patient and clear explanations of the place and activities of secularists in Leicester, and for several delightful historians' gossip sessions while I was in Leicester in January 1991. The founding date is taken from a brief history of the LSS by Gould, "Our Jubilee," *The Leicester Reasoner*, 11 (January 1902). For a photograph of the Secular Hall, see Elliott, *Leicester. A Pictorial History*, illustration 138. On the early days of Secularism and socialism in Leicester, see Barclay, *Memoirs*. On Quaker socialists, see Socialist Quaker Society Minute Book, 1898–1909, at Friends House Library, London; Ellen Robinson was a member, and Henry Hancock and Charles Wynne of Leicester were particularly active. See also Adams, "A Consideration."

49 See Gimson, "Random Recollections," and Walker's thesis, "Engineers and Secularists." On F.J. Gould, see Nash's article, "F.J. Gould and the Leicester Secular Society," and Gould's *History of the Leicester Secular Society*; Hayward, "In Memory of F.J. Gould." Samples of Gould's educational approach can be found in his regular column, "For the Children," in *The Leicester Reasoner*, as well as in the dozens of books he wrote on the subject.

50 On the Twilley-Hughes friendship, Fred to Edith, 24 January 1915. On hate mail, "A True Woman," *Leicester Pioneer*, 26 October 1917. Florrie's objection to imperialist aggrandisement was presumably on behalf of the Boers rather than the "natives," but not enough of her writing is available to be sure. Davie, "Let the Capitalists Fight," *Morning Leader*, 20 September 1899; the reservist articles included "That Fateful List," 25 November 1899, "Employment Bureau for the Wives of Men at the Front," and "Doling Out the Fund," 6 December 1899. For Florrie's authorship, Richardson, "My Canadian Letter," *MFP*, 5 December 1914. The editor of the *Echo* was fired for his antiwar stand; Whyte, *W.T. Stead, vol. 2*, 171.

51 J.M. Robertson had spoken on the war in his talk at the Secular Hall on "Christianity and Character," which was reported by the *MFP*, 9 December 1899; I do not know if Gertrude heard him. Dexter, "The Transvaal and the Boers," *Leicester Daily Post*, 22 December 1899.

52 Dexter, *Leicester Daily Post*, 2 January 1900.

53 Galbraith, "The pamphlet campaign on the Boer War." On Quaker peace
activism in Leicester, see Minutes of Leicester Monthly Meeting, 18 January 1900. Cronwright-Schreiner, *The Land of Free Speech*, describes his tour.
Although prowar individuals accused him of being a paid agent of the
Boers, by his own account he did not undertake the tour for profit: the
SACC paid him £50 and the STWC £35. 5 s. 7 d.; various other sums total-
ling £300 barely paid his expenses, he said.

54 For a detailed account of the Leicester meeting and similar events in other
venues, see Cronwright-Schreiner, *The Land of Free Speech*. The words to
"Soldiers of the Queen" are included in an appendix: "It's the soldiers of
the Queen, my lads,/ Who've been, my lads,/ Who're seen my lads,/In
the fight for England's glory, lads,/ When we have to show them what we
mean./ And when we say we've always won/ And when they ask us
how it's done/ We'll proudly point to everyone/ Of England's soldiers of
the Queen!" Cronwright-Schreiner notes that the manuscript was completed in 1901 but the book was too controversial to publish until some
years after the war.

55 See Price, *An Imperial War*, 88–9, and on mobs, 132–77. For details of similar events, see articles in Stead's *Review of Reviews*, April 1900, describing
"jingo terrorism," 307–11. Phillips, in "A Study of Attitudes," concludes
that Price's description holds for the local disruption too: the Leicester
rowdies were youths supported by middle class men, it was not a working class mob. The Leicester meeting was described in detail in "Stop the
War Weeting at Leicester," *MFP*, 24 February 1900, and "The Trades
Council," 3 March 1900. See also Rogers, "The Leicester Peace Society."
See Weller on pamphlets, free speech, and socialist organising from the
1880s on, *Don't Be a Soldier!* 20–2.

56 "Local Notes and News," "Adult Schools' United Service," and "Mr Keir
Hardie at Leicester," *MFP*, 3 March 1900; Stead's report is in "The Stop
the War Movement," *WAWSA*, 2 March 1900, 315. Wicks, "The Leicester
'Peace' Movement," *MFP*, 10 March 1900; Wicks, "The Stop the War Meet-
ing," and Hayes, "Military Glory," *MFP*, 24 March 1900; Inquisitive,
"Stop the War Meeting," and Wicks, "Military Glory," both *MFP*, 31
March 1900.

57 Davie, "Liberalism and Imperialism," *MFP*, 31 March 1900. See also
debate between "Pro-Boer" and others, *Leicester Daily Post* letters page, for
example, 27 March 1900. On John Dexter see the list of "also received"
letters, *Morning Leader*, 23 February 1900. Gertrude always called him
"Leonard" but his name appears as John Leonard Dexter on all documents I have seen, suggesting that is how he signed himself.

58 Rempel quotes Stead's free speech complaints and comments that a riot at
Birmingham in December 1901 was "the only demonstration during the
war which resulted in a death": "British Quakers and the South African

War." On attacks against the Quaker Rowntree family in Scarborough, see also Hewison, *A Hedge of Wild Almonds* 116–18.

59 Coroner's report number 63 on the inquest held 2 April 1900, Leicester-shire Record Office. "Sudden Death of a Shoemaker," MFP, 7 April 1900; see also "A True Woman: Her Life and Labour," *Leicester Pioneer*, 17 October 1917. Stead compiled lists of attacks around the country, as for example "Liberty in Britain, 1900 AD: A Disgraceful Record of Mob Savagery," WAWSA, 16 March 1900, 342; it is a curious omission. Joan Twilley Wallcraft wrote to me 6 June 1987, recounting family stories about James Twilley's attack and adding about her father Fred's reaction to it, "I know my Dad said he could never give his views from the audience, but from the platform he never suffered from stage-fright." She added, "However he was mostly making audiences laugh so it is not likely he'd get clobbered."

60 On Dexter's exclusion from the church, Melbourne Hall Committee Minute Books, 1896–1914 and Melbourne Hall Roll Book 1893–1913.

61 On Florrie, see Richardson, "My Canadian Letter," MFP, 5 December 1914.

62 Wynne's report, May 25, 1900; Socialist Quaker Society Minute Book 1898–1909.

63 Davie, "Military Glory," MFP, 5 May 1900.

64 On the free speech issue, see Koss, *The Anatomy*, 105–26. On Leicester peace activities, see Stead's comment of "no trouble" in his report in "The Stop-The-War Movement," WAWSA, 10 August 1900, 30, and Rogers, "The Leicester Peace Society." On the women's peace meeting, Lidding-ton, *Long Road*, 43–9.

65 Richardson, autobiographical letters, 1 May 1924, 102, and 6 October 193[9], 224–31, Brandon file; Gertrude Twilley Dexter's entries in the Towers Hospital recordbook, 44, Leicestershire Record Office (hereafter Towers file: thanks to Dorothy Twilley Shewfelt for permission to see these records); Fannie's recollections of Gertrude's first marriage from Connie MacDonald, September 1986 and July 1991. On farm burnings see also Fisher, *That Miss Hobhouse*, 82–95. For outcries against farm burning, see the letters page of the *Morning Leader* November and December 1900, passim; many of these correspondents quoted from letters from British soldiers in South Africa as evidence for their claims.

66 The Tories won a majority of 134 and the antiwar MPs held only about thirty-two seats (although Price puts their number at fifty-two). On the election, Tory slogans, and atrocities, Price, *An Imperial War*, 97–102, and his list of pro-Boer MPs, 250–1. Phillips, "A Study of Attitudes," points out that antiwar Liberal Broadhurst won one Leicester seat (on an upset, Tory Rolleston won the other from Liberal Hazell who soft-pedalled his [Limpish] antiwar views, angering both sides); Phillips argues that

although the war was an important issue it was not the only one: the local Liberal campaign focused on the Tory record on social legislation, and traditional issues such as temperance, land reform, and education. It was not just a Khaki election in Leicester. Hazell also lost, Phillips argues, because the ILP ran MacDonald and split the Radical vote, a trend noted in the previous (1894) by-election. For Leicester Peace Society activities, see Rogers, "The Leicester Peace Society." The WLF comment about farm burnings was by Mrs Fordham during the debate at the WLF Council Meetings held at Birmingham early in May 1901: Report of the Annual Council Meetings, 22.

67 On concentration camps, Koss, *Anatomy*, 222–49; Price, *An Imperial War*, 100–2; Hewison, *Hedge of Wild Almonds*, 187–211 and as well, Rempel, "British Quakers and the South African war." See also "The Civilised World and the English People," STWC pamphlet on the camps citing statistics on death causes and rates, published as a supplement to *The New Age*, 24 October 1901. Although the British use of these camps set the precedent for later applications, they may not deserve credit for inventing them. The "concentration camp" was reputedly invented in the late nineteenth century as a war tactic by a Spanish military leader called Weyler. The British press had denounced the tactic as an atrocity between 1896 and 1898, according to STWC leader Alfred Marks. On Weyler's use of concentration camps, Marks, *The Churches*, 35–7.

68 Robertson had gone to South Africa 2 June 1900: "Seeking Truth," MFP, 23 June 1900. The petition is reproduced in "Promotion of Peace," MFP, 29 December 1900. Activities are listed in Rogers, "The Leicester Peace Society," and Robertson's talk is mentioned in *The Leicester Reasoner*, March 1901. The *Leicester Daily Post* also reported Robertson's talk, "Mr J.M. Robertson on the war," 7 January 1901, but it did not mention his descriptions of barbarism in the conduct of the war. This account entitled the address "What is Happening in South Africa," whereas according to the version in Rogers, "The Leicester Peace Society," it was entitled "Imperialism in Action." Sydney Gimson's reaction is discussed in volume 2 of his unpublished "Recollections." The secularists and others in the audience at Robertson's talk were shocked that British soldiers could be so cruel, he reported. Perhaps the closest equivalent to Robertson's lantern slides for us would be the impact of the unforgettable images described and shown at meetings held in North America during the 1980s by Helen Caldicott's group, Physicians for Social Responsibility, on the medical consequences of nuclear war, illustrated by U.S. military film clips of the wounds of victims of the bombings by the U.S. of Hiroshima and Nagasaki. I can still recall my horror in the mid 1950s at reading John Hersey's similar descriptions, and my parents' dismay that they could neither say that these horrifying things had not happened nor offer much comfort. At that time

in the U.S., it was not even possible to say that tens of thousands of people were working to assure that such an atrocity would never happen again, as we could say to our terrified children in the 1980s. Hersey's *Hiroshima* was published in a Bantam edition in New York in 1948.

69 By the end of the war, at least 4,000 women and 16,000 children had died in the camps. Fisher, *That Miss Hobhouse*, and Koss, *Pro-Boers* 170–90, reproducing sections of the report, entitled *Report of a Visit to the Camps of Women and Children in the Cape and Orange River Districts*, and Liddington, *Long Road* 48–57; see also Rempel, "British Quakers," Jones, *Christian Socialist Revival*, 201–5, Koss, *Pro-Boers*, 191–220, Hirschfield, "Liberal Women's Organisations," 41–7. An official report by a government-appointed group (which included Mrs Fawcett of the National Union of Women Suffrage Societies, who had publicly supported the camps as "part of the fortune of war"), aptly nicknamed the "Whitewash Commission," *Report on the Concentration Camps in South Africa*, came out in the spring of 1902; mildly critical, it was carefully vague on death rates, as Liddington notes. See also Krebs, " 'The Last of the Gentlemen's Wars.' " On conscription, "Conscription," *MFP*, 25 May 1901; "Local Comments," August 1901, and "Secular Society notes," September 1901, *The Leicester Reasoner*. The arguments used against conscription in 1901 would be used again by Gertrude in the First World War.

70 Wicks tributes can be found in "Death of Mr Wm Wicks," 8 June 1901, Stanton, "The Late William Wicks: an appreciation," and "The late Mr Wicks. Funeral," 15 June 1901, "Leicester Temperance Society," Burden, "In Memoriam," and Dexter, "In Memoriam: William Wicks," 22 June 1901, all *MFP*; "William Wicks," *The Leicester Reasoner*, July 1901.

CHAPTER TWO

1 See Gertrude Twilley Dexter Towers Hospital Case book 31, pages 44, 107, 122, (Towers file). Linda McKenna discovered the Leicester Asylum records and initiated the access request. There is normally a 100-year period closure; we were ten years short. Thanks to a letter of permission from Gertrude's niece, Dorothy Twilley Shewfelt, the authorities in Leicester gave us access. J.G. Gould wrote a brief article on the Asylum, "The Borough Asylum," in the July 1901 issue of *The Leicester Reasoner*. I believe his attention was directed to the subject by Gertrude's illness and commitment. Some information is also found on her Towers Hospital stay in Gertrude Richardson's autobiographical letters, 1 May 1924, 102 and 6 October 193[9], 224–31, in her file from the Brandon, Manitoba hospital (Brandon file). See Orme and Brock, *Leicestershire's Lunatics*, for a history of the asylum, its inmates, and treatments. Also for descriptions, see "Borough Asylum extension. Formal Opening," *MFP*, 9 February 1901, and

"The Borough Lunatic Asylum. Annual report," *Leicester Daily Mercury*, 13 June 1901. On public asylums, see Showalter, *The Female Malady*, 25–50.

2 The family members who told me these stories did not wish to be identified. A record of a physical examination years later said she had never borne a child: Dr Goulden, Ward notes, 31 October 1924, Brandon file, 46. This is further confirmed in information given by her own physician, 23 April 1930, Brandon file, 7–8, and her autobiographical letters in Brandon file, 1 May 1924, 102 and 6 October 193[9], 224–31.

3 Towers file passim and Medical Superintendent's Diary, vol. 9, starting with 24 February 1905. Her later recollections are recorded in Gertrude's autobiographical letter, 1 May 1924, 102, Brandon file.

4 Towers file, 44. On chapel, library and visitors see Orme and Brock, *Leicestershire's Lunatics*, 38.

5 Towers file, 44, 107.

6 Towers file, 122.

7 Treatments prevalent at the time of her hospitalisation are discussed in Orme and Brock, *Leicestershire's Lunatics*, 38–9; they believe that the inmates were well cared for physically and there was an effort to provide a good diet. It was common practice to send people home on "trial leave." Her comment on kindness, Gertrude Richardson, autobiographical letter, 1 May 1924, 104–5, Brandon file.

8 Gertrude may never have seen Dexter, but he was still legally responsible for her support. The Poor Law Guardians ordered him to pay for her stay at the hospital, although it appears he did so only infrequently if it all. The records imply he was unemployed or unwell himself, and the Guardians do not appear to have pursued him beyond the end of 1902: Leicester Poor Law Union, Lunacy Committee Minutes, Leicestershire Record Office, G/12/8h/1 26D68/107 records contacts between Dexter and the Guardians from mid-1901 through 1902. Gertrude may not have been aware of all this.

9 Brumberg, *Fasting Girls*. On Victorian meanings of sickliness and appetite see her chapter "The Appetite as Voice."

10 Dexter, "God's Angels," *MFP*, 26 October 1907.

11 Gertrude's sister Florrie had been paid for the (unsigned) articles she wrote on reservists' families for the *Morning Leader* during the Boer War: Richardson, "My Canadian Letter," *MFP*, 5 December 1914. For information on pay rates for socialist newspapers see Steedman, *Childhood, Culture and Class*, 104, 141–55, 285 n35–6. In 1909, *Midland Free Press* editor Edwin Crew inserted a notice to would-be contributors to the "Free Speech Page" (part of which was the "Poet's Corner" where Gertrude's poems appeared) saying he did not pay for poems or letters to the editor: "Special Notice to Contributors," *MFP*, 20 February 1909.

12 It would have been unusual to resume her maiden name: since she was apparently too embarrassed to tell her sister that the marriage had not

been consummated, she was unlikely to want to raise awkward questions about the name. About support, if she had been supported by Dexter subsequent to their *de facto* separation and his alleged disappearance, surely that would have given some validity to the marriage or required a formal action (which was never initiated) to declare it null and void. The advisers she would consult in 1912 about the validity of the marriage apparently had no such hesitation, suggesting that there had been no financial support.

13 Dexter, "Sunshine and Shadow," *MFP*, 15 May 1909. On readers' appreciation see also Demos, "Sunshine and Shadow," 8 May 1909, Hardy, "Our Love Waiteth for the Lord," 31 July 1915, and Friendless, "A Worthy Tribute," 11 March 1916, all *MFP*. On the tradition of popular preaching into which Gertrude fits, and on earlier women preachers, see Valenze, *Prophetic Sons and Daughters*.

14 R.J. Campbell (1867–1956) was the subject of controversy in his own church; in one episode he was accused of being a Unitarian in his beliefs about the divinity of Christ, and labelled a "crank and adventurer" by a leading Congregational clergyman: "Congregational Union," *Leicester Daily Post*, 10 May 1910.

15 From "Babylon's Waters," the poem is indeed about weeping and hope: *MFP*, 12 December 1908.

16 "A Key of Gold," *MFP*, 30 October 1909.

17 "Laborare est Orare," *MFP*, 24 August 1907.

18 Peace Society affiliation: Dexter, "The Star in the East," *MFP*, 15 December 1906. The minute book of the Peace Society 1901–14 is held at the Marx Memorial Library in London; thanks to Tish Newland for generous access to the library's resources. The Society had a regular column in the Wycliffe Church Magazine, *Wycliffe Review* (of which unfortunately very few numbers remain); thanks to church secretary Howard Rees for access to the church's records. On the Wycliffe Church, Ellis, *Records of Nineteenth Century Leicester*, 173–8; Ernest James' activities were regularly reported in the *Midland Free Press*.

19 For a history of the central body see the pamphlet by Ingram, "Fifty Years of the National Peace Council." The British Library holds a small collection of their documents. On overall trends see Young, "Tradition and Innovation." See also the discussion in Hinton, *Protests and Visions* 27–40. Liddington, *The Long Road to Greenham* 43–84, points out that most women reformers were involved more in suffrage than peace activism during this period, although there was a peace element within suffrage internationalism. On Quaker peace activism, see Kennedy, "The Quaker Renaissance," (thanks to Tom Kennedy for a copy of this article), and also Kennedy, "The Society of Friends and Anti-Militarism" (thanks to discussant Jo Vellacott for a copy of this paper and her comments on it).

20 Gertrude's memorial poem: "In Loving Memory of Sir Henry Campbell-Bannerman," MFP, 2 May 1908. Dexter, "Within the Shadow," MFP, 23 November 1907: her title comes from Lowell, whom she quoted: "And, behind the Dim Unknown, Standeth God, within the shadow, Keeping watch above His own." Although he had not spoken out strongly on peace until the concentration camps scandals (valuing party unity), he had come out as a pro-Boer in his electrifying 14 June 1901 methods of barbarism speech in the House of Commons. As Gertrude's memorial poem eulogised him, "When England madly waged unholy war; / Thy voice was heard; / 'Twas like the calming of a tempest roar, / Thy brave true word." Boer War peace activist Sydney Gimson was president of the Leicester Peace Society in 1914, but accepted the Great War as a "just war forced upon [England] by the military aggression of Germany." He urged young men to enlist, "Stray Notes by an Old Resident," MFP, 17 October 1914.

21 She published a slightly different version of this poem in July 1918, when she was almost totally occupied with organising antiwar activities and feeling outrage and despair about the atrocities of war, including "enemy" women and children dying of hunger. The 1918 version appears in two places: first as a poem with the same title in *Canadian Forward*, 10 July 1918, dedicated to a CO who had died after three weeks imprisonment, an antiwar socialist clergyman, and a socialist newspaper editor imprisoned for publishing antiwar material; and second, as part of an article of the same title in *Leicester Pioneer*, 19 July 1918. The 1918 version included a stanza condemning the apostate clergy who served the moloch state. On religion and socialism, see Yeo, "A New Life."

22 Dexter, "Hovering Wings," dedicated to the Hague Peace Conference, MFP, 4 July 1908, and "Peace on Earth," MFP, 31 October 1908.

23 Gould, "History of the Leicester Secular Society," 4; the report on Gould's lecture on St Augustine is in the Leicester Secular Society Scrapbook held at the Leicestershire Record Office; it is on the same page of the scrapbook as items from the summer of 1900, but no date is noted on the clipping. The Melbourne Hall Roll Book shows that Gertrude was erased from the list of members (for nonattendance) 31 December 1908.

24 "Human Meaning of the Eucharist," MFP, 16 June 1900, clipping in the Leicester Secular Society Scrapbook.

25 See the detailed report, "Mr Malcolm Quin on Positivism," *The Leicester Reasoner*, April 1901, and "The Religion of Humanity," MFP, 16 March 1901. An earlier paragraph by Gould in the *Reasoner* explained that Quin represented the more orthodox strain of positivism: "Local Comments," March 1901. There had been a local positivist group holding weekly meetings in private homes at the time of Malcolm Quin's visit. On Gould's departure, David Nash explained to me, there had been other tensions within the Leicester Secular Society (LSS) between the ILP-oriented

group Gould belonged to and the more Liberal-leaning group associated with long-time president Sydney Gimson; similar tensions were to be found in Leicester electoral politics during this period of transition from a Lib-Lab to a labour position. Gould's farewell is described in "At the Secular Hall," *MFP*, 2 May 1908. Until Gould's departure from Leicester in 1910, his time would be taken up with the Church of Humanity and his work on the municipal council and the local school board. Nash's article, "F.J. Gould and the Leicester Secular Society," and book, *Secularism, Art and Freedom*, appeared after my research was completed: see especially chapter 4, "F.J. Gould: Positivist, Socialist and Pastor."

26 On the services, see Dexter, "The Church of Humanity," *MFP*, 14 November 1908, and "The Day of All the Dead," *MFP*, 9 January 1909. Lancaster, *Radicalism, Cooperation and Socialism*, 56–75, is also helpful on the positivists in Leicester. For more on the Church of Humanity, see Van Arx, *Progress and Pessimism*, 130–4.

27 Dexter, "The Piteous Sacrifice," *MFP*, 16 January 1909.

28 On heroes see her poems "The Starry Way," 16 January 1909, "The Image of God," 20 March 1909, "Thankfulness," 3 April 1909, and "For All the Great," 24 July 1909. See also her allegory "The Angel and the Seer," 23 January 1909, all *MFP*.

29 Dexter, "Requiem," *MFP*, 20 February 1909.

30 On the role of education see Hayward, "In Memory of F.J. Gould." The Secular Society scrapbook contains numerous clippings about Gould and the school board and his moral education work, largely from the *Midland Free Press*; examples are [Crew], "Secular Moral Education," *MFP*, 24 November 1900; Molesworth, "The School Board Election," *Daily Post*, 24 November 1900; "The Leicester School Board Election'" nd; "School Board: The Question of a Vice Chairman," nd [Jan. 1901]. On the parish magazine, "To the Friends of the 'Reasoner,'" *The Leicester Reasoner*, February 1902.

31 The report on the London demonstration lesson was reprinted in "Councillor Gould and Moral Instruction," *MFP*, 10 July 1909. For Gould's description of his survey of Bible lessons and the development of his secular alternative, see Gould, "The School Board," *The Leicester Reasoner*, November 1901. For details of his methods, see Gould, "Shall Leicester Give Up Moral Instruction?" *MFP*, 27 February 1909.

32 Dexter, "Among the Children," *MFP*, 10 July 1909.

33 The resolution and the debate are reported in Gould's column, "Remnants," *MFP*, 19 June 1909 and 3 July 1909.

34 Dexter, "My Dream of Peace," *MFP*, 10 July 1909, and her rejoinder to criticism of Gould's class, "Among the Children," 31 July 1909.

35 Sylvia Pankhurst in Leicester, see Richard Pankhurst, *Sylvia Pankhurst*, 77. Pankhurst's papers are held at the Archives of the Institute for Social His-

tory in Amsterdam, but are available on microfilm in the British Studies
Collection, Norlin Library, University of Colorado at Boulder. The thirty-
seven page typescript of her 1907 description of Leicester boot and shoe
women workers is in 4511 / 116; it was probably written after her visit, as it
includes references to 1908 factory inspectors' reports.

36 On the growth of the WSPU and WFL, see Linklater, *An Unhusbanded Life*,
101–16. For an excellent overview and an account of the movement from
the perspective of working class women who were radical suffragists in
the NUWSS and like groups, see Liddington and Norris, *One Hand Tied
Behind Us*. Sylvia Pankhurst, *The Suffragette*, describes the 30 July 1908
Market Square meeting, 257. On the moderates, see Vellacott, *Catherine
Marshall*. For Vicinus' insights on the suffragettes, *Independent Women*,
247–80.

37 A[gnes] S[pencer] C[larke], "Two Processions," *MFP*, 27 June 1908, describes the Northampton Square incident.

38 Agnes Clarke had been a member of the Women Workers' Union since the
Boer War period: she recited at the "Women Workers' Union Conversazi-
one at Leicester," *MFP*, 25 November 1899; moderate Edith Gittins was on
the local executive. See ASC, "Two Processions," *MFP*, 27 June 1908 on
the London marches. For one comment on multigroup societies, see
Linklater, *Charlotte Despard*, 129. See, for example, NUWSS "Quarterly
Council Meeting," *Women's Franchise*, 15 October 1908, and also regular
reports in each issue by the different groups. The two London meetings
are described in detail in Sylvia Pankhurst, *The Suffragette*, 242–9.

39 On R.J. Campbell and the suffrage, see for example his "Why the Church
League Exists," *Church League for Women's Suffrage Monthly Paper*, June
1913. Campbell preached regularly on suffrage and published pamphlets:
for example "Women's Suffrage and the Social Evil," London 1907, reproduced in Dale A. Johnson, *Women in English Religion* 261–5. In Leicester,
"Votes for women," *MFP*, 2 June 1910, records a bimonthly at-home presided over by Leicestershire WSPU organiser Dorothy Pethick. Gertrude's
contacts with Dorothy Pethick, for example, Richardson, "Housekeeping
in Canada," *MFP*, 30 December 1916. Dorothy Pethick, sister of WSPU
(and later WFL) leader Emmeline Pethick Lawrence, went to Canada and
the U.S. in October 1911 with Emmeline Pankhurst. The following summer Fred and Emmeline Pethick Lawrence went to Canada to visit Harold
Pethick who was then living on Vancouver Island: MacKenzie, *Shoulder to
Shoulder* 199. On Gittins and Ashby, see for example "Balance and Report
Sheet for the year 1912," Leicester and Leicestershire Women's Suffrage
Society, in the Fawcett Library. Although support was widespread, labour
and socialists were then split over the issue of fighting for universal adult
suffrage versus fighting for admitting qualified women to the suffrage on
the basis of the present system of property qualification, thus there were

quarrels about which organisations should work together on which issues. The Mary Wollstonecraft lecture is reported in *MFP*, 17 February 1900. Gould advocated opening all professions to women and assumed that equal pay would not be an issue because men and women were so different that they would not do the same work: "Womanhood," *MFP*, 5 October 1907. A few months later, Gould published a lengthy statement of his views on "Womanhood, Marriage, the Family, and Religion" in response to smears by his Liberal opponent during the municipal election campaign, in which he had stood as a Labour candidate: Gould, "After the Election," *MFP*, 4 January 1908. Gould's opponent had circulated a pamphlet on the views of socialist Belfort Bax, and implied that these were Gould's views; for Bax's views see "Socialism and its Consequences," a report on Bax's talk to the Secular Society, *MFP*, 26 October 1907. For one example of Gould's ideas of womanly nobility, see his brief historical tale, "For the Young: The Good Wife," *MFP*, 20 July 1907. Gould did not think married women should have to work outside the home (they should be free of economic responsibilities in order to carry out their own work), but he did not forbid it. Another example of Gould's views can be found in the report of his talk on "Human Nature," *MFP*, 22 June 1907.

40 Fred had gone to Canada in 1902, followed by Florrie, then Fannie, her husband, and daughter in 1905, and Wilfred went to Japan in 1908. On Wilfred's departure, see Gertrude's poem, "Farewell," *MFP*, 19 September 1908. I am assuming from her later activism that Eliza Twilley was then a suffragist. H.G. Twilley, "The case for the suffrage," *MFP*, 4 July 1908. On Horace, telephone interview with Gertrude's nephew Wilfred Twilley, 15 June 1990, Vancouver B.C., and interview with Mildred Ashby, who as a young matron met Horace at tea at her husband's aunt Isabel Ashby's during the late 1920s or early 1930s. Horace probably knew Isabel Ashby through the First World War peace movement in which the Wycliffe Church played an important part, although their acquaintance may have stemmed from earlier connections. After James' death in 1910 his replacement at the Wycliffe Church was F. Seaward Beddow. A follower of R.J. Campbell, he would continue James' strong peace witness and emphasise yet more strongly social and economic justice issues. Bill Lancaster identifies Beddow as "Bellow;" Lancaster cites Beddow's socialist and World War I CO comrade Fenner Brockway: *Radicalism, Cooperation and Socialism*, 202, n63. The Wycliffe Church Social Union put on theatrical and musical performances; Horace probably got his start as an actor there. Horace was keen on theatre, and worked hard at it. Keith Twilley showed us theatrical souvenirs of his great uncle Horace and told us his recollections, January 1991, Leicester. He recalled that Horace had taken elocution lessons, for example. For most of his life he regularly appeared in amateur

theatrical performances; he also was featured in various musicals. Horace was a key figure in Leicester amateur theatre after the First World War, and well known locally as a performer. Isabel Ashby was a Wyggeston student, although she left a year before Gertrude started, and was probably a fellow antiwar sympathiser during the Boer War. The Wyggeston admission register shows Isabel Ashby attended from 1882 to 1886; she was six years older than Gertrude.

41 The entry for von Petzold in the U.S. Library of Congress National Union Catalogue of pre-1956 Imprints, vol. 454, gives her birth date as 1886, which seems rather late, as it would make her only 12 or 13 years of age when she began studying at Manchester College, and only 18 or 19 when she was appointed to the pulpit at Leicester Free Christian Church (a branch of Unitarianism). Von Petzold won an exhibition (scholarship) to Manchester College in 1898, completed her degree, and from 1901 to 1904 her theological training, according to Holt, *The Unitarian Contribution*, 245. The Unitarians and Free Christians trained ministers at Manchester College, Oxford, founded as a dissenting academy during the period when other colleges at Oxford and Cambridge imposed a religious test and thus dissenters could not take degrees (although they were allowed to attend after 1854); such tests were removed generally by the late nineteenth century although they lasted until after the First World War for divinity degrees: Holt, 242–4, 338–40. Von Petzold is also mentioned as a pioneering woman minister in Dale Johnson, *Women in English Religion, 1700–1925*, 270. The main source of information about her in English is the novel by Clarke, *The First Woman Minister* a thinly disguised account of von Petzold's Leicester days by one of her young woman followers of the period, herself an avid suffragist. Although von Petzold may have completed the requirements for the Oxford M.A., she did not actually receive it, since Oxford did not grant women degrees until 1920. Mildred Ashby recalled that her aunt-in-law Isabel Ashby's brother Sidney was one of von Petzold's followers, later joined by Isabel herself. When von Petzold's replacement turned out to be promilitary, the Ashbys quit the Narborough Road church and went elsewhere. Also see Davy, "England's First Woman Minister," *Women's Franchise*, 17 September 1908. Von Petzold earned a doctorate at Giessen University in 1924; her dissertation, published in 1924, was on the portrayal of Jesus Christ in fiction, drama, and poetry. Von Petzold's publications include *John Davidson* and *Harriet Martineau*. Thanks to my colleague Renate Peters for help with German sources.

42 Richardson, "Housekeeping in Canada," *MFP*, 22 November 1913; and "Harvest Gold," *MFP*, 30 September 1916; von Petzold was by then preaching at the American Church in Berlin.

43 See for example A.S.C., "The First Woman Minister," *MFP*, 16 May 1908. The Leicester Reference Library had copies of Clarke, *Glenroyst* and *Seven*

Girls; see also the British Museum catalogue for other works. *Glenroyst* is a historical novel about seventeenth century Leicestershire; *Seven Girls* is about a group of jolly young working class women. Clarke also published a serial novel in the *Midland Free Press* in 1907 (she was in good company; the paper ran a serial of Rider Haggard's, among others) about a splendid orphan girl with intellectual ambitions who is rescued by an impecunious but honourable lodger from her drink-sodden aunt's unsuitable house, to be raised by her newly rediscovered relations in the north of England. The serial novel was A[gnes] S[pencer] C[larke], "The Wooing of Thea," running weekly in the *MFP* beginning 17 August and concluding in mid-December 1907.

44 A.S.C., "Women's Social and Political Union," *MFP*, 22 August 1908, and "The Sex in Olden Times," *MFP*, 22 August 1908. A.S.C., "Reply to "Semper Fidelis," *MFP*, 25 April 1908, and "Rejoinder to Semper Fidelis," *MFP*, 9 May 1908 and his further comments in "Temperance Talks," 16 May 1908.

45 On Selina Cooper's work see Liddington and Norris, *One Hand*, for example 213–5 and passim, and Liddington, *Selina Cooper*. "Voteless Women," *MFP*, 17 October 1908; "National Union of Women Workers," *MFP*, 4 July 1908.

46 Antisuffrage: Brown, "Votes v. Citizenship," *MFP*, 23 May 1908; also see his letter, "The Case For the Suffrage," *MFP*, 27 June 1908. Preston, "Suffragettes, What I Think of Them," is an antisuffrage opinion from a lady, *MFP*, 22 August 1908.

47 Dexter, "An Appeal" and "Virginia's Cry," *MFP*, 5 September 1908 and "Virginia's Cry II," 12 September 1908. For examples of reports on WFL activities for Daisy Lord, "Notice of a Protest Demonstration by the Women of England Against Sentence on Daisy Lord," 10 September 1908, "Daisy Lord Defence Fund," 17 September 1908, and "Caravan Tour," 24 September 1908, all in *Women's Franchise*. There were WFL caravan reports in each issue; in the summer of 1909 a second caravan was added. Also on Daisy Lord and on the caravans see Linklater, *Charlotte Despard*, 122, 127–9. Charlotte Despard was an ILP Christian Socialist after about 1901 (and later interested in theosophy); before that she was in the Women's Liberal Federation. Linklater describes the WFL-WSPU split and WFL activities, 101–75.

48 Dexter, "The Crimson Curtain," *MFP*, 10 October 1908.

49 Dexter, "Christ and Womanhood," *MFP*, 24 October 1908; Hinde, "The Crimson Curtain," 17 October 1908 and "Christ and Womanhood," 31 October 1908, both *MFP*. Daisy Lord was released conditionally in April 1910: see Gertrude's note of thanks to those who signed her petition, "Release of Daisy Lord," *MFP* 23 April 1910. On Holloway, see Lytton, *Prisons and Prisoners*.

50 Dexter, "The Death of Hypatia," *MFP*, 28 March 1908.

51 Dexter, "Per Ardua ad Astra," *MFP*, 27 June 1908.

52 Dexter, "God With Us," *MFP*, 4 January 1908. On this theme see also "Eloi, Eloi, Lama Sabacthani," *MFP*, 11 April 1908, "Feed My Lambs," *MFP* 5 December 1908, "My Wishes," *MFP* 8 August 1908, and "Our Daily Bread," *MFP* 31 October 1908.

53 "Ye Did It Not. A Dream," *MFP*, 23 January 1909.

54 Dexter, "Unemployment" and "Christ at the Workhouse," *MFP*, 22 May 1909. Thanks to local historian and long-time Loughborough resident Wallace Humphrey who walked the entire street in an unsuccessful attempt to locate Gertrude's Loughborough address, given only vaguely as "Ivy House, Victoria-street," where she apparently lived for several months in 1909 for reasons we were unable to determine.

55 Dexter, "To Arms!" *MFP*, 29 January 1910. Polling took place from 14 January to 10 February. Dexter, "Love and the World," *MFP*, 5 March 1910.

56 The committee took its name from the subtitle of part one of the minority report: "The Break-up of the Poor Law"; it was later changed to the National Committee for the Prevention of Destitution. The poor law abolition meeting is discussed in "Break-up of the Poor Law," *MFP*, 16 April 1910. For a later meeting from the majority report perspective see "Charity Organisation," *MFP*, 19 November 1910. On the minority report and controversies, see Thane, "The Labour Party and State 'Welfare.'" On Donaldson, see Richardson, "Housekeeping in Canada," *MFP*, 30 May 1914.

57 Gertrude recommended Rauschenbusch's *Christianity and the Social Crisis* to Leicester readers, "Housekeeping in Canada," *MFP*, 6 June 1914. His *Christianizing the Social Order* was a social gospel mainstay. For Horace's views, Twilley: "Society and the Social Problems," 19 December 1908, 2 January 1909, 16 January 1909, and 30 January 1909.

58 Twilley, "Why I Have Become a Socialist," 19 March 1910; "Socialism," 16 April 1910, 23 April 1910, and 30 April 1910, all *MFP*. His opponents' views can be found under letters of the same titles in these issues of the paper. There was a labour church in Leicester; it is unclear whether Gertrude or Horace ever attended. On the church's doings see for example, "Problem of Poverty," *MFP*, 7 March 1908.

59 Unfortunately Wycliffe Church membership records are incomplete and ledgers are missing for certain periods, so Gertrude's and Horace's attendance is unclear. However, Mrs Alice Bradley recalled Horace as a member during the First World War when she was a schoolgirl: personal communication, Leicester, September 1993. When I first looked through Gertrude's collection of clippings in a box at her niece Joan Twilley Wallcraft's house in September 1986, I found an envelope bearing the return address of the Blind Cottages on Gwendolen Road. Her niece Connie

313 Notes to pages 72–5

Livesey MacDonald and later her son Eric Richardson told me how fascinated they had been as children watching Gertrude use her Braille writing board to write letters or transcribe poems to send to a pen pal. Dexter, "The Shadow-World," *MFP*, 9 October 1909, records her attendance at a Wycliffe Church social for the blind and her admiration for the society. Regular reports in the *Midland Free Press* provide information about the society's members, history, and activities. See for example "Wycliffe Homes for the Blind Opening Ceremony," 28 July 1900; "Entertaining the Blind," 10 March 1900; "Wycliffe Blind Society, the Year's Record," 25 May 1901; "The Wycliffe Society for Helping the Blind," 23 May 1908. Gertrude appears in the list of attenders at the annual meeting in an undated clipping from Joan Wallcraft's collection, "Wycliffe Blind Society," probably May 1910 from internal evidence. See also in later years: "Wycliffe Society for Helping the Blind: Coming of Age," which gives a history of the society, 23 May 1914; "Wycliffe Society for Helping the Blind," 17 October 1914; "To Help the Blind," 3 June 1916. Hamilton Donisthorpe ("president of the Leicestershire Christian Endeavour Union") is among the listed "New Adherents," *WAWSA*, 23 February 1900, 302. Jessie Donisthorpe was a regular speaker at Temperance Society meetings, see for example "Leicester Temperance Society," *MFP*, 7 April 1900. Gertrude refers to Jessie Donisthorpe in "Housekeeping in Canada," *MFP*, 29 November 1913. The Blind Society activities were reported in some detail in their regular column in the church's monthly magazine *Wycliffe Review*, started by J. Ernest James in 1892. James' Blind Society involvement is mentioned in all his obituaries, including the tribute by a key figure in the congregation and the Peace Society, Emma J. Hawley, "Mr J. Ernest James. An Appreciation," *Wycliffe Review*, November 1910. Gertrude's undated poem "Kyrie Eleison," from the collection of her poems given by Fred Twilley to the Swan Valley Historical Museum in the 1970s, is dedicated to memory of the Blind Society. Signed Gertrude Dexter, it was probably written between the spring of 1911 when she left Leicester, and the fall of 1912 when she remarried and changed her name. She sent a donation of four shillings to the Cottage Homes during that period: "Wycliffe Society for Helping the Blind, New Issue March 1914," in the Society's papers at the Leicestershire Record Office.

60 These events are described in Vellacott, *Catherine Marshall*.
61 Dexter, "Womanhood," *MFP*, 24 April 1909.
62 The address was given to the Undenominational Men's Meetings: "The Meaning of Evolution," *MFP*, 17 December 1910.
63 Dexter, "A Defence of Womanhood," *MFP*, 21 May 1910.
64 Dexter, "A Defence of Womanhood," *MFP*, 21 May 1910. Christabel Pankhurst's campaign is widely discussed by writers on the suffragettes; she is usually wrongly dismissed as a merely a man-hating hysteric.

Although the statistics she cited on infected men were exaggerated, the problem was a real one. Other of Gertrude's poems on motherhood dealt with its portrayals in paintings, literature, and Egyptian religion: *MFP*, "Motherhood," 28 May 1910 and "The Madonna of Egypt," 31 December 1910.

65 Clarke, "Mrs Pemberton Peake," *MFP*, 12 November 1910. Also see Clarke, "Miss Marie Brackenbury in Leicester," *MFP*, 29 October 1910, for another of Clarke's reports on WSPU speakers in Leicester.

66 Adela Pankhurst was then in Leicester to speak at the Trade Hall, and to meet local WSPU women preparing for the deputation to Parliament: Clarke, "Adela Pankhurst," *MFP*, 19 November 1910. Charlotte Despard was also in town that week for the Catholic Women's League for Women Suffrage, but Gertrude's reaction calls up a younger woman.

67 Dexter, "A Suffragette," *MFP*, 19 November 1910.

68 For the planning and execution of the Congress see the Leicester Society for the Promotion of Peace Minute Book for 1909 and 1910, passim.

69 Sessions of the Congress are described in *Leicester Daily Post* reports: "The Peace Congress: Mass Meetings in Leicester," 14 June 1910, "National Peace Congress," 15 June 1910, and "The Peace Congress," 16 June 1910.

70 A collection of James' sermons, *The Socialism of Jesus and Kindred Addresses*, illustrates his ideas; from the Wycliffe Church papers. Dexter, "Love's Portal," *MFP*, 15 October 1910, is her memorial poem. On family visits at Rood House, Fred to Edith, 29 June 1913. James' photograph, "Housekeeping in Canada," *MFP*, 7 June 1913. For a lengthy account of the funeral service and a memorial service at the Wycliffe Church see "Funeral of the Rev. J. Ernest James," *MFP*, 15 October 1910. Campbell "preaching in" Beddows is recounted by Beddows in his forty-first anniversary sermon, 3 February 1952: Wycliffe Church papers. Campbell discussed his views of Christianity and its connection with social and political issues and reiterated his decision not to enter electoral politics, in "The Rev. R.J. Campbell's Position: Liberal Christianity," *Leicester Daily Post*, 16 May 1910.

71 Another cousin on the Richardson side, Nellie Simpson Carter, had settled with her husband in Saskatchewan: Fred to Edith, 10 January 1913. On Horace's possible marriage, his brother Fred later referred to Horace's serious romance with someone called Florence, who may have been an amateur dramatics colleague: Fred's letters to Edith mentioning Horace's plans, 1 September 1912, 3 November 1912, 4 December 1913, 5 April 1914, 12 April 1914, and the end of the relationship, probably early 1915 (and, I speculate, possibly over Horace's pacifism or its disruptive consequences) is discussed, 27 May 1915. On general patterns of Leicester working class emigration see Page, "Emigration and Poverty."

72 One farewell gift, a book entitled *The Women of Israel*, inscribed "To Gertrude Dexter from Mary McIntosh, Leicester, England, 1911," is still in

Gertrude's niece Connie MacDonald's possession. On legislation, see the excerpts from documents of the period in "Turning Away From the Poor Law," in Rose, *The Rise of the Welfare State*, 129–95, and "The Poor Law Under Attack 1870-1914," in Rose, *The English Poor Law*, 222–82. Edwin Crew's fine writing paper, Fred to Edith, 27 July 1913.

CHAPTER THREE

1 Information in this chapter is drawn in part from interviews with family members and from their papers and mementos. Fred Twilley's daughters Dorothy Twilley Shewfelt and the late Joan Twilley Wallcraft were key sources of information and material; Grant Shewfelt made photocopies for me of Gertrude's clippings that Joan Wallcraft had organised; Connie Livesey MacDonald, with help from her daughters Myrna and Peggy, also showed me letters, photographs, and other material. The list of Swan River people who helped me gather and understand this information is lengthy (it is provided in my earlier publications on Gertrude), but I am especially indebted to Eric Richardson and Isobel Martin McKay, the late John Booth, and John Dubreuil. The correspondence between Edith Watson and Fred Twilley is a particularly rich source of information about the Twilley family and life in Swan River. Luckily, Edith saved her letters from Fred, Gertrude, Fannie, and May Minchen, and took them to Swan River when she came to Canada from England with Fred after the First World War. Fred kept them in a drawer in his little museum in La Rivière, Manitoba where his son-in-law Bob Wallcraft and I unearthed them in 1991. I am grateful to Dorothy Shewfelt and him for permission to copy them, and to Nancy Kariel for doing the photocopying. Fred's introduction to Edith is discussed in the letter from May Minchen to Edith Watson, 3 September 1912. May Minchen had read out bits of or handed over Edith's earlier letters to various Twilleys, long before Fred first wrote to Edith, as Fannie Livesey reminded Edith years later: Fannie Livesey to Edith Watson, 24 February 1917. Fred Twilley first wrote to Edith Watson, 7 June 1912; additional information is in Edith to Fred, 3 July 1912. Information on the valley's features and residents' history is taken in part from Twilley, *Between the Hills: Life in the Swan River Valley 1787–1958*; Swan River Board of Trade, "Swan River Valley: The Garden of The Canadian West." For biographical details on the Minchens see Adamchuk and Iwanchuk, *Tent Town 1898–1979*, 161. On the early Swan River Valley period and the development of farming, see her introduction in Owen, *The Wheat King*.

2 Information on the town is drawn from: Swan River Valley History Book Committee, *Eighty Years in the Swan River Valley*; Palmer and Dobbyn, *Lasting Impressions*; Dauphin Presbyterial United Church Women,

"Church Histories 1880–1925"; "Housekeeping in Canada," *MFP*, 11 April 1914.

3 Emily Murphy took part in this effort for the new hospital when she lived in Swan River from 1904–7 while her husband was involved in timber cutting and acted as a volunteer assistant Anglican minister. Murphy accompanied her husband on his trips in the region, and wrote amusingly about them. She records that on one occasion he stood on a stump to preach a sermon on the mother-heart of God to an audience of lumber camp workers in the bush. For her impressions of Swan River and her stories about her trips with "the Padre," as she called her husband, see her *Janey Canuck in the West*; the "mother-heart of God" sermon is on page 110.

4 A rival newspaper was bought out around 1908. The Swan River *Star* editor of Gertrude's day, Andrew Weir, supported progressive causes and admired Gertrude's literary and other abilities. He was also the Presbyterian minister for about a year in 1912–13.

5 Fannie Livesey to Edith Watson, 24 February 1917.

6 Fred to Edith, 21 September 1912; Fred discusses anti-English feeling in Ontario in his letter.

7 Twilley, *Between the Hills*. Fred wrote to Edith on letterhead from "S. Harvey and Son, Dealers in General Merchandise and Hardware, Durban," 24 August 1912, but I am not sure at which Swan River store he worked.

8 Fred's and Fannie's opinions of Charlie from interviews with Dorothy Twilley Shewfelt, Joan Twilley Wallcraft, and Connie Livesey MacDonald, September 1986 and July 1991; Fred to Edith, 31 May 1914. Information on Charlie's addresses, occupations, and death is from city directories, voters' lists, and the death certificate. Some information on the family can be found in Minitonas Community Centre Committee, *Notes From Tent Town*.

9 Information on Florrie is in Richardson, "Housekeeping in Canada" *MFP*, 21 March 1914; Fred to Edith, 22 January 1913; "Housekeeping in Canada" *MFP*, 16 May 1914; May Minchen to Edith Watson, 4 September [1912]; Fred to Edith, 21 September 1912, and from Dorothy Twilley Shewfelt, discussion on 8 November 1990.

10 Jackel, "Introduction," to Binnie-Clark, *Wheat and Woman*, ix.

11 "My Trans-Atlantic Voyage," *MFP*, 3 June 1911; "My Trans-Atlantic Voyage (Continued)," *MFP*, 10 June 1911; "My Trans-Atlantic Voyage (Continued)," *MFP*, 17 June 1911.

12 "My Trans-Atlantic Voyage (Continued)," *MFP*, 17 June 1911; Roberts, "Doctors and Deports," and *Whence They Came*; the 1902 Immigration Act established those suffering from or with a history of mental illness as prohibited immigrants.

13 18 May 1911 Swan River *Star* (hereafter referred to as the SR *Star*) records the arrival of Mrs Twilley and Mrs Dexter; Fred to Edith, 2 December

1912; "A Canadian Wedding," MFP, 1 July 1911. On not wanting to emigrate see "My Canadian Letter: Mutual Helpfulness," MFP, 4 September 1915.

14 "Life on a Canadian Farm," MFP, 22 July 1911; "Summer in Canada," MFP, 12 August 1911; "Summer in Canada (Con't [sic])," MFP, 19 August 1911; "The Cry of the Flowers," MFP, 7 October 1911 and "Harvest Time in Canada," MFP, 30 September 1911 on death and seasons.

15 "The Promise of Hope," MFP, 18 November 1911.

16 "People I Have Met: American Indians," MFP, 26 August 1911; "People I Have Met: Galicians," MFP, 18 November 1911; "Verigin, the Story of the Doukhobors," MFP, 14 October 1911.

17 On the evangelical liberals' views, Fraser, The Social Uplifters, 32; "People I Have Met III: Scandinavians," MFP, 16 September 1911.

18 "Coronation Prayer," MFP, 17 June 1911.

19 See for example her poem "Snow Jewels," MFP, 10 February 1912; "A Prayer for Winter," MFP, 16 March 1912.

20 "My Canadian Christmas," MFP, 17 February 1912; "Phases of Canadian Social Life: I. A Bible-Class Social," MFP, 24 February 1912; "A Canadian Surprise Party," MFP, 9 March 1912; "Social Life in Canada. A Valentine Party," MFP, 13 April 1912.

21 "Housekeeping in Canada," MFP, 19 April 1913; "Silent Voices," MFP, 20 April 1912; "Housekeeping in Canada," MFP, 26 April 1913.

22 "Woman Suffrage," SR Star 29 March 1912. Grace Shaw's father was a minister at Dauphin; schoolteacher Margaret Knox, from a valley family, married Thomas Martin, an early settler from Ontario, in 1910: biographical details are scattered in 80 Years; "Summer in Canada (Con't)," MFP, 19 August 1911. On Grace Shaw, Fred to Edith, 2 April 1913. Some details of the early suffrage campaign are included in "Women Have Had Vote For Seventy-Five Years," SR Star, 2 May 1991, reporting a speech by Margaret Martin's daughter Isobel McKay; unfortunately the reporter had the dates wrong and described the movement as "suffragettes." I am grateful to Isobel McKay for this clipping.

23 "Woman Suffrage in Canada," MFP, 27 April 1912; on the earliest claim, "Housekeeping in Canada," MFP, 27 September 1913; see also Fred to Edith, 17 July 1912; on the Icelandic women, see Kinnear, "The Icelandic Connection."

24 May to Edith, 3 September 1912. Grace Shaw's article "Women's Suffrage," SR Star, 28 February 1913, gives numerous examples of discrimination against women. See also Fred to Edith, 16 March 1913.

25 Fred to Edith, 16 March 1913. The complexities of government positions and intentions, of the range of possible forms that a woman suffrage bill might take, and of suffragists' hopes and strategies in this period, are clearly discussed by Vellacott, From Liberal to Labour.

26 "The Opening of Spring in Canada," *MFP*, 8 June 1912; "Housekeeping in Canada," *MFP*, 10 May 1913.

27 "Our Suffrage Picnic" *MFP*, 20 July 1912.

28 "Dominion Day in Canada," *MFP*, 2 August 1912; on the 1913 celebration, see "Housekeeping in Canada," *MFP*, 2 August 1913.

29 Gertrude discusses Braille in "The West," *Woman's Century,* May 1916. Her Braille pen pals were mentioned by family members, and some remnants of the correspondence were in material that Joan Wallcraft showed me in September 1986. "Our Canadian Missionary Society," *MFP*, 13 July 1912; "Meeting of the Presbyterian Ladies Aid," SR *Star*, 21 May 1912; "Housekeeping in Canada," *MFP*, 24 January 1914.

30 "A Canadian 'Corn-Feed,'" *MFP*, 21 September 1912.

31 "Housekeeping in Canada," *MFP*, 11 October 1913; "Housekeeping in Canada," *MFP*, 24 January 1914.

32 "The Boy in his Teens. What and How Shall we Teach Him," SR *Star*, 26 July 1912.

33 I am grateful to Melinda McCracken, who unearthed various biographical details about Gertrude's associates, and to Diane Haglund, United Church Archives, University of Winnipeg, for information on Andrew Weir's church career. Weir's praise is in "Local News," SR *Star*, 4 October 1912.

34 Originally from Ontario, his family had settled in the Dauphin area for a time. Robert and his sisters and brother had come up to the Swan Valley area with their father to work on the survey; the father had died in the spring of 1899, but Robert was hired in his place. Robert registered his homestead in April 1899, while brother James took up an adjoining quarter section the next April. Robert's homestead file number was 75616, South West 24, Township 36, Range 27 West, James' was SE24; the records are in RG1 H1, Department of Agriculture, Debt Adjustment Board, at the Provincial Archives of Manitoba; according to the Land Records Office, Robert proved up in 1903 and gained clear title. For Presbyterian activities see Dauphin Presbyterial United Church Women, "Church Histories"; "Bells Across the Snow: Church Going in Canada," *MFP*, 16 December 1911.

35 Fred to Edith, 25 January 1914; A propos of reciting poetry, Fred wrote that Jim's memory was even better than Robert's and were it not for the speech impediment, Jim's capacity would be greater still. Maggie moved away after Robert married Gertrude; family information is mainly from interviews with Joan Wallcraft and Dorothy Shewfelt, September 1986, and Eric Richardson, September 1986, July 1991.

36 Interviews with Connie Livesey MacDonald, September 1986, and July 1991, and on her decision to marry, Gertrude to Dr Goulden, 1 May 1924, Brandon file, 105–6.

37 On Robert Richardson's holdings, see Fred to Edith, 20 October 1912. Re Gertrude's occupation, she may have worked as a seamstress during her first year in Swan River, but she never refers to having done so. She gives seamstress pay rates in the Valley as $1.50 to $2.00 a day plus meals; the seamstress generally stayed in the home of the customer while doing the work: "Housekeeping in Canada," *MFP*, 19 April 1913.

38 Fred discussed problems of cash shortage, high cost of credit, and the usual vagaries of weather, prices, etc., in his correspondence with Edith Watson, passim, 1912–16. See for example 27 July 1913, wherein he discusses the outlays needed to bring the newest quarter section into production; at that point he and John Livesey jointly owned 480 acres, of which only sixty were cultivated, and that summer, thirty-five in crop. Quotes are from Fred to Edith, 20 October 1912; 27 July 1913; 4 December 1916; Gertrude to Edith, 26 December [1912]. The high cost of credit was an even worse problem after the First World War. Fred commented bitterly that it took him fifteen years and cost twice what he had borrowed, to regain clear title to his homestead: *Between the Hills* 118–19. On women buying land, Georgina Binnie-Clark and her sister Ethel operated a wheat farm in Saskatchewan for many years. Binnie-Clark set out practical step-by-step farm acquisition and development plans for women ranging from five acres at one hundred pounds capital investment (on Vancouver Island near a town) to one hundred acres at one thousand pounds (the Qu'appelle Valley). But £100 sterling was more than $500 Canadian, an impossible sum for most women, and that was only the initial investment. See Owen's discussion of capital and operating costs in "The Cost of Farm-Making in Early Manitoba." On homesteading costs and failure rates see Friesen, *The Canadian Prairies*, 309–12.

39 Maybe any man could get one, but about 40 percent of homesteaders never successfully "proved up," or gained permanent title; see Friesen, *The Canadian Prairies*, 209–11, for a discussion of research on failures. Oliver's comments to Hind are cited by Binnie-Clark, *Wheat and Woman*. This state of affairs did not go unchallenged. As Susan Jackel describes in her excellent introduction to the Binnie-Clark book, there was a movement to pressure the government to change the homestead regulations, strongest between 1909 and 1913, but continuing through the 1920s, led by farm activists and journalists. Far from being successful in bringing reform, early complaints about the regulations led the minister of the interior to tighten what few loopholes existed. Subsequent federal ministers refused to make changes. When land jurisdiction passed to the provinces in 1930, Manitoba and Saskatchewan cancelled the homestead system completely, and Alberta opened it up to all "persons," which by then (after the famous "Persons Case" led by five Alberta women, one of whom was Gertrude's suffrage friend Nellie McClung) had been established to

include women. See also such Western press discussions as the "Land Values" column in the Winnipeg *Voice*, 19 May 1916, entitled "What the Women of Canada Want," and in the 10 August 1917 issue, in the "Current Events" column, the paragraph headed "Homesteads for Women." In the U.S. single women had the same privileges as men for homestead access, but to my knowledge no comparative study has been done, although Sandra Myers was apparently working on one. See her preliminary article, "Victoria's Daughters." Thanks to Catherine Cavanaugh for this reference.

40 Roberts, "A Work of Empire," and "Ladies, Women and the State."

41 Jackel, "Introduction," *A Flannel Shirt and Liberty*, xiii–xxvii; see also especially Binnie-Clark's three articles in this volume. On Gertrude's "widowhood," Fred told John Dubreuil of the Swan Valley Museum that Gertie's first husband had been killed in the First World War; perhaps by the 1970s Fred had forgotten, or thought Dubreuil had, that the second marriage took place in 1912. This information is repeated on the cover of a manuscript book of Gertrude's poems held in the museum.

42 Interview with Connie Livesey MacDonald, September 1986.

43 Gertrude to Dr Goulden, 1 May 1924, Brandon file; the marriage licence form offers the alternatives of "spinster" or "widow" for women; "widow" was written in.

44 Gertrude to Dr Clement, 6 October [1939], Brandon file; the marriage witnesses were Hazel Addy Hope Lloyd, and C.A. Bowman, the wife of presiding minister James Bowman. Information is taken from the marriage certificate and from Winnipeg city directories; thanks to Melinda McCracken for help.

45 Fred to Edith, 1 September 1912.

46 Fred to Edith, 20 October 1912; but Fred was a terrible tease. He told Edith that he had planned to write her on suffrage stationery which he pinched from Gertie for the purpose; "How will you like to receive an envelope with 'Votes for Women' on," he enquired: Fred to Edith, 1 June 1913. He later did so, and in a subsequent discussion said the group did not plan to alter the colour of the stationery until they got the vote; he claimed that its scent, which he did not describe, was intended to attract attention to the cause: Fred to Edith, 27 July 1913.

47 May to Edith, 4 September 1912.

48 "Housekeeping in Canada," *MFP*, 7 June 1913 on the sweet and restful countryside. Gertrude's transport, May to Edith, 4 Sept 1912.

49 Family interviews helped to fill in details here. The house's name is on her 1916 Christmas card to Edith, 7 December 1916. On telephones in the valley see Palmer and Dobbyn, *Lasting Impressions* 130–1. On scarcity of time for writing see "Housekeeping in Canada: Visitors," *MFP*, 17 May 1913 and "Housekeeping in Canada," 30 August 1913; the latter mentions the

arrival of the telephone in the valley. Fannie's phone is mentioned in "Housekeeping in Canada," *MFP*, 20 June 1914.

50 Fred to Edith, 27 December 1912; the telephone installation and city poverty are described in "Housekeeping in Canada," *MFP*, 15 November 1913.

51 On rural adult education and farm women see Jeffery Taylor, "Professionalism, Intellectual Practice, and the Educational State Structure," 36–45; "Home Economics [Society Reports]: Swan River," *Canadian Thresherman and Farmer* (hereafter *CTF*), November 1913.

52 "The Agricultural Train," *MFP*, 27 July 1912; "Housekeeping in Canada," *MFP*, 26 July 1913; see also Taylor's article, "Professionalism, Intellectual Practice and the Educational State Structure," and "A Big Educational Course on Wheels," *Canadian Thresherman and Farmer* September 1915, for a description of the trains' operation.

53 Information on the Home Economics Society and its activities is taken from the following: Departments of Social Service and Evangelism of the Methodist and Presbyterian Churches, *Report on a Rural Survey* 26–8; "Housekeeping in Canada," *MFP*, 7 June 1913, 21 June 1913, 23 August 1913. See also Taylor, "Dominant and Popular Ideologies." On the Rest Room fund raiser, "Housekeeping in Canada," *MFP*, 29 November 1913. Miss E. Baldwin's paper, "Women in the Business World," was published in the Swan River *Star*, 4 December 1913 and the event was reported in "Women in the Business World," *CTF*, November 1913.

54 "Town Items" announcement of the monthly meeting submitted by Livesey, SR *Star*, 7 February 1913.

55 "G. G. Association," SR *Star*, 14 March 1913.

56 Shaw, "Women's Suffrage," SR *Star*, 28 February 1913. A description by Mansell-Moullin, MD, of forcible feeding methods, "Artificial v. 'Forcible' Feeding," *The Suffragette*, 4 April 1913, is in MacKenzie, *Shoulder to Shoulder*, 233–4. Miss Higgins' visits with Gertrude are described in "Housekeeping in Canada," *MFP*, 14 March 1914, and 23 May 1914. I am grateful to Diana Chown for the information on Miss Higgins; she and Mary Walters Riskin have written a history of the VON in Alberta which is still unpublished; the manuscript is held by the Edmonton branch of the VON. On the Women's Freedom League paper, see "In Time of War," *MFP*, 31 October 1915.

57 "Letter to the Editor," SR *Star* 23 May 1913. Vellacott's biography of Catherine Marshall, *From Liberal to Labour*, and numerous other sources, suggest that militant tactics were considered to be damaging to public opinion. Vicinus, *Independent Women* 260.

58 I have not been able to track down further information about Mr Middleditch: "In Answer to Mrs Gertrude Richardson," SR *Star*, 30 May 1913.

59 Richardson, "Letter to the Editor," SR *Star*, 6 June 1913; Shaw, "Communication," SR *Star*, 20 June 1913.

60 Anthony Mardiros, *William Irvine*; thanks to Betty Mardiros for information on Irvine and his associates, access to her own copies of early newspapers, and the gift of this book; on visits with Irvine, for example,
   "Housekeeping in Canada," MFP, 23 August 1913, 13 September 1913,
   18 October 1913.
61 Irvine, "Communication," SR *Star*, 6 June 1913.
62 Shaw to Dear Editor [*sic*], 27 March 1975. At that time she was living in
   Toronto; the copy of the letter was found in Fred's museum, and I do not
   know if it was ever published. On contact with the Winnipeg PEL see for
   example PEL Minute Book 1912–14, 192, PEL Papers, PAM. The British
   Dominions Woman Suffrage Union (BDWSU) sent material to overseas
   groups; see the discussion in Duley, *Where Once Our Mothers Stood We
   Stand*, 55. Gertrude also knew the BDWSU's Dorothy Pethick from
   Leicester days.
63 On the picnic see "Housekeeping in Canada," MFP, 19 July 1913; Fred to
   Edith, 27 September 1913; information on the group's fund-raising success is in the annual report, discussed in "R. R. Woman's Suffrage,"
   SR *Star*, 26 March 1914.
64 "Housekeeping in Canada," MFP, 27 September 1913 contains details of
   the tea.
65 The meetings are described in: "Visit of Lillian Lawrie [*sic*]," SR *Star*,
   29 August 1913; "Woman Suffrage Meeting" and "Minitonas," SR *Star*,
   12 September 1913; Fred to Edith, 1 September 1913; see also "Housekeeping in Canada," MFP, 6 September 1913, and 13 September 1913. For
   an example of how Thomas was portrayed in farm press see Hamilton,
   "Our Winnipeg Press Women," CTF, July 1913, 82–4.
66 A similar situation existed when the wood-sawing engine and crew arrived to saw the wood pile; this occurred in late winter, used smaller
   crews, and lasted about a day so the volume of work was less; on feeding
   a sawing crew, "Housekeeping in Canada: Sawing the Woodpile," MFP,
   15 March 1913. On the harvest, Fred wrote about snapshots he taken of a
   harvest crew he worked on, that Gertrude had helped a neighbour feed,
   Fred to Edith, 9 October 1913. The fall harvest is described in "Housekeeping in Canada," MFP, 18 October 1913 and 25 October 1913. For a
   captivating description of the work and especially the machinery of
   the threshing crew (with a steam combine harvester), see Robert Stead's
   novel, *Grain*.
67 On economic problems, "Housekeeping in Canada," MFP, 24 January 1914.
68 "Housekeeping in Canada," MFP, 5 December 1913; "Public Monthly
   Meeting of the Woman Suffrage Association in the Roaring River Schoolhouse," SR *Star*, 12 November 1912; "Literary Society," SR *Star*, 11 December 1913; "Housekeeping in Canada," MFP, 27 December 1913;
   "Housekeeping in Canada," MFP, 17 January 1914.

69 As it turned out, Horace and his fiancée did neither; Horace married someone else, lifetimes later after the war, but luckily for the sake of a last happy holiday season before the family's world changed forever, no one could foresee any of that. Fred mentioned later that there had been obstacles to Horace's planned marriage but not their nature; it may have been related to the war. Information on Horace comes from Fred to Edith, 28 December 1913; also on Horace's plans, 1 September 1912, 4 December 1913, 17 February 1914, 5 April 1914, 24 January 1915. I do not know the identity of Horace's sweetheart, but in 3 November 1912 Fred wrote to Edith that Horace was madly in love with someone called Florence. Gertrude writes about the holidays in "Housekeeping in Canada," *MFP*, 17 January 1914, 24 January 1914, 31 January 1914.

70 "At the 'Gateway of the West,' " *MFP*, 10 January 1914; J.A. Bowman's obituary is found in Winnipeg *Tribune* and *Free Press*, 20 September 1960; copies of the clippings are in the biography scrapbooks in the Manitoba Legislative Library. I am grateful to Melinda McCracken for tracking down these.

71 "Housekeeping in Canada: A Bridal 'At-Home," *MFP*,14 February 1914; "Housekeeping in Canada: IV," *MFP*, 8 March 1913.

72 "Housekeeping in Canada," *MFP*, 21 March 1914.

73 "Housekeeping in Canada: A Miscellaneous Shower," *MFP*, 27 December 1913; "Housekeeping in Canada: A Bridal At-Home," *MFP*, 14 February 1914.

74 "R. R. Woman's Suffrage," SR *Star*, 26 March 1914; "Housekeeping in Canada," *MFP*, 11 April 1914.

75 "Housekeeping in Canada," *MFP*, 4 April 1914.

76 Gertrude mentioned that she had begun to write for the magazine, "Housekeeping in Canada," *MFP*, 11 April 1914. On the magazine see Reynolds, "History of 'Woman's Century,' " *Woman's Century*, September 1918.

77 These events are described in "Housekeeping in Canada," *MFP*, 18 April 1914, and 2 May 1914.

78 "Housekeeping in Canada," *MFP*, 9 May 1914, and 30 May 1914; William Sims replaced Tory MLA Daniel McDonald and was himself ousted in 1920 by an independent. Sims had been on the municipality council for several years before his election.

79 The Church League for Woman's Suffrage grew out of the experience of an all-night vigil series in the summer and fall of 1905 to try to force the government to receive a petition from Women's Freedom League members. (The petition consisted of resolutions passed at a huge outdoor meeting held near Westminster 5 July 1905.) A Church of England minister, Claude Hinscliff, was struck by the importance of the petition (some C of E men helped their female relatives with the vigil, and so did the Rever-

end Mr Hinscliff). He helped churchwomen who had been involved in the vigil to organise the Church League, in the fall of 1909. Hinscliff was also a member of the Men's League for Women's Suffrage. Nevinson, "How the Church League was founded," *Church League for Woman's Suffrage*, May 1913, held by the British Library in the Maud Arncliffe Sennett Collection; she was a National Executive Council member for the WFL. She was an actress under the name Mary Kingsley; her father was reputedly an associate of Garibaldi: "Eastbourne and Sussex Society," 13 April 1909, clipping in volume 7 of the collection, 25 February-13 July 1909.

80 "Housekeeping in Canada," MFP, 9 May 1914, and 23 May 1914.

81 "To the Editor of the Swan River Star," SR *Star*, 14 May 1914. Although the British government claimed it only force fed the women when their health was in danger because of hunger strikes, there were cases where force feeding was used when the women had not hunger struck; it was clear that the government was using this as a form of punishment, perhaps as a deterrent. Whatever the motivation, it amounted to legally sanctioned torture; the methods were brutal, painful, and dangerous. The leader of the doctors was Charles Mansell-Moullin, a member of the nonmilitant Men's League for Women's Suffrage. His wife Edith was a WSPU activist. He began making public statements against forced feeding in 1909, coauthored the medical journal article in 1912, and another to the highly respected journal *Lancet* in August 1912. See Stanley with Morley, *The Life and Death of Emily Wilding Davison*, on the Mansell-Moullins, 102–4, 121–3, on overlaps, 152–4. On the prison experience, see Lytton, *Prisons and Prisoners*, and Vicinus, *Independent Women*, chapter 7.

82 Fred to Edith, 21 June 1914; "Housekeeping in Canada" MFP, 27 June 1914, 4 July 1914, and 11 July 1914.

83 The impending visit is mentioned in "Housekeeping in Canada," 20 June 1914; "Mrs McClung's Visit," SR *Star*, 11 June 1914.

84 Gertrude had greatly admired McClung's writings, comparing her to Dickens; she was familiar with *Sowing Seeds in Danny*, and considered Pearlie Watson an immortal character. Pearlie Watson first appeared as a child in McClung's 1908 novel *Sowing Seeds in Danny*; by the end of *The Second Chance* Pearl is a transformed enlightened and mature fifteen, for whom is prefigured a happy marriage and a useful life. The story is continued in the 1921 novel *Purple Springs* in which Pearl goes to normal school and becomes converted to political activism in the suffrage movement. *Purple Springs* includes the story of the Winnipeg "Women's Parliament" of January 1914, when a Political Equality League deputation to Premier Roblin had memorised his sexist words and gestures, and used them to great effect in a satire wherein men unsuccessfully requested to be given the franchise, performed three evenings to packed houses at the Walker Theatre. Although Gertrude was not on the delegation in 1914 and

did not mention the event in her columns, she would certainly have been aware of it, and no doubt she and her Roaring River associates had passed some merry minutes relishing the *tour de force*. I am indebted to Randi Warne for information about McClung; Warne's reissue of *Purple Springs*, with an important introduction, was published in 1992 by University of Toronto Press.

85 Details are in "Housekeeping in Canada," *MFP*, 18 July 1914.

86 "Housekeeping in Canada," *MFP*, 18 April 1914, and 9 May 1914; the sacred work of editors is discussed in "Housekeeping in Canada: Canadian Newspapers," *MFP*, 16 May 1914. For the record they ate meat loaf, scalloped potatoes, lobster, tomatoes, pickles, bread and butter, layer cake, white nut cake, biscuits, strawberries and cream, olives, homemade candies, nuts, chocolates, and tea; "Housekeeping in Canada," *MFP*, 18 July 1914.

87 Her version that evening differed in some respects from the essay of that same title published in the collection *In Times Like These* a few years later. McClung often gave talks on a theme as part of the process of developing it for its written version. Unfortunately, Randi Warne explained to me, her archival records of speeches tend to be seven words jotted on the back of an old envelope, so it is difficult to ascertain how the versions differed.

88 "Housekeeping in Canada" *MFP*, 18 July 1914; "Mrs McClung's Address," SR *Star*, 24 July 1914.

89 "Housekeeping in Canada, *MFP*, 18 July 1914.

90 "Seek Ye First the Kingdom of God" is in her 25 July 1914 column.

91 "Housekeeping in Canada," *MFP*, 1 August 1914.

92 "Housekeeping in Canada: A Digression," *MFP*, 8 August 1914; see "Observer," rejoinder under the same title, 22 August 1914.

93 "Housekeeping in Canada," *MFP*, 29 August 1914. The Tories won a minority of the popular vote but won the "non-British" ridings in this election. It is worth noting that there was a nasty underside of racism in the Liberals' progressive reforms, such as the removal of educational and cultural rights from non-Anglophones; the Liberal government's violations of the bilingualism provisions in the Manitoba constitution were not reversed until a Supreme Court decision in 1979. On Manitoba voting patterns see Peterson, "Ethnic and Class Politics in Manitoba."

CHAPTER FOUR

1 See Roberts, "Women's Peace Activism in Canada," and "Why do Women do Nothing to End the War?"

2 "In Time of War: Letter From an Englishwoman in Canada," *MFP*, 12 September 1914; the aunties who told Gertrude the story were probably her mother's sisters, including Eliza's younger sister Charlotte Richardson,

according to the family tree worked out by Gertrude's maternal cousins Olive Burrell and Margaret Bailey whom I visited in Scarborough in January 1991. In addition to their invaluable help with the family history, I am grateful to them for warm hospitality, delicious meals, and fascinating conversation about their own experiences in the British Women's Total Abstinence Society, the British branch of the WCTU. Eliza Richardson Twilley's sister Charlotte (1837–1917) married Lomas Flude; they had seven children. Their daughter Charlotte Flude married Arthur Bailey in 1910; Olive Bailey Burrell and Margaret Bailey are their daughters. The grandmother who divided the loaf during the Crimean War was probably Charlotte and Eliza's mother, about whom we know virtually nothing.

3 Of course a man could claim to be single and enlist without consent, but then his family would not receive the allowances to which they were entitled. The women's consent regulation was abolished in August 1915 but by mid-1916 authorities were still concerned over women's refusal to allow men to enlist. Whether the authorities had grounds for such concern by then is not clear. Wilson, *Ontario and the First World War*, on women's consent and men lying, xxxv; quoting *Canadian Annual Review*, 1914, 190; on women's refusal, lxxxvi. Wilson believes women in general were pro-war.

4 "In Time of War: Letter From an Englishwoman in Canada," *MFP*, 12 September 1914; "Housekeeping in Canada," *MFP*, 19 September 1914.

5 "My Canadian Letter: A Service of Intercession," *MFP*, 3 October 1914. On Dr Murray, see the account of his visit with Gertrude in late December 1914, "In Time of War," *MFP*, 9 January 1915.

6 "In Time of War," *MFP*, 31 October 1914.

7 The Manifesto urged alternative methods of dispute resolution, an international court, and other institutions that recognised that all nations are inextricably bound together in the human family. See Fraser, *The Social Uplifters*, 155–64.

8 "In Time of War," *MFP*, 31 October 1914; "My Canadian Letter," *MFP*, 12 December 1914. Belgian refugee story, Fred Twilley to Edith Watson, 11 October 1914, in the collection of family letters found in the Fred Twilley museum, courtesy of Dorothy Twilley Shewfelt and Bob Wallcraft.

9 "In Time of War," *MFP*, 31 October 1914; "My Canadian Letter," *MFP*, 12 December 1914.

10 "In Time of War," *MFP*, 7 November 1914. Nellie McClung's remarks are reported in "Auspicious Opening of the People's Forum," Winnipeg *Voice* 30 October 1914.

11 Richardson, "Swan River: Rest Room Opening," *CTF*, November 1914. For the development and functions of Rest Rooms in the province, see Norell, " 'The Most Humane Institution.' " Norell apparently did not use the *CTF*, which contains reports of early Rest Rooms.

12 "My Canadian Letter," *MFP*, 14 November 1914. The War Office request for socks was made in October 1914; see Duley, *Where Once Our Mothers Stood*. For Home Economics Society activities, see the annual convention report, "Home Economics," *CTF*, March 1915, and Gertrude's report, "Swan River Home Economics Society," *CTF* May 1915.

13 "My Canadian Letter," *MFP*, 21 November 1914, and 28 November 1914.

14 On Britain, see Vellacott, "Feminist Consciousness and the First World War"; Vellacott points out that all the NUWSS executive resigned over the issue, except the president and honorary treasurer. See Liddington, *The Long Road to Greenham*, especially chapters 4 and 5; Wiltsher, *Most Dangerous Women*. For Mary Sheepshanks during the war, see Oldfield, *Spinsters of This Parish*, 176–98.

15 "My Canadian Letter," *MFP*, 28 November 1914, 19 December 1914, 10 July 1915. On Sylvia Pankhurst and the *Dreadnought*, "In Time of War," *MFP*, 2 January 1915; it is not clear whether Gertrude received the *Dreadnought* all through the war. For Australia see an excerpt from an editorial describing the raids and censorship, by Goldstein and John, *Woman Voter* 16 September 1914, in Daniels and Murnane, *Uphill All The Way*, 288–9. See also Weiner, "Vida Goldstein: the Women's Candidate" in Spender, *Feminist Theorists*.

16 The BDWSU had grown out of the Australian and New Zealand Women Voters Association (ANZWVA), of women from those countries (where women could vote) who were living in London (where they were disenfranchised) and were active in the British suffrage movement. A small ANZWVA contingent had participated in the first big woman suffrage procession in London, and had grown into the BDWSU. Gertrude mentions the BDWSU day of prayer request in "In Time of War," *MFP*, 2 January 1915; the July 1914 BDWSU conference is discussed in "Housekeeping in Canada," *MFP*, 13 June 1914. The 1913 *Women's Who's Who* describes Newcomb's work in organising Australian women into the London suffrage campaign: 319. Newcomb's endorsement: see the March and April 1915 issues of *Woman's Century*. Newcomb had corresponded with the Winnipeg suffragists; see for example Minutes of the PEL Executive Meeting, 11 May 1914, PEL Papers, File Miscellaneous nd 1913–14, PAM. After July 1914 the BDWSU regularly contacted suffrage groups throughout the empire.

17 "In Time of War," *MFP*, 9 January 1915; "Christmas in War Time," *MFP*, 23 January 1915; "Lillian Laurie," "Women's Organizations in Rural Districts," Manitoba *Free Press*, 7 February 1915.

18 "My Canadian Letter: A Letter to my Women Friends," *MFP*, 13 February 1915. The bayonet phrase sounds like Nellie McClung, but Randi Warne is unable to attribute it to McClung's written work; if it were McClung, it would likely have been in one of her speeches.

19 "My Canadian Letter," *MFP*, 20 February 1915; Departments of Social Service and Evangelism of the Methodist and Presbyterian Churches, *Report on a Rural Survey.* John Murchee joined the Manitoba Agricultural College staff in 1915 as a rural sociology expert. On the rural survey movement see Taylor, "Dominant and Popular Ideologies," 200–5. See also Allen, *The Social Passion*, 12–14.

20 The meeting is mentioned in "My Canadian Letter," *MFP*, 20 February 1915. Jackel, "First Days, Fighting Days," discusses the important part played by feminist journalists in the women's movement. For information on The Hague and subsequent WILPF activities, see Wiltsher, *Most Dangerous Women*, Liddington, *The Long Road to Greenham*, and also see WILPF papers, Norlin Library, University of Colorado at Boulder; the 1915 lists are in I-6, and the invitation in I-13–1. Murphy's letter, dated 5 April 1915, is in III-4/7. The lists are not exhaustive or complete; for example, Emily Murphy's papers in the Edmonton City Archives contain an invitation to the conference, and her name is not on this 1915 list although it appears on others later that year for the Circular Letter No. 1 sent out before 5 August 1915, and Circular Letter No. 11 send out 17 December 1915. The invitation itself was entitled "Call to the Women of All Nations" and was sent out over the signatures of women affiliated with a wide range of women's organisations, representing interests from health care, fine arts, education, trade unions of various occupations, and national and international feminist groups. It is clear that Gertrude was in touch with this group that later became the Women's International League for Peace and Freedom, from its earliest days as an IWSA peace splinter.

21 See "What Twelve Canadian Women Hope to See as the Outcome of the War," *Everywoman's World*, April 1915. The views of the twelve women are noteworthy for the absence of pacifism: although they are not uniformly prowar, only Murphy and Halifax writer Marshall Saunders are overtly antiwar in their replies. The letters from Murphy to Ryckman, 25 May 1915, and Wales to Murphy, 29 October 1915, are in the Julia Grace Wales papers, MG30 C238, unsorted when I saw them in June 1991. I am grateful to archivists David Fraser and Robert Albota for their help. On Murphy and the U.S. connection to Canadian WILPF sympathisers, see Harriet Thomas to Chrystal Macmillan, 30 December 1915, WILPF papers III-31–5. The ICWPP peace envoys were Rosika Schwimmer's idea: see Addams, Balch and Hamilton, *Women at The Hague*.

22 "Women and Peace" editorial, presumably by Jessie MacIver, *Woman's Century*, April 1915.

23 Barker, "Agitation for Peace," *Woman's Century*, April 1915. Lang, "National Union," *Woman's Century.* The events leading up to the congress, its activities, and outcomes, are discussed in Addams, Balch, and Hamilton; Liddington, *Long Road to Greenham*. See also Sylvia

Pankhurst, *The Home Front*, 147–9, and Wiltsher, *Most Dangerous Women*. For Canada see Roberts, "Women's Peace Activism in Canada" and CRIAW paper.

24 "People I Have Met I: American Indians," *MFP*, 26 August 1911; Johnson's death, "Housekeeping in Canada," *MFP*, 7 February 1914; conquest poem quote and rethinking the Empire, "My Canadian Letter," *MFP*, 20 February 1915. The Johnson poem is "A Cry From an Indian Wife," from *Flint and Feather*, 15–17. The poem was first published in *White Wampum* in 1895. The sympathetic article is "Pauline Johnson," *CTF*, September 1912.

25 The SR *Star* noted on 19 February 1915 that "Mr and Mrs Robert Richardson are in the city." For Gertrude's account see "In Time of War," *MFP*, 20 March 1915 and "My Canadian Letter: A Visit to the Premier of Manitoba," *MFP*, 27 March 1915.

26 "My Canadian Letter: A Visit to the Premier of Manitoba," *MFP*, 27 March 1915; for a discussion of Bland's sermon, see "My Canadian Letter," *MFP*, 3 April 1915. For Miss Brown's antiwar views, see her People's Forum talk, reported in the *Voice*, 24 December 1915.

27 "My Canadian Letter," *MFP*, 10 April 1915; in England Asquith's government wriggled out of woman suffrage commitments for years. For a lucid account of the British situation see Vellacott, *From Liberal to Labour*.

28 Evans quoted by Steinson, "The Mother of Half of Humanity," 269; "R.R. Woman Suffrage Association," SR *Star*, 19 March 1915. On antiwar news see the column reporting a pacifist talk on "Women and War" given at a regional suffrage meeting in Indianapolis by Rosika Schwimmer, a Hungarian feminist who had visited the U.S. in late 1914 to help organise support for feminist peace groups and the Hague Congress: "Political Equality League," Winnipeg *Voice*, 2 April 1915.

29 "My Canadian Letter," *MFP*, 19 June 1915, and 3 July 1915. On MacIver's hostility to pacifism, see for example Jessie MacIver's prowar editorials, both entitled "Women and Peace," in the *Woman's Century* for April 1915 and January 1916. On scientific ideas about gender and nature, Conway, "The Woman's Peace Party and the First World War." Geddes' 1900 lecture tour of the States had included particular attention to audiences involved in the settlement house movement and other sectors of social reform: educated active women reformers. For additional uses made of Geddes and Thomas' theories by some British feminists to support "sex war" analyses, and presumptions about the innate superiority of the female sex, see Kent, *Sex and Suffrage in Britain*, 35, 161–7. See also Byles, "Women's Experience of World War One," and "My Canadian Letter," *MFP*, 6 February 1915. Byles drew upon Reilly, *Scars Upon My Heart*, which is based on Reilly's bibliographical research which turned up 532 British women who had written war verses; the collection includes sev-

enty-nine of these. Gertrude is not among them. Reilly did not include
newspapers, which is where Gertrude's wartime poems appeared.

30 "My Canadian Letter," MFP, 8 May 1915; "My Canadian letter: The Kindness of God," MFP, 15 May 1915.

31 The 1915 ICWPP News Sheets reprinted the peace messages throughout
the fall: WILPF papers, V-2–11. For a chronology of women's antiwar activities, see the WIL newsletter which began with the January 1916 issue:
"Some Facts About Women's Peace Work During the World's War," Internationaal, 1.5, Aug.-Sept.-Oct. 1916, 47–50. Gertrude was a subscriber. It
was intended to be a monthly but due to problems getting news, and in-
sufficient money for printing and mailing, it was irregular. On Jus Suffragii, Liddington, Long Road, 88–98, and Wiltsher, Most Dangerous Women,
126–53. For women's antiwar activities in France and Germany see Wishnia, "Feminism and Pacifism," and Hermann, "Social Democratic Women
in Germany."

32 "My Canadian Letter," MFP, 19 June 1915, and 3 July 1915; for the Home
Economics Society, "Swan River," CTF, October 1915, and "My Canadian
Letter," MFP, 30 October 1915.

33 Corresponding Secretary Gertrude Richardson to Premier Norris, [June
1915], and Norris to Richardson, 16 June 1915, Norris Papers, MG13
H1 157–8, PAM; Gertrude's original is written in ink; the underlining is in
pencil, presumably added by the recipient.

34 "My Canadian Letter," MFP, 3 July 1915, and 17 July 1915; "Political
Equality Meeting," SR Star, 21 May 1915; Minutes of the Ninth Annual
Convention, Manitoba Grain Growers Association, Brandon Manitoba,
1912, MG 10E1 Box 15, PAM. The establishment of the Oakhurst branch is
recorded in "Political Equality League Inaugurated," SR Star, 16 July
1915; petition appeal, "Suffrage Petition Form," SR Star, 27 August 1915
and "Political Equality League," SR Star, 24 September 1915; the Grain
Growers picnic is reported under the heading "The Western Awakening,"
also featuring a sketch of Lillian Beynon Thomas, under the subheading
"Women of the Awakening," which may have been intended as a regular
feature (but did not subsequently appear as such) of Gertrude's column,
"The West," Woman's Century, August 1915. Mrs Wright's lecture, "Political Equality League," SR Star, 10 September 1915, "My Canadian Letter,"
MFP, 2 October 1915; new branches founded, "My Canadian Letter:
Mutual Helpfulness," 4 September 1915.

35 Discussion of future plans, "My Canadian Letter," MFP 14 August 1915.

36 After the conference, the ICWPP headquarters sent out copies of a report,
which included the resolutions passed and a description of their international mediation project which they carried out in subsequent months.
Gertrude may well have received the report from them, although the
records show several mailing lists and it is not clear from scribbled nota-

tions which material was sent to which lists. See Circular Letter No. 1, International Committee of Women for Permanent Peace, which accompanied the first mailout of Congress documents in the late summer of 1915, in WIL papers, Boulder, I-6–1915; Emily Murphy's name is also on a list of those to whom this was sent. A memo by Rosika Schwimmer and Chrystal Macmillan, describing the activities of the peace envoys and the reaction of heads of state to their visits, may have been sent out: headed "strictly private and confidential," it is dated 2 August 1915; WIL papers, I-6–1916. Gutteridge, "Women and Their Attitude to the War," Winnipeg Voice, 9 July 1915; the subtitle is "Fundamental Instinct of Maternity Comes Out Strong As Ever." For more on Gutteridge see Howard's biography, Helena Gutteridge. Edith Lang's column was regularly headed "National Equal Franchise Union," Woman's Century, September 1915. See Ellis' ambiguous poem, "An African Legend," Wyggeston Girls' Gazette, December 1892, 177. Charlotte Ellis was on the executive of the Leicester and Leicestershire Women's Suffrage Society; their annual reports are in the Fawcett Library, London. Both Ellises appear in the minutes of the local Quaker meeting, for example, 18 January 1900 and 20 June 1901, Minutes of the Leicester Monthly Meeting of the Religious Society of Friends, Leicestershire Record Office. I am grateful to Malcolm Elliott, historian of Leicester and coclerk of the Meeting, for permission and help with this and other material. For Charlotte Despard, see Linklater, An Unhusbanded Life. The British WIL report is entitled "Towards Permanent Peace," and is found in several places in the WILPF papers, I-13–2 for example. For Gertrude's comments, "My Canadian Letter," MFP, 29 August 1915

37 "My Canadian Letter," MFP, 28 August 1915. In fact, there had been a meeting of the International Congress of Socialist Women in late March 1915, who sent sisterly greetings to the Hague Congress. This women's meeting was the first organised socialist opposition to the war. The hostile letter from Adelaide Plumptre, secretary of the National Committee of Women for Patriotic Service, to Jane Addams, refusing the Hague invitation and enclosing the "Open Letter," 15 April 1915, is in WIL papers, III-4/7; "My Canadian Letter," MFP, 11 September 1915, and 6 November 1915.

38 "In Time of War," MFP, 2 January 1915. The poem is "The Benediction," by Gerald J. Lively. It was later reprinted in the SDP antiwar paper, Canadian Forward, 24 July 1917. Gertrude does not say where the first copy came from, to which she had referred in "My Canadian New Year's Letter," MFP, 30 January 1915.

39 "My Canadian Letter," MFP, 6 February 1915 and 10 July 1915; "My Canadian Letter: Patriotic Sunday," MFP, 24 July 1915; "My Canadian Letter," MFP, 31 July 1915, 28 August 1915. On this view of the press'

leadership role, see the discussion by Steedman, *Childhood, Culture and Class*, 148.

40 "The Justice of Jesus," *MFP*, 4 September 1915.

41 Lang's report on a circular letter sent out by the National Equal Franchise Union, asking members to abandon suffrage work for war work; most suffragists agreed that war work should be focused on some particular area which would be seen as the specific "gift of suffragists," but western women refused to stop suffrage organising. Lang commented that since they were "within sight" of getting the vote, it made sense for them to make that choice. In other areas where winning suffrage was not imminent, postponement might seem reasonable. In either case, Lang wrote, "It is clearly a matter of conscience which each individual must settle for herself." "Suffrage and Patriotism," *Woman's Century*, September 1915.

42 "The Coming of the Angel," *Woman's Century*, September 1915.

43 "My Canadian Letter," *MFP*, 2 October 1915, 20 November 1915, 27 November 1915, 4 December 1915, 18 December 1915, 25 December 1915.

44 "My Canadian Letter," *MFP*, 20 November 1915, and 18 December 1915.

45 "My Canadian Letter," *MFP* 6 November 1915, 20 November 1915, 27 November 1915, 18 December 1915, 25 December 1915.

46 Thomas, "Have You Signed the Petition?" and Dixon, "Why Manitoba Women Want to Vote," in *CTF*, September 1915; Laurie, "Forty Thousand Women Want to Vote," Manitoba *Free Press*, 9 October 1915; Richardson, "The West," *Woman's Century*, January 1916.

47 "My Canadian Letter," *MFP*, 22 January 1916, 29 January 1916; The story of the last-minute change is told in Cleverdon, based on a 1944 letter from Lillian Beynon Thomas: *The Woman Suffrage Movement in Canada*, 60–3.

48 "My Canadian Letter," *MFP*, 22 January 1916; "My Canadian Letter: The Woman Suffrage Movement and the War," *MFP*, 29 January 1916. "The West," *Woman's Century*, February 1916.

49 Fred to Edith, 1 November 1914, 24 January 1915, 17 February 1915, 13 June 1915, 12 September 1915, 7 November 1915.

50 Fred to Edith, 7 November 1915, 13 December 1915, 12 April 1916.

51 Gertrude records the departure in "My Canadian Letter," *MFP*, 15 January 1916; the Boston cousins were the same ones whom Florrie had stayed with for four years. Fred to Edith, 27 September 1914, 24 January 1915, 17 February 1915, 21 November 1915, 13 December 1915, 25 February 1916, 26 January 1918.

52 Gertrude Richardson, "My Canadian Letter," *MFP*, 1 January 1916; "My Canadian letter: New Year, 1916," *MFP*, 8 January 1916; "My Canadian Letter: The Woman Suffrage Movement and the War," *MFP*, 29 January 1916.

53 Beynon, "Country Homemakers," *Grain Growers' Guide* (hereafter *GGG*), 9 February 1916, 23 February 1916, 1 March 1916; I am grateful to Gloria

Geller for her notes from Beynon's columns. "My Canadian Letter," *MFP*, 18 March 1916; 19 February 1916; "My Canadian Letter: Problems Arising Out of the War," *MFP*, 8 April 1916; "The West," *Woman's Century,* March 1916, 5, and April 1916, 22. For a contemporary account of the Alberta campaign see L.C. McKenney [*sic*], "Alberta's Triumph," WCTU *White Ribbon Bulletin*, October 1916.

54 "My Canadian Letter," *MFP*, 6 May, 13 May, 3 June, and 5 August 1916; see also Fred to Edith, nd but probably spring 1913, 5 May 1916, and nd but probably June 1917. Eva remained in England for a number of years, while Wilfred went briefly to West Africa to survey possibilities for Salvation Army work there. He wrote that he "found it very hot and was feeling lonely and wishing he was home with his wife," Fred reported to Edith. After the war, Wilfred and Eva went to the West Indies, where they eventually were fêted for their long years (forty in his case, thirty-four in hers) of Salvation Army service. Some career information is taken from a newspaper clipping describing the anniversary celebration, entitled "Proud Record Celebrated," but its publication source (probably the English *War Cry*) and date are uncertain. It was among Fred's unsorted papers, in the Fred Twilley museum on the Wallcraft farm. The younger Wilfred Twilley joined up soon after his birthday: Fred to Edith, nd but early April 1917. The same Wilfred Twilley, then in his nineties, was kind enough to tell me some of his recollections about that visit in a telephone discussion, 15 June 1990. About West Africa, Fred to Edith, 8 February 1917, and Gertrude's comment, "My Canadian Letter" *MFP*, 10 March 1917.

55 Edith Lang, "National Equal Franchise Union," *Woman's Century,* March 1916, for the announcement of program topics; Lang discusses the conference report in her EFU column, *Woman's Century,* September 1917, 20. Richardson, "The West," *Woman's Century* July 1916, 18; Eliza to be a delegate, "My Canadian Letter," *MFP*, 24 June 1916; "My Canadian Letter: New Year's Letter," *MFP*, 30 December 1916 and "The West," *Woman's Century,* January 1917, on Dorothy Pethick's report.

56 Pugsley was from St John, New Brunswick. See Lang's column, "National Equal Franchise Union," *Woman's Century,* March 1916, and *Woman's Century,* April 1916.

57 Lillian Beynon Thomas wrote a guest column while Francis was on holiday: "Country Homemaker," *GGG*, 2 August 1916, and 9 August 1916. Long, "Canadian Suffrage Association" column, *Woman's Century,* September 1916. Long gives the date as 23 September 1912; but I have relied on Cleverdon, *The Woman Suffrage Movement in Canada*.

58 "Country Homemaker," *GGG*, 18 October 1916. The B.C. date is confusing. The Bowser Tory government passed legislation giving women the vote, and it gained royal assent 31 May 1916; but the implementation of

the franchise law depended on a referendum which took place during the provincial election 14 September 1916. Because of technicalities, when the new Liberal legislature convened 1 March 1917, the law had not been actually proclaimed, and a new one was passed and given royal assent 5 April 1917. However, many suffragists assumed that B.C. women had the vote as of September 1916, and discussed the federal eligibility issue on that premise. About women's eligibility, it is noteworthy that no one seems to have given a thought to aboriginal women. Western women pressed for the removal of gender limits, assuming that then "all women" meeting age, citizenship, and residence requirements could vote. Status Indian women were penalised as citizens similarly to other British subjects in many respects (i.e., women's loss of nationality when marrying out, the last vestiges of which for non-aboriginal Canadian women endured until the 1970s), but despite the fact that they were Canadian born, aboriginal women did not automatically enjoy various rights of citizenship supposedly for "all" women, such as the vote.

59 The essays in Willms, Cook, et al. *Conscription 1917*, are helpful for the men's history version of this question, although the same cannot be said for the women's side of things. Cleverdon, *The Woman Suffrage Movement in Canada*, 117–31, provides a balanced account. Craig Brown and Ramsay Cook say that Meighen had reputedly had the idea of two-stroke gendered gerrymandering of the electorate as early as October 1916, *Canada 1896–1921*, 271, citing a letter from Meighen to Borden. Gertrude's description is in "The Canadian Crisis," *Leicester Pioneer*, 7 September 1917.

60 See Brown and Cook's discussion of the legislation, *Canada 1896–1921*, 269–73. Gloria Geller's article, "The Wartimes [*sic*] Elections Act," 88–106, is a good account of the issues and events (although Geller sees women as having fallen into the divide-and-conquer partyist trap, she implies there was at least potentially a common-interest-as-women stance, a view that is less widely accepted today). A less accessible but important source is *Woman's Century*. Accounts can be found in Cleverdon, *The Woman Suffrage Movement in Canada*, Beynon, "Country Homemaker," the more than 200 pages of the House of Commons debate recorded in the 1917 *Hansard*, and biographies of the leading politicians. Borden's speech was reproduced as a pamphlet, "The War-Time Election Act," by the Federal Press Agency, nd [1917]; thanks to Nanci Langford for a copy. See also the act itself in *Statutes of Canada 1917*.

61 Isabel R. Erichsen Brown, "National Equal Franchise Union," *Woman's Century* December 1916; MacIver, "What Do Men Fear?" *Woman's Century*.

62 Richardson, "The West," *Woman's Century*, May 1917; McClung's optimistic letter is cited by MacIver, "What Do Men Fear?" *Woman's Century*, December 1916. Cleverdon, *The Woman Suffrage Movement in Canada*, 112–23.

63 The proconscription resolution was decried by Gertrude in "The West," *Woman's Century*, November 1916; see also "Women Do Not Follow Lead," *Woman's Century*, December 1916.

64 See especially Warne, "Nellie McClung and peace." McClung, "Mrs Mc-Clung's Reply," in "Country Homemaker," *GGG*, 24 January 1917; Clever-don, 118; Richardson, "The West," *Woman's Century* March 1917.

65 Beynon, "The Foreign Women's Franchise," 27 December 1916, and Mc-Clung, "Mrs McClung's Reply," in "Country Homemaker," *GGG*, 24 Janu-ary 1917; and see also Beynon's response to McClung's reply, *GGG*, 24 January 1917.

66 For the reactions of other western suffragists, see Lillian Beynon Thomas to Violet McNaughton, 21 December 1916, McNaughton papers, Saskatchewan Archives Board, A1 E18; "The West," *Woman's Century*, February 1917; Gertrude's Leicester column, "The Canadian Crisis," *Leicester Pioneer*, 7 September 1917. Lillian Beynon Thomas, "A Woman's Talk to Woman," *CTF*, February 1917.

67 "Premier Borden and the Federal Franchise: Difficulties Discussed with National Council Women," *Woman's Century*, September 1917. Local Council revolts and the NCWC attempt to renege are discussed in Strong-Boag, *Parliament of Women*, 325–35. See also *Canadian Annual Review*, 1917, on the Victoria LCW, the Regina WCTU, and the Alberta WCTU, advanc-ing similar protests: 428, 430. Lang, "The Human Basis," *White Ribbon Bul-letin*, October 1916.

68 Gordon is quoted by Bacchi-Ferraro, "The Ideas of the Canadian Suffrag-ists," 125. For another example of this view see "Canadian Suffragists Bit-ter Against the 'Suffrage' Law," *Seattle Daily Call*, 16 November 1917.

CHAPTER FIVE

1 For the early days of the NCF see Kennedy, *The Hound of Conscience*; I am grateful to Tom Kennedy for a number of details about the CO experience, and for his helpfulness in interpreting obscure comments in my sources. See also Vellacott's important study, *Bertrand Russell and the Pacifists*, and Brockway, *Inside the Left*. For Horace, "My Canadian Letter," *MFP*, 5 June 1915. On labour and socialist advocacy and testimony at tribunals, see Bush, *Behind the Lines*, 56–64.

2 Vellacott's two books are the source for Marshall and Russell, supple-mented by Tom Kennedy. *The Hound of Conscience*. Vellacott's forthcoming second volume of her biography of Catherine Marshall will shed further light on the NCF and other women's peace activism during the war. Vari-ous incidents of Quaker involvement above are described in Hirst, *The Quakers in Peace and War*, in particular 504–10. On Nellie Best, see Lidding-ton, *The Long Road to Greenham*, 108; this is an excellent source for British

women's peace activity. For various groups in the English antiwar movement, see Rowbotham's lengthy essay, "Rebel Networks in the First World War," in her *Friends of Alice Wheeldon*. See also James Hinton, *Protests and Visions*, chapters 5 and 6; and Young, "War Resistance and the British Peace Movement Since 1914." On the Wycliffe Church, Ellis, "Records of Nineteenth Century Leicester," 173–8. The Ellises were Quakers, keen Liberals, and keen feminists.

3 Twilley, "Socialism," MFP, 16 April 1910.

4 Minute Book of Leicester Monthly Meeting (hereafter LMM Minutes), 1914–33; petition discussed 15 April 1915; FOR meeting discussed 20 January 1916, 16 March 1916; CO issues appear in the minutes for the wartime period passim. The Monthly Meeting Minutes report on the equivalent of the congregation's monthly business meeting. See also Minutes of the Ministry and Evangelism Committee, 4 January 1916, Leicester Monthly Meeting, 1913–19 (hereafter M&E Minutes). The local records are at the Leicestershire Record Office. I am grateful to Malcolm Elliott for help in finding and understanding this and other material.

5 Apparently in Leicester the only Friends in jail were COs. The M&E Minutes, passim, contain a number of discussions of CO issues and actions taken by Friends, including a few individual cases.

6 "My Canadian Letter," MFP, 29 April 1916. Information on the conscription legislation and on early numbers is taken from the No-Conscription Fellowship magazine *The Tribunal*, passim; Kennedy, *The Hound of Conscience* and other sources mentioned above. Fred to Edith, 19 May 1916, 1 June 1916, and nd ("Sunday 4th/16," probably June 1916, from Fred's mention of the amended conscription act passed 25 May 1916). The househunting is mentioned Fred to Edith, 26 January 1916.

7 Kennedy, *The Hound of Conscience* is a good source on the workings of the act. Fred to Edith, 1 June 1916, 4 [June] 1916. The money from the business is discussed in 12 June 1916. Wilfred Twilley (the younger) gave me information about Horace's business, 15 June 1990.

8 Accounts of Horace's early captivity, "More 'Horseplay'," *The Tribunal*, 15 June 1916; "Horace Gladstone Twilley: Conscientious Objector to Military Service, Leicester, England," *Canadian Forward*, 12 June 1917; Richardson, "The West: Canada and Conscription," *Woman's Century*, November 1916; Fred to Edith, 12 June 1916.

9 Fred to Edith, 21 June 1916 and nd but probably about 4 July 1916.

10 Fred to Edith, 12 June 1916, 21 June 1916, and nd but probably about 4 July 1916; on MacDonald's troubles see Brockway, *Inside the Left*, 56–9, and "Mr R. MacDonald on the War," MFP, 3 April 1915 and "Mr MacDonald, MP," MFP, 2 October 1915. The Leicestershire Record Office holds a copy of the petition, circulated by Percy Hagon, Hon. Secy, Leicester Committee for National Patriotic Organizations.

11 Mabel Horner Thompson to Mrs Bigland, 16 June 1916 report, and 24 July 1916 report, Visitation of Prisoners Committee: Quaker Chaplains Reports, Case File #8 Tur-Wal, Friends House Library, London. Horace was case #723 in these records, which cover 1916–19. They are an extensive collection and a superb source of information on CO conditions. For material on the formation of the system and records kept by observers at the tribunals, the Prison Visitors Committee, and other Quaker peace work during the war, see Friends Service Committee, Minutes, Records of Work, and Documents Issued June 1915-July 1916, and vol. 2, August 1916-December 1917. I am grateful to librarian Sylvia Carlyle, who spent a good deal of time and energy going through material, who helped me with these and other records.

12 Mabel Thompson, 13 July 1916 report, Friends Service Committee, Minutes, June 1915–July 1916.

13 Horace to Fred, nd but between 3 and 12 July, 1916. On Horace at Durham, Fred to Edith, 28 July 1916.

14 Horace's first court-martial is recorded in "Latest Courts-Martial Sentences," The Tribunal, 27 July 1916. Gertrude published excerpts from Horace's diary in "Horace Gladstone Twilley: Conscientious Objector to Military Service, Leicester, England," Canadian Forward, 12 June 1917. Fred mentions the mid-October interim, Fred to Edith, 22 October 1916. The details of the Rotherham visit came from Margaret Bailey and Olive Bailey Burrell, 26 January 1991.

15 Information on prison conditions can be found in Kennedy, especially chapter 9; the NCF newsletter, The Tribunal, passim; and the biographies and autobiographies of COs such as Brockway, Allen, and Catchpool. On the Scrubs, see Hughes, Indomitable Friend, chapter 3, "On the Prison Front."

16 Numbers of deaths etc given from COIB 1920 statistics by Robert Mennell, "The CO in Prison," in Troublesome People.

17 On joy and fellowship, Robert Mennell, "The CO in Prison"; Allen from Kennedy, Vellacott, and Brockway; Horace's sighting, visits, and Christmas from his chronology, "Horace Gladstone Twilley: Conscientious Objecter to Military Service, Leicester, England," Canadian Forward, 12 June 1912.

18 "In Time of War: An Answer to 'A Constant Reader,'" MFP, 26 December 1914, "My Canadian Letter," MFP, 10 July 1915.

19 Excerpts from Shaw's speech to the January 1915 WPP mass meeting in Washington DC quoted by Steinson, "'The Mother Half of Humanity.'"

20 "My Canadian Letter: Advice and Advisors," MFP, 18 September 1915, "My Canadian Letter," 25 September 1915, 6 November 1915. On unequal suffering from food shortages and insulting admonitions to be thrifty, see Braybon and Summerfield, Out of the Cage, 98–104.

21 "My Canadian Letter," *MFP*, 13 November 1915.

22 Minchen, "Shall Christians go to War?," S R *Star*, 7 April 1916; Weir's response, "Fight or Lie Down – Which?," S R *Star* 14 April 1916.

23 "My Canadian Letter," *MFP* 29 April 1916.

24 "My Canadian Letter," *MFP* 6 May 1916.

25 Gertrude to Edith, 7 December 1916; Fred to Edith, 25 March 1917. "The West," *Woman's Century,* May 1916; "My Canadian Letter," *MFP* 3 June, and 24 June 1916.

26 "My Canadian Letter," *MFP*, 14 October 1916.

27 "The West," *Woman's Century,* July 1916. The text of the "call" was printed in the Aug.-Sept.-Oct. 1916 issue of the I C W P P newsletter, the *Internationaal*. On the negotiated peace campaign, see Hinton, *Protests and Visions,* 54–5. The conference was postponed, due mainly to Jane Addams' illness, and eventually cancelled for various reasons. Re the circular letter sent out by Laura Hughes and Elsie Charlton, a similar letter is in Violet McNaughton's papers; McNaughton circulated it among her friends. Although the letter's date is given only as 12 July, other correspondence to and from McNaughton which refers to the letter sets the year as 1916: McNaughton Papers, Saskatchewan Archives Board, A 1 E 52, passim. Hughes, "The Women's International Congress," *White Ribbon Bulletin,* March 1916.

28 The Dutch spelling of international was used to make a title that made sense in English, French, and German, the three working languages of the I C W P P. Gertrude was a regular reader of the newsletter, according to a letter she wrote to the organisation 10 October 1920, although it is not clear when she began to receive it: the letter is in W I L P F papers, II-3-17. The 1 January 1916 report of Hughes' activities is on 8–9 of the first issue of the *Internationaal*. There are letters and other material sent to Prime Minister Borden by Laura Hughes, 11 February 1916 and 9 June 1916, in Borden's papers. The February letter makes it clear that Hughes had previously been lobbying Borden. (Borden remained hostile.) Borden Papers, M G 26, II 1(a), 22643, 22651, 22699. Laura Hughes reports, *Internationaal* Aug.-Sept.-Oct. issue 1916; Nov.-Dec. issue, 1916. Lawrence, "Julia Grace Wales: The Canadian Girl who has Won World-Wide Fame," *Woman's Century,* July 1916.

29 "For Conscience Sake," *MFP*, 12 August 1916, and "Harvest Gold," *MFP*, 30 September 1916.

30 "My Canadian Letter," *MFP*, 9 December 1916.

31 "The West," *Woman's Century,* November 1916. The front of her Christmas card displayed the phrase, "With Unforgetting Love ... Christmas 1916" and her and Robert's names and address. "A Christmas Vision" was the text inside. She sent the card along with a letter to Edith, 7 December 1916; they were in the shoebox with Fred's letters.

32 The ICWPP leaders decided not to take any action on the German peace feelers, since a partial canvass of their members revealed mixed advice and a complete canvass was impossible. Some fears were expressed that the organisation would appear to be taking sides and would be destroyed as a consequence. This is discussed in *Internationaal* Jan.-Feb.-Mar. 1917. Discussion of the never-held planned meeting's ups and downs can be found in *Internationaal* 1917 issues Nov.-Dec. 1916; April-May-June; July-Aug.-Sept.

33 On the Germany-Mexico fiasco see Tuchman, *The Zimmermann Telegram.*

34 Gertrude comments on registration in detail, "My Canadian Letter," MFP, 10 March 1917. See Robin, "Registration, Conscription, and Independent Labour Politics, 1916–1917," in Willms, Cook, et al., *Conscription 1917.* For example, Gertrude reported the Winnipeg Trades and Labour Council's anticonscription resolution, "My Canadian Letter," MFP, 20 January 1917. On the demise of her paper, see "Midland Free Press Suspended," MFP, 31 March 1917.

35 "The West," *Woman's Century,* February 1917; "Educational League Convention," GGG, 21 February 1917. Gertrude wrote about Lillian Beynon Thomas' departure in "The West," *Woman's Century,* May 1917. On the Dixon recall campaign, see the "Anti-Registration and Recall Clippings" scrapbook in the Dixon papers, MG14 B25, PAM. On Westwood, see "My Canadian Letter: The Tragedy We Share," MFP, 17 February 1917. For early examples of Westwood's speeches, see the report on his "Labor and War," *Voice,* 20 November 1914; "Retail Clerks Strong Organization," and "On the Eve of Conscription Shall We Tamely Submit?" *Voice,* 25 May 1917; "Woolworth Strikers," *Voice,* 8 1917.

36 See Martin Robin, "Registration, Conscription, and Independent Labour Politics." "Women Endorse General Strike," *Voice,* 27 July 1917. A number of these women were associated with Gertrude's old ally William Irvine, now a Calgary Unitarian minister. See Tony Mardiros, *William Irvine.*

37 "If There is a Semblance of the Freedom of Citizenship Left," *Voice,* 1 June 1917; "Speeches Drowned in Yells," *Voice,* 8 June 1917.

38 "Meeting Proscribed," *Voice,* 23 June 1917; "Prussianism in Winnipeg," *Voice,* 23 June 1917.

39 Beynon, "Freedom," GGG, 20 June 1917; see also Ramsay Cook, "Francis Marion Beynon." Beynon's column was taken over by Mary McCallum, who fussed a bit about the Wartime Elections Act as "a disgrace" but came down in favour of the Union government in the end.

40 The *Forward* began as a temperance paper called the *Observer* published in Cowansville, Quebec, founded 17 September 1908; its title was changed to *Cotton's Weekly* that December. It moved to Toronto in 1913, and was edited for several years by A.W. Mance. The name was changed to *Canadian Forward* in 1915: Wallace, "History of Socialism in Toronto," nd [March

1916], unpublished typescript, Metro Toronto Public Library. Examples of antiwar material include Prenter, "Women's Column," 24 March 1917; "Society of Friends Deliberates on Freedom, Conscience and State," 10 May 1917; "A Protest Against All Wars and Fighting and the Spirit Thereof, From the Society of Friends, (called Quakers), Addressed to the People of Canada," 12 June 1917. On Hughes see "Attack by Miss Laura Hughes on Bonar Law and Noted Britishers," reporting a speech she gave in Rochester, NY about British leaders' investments in the international arms and war materials trade, in the same issue.

41 Gertrude's first three pieces were "Horace Gladstone Twilley, Conscientious Objector to Military Service, Leicester, England," 12 June 1917; "An English Pacifist and His 'Glory,'" 25 June 1917; "The Cruelty of Conscription," 10 July 1917. She also described this sequence of events in a letter to ICWPP headquarters probably written in September 1917 (received in Amsterdam 12 October 1917), published in *Internationaal* Jan.- Feb.- Mar. 1918. German women led hunger riots in over twenty cities in 1915–16, and the situation continued later in the war: Hermann, "Social Democratic Women in Germany." It is interesting to note that in her 2 January 1915 column for the *Midland Free Press* Gertrude quoted a few lines from an antiwar poem she had read in that day's mail (this would have been written in December 1914); the same poem is quoted at greater length in her 9 November 1917 column for the Leicester *Pioneer*. "The Benediction" by Gerald Lively, it was reproduced in the *Canadian Forward* 24 July 1917.

42 The first three paragraphs are reproduced in her letter to the ICWPP published in *Internationaal* Jan.-Feb.-Mar. 1918. "Letter to Women," *Canadian Forward*, 10 July 1917. The second version of the pledge is from "Unto This Last the Mother Cry is Supreme," *Canadian Forward*, 24 August 1917. Those who read it in the journal itself will note that an extra line, which reads "life of international Socialism it has," has been inserted in the phrase "workers, to whom [insert] it belongs." This is almost certainly an error made in the composing room while setting up the page, by inserting a metal line of type into the wrong article; the proofreader did not catch it.

43 Information on Wellock and the Christian Peace Crusade is scanty but there is an entry for him in Josephson, Cooper, et al, *Biographical Dictionary of Modern Peace Leaders* and some mention in Caedel, *Pacifism in Britain*.

44 Wiltsher, *Dangerous Women*, gives biographical information about WPC founders Helen Crawfurd and Agnes Dollan, 148–53; Wiltsher cites *Dreadnought* stories on WPC events in June and July 1916. Gertrude mentions that Sylvia sent her the *Dreadnought* but it is not clear whether she received it regularly or relied on clippings or news from other sources, such as her mother.

45 Accounts of the British WPC are drawn from Liddington, *Long Road to Greenham*, chapter 6, and Wiltsher, *Dangerous Women*, 151–2, 184–90. The

Dreadnought reporter from Glasgow was married to suffragette Agnes Dollan, one of the WPC founders. On coverage (or the lack of it) of peace activities by the press, see Liddington, 120–1, 123, and Wiltsher citing Swanwick, 135–6.

46 The attack on Hughes and Prenter is untitled, beginning "In the Toronto Telegram," *Woman's Century,* September 1917.

47 The Nyria instalments are in the following issues of *Woman's Century*: March 1916, chapters 1–2; April 1916, 3; May 1916, 4–5; July 1916, 6–7; August 1916, 8–9; September 1916, 10–11; October 1916, 12; November 1916, 13–14; December 1916, 15; March 1917, 16; April 1917, 17–18; August 1917, 19; September 1917, 20–2. Gertrude to Violet McNaughton, 12 January 1918, V.M. papers, Saskatchewan Archives Board, Saskatoon, A1 E52. The letter shows that Gertrude and Violet had not previously corresponded or met, although Gertrude and Violet knew each other's work.

48 Cahan's comment is found in the Militia papers, MG26 H1(a) OC519(1) con't, page 6.

49 "Canadian Women and the War," Leicester *Pioneer* (hereafter *LP*), 31 August 1917. Gertrude's subsequent *LP* articles discuss the changes in the political scene; her style is less flowery than formerly, and her accounts of events show her to have an excellent understanding of them. For example, "The Canadian Crisis," *LP*, 7 September 1917.

50 "Canadian Women and the War," *LP*, 31 August 1917.

51 "Unite in Workers Council," 14 September 1917, and "Workers Council Platform," *Voice*, 21 September 1917. Farmer, "Free Speech and the Coming Peace," *Voice*, 28 September 1917.

52 On Workers' Councils in the U.K., see Bush, *Behind the lines*, 74–83. For an account of the July 1917 Chicago meeting see "The People's Council of the U.S.A.," *Canadian Forward*, 10 September 1917. Richardson, "The Workers' Council of Canada," *LP*, 7 December 1917. On Bainbridge's attendance, Richardson, "Chains of Gold," *LP*, 28 June 1918. Gertrude may have heard about the People's Council from Laura Hughes; on the organisation see Steinson, *American Women's Activism*, 265–79. See also Early, "Feminism, Peace, and Civil Liberties." See also Nearing, *The Making of a Radical*, 109–11.

53 Gertrude described the baby's situation and the adoption in a postcard to Fred, 26 September 1917, in Joan Wallcraft's possession in September 1986.

54 On her "public" visit, see her "The War-Time Election Act," *LP*, 26 October 1917; "The Women's Crusade," *LP*, 2 November 1917.

55 "A Letter to Women," *Voice*, 19 October 1917, and "To the Women Crusaders," *Canadian Forward*, 24 October 1917. A similar suggestion was made by Minnie Singer of Toronto, concerning Unionist sermons: Naylor, *The New Democracy* 89.

56 "To the women Crusaders," *Canadian Forward*, 24 October 1917.

57 The excerpt from Horace's letter is in "To the Women Crusaders," *Canadian Forward*, 24 October 1917; the U.S. spelling appears in the printed version.

58 Horace's transfer to Wandsworth and subsequent weeks: Visitation of Prison committee, Minutes 1916–19, entry for 1 February 1917 notes the transfer of sixty-six prisoners on the visit list; "Horace Gladstone Twilley: Conscientious Objector to Military Service, Leicester, England," *Canadian Forward*, 12 June 1917; Fred to Edith, 8 February 1917. On Catharine Gittins, see Ellis, "Mary Catharine Gittins, 1840–1930, and Edith Gittins, 1845–1910"; Papers of the Great Meeting Unitarian Chapel, Roll of members of Great Meeting, 1897–1916, Leicestershire Record Office. This congregation was split over the war, and the opposition of several leading members (and key financial supporters) to young minister Sidney Spicer's pacifism led to a crisis. A mediator had to be called in and a compromise worked out. It is unclear whether it held for the remainder of the war. In any case there was substantial support for COs among individual members. Gittins apparently had to resign her post as secretary of the Local Council of Women in 1916, over her pacifist views. See also Ellis, "Records of Nineteenth Century Leicester," 143–6.

59 On the March visit and end of sentence, Fred to Edith, 9 March 1917 and nd but between 30 March and 6 April 1917, and two letters nd but shortly after 6 April 1917.

60 COIB statistics are reported in Kennedy, 302. Prison conditions in the period are described by Vellacott, *Bertrand Russell* 190–4; see also Kennedy. The prison governor's comments to Appleton and some information about Beddow's status are recorded in Appleton's reports to the Visitation of Prisoners Committee, which were not available when I was at Friends House Library, but were later disinterred and read by Sylvia Carlyle, Assistant Librarian, who sent me a report on her findings, 20 February 1991. Richardson, "An English Pacifist and His 'Glory,' " *Canadian Forward*, 25 June 1917; "The Red Flag" had practically become a CO anthem, and it was sung by similar choirs all over England. See reports in *The Tribune*, passim. Fred to Edith, 8 July 1917.

61 "The Call and the Response," *Canadian Forward*, 24 September 1917; the huge Leicester meeting was reported in *Labour Leader*, 30 August 1917, cited by Liddington, *Long Road*, 125, 303.

62 Re WPC banners, similar slogans were used in various cities; see Wiltsher, citing Helen Crawfurd's descriptions of Glasgow activities, 187. Death figures are cited by Wiltsher, 153, 191. Gladdening news is from "To the Women Crusaders," *Canadian Forward*, 24 October 1917. The poem is "In Prison," "dedicated reverently to the conscientious objectors." *LP*, 2 November 1917.

63 I am indebted to Anne Molgat, whose unpublished research on Helen Armstrong is the source for most of this discussion. She points out that Ada Muir had been involved in an earlier and somewhat less union-oriented incarnation of the WLL around 1910, which appears to have evaporated with Muir's departure. The characterisation of Helen as the leading figure is Molgat's. "Women's Labor League," *Voice*, 23 March 1917 (editor Arthur Puttee's wife was on the WLL founding executive). On the Woolworth's strikers see "Woolworth Girls Strike," *Voice*, 1 June 1917; see also another successful advocacy action by Armstrong discussed in her letter "Alien Families Relief," *Voice*, 14 September 1917. Several of these exploits are mentioned by Gertrude, "Progress in Canada," *LP*, 14 December 1917. On Armstrong's Crusade membership, "In the Name of Freedom," *LP*, 11 January 1918. On allowances, see "The Alternative," *Voice*, 10 August 1917; the mass meeting episode is described in "Some of the Women," *Voice*, 31 August 1917.

64 Hughes' own brother had enlisted and been killed early in the war. Her mother was antiwar, her father pro. For more on Hughes see Roberts, "Women against War," and "Women's Peace Activism in Canada." Gertrude discusses Hughes and the winter study program in "Progress in Canada," *LP*, 14 December 1917. It is not clear whether this item came via the Chicago WPP women's forwarding service, or whether Gertrude got it from her British contacts, which could mean her mother, the BDWSU, or WIL.

65 For details on the authors and the text see Kamester and Vellacott's introductory sections to their edition of Sargant Florence, Marshall, and Ogden, *Militarism Versus Feminism*, 21–9. The text of the pamphlet that Gertrude and her friends read is from 53–140 in the Vellacott-Kamester collection.

66 Ogden and Sargant Florence in Kamester and Vellacott, *Militarism*, Introduction, 56–8, 61–2. Jo Vellacott generously gave me information about British pacifism and Catherine Marshall, and gave me a photocopy of the 1915 pamphlet before her and Kamester's book was out; I am grateful to her for her intellectual and spiritual generosity, friendship, and splendid example over the years. See Enloe, *Does Khaki Become You?* and her *Bananas, Beaches and Bases*, and Mies, *Patriarchy and Accumulation*. Concerning happy exceptions, see Socknat, *Witness Against War*; most of his focus here is on men, but his later work has contributed to women's peace history. See also Williamson and Gorham, *Up and Doing*, and Pierson, *Women and Peace*, and my own work previously cited.

67 "A Letter to the Women," *Voice*, 30 November 1917.

68 "Motherhood and War," *Canadian Forward*, 24 November 1917; "A Letter to the Women," *Voice*, 30 November 1917. The flyer was sent to various supporters apparently in that form; this example was taken from Violet

McNaughton's papers, sent to her by Gertrude in January 1918. On "preservative love" see Ruddick, *Maternal Thinking*.

69 Beynon, "Democracy," *Canadian Forward*, 10 December 1917; and "Message of the Women Grain Growers of Western Canada: Democracy," *Voice*, 17 December 1917. See Ramsay Cook's article, "Francis Marion Beynon," and my "Women against War" for more details.

70 "My Fourth War Christmas," *LP*, 1 February 1918. See Morton, "World War I," *Canadian Encyclopaedia*, 2nd ed., Edmonton, Hurtig, 1988, 2343. See also Brown and Cook, *Canada 1896–1921*, 272–4.

71 "The Piteous Sacrifice," *LP*, 11 January 1918.

72 "My Fourth War Christmas," *LP*, 1 February 1918.

73 "My Fourth War Christmas," *LP*, 1 February 1918.

CHAPTER SIX

1 The verse is quoted in "An Appeal to Women," *Canadian Forward*, 25 January 1918; the sons' seizure is from "In the Name of Freedom," *LP*, 11 January 1918. The distraught mother may have been Mrs R.S. Wainwright, who sent a telegram about her son Francis Cedric Wainwright, but perhaps the similar names are coincidental.

2 In October 1918 the authorities ruled that Mennonites who came to Canada after 1873 were not exempt. About 152 COs were held in Canadian prisons. I have relied on Thomas Socknat's discussion, *Witness against War*, 60–90. Despite the fact that all but CO exemptions were officially cancelled, about half the total men called up got exemptions of one kind or another, few as COs. On farmers' outrage when their sons were called up in the spring of 1918, "Friends Old and New," *LP*, 21 June 1918.

3 "An Appeal to Women," *Canadian Forward*, 25 January 1918, "In the Name of Freedom," *LP*, 11 January 1918, "Freedom in the Empire," *LP*, 1 March 1918. On the idea that returned soldiers would be a positive influence for social change, see Braybon and Summerfield, *Out of the Cage*, 116–18. For Canada, see Richard Allen's discussion, *The Social Passion*, 41–2. Protestant chaplains foresaw this progressive role for soldiers as an outcome of heightened social consciences brought about by the unifying experiences of the trenches.

4 "Modern Slavery," *LP*, 18 January 1918, "The New World," *LP*, 15 February 1918.

5 Swan River editor Andrew Weir became preoccupied with supply preaching to replace clergymen gone to war, and leased the Swan River *Star* to a Mr Noble, who published it until 1926. Noble would publish a handful of Gertrude's religious poems during his reign, but the paper carried nothing else by or about her. On Weir's lease of the *Star* see Pratt, *The Story of Manitoba's Weekly Newspapers*, 538. Olivereau was released in 1920. Near-

ing calls her "gentle Louise Olivereau" in his brief discussion of her case: *The Making of a Radical*, 113–14. For details see "Miss Olivereau Confesses Guilt," *Seattle Daily Call*, 8 September 1917, and in subsequent issues, a letter from her in "The Editor's Mail," 15 September 1917; "Louise Olivereau Declared Guilty," 1 December 1917 (her lengthy defence statement was printed in this and the next two issues); a letter from Louise Olivereau in "The Open Forum," 10 December 1917; an announcement of an "Appeal in Olivereau Case" in "The Open Forum," 12 December 1917; and "On the Face of the Waters," on the appeal, 31 December 1917. The legislation disfranchising COs is reproduced in "COs and their Votes," *The Tribunal* 20 February 1919. In theory this disfranchisement was to last until 1926, but it was apparently laxly enforced.

6 I did find one trace of her in the socialist *Seattle Daily Call*: a reprint under the title "A Canadian Mother on Conscription," 4 August 1917, of her 24 July 1917 column from the *Canadian Forward*, which includes the Gerald Lively poem excerpt. See her "The 'Christian Pacifists' of America," *LP*, 15 March 1918, "The Seed of the Church," *LP*, 10 May 1918.

7 Conscripts on the train are mentioned in Richardson, "The United Empire Loyalists of 1776," *LP*, 22 February 1918. Chinese labourers are in Richardson, "Freedom in the Empire, "*LP*, 1 March 1918." See also Tancock, "Secret Trains Across Canada 1917–1918." I am indebted to David Millar for this article.

8 "The Under-Current," *LP*, 15 February 1918; the Australians had a strong distrust of English imperialism and their Pommie "betters"; a coalition of labour, socialist, and feminist pacifist groups was an important factor in the defeat. However Australia had a high percentage of enlistment, so defeat of conscription does not necessarily translate into a majority antiwar opinion. Thanks to Jeremy Mouat for his help with the Australian material.

9 Gertrude to Violet McNaughton, McNaughton papers, Saskatchewan Archives Board, Saskatoon, 12 January 1918, in A1 E 52, and "The Women's Crusade (International)" flyer in A1 H 23. Wellock's Crusade was being run by Quaker feminist radical Theodora Wilson Wilson of the WPC and WIL. Laura Hughes had by then married Chicago CO Erling Lunde and was living in Chicago, although she stayed in touch with Toronto pacifists. Gertrude probably learned about Australian activities mostly through the socialist press (the *Forward* reprinted material from time to time, for example Adela Pankhurst, "The Women's Revolution," 24 October 1917, reprinted from the *Melbourne Socialist*) and the *Internationaal* carried reports of doings of groups in most countries. There were two groups in Australia, the more radical being the Women's Peace Army: see Gowland, "The Women's Peace Army." Chesley, "Report of Department of Peace and Arbitration," *WCTU Convention Report*, 1918, 111–12, Provincial Archives of Ontario, MU 8398.

10 "Torture of Conscientious Objectors," *Voice*, 25 January 1918, and "Conscientious Objectors Said to Have Been Roughly Handled," *Winnipeg Free Press*, 25 January 1918. The Borden papers, vol. 238, 132765–6, contain Robert Clegg's affidavit and a supporting affidavit by soldier Paul Case. The latter account included a statement from a Mrs E.C. Tingling who had interviewed Naish and Clegg and had visited General Ruttan at his home and gotten his promise to investigate. Correspondence between Borden and Newburn is in vol. 238, 13276–7. Court martial and acquittal were discussed in Gertrude's column "Suppression and its Effects," *LP*, 12 April 1918. The Grain Growers' motion, which was seconded by Roaring River PEL suffragist Alice Cox's husband Ben, is recorded in their minutes for 20 February 1918, *Minute Book* of Roaring River Grain Growers' Association 14 June 1916 to 11 October 1932, from the Fred Twilley Museum; PAM has a photocopy. Thanks to Dorothy Shewfelt and Bob Wallcroft for permission to photocopy the minute book. The RRGGA had previously sent a resolution to Borden and Crerar that alien labour be conscripted into labour battalions and distributed as needed, and that such workers be paid the same amount as soldiers at the front: 28 November 1917. They sent Crerar another letter the following month wanting to know why they had not received an answer to this resolution (19 December 1917).

11 On David Wells, Ivens' letter to Crerar and various interdepartmental correspondence concerning his letter and the investigation are in Borden papers, vol. 238, 132779–90, 25 February 1918 to 8 April 1918. See "Conscientious Objector Done to Death," *Voice*, 1 March 1918; "Making the World Safe for Democracy," *Canadian Forward*, 10 March 1918; Gertrude wrote about cases in "The United Empire Loyalists of 1776," *LP*, 22 February 1918, "A Letter to Women," *Voice*, 22 February 1918, and on David Wells, "Canada's First Martyr," *LP*, 19 April 1918. See Socknat, *Witness against War*, 76–87.

12 Gertrude wrote about this in "Suppression – and its Effect," *LP*, 12 April 1918. Francis Beynon to Violet McNaughton, McNaughton papers, 11 January 1918, A1 D1.

13 William Ivens, "The Ministry of Murder," *Voice*, 12 April 1918. Ivens had been at McDougall Methodist since 1916, located in the immigrant and working class North end section of Winnipeg.

14 A similar petition was sent to Borden from the Winnipeg TLC on 8 April 1918: see Borden papers, vol. 238, 132798–9. See also Gertrude's columns "The Seed of the Church," *LP*, 10 May 1918, and "Within the Shadow," about CO martyrdom and repression of pacifists, concluding "With a great and awful vengeance / God is coming to the world, / Downward, from their long usurping / shall His enemies be hurled; / And their prayers shall be unheeded, / god shall speak in majesty,'/ 'Ye have crucified My children – / ye have done it unto ME!' " *LP*, 19 July 1918.

15 Report of Ivens' farewell sermon, "What is True Patriotism?" *Voice*, 28 June 1918. I have relied on Richard Allen's analysis of Ivens' negotiations with the committee, *The Social Passion*, 51–4.

16 "J.S. Woodsworth withdraws from ministry," *Voice*, 28 June 1918. "The Seed of the Church," *LP*, 10 May 1918, "A New 'Creedless Church'," *LP*, 23 August 1918. The labour church was popular, and by October 1918 it had grown so large it had to meet in theatres; by mid-1919 it had grown sufficiently to split into eight local congregations. Westwood's members and growth of the new church, from Richard Allen, *The Social Passion*, 83–4. Westwood preached a series of peace sermons in 1918; these included "Great Women of Modern Times" (reported in the *Voice*, 25 January 1918), "The Foundation of International Peace" in April (reported as "A Historical Survey of the Growth of the Idea of Universal Peace," *Voice*, 12 April 1918, and "The Voice of Labor and World Peace," *Voice*, 16 May 1918), and "A Rich Man's View of the Church of God: Will it Suffice?" (reported in "Local News," *Voice*, 21 June 1918).

17 Socknat, *Witness against War*, 85–6; Borden papers, vol. 328, 132793–5,7, 5 and 6 April 1918. Gertrude wrote of the shipments in "The Cruelty of the Day of War," *LP*, 22 March 1918; "Progress and Retrogression in Canada," *LP*, 22 March 1918; "Democratic Militarism," *LP*, 14 June 1918; on the Bible students in chains, "The Spring – and the Breaking of Chains,'" *LP*, 31 May 1918, and "The Reign of Force," *LP*, 21 June 1918.

18 On Wandsworth conditions, "Canadian COs in England," *The Tribunal*, 27 June 1918, and "Canadians in Wandsworth," *The Tribunal*, 17 October 1918; Gertrude's "Women's Crusade News," *WLN*, 16 August 1918; for details on torture of Canadian COs by British soldiers, see Pimlott's account in "Canadian Courage," *The Tribunal*, 19 December 1918.

19 "Modern Idols," *LP*, 14 June 1918.

20 See her columns, "Democratic Militarism," *LP*, 14 June 1918, "Friends Old and New," *LP*, 21 June 1918; Socknat, *Witness against War*, 86. Ralph Naish's sister wrote the NCF on 20 December 1918 that the returned COs were held incommunicado, mostly on bread and water, for four weeks, then released: "Canadian COs Discharged," *The Tribunal*, 6 February 1919. New Zealand COs had it worse; some of them were sent to France where they refused to cooperate: see "The New Zealand COs," *The Tribune*, 17 January 1918, and Gertrude's "The Spring – and the Breaking of Chains." Some early British COs had been sent to France; they were sentenced to be shot, apparently as a scare tactic, but a huge public fuss and representations by NCF and other leading figures put an end to this. On British COs sent to France see Vellacott, *Bertrand Russell* 72–7. See "Women's Labor League Wires Ottawa," *WLN*, 13 December 1918, about post-Armistice demands for CO release. In January 1919 there were still 117 COs in prison in Canada: Socknat, *Witness against War*, 86.

21 On the ghostwriting, see Vellacott Newberry, "Russell as Ghost Writer: A New Discovery," and on the pamphlet, campaign, and improvements, see Kennedy, *The Hound of Conscience*, 187–98. On medically unfit releases as a sham, see "More Home Office Delay," *The Tribunal*, 10 January 1918. Despite lower levels of hostility there were still strong feelings: in May 1918 CO Fred Watson and some of his comrades were visiting with Mrs Starnes, a widow with ten children who was a Quaker CO supporter in Wakefield, when a mob attacked the house and the COs had to escape through some old underground passages leading out of the cellar. Mrs Starnes had to flee with her family to a cottage in the countryside. The Riot Act was read the next day in the town. Fred Watson was assigned to work as the secretary to the prison governor. After the war he married the eldest Starnes daughter. He was secretary to the Workers Education Association for sixty years. Watson wrote to Mrs Starnes about the events, 29 May 1918; daughter Jean M. Watson has his wartime letters to her grandmother. I am grateful to Clive Sutton who loaned them to me in Leicester, January 1991.

22 "A Letter to Women," *Voice*, 22 February 1918; carol singers, "The United Empire Loyalists of 1776," *LP*, 22 February 1918. On the Leicester NCF choir, letter from F.G. Blockley, "Dear Comrade," *The Tribunal*, 10 January 1918.

23 "A Letter to Women," *Canadian Forward*, 10 April 1918; "Democratic Militarism," *LP*, 14 June 1918; "Friends Old and New," *LP*, 21 June 1918; "The Reign of Force," *LP*, 21 June 1918; "Chains – of Gold," *LP*, 28 June 1918.

24 Fred to Edith, 24 March 1918, 2 April 1918. CO vegetarian diets were available but they were dreadful, scantier, and even less healthy than the regular diets; there is no way to learn who requested them. Ella Stevens is listed in "Divisional and Branch Secretaries of the NCF, 1917," Kennedy, *Hound of Conscience*, Appendix A, 297. I am grateful to Tom Kennedy for photocopies of his research material including prison diet sheets. There was a longstanding Vegetarian Society in Leicester; in 1883 Mayor Hewitt had chaired its annual banquet: see for example "Vegetarian Society," *Leicester Daily Post*, 11 May 1910. On Horace's vegetarianism, letter from Connie MacDonald, 14 February 1992, and letter from Keith Twilley, 7 May 1992. But apparently they were not lifelong vegetarians. Connie MacDonald recalled, "In 1956 Horace and Ella came over and stayed with me [in Manitoba] for two weeks. I know they weren't vegetarians as I recall cooking bacon for them and Horace remarked that he wished Ella would learn to cook bacon like that – hers always curled up." On the issue of giving in, after 1916 there were differences of opinion about the legitimacy of trying to secure releases or improved conditions for COs; the Friends Service Committee (FSC) (including Edith Ellis who with her sister Marian had previously been a major donor to NCF) and other Quakers feared that such activities would take energy and attention away from broader anti-

militarist work which was more central to the peace testimony. Some worried that attempts to ameliorate conditions were weakening witness, or a tacit acceptance of the right of the state to conscript or imprison. Official Quaker support for CO prison issues diminished. Opinion among the imprisoned COs themselves varied. This was a highly contentious decision and many Quakers involved in the NCF disagreed with it, believing the CO work was a crucial form of peace testimony or did not weaken it. The NCF was heavily Quaker: for example Marshall, and Russell's replacement after his January 1918 resignation, Alfred Salter, an obstetrician and bacteriologist who had been Russell's "shadow." Russell was sentenced to six months in prison in February 1918 and began his sentence in April 1918. The NCF continued agitation for exemption, better treatment, and release of COs, while also attempting to do additional antiwar work, but the CO support came first. However, the London Yearly Meeting (the national Quaker body) did eventually engage in a national campaign for CO release, or better treatment, circulating "An Appeal to the Conscience of the Nation from the London Yearly Meeting of the Society of Friends, May, 1918." A copy is published in *The Tribunal*, 1 August 1918. On criticism of the FSC position, see T.H. Ferris, "Friends and the Release of COs," *The Tribunal*, 10 January 1918. No one claimed non-CO Quakers were cowards; in fact several leading Quakers, including Joan Beauchamp, publisher of *The Tribunal*, and Edith Ellis, clerk of the Friends Service Committee, served prison terms for violations of the Defense of the Realm censorship regulations. See for example, all from *The Tribunal* "Making History," 30 May 1918; "The FSC Appeal," 11 July 1918; "Joan Beauchamp, Printer," 29 August 1918, and "Our Appeal," 17 October 1918, on raids and sentences. For a discussion of these splits see Thomas Kennedy, "Fighting About Peace," and also his "The Quaker Renaissance."

25 "A Letter to Women," *Canadian Forward*, 10 April 1918; "A Letter From Winnipeg," *LP*, 17 May 1918.

26 Presbyterian Church in Canada, General Assembly, Commission on the War and Spiritual Life of the Church, *The War and the Christian Church*, Toronto, Presbyterian Church in Canada, [1917].

27 The meeting is described in "The Women's Crusade," *LP*, 24 May 1918. Gertrude also attended a Women's Labour League meeting which featured a lecture on the cooperative movement in various countries, and a discussion of high bread prices, at the conclusion of which a number of women decided to learn to make their own bread. All women present were given recipe booklets and yeast cakes.

28 "A Letter to Women," *Canadian Forward*, 10 April 1918.

29 "The Call," *Voice*, 5 April 1918.

30 "The Hand of Militarism (A Letter to Women)," *Canadian Forward*, 10 March 1918. Beynon had expressed similar views in "Military Train-

ing," *GGG*, 20 June 1917, concerning the militarist tenor of the discussions at the 1917 NCWC annual convention. It was apparently the reactions to columns like this that led Beynon to decide to flee Winnipeg.

31 For the context of discontent and its management by the authorities, Hinton, *Protests and Visions*, chapter 7; Rowbotham discusses Lloyd George's tactics, radical movements and their failure to form the necessary links to provide any real threat to established power, in her essay "Rebel Networks in the First World War," in *Friends of Alice Wheeldon*.

32 "Women's Crusade News," *Voice*, 31 May 1918; "Items of News of all Parts: To Women," *Canadian Forward*, 10 June 1918. On Russell's views, Vellacott, *Bertrand Russell*, 230–1. Liddington, *Long Road*, 127–9, gives details of the campaign. On the ups and downs of the peace movement, see Julia Bush, *Behind the Lines*, 83–102.

33 On German women's antiwar activism, see Herrmann, "Social Democratic Women in Germany." Wishnia, "Feminism and Pacifism," describes the antiwar activism of Helene Brion's socialist feminist comrades, 103–13. On the *Canadian Forward* as a source of information about foreign socialist antiwar activities, see for example "German Women Issue Manifesto," *Canadian Forward*, 24 July 1918.

34 "War, Womanhood, and Morals," *LP*, 14 June 1918; see also Braybon and Summerfield, *Out of the Cage*, 107–10.

35 "War and Industry," *LP*, 19 July 1918, and "Of Interest to Women, *LP*, 12 July 1918. Letter from Helen Armstrong, *Voice*, 17 May 1918; "Trades Council Report," *Voice*, 21 December 1917. "Manitoba News," *Woman's Century*, July 1918, describes LCW members scabbing during the telephone strike, denying that it was scabbing and excusing it as providing an essential war service. Margaret McWilliams was a member of a rightwing "citizens committee" that negotiated a settlement, according to this article. The event is not mentioned in Kinnear, *Margaret McWilliams*. On postwar society, see "Labor [*sic*] and the New Social Order," a pamphlet by the Labor [*sic*] Board of Great Britain, sent Gertrude by Isaac Bainbridge in the spring of 1918. She discusses the program in "Labor and the New Social Order," *LP*, 28 June 1918. The statement was adopted by the British Labour Party in June 1918 (James Simpson from Toronto had attended as an observer), and was similar to the policy of the Canadian SDP.

36 "Of Interest to Women," *LP*, 12 July 1918.

37 NCWC papers, MG28 I 25, NAC, NCWC Minutes, vol. 27, June 1918-June 1919: the original resolution moved by the IODE is #4, page 123; the compromise version, resolution #5, on page 122. For the annual conference's action on this issue and a critique of the IODE intransigency, see Muir Edwards, "Imperial or National?" *Woman's Century*, August 1918. On greetings from Austrian suffragists, see Gertrude's column "Of interest to Women," *LP*, 12 July 1918.

38 "Friends – Old and New," *LP*, 21 June 1918; Beynon's discussion is in her "Military Training," *GGG*, 20 June 1917. Gertrude's vision of women standing between armies recalls her description of Helen Armstrong's bravery on the anticonscription platforms in the face of attacks by prowar bullies in the summer of 1917; the poem is from "Items of News of all Parts: To Women," *Canadian Forward*, 10 June 1918.

39 "A Call to Women," *Canadian Forward*, 24 August 1918.

40 Gertrude's columns "Women's Crusade News," *Western Labor News* (hereafter *WLN*), 16 August 1918, and "An Appeal to Women," *WLN*, 28 September 1918.

41 "Women's Crusade Notes," *WLN*, 9 August 1918, "A Brave Canadian Editor," *LP*, 16 August 1918, and "A New 'Creedless Church'," *LP*, 23 August 1918. Bulletins about Bainbridge's arrests, hearings, releases and imprisonments are recorded in the paper, for example "Bainbridge Wins Out," 10 March 1918; "What is Sedition," 10 May 1918, "Get Bainbridge Again," 24 May 1918, "Editor Bainbridge Liberated," 10 July 1918. See Naylor, *The New Democracy*, 44–5, for the Bainbridge case: Bainbridge was first arrested in April 1917 and found guilty of seditious libel for publishing peace literature; he got a suspended sentence. He was arrested 12 September 1917, convicted of seditious libel, and sentenced to prison; he was released after three months due to an impropriety in the proceedings. He was charged again late in 1917, and his trial resulted in a three-month sentence. The minister of justice ordered his release in June 1918. For example, Kate Richards O'Hare became a prison reformer after her imprisonment as an antiwar radical in the U.S., see Foner and Miller's introduction to *Kate Richards O'Hare*.

42 "A new 'Creedless' Church," *LP*, 23 August 1918. Puttee had been a co-founder of the local trades council and the labour party and became editor of the council's paper in 1899. He was elected to Parliament as a labour candidate in a 1900 by-election, and reelected in the general election in November 1900, with Liberal support. He had lost his seat in the 1904 election, amid accusations that he had made Boer War deals with the Liberals, who by then had recovered from their previous disarray and nominated their own candidate. On Puttee and his relationship to the labour and socialist movement, see McCormack, *Reformers, Rebels, and Revolutionaries*, 79–97, and on the *WLN* takeover, 146. Ross McCormack describes Puttee's political philosophy as "an amalgam of Marxism and Christianity, populism and liberalism," not unlike Gertrude's own, although she had surpassed him in radicalism by the mid-war period. David Bercuson's account provides more details of the *WLN* takeover: *Confrontation at Winnipeg*, 59–67. The changeover is discussed in *Voice*: "Trades Council," 21 June 1918, "Local News," 5 July 1918, "Last issue of The Voice," 26 July 1918. Beynon, "The New Womanhood," *WLN*, 23 August 1918. The TLC

fired Ivens as editor in August 1920: Richard Allen, *The Social Passion*, 98. On religion among antiwar socialists, Naylor notes that the Christian socialist movement was lively in Toronto and most Christian socialists were SDPers: *New Democracy*, 89–90. See also Newton, "The Alchemy of Politicization."

43 "Valedictory" (farewell editorial), *LP*, 30 August 1918; "Editorial," *LP*, 6 September 1918.

44 The correspondence in the Borden papers between Borden, Rowell, Crerar, Doherty, and Cahan is found in vol. 104, 56698–56709, 18–29 October 1918, and vol. 246, 137871–137878, 31 October–4 November 1918. October 1918, Borden papers vol. 104, 56702. On the 1917 hesitation by authorities, see McCormack, *Reformers* 129–31, and on the *WLN*, 152–3, citing Press Censor's papers.

45 Cahan's citation (in a letter to Doherty dated 22 October 1918) from Gertrude's writings is from her "An Appeal to Women," from the 25 January 1918 issue. Cahan juxtaposes her excerpt with another by someone else about the Russian Revolution and repression at home, in such a way that it could imply these two paragraphs were from the same article; he cites neither titles nor authors. It is not clear what conclusion was intended to be drawn.

46 On Fenner Brockway's defence statement as seditious, see Cahan to Borden, 22 September, 1918, vol. 279–12, Chambers to Ivens, 24 September 1918. The *Western Clarion* was raided in May by military intelligence, warned by the press censor (the editors ignored the warning), outlawed in September 1918 and published its last issue 15 October 1918; the *BC Federationist* was merely warned, and complied, like the *WLN*. The authorities feared tackling the B.C. Federation of Labour and did not ban it, despite urgings. On the government's fear of tackling labour centrals' newspapers, see RCMP Controller to Deputy Minister of Labour, 6 March 1919, RCMP papers, RCMP Letterbooks, vol. 878, Labour Organisations and Communism, 47. Toronto SDP information is provided by Naylor, *The New Democracy*. The ban against the SDP was lifted in late 1918 and some of the prisoners who had been convicted of membership offences were released: see for example Tom Holm's case. From the Soo, on 19 October 1918 he had been sentenced to three years for being an SDP member; his release was ordered 23 December 1918, "as it was then no longer an offence for anyone to be a member," as his case is described in a department of justice memorandum for the solicitor general dated 20 June 1919, concerning various sedition cases from 1918 and early 1919, found in Borden papers, vol. 559, 60974–8. Some of the cases described therein are discussed by Naylor, *The New Democracy*, 44–7. The Toronto Central Committee of the SDP briefly published *The Social Democrat*, beginning 31 December 1918, as part of the municipal election campaign, after the

Forward's banning. It pointed out somewhat disingenuously that it had only received one notice of objection from the Press Censor "and that of a purely technical nature."

47 On the flu epidemic in Swan River see the mention of the experience of John Lambert in Pettigrew, *The Silent Enemy,* 60. For an overview of the epidemic see McGinnis, "The Impact of Epidemic Influenza." PC 2384 was rescinded by an Order-in-Council, 2 April 1919.

48 On the campaign to appoint a woman representative, see Borden papers, vol. 245, for example 137720–30, Emily Murphy to Borden, 5 November 1918, telegram from Calgary women 9 November 1918, telegram from Vancouver Women's Liberal Association, 9 November 1918, from the Dominion WCTU president in Halifax, 20 November 1918. Borden cabled back to his office, "Cannot see any possible advantage … Do not know of any work that they could do if they came." Violet McNaughton's papers contain correspondence on the campaign, A1 E52, passim November and early December 1918. See also McClung, "Alberta News: Do we Want Women at the Peace Conference? Please Yes," *Woman's Century,* February 1919. On Manitoba conservative women's belief that there were no qualified Canadian women, see Mary McCallum to McNaughton, 19 November 1918; Christina Murray to McNaughton, 5 December 1918. On the Women's Party question, see AAP (Anne Anderson Perry?), "Are We to Have a Woman's Party in Canada?" and "The Women's Party," *Woman's Century,* December 1918; the magazine agreed to publish party information; it appears that some Toronto enthusiasts presumed in print that the magazine would become the official party magazine, but that claim was retracted. On the anti side, see Violet McNaughton to Jessie MacIver, McNaughton papers, 7 December 1918, A1 E 54. MacIver had refused to print an anti article by McNaughton. See Naylor, *New Democracy,* 139–40. On the postwar hope for a better world, see Thomas, "Education to the Fore," *WLN,* 20 December 1918.

49 A conference planning committee had recommended that the NCF disband and retain a few committees, of which only the reunion committee continued its work for any length of time. On the last days of the NCF see Kennedy, *Hound of Conscience,* 262–81; *The Tribunal,* passim, November 1918 to June 1920. On Gertrude in *The Tribunal* see for example "A Canadian Mother's Appeal," 20 August 1917; "News from Canada," 15 May 1919; "Messages From Home and Abroad," 8 January 1920 (this is the report of the November 1919 convention).

CHAPTER SEVEN

1 Richardson, "Lovest Thou Me?," SR *Star,* 6 February 1920.

2 Food Controller for Canada (W.J. Hanna), "Europe Starves While we Talk of Sacrifice," *Woman's Century,* August 1918.

3 "Great Britain," the *Internationaal*, Oct.-Nov.-Dec. 1918; the German women's appeal was published in the British WIL monthly newsletter in February 1919 and was reproduced in the same issue as Ellen Key's "Appel aux femmes des pay victorieux," the *Internationaal*, Jan.-Feb.-Mar. 1919, with various messages of support: WILPF papers. Details on the rubber nipple collection and shipment, protests, and Save the Children are found in Liddington, *The Long Road to Greenham*, 134–5. On Save the Children, Eric Richardson recalls Gertrude's huge bundles. My grandfather Charles A. Bowman, editor of the *Ottawa Citizen*, was seconded to Save the Children for several months and also served on its board of directors; I searched the organisation's records in Ottawa and found him, but no mention of Gertrude.

4 I am grateful to Jo Vellacott for giving me a manuscript chapter of the second volume of her biography of Catherine Marshall, on which I have relied for the discussion of the food blockade and the Zurich conference: the quotes are from Vellacott, "Postwar World: 1919–20," typescript pages 17–19. The first volume is *From Liberal to Labour*. Emily Balch's comments and the Red Cross report are from "A," *News-Sheet No. 3*, WILPF, nd but mid-July 1919, WILPF papers V2-Bundle 1, 1919.

5 *Pax et Libertas*, First supplement, May 1920, WILPF papers, V2 Bdl 1. Gertrude to Dear Friends, nd, and Balch's reply, 29 May 1920, WILPF papers II-2–7. "The Call" is included in Chapter 6; it was published in *The Voice*, 5 April 1918. Gertrude's October 1917 letter is in the *Internationaal* for Jan.-Feb.-Mar. 1918.

6 On Toronto WILPF see Roberts, "Women's Peace Activism in Canada." Emily Balch to Laura Hughes, 6 July 1919, WILPF papers II-1–20; Hughes to Eva Macnaghten, 9 August 1919, WILPF papers II-1–23; Balch to Harriet Prenter, 17 September 1919, III-4/7; Hughes to Balch 7 November 1919, III-4/7, and 25 February 1920, II-1–23. Prenter had written Balch, 13 January 1920, III-4/7, claiming various individuals were organising branches here and there (for example Rose Henderson in Montreal and Winona Dixon in Winnipeg). But Hughes wrote Balch that Rose Henderson no longer lived in Montreal and "had no more use for Mrs Prenter than she did two years ago," while Winona Dixon had written Hughes that she had not even been in Winnipeg that winter, but in the States for her health. If these two example are representative, then Prenter did little or nothing effective to spread WILPF. Prenter resigned in June 1922; her explanation is in a letter to Balch with an attached copy of her letter of resignation to the Toronto executive, nd but attachment dated 16 June 1922, III-4–9. Prenter's correspondence in the WILPF papers does not refer to Gertrude.

7 On Gertrude's health problems, Robert's discussion with Charles Baragar, 1 April 1922, 23–4, and Fannie to Dr G.G.G. (no name given), 15 June 1921, 19–20, Brandon file. Gertrude refers to her illness in a letter to Emily

Balch, 10 October 1920, WILPF papers, II-3–17. "The Children's Cry," Swan River *Star*, 11 June 1920.

8 Richardson, "Our Communion," SR *Star*, 29 July 1920. Information on Minitonas war losses, Mrs Lorne (Lizzie Fraser) Henderson, *Tweedsmuir History of the Swan River Valley.*

9 Richardson, "Bye and Bye," SR *Star*, 20 August 1920.

10 Balch to Gertrude, 29 October 1920, WILPF papers, II-3–7. Fannie's comment, "Records of Interviews" with Gertrude, Fannie, and Robert, 15 June 1921, 18, Brandon file.

11 Gertrude to Emily Balch, 10 October 1920, WILPF papers, II-3–7. Dr Cameron practised in Minitonas until about 1924 when he moved to Swan River. Dr Bruce practised in Swan River from earliest days until after the Second World War.

12 On Winnipeg socialist and labour circles, Millar, "The Winnipeg General Strike," 338–55. On absolute pacifist networks see Alonso, *The Women's Peace Union*, and Early, " 'War is a Crime against Humanity.' " On interwar peace activism, see also Roberts, "Women's Peace Activism"; Socknat, "For Peace and Freedom"; and Strong-Boag, "Peace-Making Women."

13 Brittain, *Testament of Youth*, 467–8.

14 Swanwick, *I Have Been Young*, 323, quoted by Wiltsher, *Most Dangerous Women*, 199. On U.S. women, Early, "Feminism, Peace, and Civil Liberties." I am grateful to Frances Early for happy hours of hot gossip about long dead feminist peace activists of this period. For more on the backlash, see Jensen, "All Pink Sisters."

15 Hughes, "The Women's International Congress," *White Ribbon Bulletin* March 1916. Catherine Marshall is discussed by Vellacott in "Feminist Consciousness and the First World War." Vellacott's forthcoming second volume of the Marshall biography will discuss this period in more detail.

16 Bertrand Russell to Ottoline Morrell, in Vellacott, *Bertrand Russell*, 221.

17 Bertrand Russell in his autobiography, quoted by Kennedy, *Hound of Conscience*, 286. Clifford Allen, "The Presidential Address to the Convention," *The Tribunal*, 8 January 1920.

18 Woodsworth on the sin of indifference: Millar, "The Winnipeg General Strike," 329, quoting from the *Western Labor News* of 12 June 1919.

19 I am indebted to pharmacist Dawn Grushy and two physicians who do not wish to be mentioned, for information about thyroid and kidney dysfunction. "Extract from Admission Form," 14 June 1921, 15–17; "Records of Interviews" with Gertrude, Fannie, and Robert, 15 June 1921, 18–20; Brandon file. Thyroid deficiency symptoms can include heart palpitations, pain all over, lightheadedness, dry skin, hair loss, exhaustion, intolerance to cold, weight fluctuation (obesity is common but not universal), digestive problems. Severe form (myxedema) can cause memory loss, mental instability, skin thickening, puffiness, decreased cardiac output,

slow pulse, poor circulation, arteriosclerosis, enlarged heart, anorexia, infertility, decreased libido. Coma can result. Stress can aggravate symptoms or hasten increased severity.

20 On horrible visions see Showalter, *Women, Madness and English Culture*, 168–94; the quote is from 170. "Extract from Admission Form," based on interviews with Gertrude, Fannie, and Robert, 14 and 15 June 1921, 15–20; Dr Kerr's review of her file, 8 January 1925, 21; Brandon file. On the reforms and Mather, see Refvik, *History of the Brandon Mental Health Centre* (BMHC), 45. Kurt Refvik happened to be at Brandon finishing up some research while I visited the BMHC in July 1991; I am grateful to him for filling in details. Jessie Little was enormously helpful in guiding me through access to archives and museum records and arranging for me to attend the reunion of BMHC nurses that took place in conjunction with a centenary celebration. Various nurses shared their reminiscences about working there in the 1930s. On prior visits, Lloyd Henderson was an excellent guide.

21 Information on Gertrude's health in this period came from interviews with family members and from her case file from the Brandon Mental Health Centre (as it is now called), which includes material from the Winnipeg hospital to which Robert and Fannie took Gertrude in June 1921. I am grateful to Dorothy Twilley Shewfelt for permission to make use of these records. I had not expected to find such a source. My original interest in the records was as a source of biographical and family information, but as I learned more about Gertrude's illness, it became an intriguing puzzle. During the period I had spent in Leicester in January 1991, Linda McKenna and historian Karen O'Rourke and I had talked at length about Gertrude's illnesses, and speculated on their causes and consequences. Karen had previously had occasion to read systematically on thyroid dysfunction, and she thought that Gertrude's lengthy episodes of manic depressive illness fit nicely into the pathologies of extreme hypothyroidism. I have subsequently gone through her medical records carefully, ploughed through present-day endocrinology texts, and discussed this possibility with medical acquaintances (who do not wish to be named); the verdict seems to be that Karen was probably right. "Extract from Admission Form," based on interviews with Gertrude, Fannie, and Robert, 14 and 15 June 1921, 14–20; Dr Kerr's review of her file, 8 January 1925, 21–2; information written up by Charles Baragar interviewing Robert, 1 April 1922, 23–4; Brandon file.

22 On shell shock, see Showalter's chapter on "male hysteria" in *Women, Madness and English Culture*, 167–94. "Extract from Admission Form," interview with Gertrude, 14–17; Brandon file.

23 "Report on Condition of Patient When Admitted," 1 April 1922, 3; Information written up by Charles Baragar, interview with Robert, 1 April 1922, 23–4, Brandon file.

24 "Report on Condition of Patient When Admitted," 1 April 1922, 3; Information written up by Charles Baragar, interview with Robert, 1 April 1922, 23–4, Brandon file.

25 Letter from [blanked out: magistrate] to Robert Richardson, 28 February 1922; Fred Twilley to Brandon Hospital, 1 March 1922; Charles Baragar to Fred Twilley, 4 March 1922; Alvin Mathers to Fred Twilley, 9 March 1922; Baragar to Mathers, 29 March 1922; "Report on Condition of Patient When Admitted," 1 April 1922, 3, Brandon file.

26 Ward notes, 42, and correspondence from Fannie, Robert, and Charles Baragar, 21 April 1922 to 30 July 1923, 76–89, Brandon file.

27 On the features of case files and their consequences, see Smith, *The Conceptual Practices of Power*, especially her chapter, "Ideological Methods of Reading and Writing Texts: A Scrutiny of Quentin Bell's Account of Virginia Woolf's Suicide," 177–88. Smith's analysis of the social construction of mental illness explicitly excludes organic disorders; nonetheless her comments about disruptive consequences of dissenting realities are useful. See also Matthews, *Good and Mad Women*, her discussion of methodology, 20–9.

28 Gertrude to Baragar, 27 August 1923, 90, Brandon file.

29 Ward notes, 2 August 1923–21 September 1923, 42–3; correspondence between Robert Richardson and Charles Baragar, 30 July 1923 – 28 September 1923, 89–97.

30 Ward notes, 12 November 1923 – 27 April 1925, 43–5, Brandon file.

31 Gertrude to Dr Goulden, 1 May 1925, 102–7, Brandon file.

32 Information on treatments at this time, Schultz and Henderson, *Evaluation of Treatment*, 3–4. On masturbation and mental illness, see Mitchinson, *The Nature of their Bodies*, 111–15; see also Bliss, " 'Pure Books on Avoided Subjects.' "

33 Gertrude to Dr Goulden, 1 May 1925, 102–7, Brandon file.

34 Gertrude to Robert Richardson, 26 August 1924, 111.

35 Ward notes, 3 December 1923 – 16 November 1924, 44–7; correspondence Robert Richardson and Charles Baragar, passim 1924, 100–18, Brandon file.

36 Review of the case, 8 January 1925, 21–2; Ward notes, 20 October 1924 – 11 January 1925, 46–7; correspondence of Robert Richardson and Charles Baragar, 4 November 1924 – 26 December 1924, 113–18; Release form, 121, Brandon file.

37 From case history taken by Ewen Cameron, and his interviews with Fannie and Fred, 25 April 1930, 31; anamnesis by Cameron, based on Fannie and Fred's information, 25 April 1930, 35, Brandon file.

38 Eliza Twilley to Lottie Bailey, 7 December 1927; thanks to Lottie Bailey's daughters Margaret Bailey and Olive Burrell, 26 January 1991, Scarborough, England, for access. Information on the late twenties comes from

interviews with Eric Richardson, September 1986 and July 1991; Elmer McLean, September 1986; and on family holidays, as well from Dorothy Twilley Shewfelt and the late Joan Twilley Wallcraft, September 1986; John Dubreuil, July 1991. This description also draws on a case history taken by Ewen Cameron, his interview with Fannie and Fred, 25 April 1930, 31; anamnesis by Cameron, based on Fannie and Fred's information, 25 April 1930, 35–6, Brandon file.

39 Interviews with Eric Richardson, September 1986 and July 1991; John Dubreuil, July 1991.

40 Case history taken by Ewen Cameron, interview with Fannie and Fred, 25 April 1930, 31; case conference by Cameron, 34; anamnesis by Cameron, based on Fannie and Fred's information, 25 April 1930, 35–6. Correspondence from individuals involved in the case and forms concerning this particular admission and hospitalisation can be found passim April 1930, 5–13, 122–3, Brandon file.

41 Information on Ewen Cameron and his therapeutic approaches from Collins, In the Sleep Room, and Gillmor, I Swear by Appollo. Information on treatments and efficacy, Schultz and Henderson, Evaluation of Treatment, and passim, Brandon file case conference and ward notes. Lloyd Henderson describes the early days of doing that research, begun when he was a ward attendant, in "Hospital History," his transcribed typescript account of his experiences at the hospital, found in the oral history collection at the hospital archives. For more on treatments, see also interviews by Lloyd Henderson of retired nurses Evelyn McKenzie and Kay McInnis, 26 April 1983, BMHC Archives.

42 Information on Gertrude's condition, Ward notes and other clinical reports, May – September 1935, 33–56, and correspondence 8 May 1930 – 24 March 1935, 124–200, Brandon file.

43 Fannie Livesey to Dr Goulden 6 July 1931, 153–5; reply 9 July 1931, 156; information on this period is drawn from: Ward notes and other clinical reports, May 1930 – September 1935, 33–56; Correspondence 8 May 1930 – 24 March 1935, 124–200, Brandon file.

44 Dr Goulden to Robert, 24 September 1930, 129; Ward notes and other clinical reports May 1930 – September 1935, 35–56; Correspondence 8 May 1930-September 1935, 124–200, Brandon file.

45 Fannie Livesey to Dr Pincock, 15 October 1933, Brandon file, 133.

46 Eric did not remember when this poem was written. Eric Richardson, interviews September 1986 and July 1991; Dorothy Shewfelt and Joan Wallcraft, interview September 1986; information on general conditions in the valley from various local history and personal reminiscences, for which I am indebted to Isobel McKay, John Dubreuil, the late John Booth, and others whose names I never knew who told me about their families and neighbours during my visits to Swan River. Robert's political partici-

pation is reflected in the Rainy Rivers Grain Growers Minutebook, passim, now at the Provincial Archives in Winnipeg.

47 Information on the Richardson family from interviews with Eric Richardson, Dorothy Shewfelt, John Dubreiul, the late Joan Wallcraft, and from correspondence from family members to the hospital, passim. The undated birthday thank you letter, in Gertrude's hand to "My Darling Eric," 194–7, Brandon file.

48 Correspondence 1934 and 1935 passim, 183–201; Ward notes 1934 and 1935 passim, 54–5, Brandon file.

49 Interviews with Eric Richardson, Dorothy Shewfelt, Connie MacDonald, Isobel McKay, John Dubreuil, and the late Joan Wallcraft and John Booth, September 1986.

50 Interviews, September 1986; see also correspondence between Robert, Fannie, and the doctors, late 1936 to late 1937, 202–15, Brandon file.

51 Robert to Dr Pincock, 30 December 1936, Pincock's reply 2 January 1937; Robert's response 6 January 1937, Brandon file, 202–4. Interviews with Eric Richardson.

52 House of Commons Law Commission, "Family Law. Report on Nullity of Marriage," Jackson, *The Formation and Annulment of Marriage*, and Horstman, *Victorian Divorce*, 103–67.

53 Information from marriage certificate of John Leonard Dexter and Edith Mary Lyne, 24 March 1920, and birth certificates of Peter Lyne Dexter and Claude Dexter, 4 July 1920, Loughborough Registry Office. I am grateful to Mrs S.M. Paton, Superintendent Registrar, Loughborough District, for superb detective work, exceptional interpretive skills, wise counsel. Dexter may in fact have been a widower, but the registrar and I were unable to find any record of an intervening marriage and death, so it seems his was a title of convenience. Could he have presumed that Gertrude was dead? Absolutely not; although he probably had no contact with her after 1901, she wrote regularly in the Leicester paper for most of the intervening years, and the slightest effort on his part would have revealed her whereabouts. Dexter and his new wife remained at Rose Cottage until 1929, according to city directories.

54 Union information from papers of the Amalgamated Society of Carpenters, Cabinetmakers, and Joiners, Loughborough Branch, Minute Book, January 1921 – September 1922, Leicestershire Record Office. Janice Dickin McGinnis finally solved the mystery of the malady "hyperiesis" by spotting the misspelling of "hyperpiesis" on the death certificate.

55 Dexter's death certificate is in Robert's file at the Swan River law firm that took over from Wright's successor; thanks to Eric for permission to see this material. Information came primarily from interviews with Eric Richardson, Joan Wallcraft, Dorothy Shewfelt, Connie MacDonald, John Dubreuil, September 1986 and July 1991.

56 Interviews with Eric Richardson, Joan Wallcraft, Dorothy Shewfelt, Connie MacDonald, John Dubreuil, September 1986 and July 1991; Correspondence 1 March 1937 – 3 September 1937, 206–14, Brandon file.

57 Gertrude to Dr [illegible], 6 October [1939], 224–31; correspondence to and from Fannie, 7 September 1937 – 2 December 1938, 215–23; ward notes and other records, 25 August 1937 – 15 February 1939, 57–8, Brandon file. On the hospital diet see interviews by Lloyd Henderson of retired nurses Evelyn McKenzie and Kay McInnis, 26 April 1983, BMHC Archives, and discussion by Refvik, *History of the Brandon Mental Health Centre*, 86–7 and menu plans 182–6. I am grateful to Jean Findley McGregor, Helen Pelchar Gilmour, and Hazel Wright Moffat for telling me about their experiences nursing in the 1930s.

58 Manitoba legal records show that nothing had yet been initiated in the courts at the time of Robert's death; I obtained the information on Robert's death certificate from the records of Paull Funeral Directors in Swan River. See also "Robt Richardson, Swan Valley Farmer, Passed Away Suddenly on Tuesday," Swan River *Star*, 10 November 1938. Other information comes from Eric Richardson, Joan Wallcraft, Dorothy Shewfelt, John Dubreuil, and various longtime residents of Swan River who told me bits and pieces when I visited there in 1986 and 1991.

59 Correspondence between Fannie and Gertrude's doctors, 3 January 1940 – 21 February 1946, 232–47, and ward notes, 1 August 1940 – 11 February 1946, 58–60, Brandon file.

60 Connie showed me the two letters from Gertrude, one not dated, the other 21 February 1945. Correspondence between Fannie and the doctors, 3 January 1940 – February 1946, Brandon file.

61 Correspondence between Fannie and Gertrude's doctors, 1 June 1946 – 12 March 1947, 248–58, and ward notes, 4 June 1946 – 5 September 1946, 60–1, Brandon file. See also "Mrs G. Richardson Passes Away," Swan River *Star*, 19 September 1946. Horace after the First World War had continued to work as a travelling manufacturer's agent selling yarn; in 1935 he went into business for himself, producing and marketing cotton yarn and instructions for home knitting. He worked out of their home at first, and Ella kept the books. Within two years business had expanded sufficiently to necessitate a move into larger quarters, at which point he and Ella moved to Stamford. After the Second World War he built a large modern factory; he served on the borough council for several years, and was on school boards and the executives of several service and cultural organisations including the dramatics society. During the 1940s Ella had worked (probably as a volunteer) at a child welfare centre, and both had been active in the archaeological society. His obituary is in "Mr H.G. Twilley's Death: Business Romance," an undated clipping [1961] from an unnamed Stamford newspaper, given to me by Connie MacDonald.

EPILOGUE

1 Richardson, *The Leicester Pioneer*, 9 November 1917.
2 Quotes are from Richardson, "The Women's Crusade," *Leicester Pioneer*, 9 November 1917.
3 Richardson, "My Canadian Letter," *MFP*, 5 December 1914.
4 Clifford Allen, "The Presidential Address to the Convention," *The Tribunal* 8 January 1920.
5 Welch, *A Feminist Ethic of Risk*, 20.
6 Smith, *The Conceptual Practices of Power*, 134.
7 Editor Ernest J. Hunter, "Good-Bye to Our Readers," *The Tribunal*, 8 January 1920.
8 McCullough, *Think on Death*, 256.

Bibliography

INTERVIEWS

Mildred Ashby, Leicester, England
Margaret Bailey, Scarborough, England
John Booth, Swan River, Manitoba
Olive Burrell, Scarborough, England
John Dubreuil, Swan River, Manitoba
Helen Pelchar Gilmour, Brandon, Manitoba
Connie MacDonald, Brandon, Manitoba
Jean Findley McGregor, Brandon, Manitoba
Isobel Martin McKay, Swan River, Manitoba
Hazel Wright Moffat, Brandon, Manitoba
Eric Richardson, Swan River, Manitoba
Dorothy Twilley Shewfelt, Somerset, Manitoba
Wilfred Twilley, Vancouver BC
Jean Twilley, Leicester, England
Keith Twilley, Leicester, England
Joan Twilley Wallcraft, Somerset, Manitoba
Robert Wallcraft, LaRivière, Manitoba

PRIVATE PAPERS

Margaret Bailey, Scarborough, England
Olive Burrell, Scarborough, England
Connie MacDonald, Brandon, Manitoba

Melbourne Hall Evangelical Chapel, Leicester, England
Paull Funeral Directors, Swan River, Manitoba
Dorothy Twilley Shewfelt, Somerset, Manitoba
Keith Twilley, Leicester, England
Joan Twilley Wallcraft and Robert Wallcraft, LaRivière, Manitoba
Jean M. Watson, courtesy of Clive Sutton, Leicester, England
Wycliffe Congregational Church, courtesy of Howard Rees, Evington, Leicester, England

ARCHIVAL MATERIALS

Amalgamated Society of Carpenters, Cabinetmakers, and Joiners (Loughborough Branch) Papers, Leicestershire Record Office
Biography Scrapbooks, Manitoba Legislative Library
Robert Borden Papers, National Archives of Canada
Brandon Hospital Oral History Collection, Brandon Hospital Records, Brandon Mental Health Centre Archives
Fred Dixon Papers, Provincial Archives of Manitoba
Congregational Church Records, Leicestershire Record Office
Great Meeting Unitarian Chapel Papers, Leicestershire Record Office
Leicester and Leicestershire Women's Suffrage Society Annual Reports, Fawcett Library, London
Leicester Burgess Lists, Leicestershire Record Office
Leicester Peace Society Minute Book, Marx Memorial Library, London
Leicester Records of Births, Marriages and Deaths, Registry Office
Leicester Poor Law Union Records, Leicestershire Record Office
Leicester Secular Society Papers, Leicester Secular Society
Leicester Secular Society Scrapbook, Leicestershire Record Office
Loughborough Records of Births, Marriages, and Deaths, Registry Office
Manitoba Department of Agriculture, Debt Adjustment Board, Provincial Archives of Manitoba
Manitoba Grain Growers Association Papers, Provincial Archives of Manitoba
Manitoba Land Records Office, Provincial Archives of Manitoba
Violet McNaughton Papers, Saskatchewan Archives Board
Militia Papers, National Archives of Canada
Emily Murphy Papers, Edmonton City Archives
National Council of Women of Canada Papers, National Archives of Canada
Tobias Norris Papers, Provincial Archives of Manitoba
Sylvia Pankhurst Papers, Norlin Library, University of Colorado at Boulder
Political Equality League Papers, Provincial Archives of Manitoba
Religious Society of Friends (Quakers), Friends Service Committee Papers, Friends House Library, London

Religious Society of Friends (Quakers), Leicester Monthly Meeting Papers, Leicestershire Record Office

Religious Society of Friends (Quakers), Socialist Quaker Society Papers, Friends House Library, London

Gertrude Twilley Richardson, manuscript book of poems, Swan Valley Historical Museum

Maud Arncliffe Sennett Scrapbook Collection, British Library

W.T. Stead Collection, "Collection of Newspaper Cuttings on Death of W.T. Stead," W.H. Fairbarns, compiler, British Library

Towers Hospital Records, Leicestershire Record Office

Julia Grace Wales Papers, National Archives of Canada

Women's Christian Temperance Union Papers, Provincial Archives of Ontario

Women's International League for Peace and Freedom Papers, Norlin Library, University of Colorado at Boulder

Women's Liberal Federation Papers, Bristol University Library Special Collections

Wycliffe Society for Helping the Blind Papers, Leicestershire Record Office

Wyggeston Girls' School Records, Wyggeston Girls School and Leicestershire Record Office

PERIODICALS AND SERIALS

Canadian Annual Review

Canadian Forward

Canadian Thresherman and Farmer

Everywoman's World

Free Press (Manitoba)

Grain Growers' Guide

ILP News

The Internationaal

Leicester City Directories

Leicester Daily Post

Leicester Pioneer

The Leicester Reasoner

Midland Free Press

Morning Leader

Pax et Libertas

Peace and Goodwill

Review of Reviews

Seattle Daily Call

Star (Swan River)

The Tribunal

Voice (Winnipeg)
War Against War: A Chronicle of the International Crusade for Peace
War Against War in South Africa
Western Labor News
White Ribbon Bulletin
Woman's Century
Women's Franchise
Wycliffe Review
Wyggeston Girls' Gazette

BOOKS, ARTICLES, PAPERS

Abella, Irving, and David Millar, eds. *The Canadian Worker in the Twentieth Century.* Toronto: Oxford University Press, 1978.

Adamchuk, Jean, and Ruth Iwanchuk, eds. *Tent Town 1898–1979: A History of Minitonas and District.* Minitonas: Minitonas Community Centre, nd [1979].

Adams, Tony. "A Consideration of Factors Influencing the Origins and Development of the Socialist Quaker Society." Master's thesis, History Department, Leicester University, 1985.

Addams, Jane, Emily Balch, and Alice Hamilton. *Women at The Hague: The International Congress of Women and Its Results.* New York: Garland, [1915] 1972.

Allen, Richard. *The Social Passion: Religion and Social Reform in Canada 1914–28.* Toronto: University of Toronto Press, 1971.

Alonso, Harriet. *The Women's Peace Union and the Outlawry of War 1921–1942.* Knoxville: University of Tennessee Press, 1989.

Amenicida Collective. *Revolutionary Forgiveness. Feminist Reflections on Nicaragua.* Maryknoll: Orbis, 1987.

Bacchi-Ferraro, Carol. "The Ideas of the Canadian Suffragists 1890–1920." Master's thesis, History Department, McGill University, 1970.

Barclay, Tom. *Memoirs and Medleys: The Autobiography of a Bottle-Washer.* Leicester: Edgar Backus, 1934.

Beales, A.C.F. *The History of Peace. A Short Account of the Organised Movements for International Peace.* London: G. Bell, 1931.

Bercuson, David. *Confrontation at Winnipeg: Labour, Industrial Relations, and the General Strike.* Montreal and Kingston: McGill-Queen's University Press, 1974.

Binnie-Clark, Georgina. *Wheat and Woman.* Intro. Susan Jackel. Toronto: University of Toronto Press, [1914] 1979.

Braybon, Gail, and Penny Summerfield. *Out of the Cage: Women's Experiences in Two World Wars.* London: Pandora, 1987.

Brockway, Fenner. *Inside the Left: Thirty Years of Platform, Press, Prison, and Parliament*. London: New Leader, 1947.

Brown, Craig, and Ramsay Cook. *Canada 1896–1921: A Nation Transformed*. Toronto: McClelland & Stewart, 1974.

Brumberg, Joan Jacobs. *Fasting Girls: The History of Anorexia Nervosa*. New York: New American Library, 1989.

Busfield, Joan. *Managing Madness: Changing Ideas and Practice*. London: Hutchinson, 1986.

Bush, Julia. *Behind the Lines. East London Labour 1914–1919*. London: Merlin Press, 1984.

Byles, Joan Montgomery. "Women's Experience of World War One: Suffragists, Pacifists and Poets." *Women's Studies International Forum* 8, no. 5 (1985): 473–87.

Caedel, Martin. *Pacifism in Britain 1914–1845: the Defining of a Faith*. Oxford: Clarendon, 1980.

Campbell, R.J. "Why the Church League Exists." *Church League for Women's Suffrage Monthly Paper*. June 1913.

Clarke, Agnes Spencer. *Glenroyst*. Leicester: Batty & Company, 1898.

– *Seven Girls: Sketches of Factory Life*. Leicester: Spencer & Greenhough, 1899.

– *The First Woman Minister*. London: Stockwell, 1941.

Cleverdon, Catherine. *The Woman Suffrage Movement in Canada*. Toronto: University of Toronto Press, [1950] 1974.

Colegate, Isabel. *Deceits of Time*. New York: Viking, 1988.

Collins, Anne. *In the Sleep Room. The Story of the CIA Brainwashing Experiments in Canada*. Toronto: Lester and Orpen Dennys, 1988.

Conway, Jill. "The Woman's Peace Party and the First World War." In *War and Society in North America*, ed. J.L. Granatstein and R.D. Cliff, 52–68. Toronto: Thomas Nelson & Sons, 1971.

Cook, Blanche Wiesen. "Biographer and Subject: A Critical Connection." In *Between Women*, ed. Carol Ascher, Louise de Salvo, and Sara Ruddick, 397–412. Boston: Beacon, 1984.

Cook, Ramsay. "Francis Marion Beynon and the Crisis of Christian Reformism." In *The West and the Nation*, ed. Carl Berger and Ramsay Cook, 187–208. Toronto: McClelland & Stewart, 1976.

Cooper, Sandi. "The Work of Women in Nineteenth Century Continental European Peace Movements." *Peace and Change* 9, no. 4 (1984): 11–28.

Creighton, Donald. *John A. Macdonald. The Young Politician*. Toronto: Macmillan, 1952.

– *John A. Macdonald. The Old Chieftan*. Toronto: Macmillan, 1955.

Cronwright-Schreiner, S.C.. *The Land of Free Speech. Record of a Campaign on Behalf of Peace in England in Scotland in 1900*. London: New Age Press, 1906.

Daniels, Kay, and Mary Murnane, eds. *Uphill All The Way: A Documentary History of Women in Australia*. St Lucia: University of Queensland Press, 1980.

Dauphin Presbyterial United Church Women. "Church Histories 1880–1925." N.p. [Dauphin]: Author, 1967.

Davies, Megan Jean. "The Patients' World: British Columbia's Mental Health Facilities, 1910–1935." Master's thesis, History Department, University of Waterloo, 1989.

Departments of Social Service and Evangelism of the Methodist and Presbyterian Churches. *Report on a Rural Survey of the Agricultural, Social, and Religious Life [of the] Swan River Valley.* N.p.: The Departments [August–September 1914].

Duley, Margot I. *Where Once Our Mothers Stood We Stand. Women's Suffrage in Newfoundland 1890–1925.* Charlottetown: gynergy, 1993.

Dyhouse, Carol. *Girls Growing Up in Late Victorian and Edwardian England.* London: Routledge & Kegan Paul, 1981.

Early, Frances. "Feminism, Peace, and Civil Liberties: Women's Role in the Origins of the World War One Civil Liberties Movement." *Women's Studies* 18 (1990): 95–115.

– "'War is a Crime Against Humanity': The Radical Pacifist Activism of Frances Witherspoon, Tracy Mygatt and Jessie Wallace Hughan." Paper presented to the Canadian Historical Association. Charlottetown, 1992.

Eck, Diana, and Devaki Jain, eds. *Speaking of Faith. Cross-Cultural Perspectives on Women, Religion and Social Change.* London: Women's Press, 1986.

Elliott, Malcolm. *Victorian Leicester.* Leicester: Phillimore 1978.

– *Leicester. A Pictorial History.* Leicester: Phillimore, 1983.

Ellis, Isabel C. "Mary Catharine Gittins, 1840–1930, and Edith Gittins, 1845–1910, a Memoir." 1931. Unpublished typescript. Leicester University Library.

– "Records of Nineteenth Century Leicester." Privately Printed. Leicester, 1935.

Enloe, Cynthia. *Does Khaki Become You? The Militarisation of Women's Lives.* London: Pluto, 1983.

– *Bananas, Beaches and Bases: Making Feminist Sense of International Politics.* London: Pandora, 1989.

Fisher, John. *That Miss Hobhouse.* London: Secker & Warburg, 1971.

Foner, Phillip, and Sally Miller, eds. *Kate Richards O'Hare. Selected Writings and Speeches.* Baton Rouge: Louisiana State University Press, 1982.

Forster, Margaret. *Significant Sisters: the Grassroots of Active Feminism 1839–1939.* Harmondsworth: Penguin, 1984.

Franklin, Ursula. *The Real World of Technology.* CBC Massey Lecture Series. Toronto: CBC Enterprises, 1990.

Fraser, Brian. *The Social Uplifters: Presbyterian Progressives and the Social Gospel in Canada 1875–1915*. Waterloo: Wilfrid Laurier University Press, 1988.

Friesen, Gerald. *The Canadian Prairies: A History.* Toronto: University of Toronto Press, 1984.

Galbraith, John S. "The Pamphlet Campaign on the Boer War." *Journal of Modern History* 24, no. 2 (1952): 111–26.

Geller, Gloria. "The Wartimes [*sic*] Elections Act of 1917 and the Canadian Women's Movement." *Atlantis* 2, no. 1 (1976): 88–106.

Gillmore, Don. *I Swear by Apollo, Dr Ewen Cameron and the CIA Brainwashing Experiments*. Montreal: Eden, 1987.

Gimson, Sydney A. "Random Recollections of the Leicester Secular Society." 1932. Bound typescript. Leicestershire Record Office.

Gorham, Deborah. "English Militancy and the Canadian Suffrage Movement." *Atlantis* 1, no. 1 (1975): 83–112.

– *The Victorian Girl and the Feminine Ideal*. London: Croom Helm, 1982.

Gould, F.J. *History of the Leicester Secular Society.* Leicester: The Society, 1900.

Gowland, Pat. "The Women's Peace Army." In *Women, Class and History: Feminist Perspectives on Australia 1788–1978*, ed. Elizabeth Windschuttle, 216–33. Melbourne: Fontana/Collins, 1980.

Grant, Linda. *Blind Trust*. New York: Scribner's, 1990.

Halevy, Elie. *Imperialism and the Rise of Labour*, 2nd ed. Trans. E.I. Watkin. London: Ernest Benn, [1926] 1951.

Hayward, F.H. "In Memory of F.J. Gould, Who Passed Away 6 April 1938, Aged 82 Years." Typescript. Leicester Reference Library.

Henderson, Mrs Lorne (Lizzie Fraser). *Tweedsmuir History of the Swan River Valley.* Np: Women's Institute, 1952.

Herrmann, Ursula. "Social Democratic Women in Germany and the Struggle for Peace Before and During the First World War." In *Women and Peace: Theoretical, Historical and Practical Perspectives*, ed. Ruth Roach Pierson, 90–102. London: Croom Helm, 1987.

Hewison, Hope Hay. *Hedge of Wild Almonds: South Africa, the Pro- Boers and the Quaker Conscience 1890–1910*. London: James Currey, 1989.

Heyward, Carter. *The Redemption of God. A Theology of Mutual Relation*. Lanham, MD: University Press of America, 1982.

– *Our Passion for Justice. Images of Power, Sexuality, and Liberation*. New York: Pilgrim, 1984.

Hinton, James. *Protests and Visions: Peace Politics in Twentieth-Century Britain*. London: Hutchinson, 1989.

Hirshfield, Claire. "Liberal Women's Organizations and the War against the Boers, 1899–1902." *Albion* 14:(1984) 27–49.

Hirst, Margaret. *The Quakers in Peace and War: An Account of their Peace Principles and Practice*. London: Swarthmore Press, 1923.

Hogg, V.W. "Footwear Manufacture." In *A History of the County of Leicester, vol. 4, The City of Leicester*, ed. R.A. McKinley, 314–26. London: Oxford University Press, 1958.

Holt, Raymond. *The Unitarian Contribution to Social Progress in England*, 2nd ed. London: Lindsey Press, 1952.

Hosgood, Christopher. "Shopkeepers and Society: Domestic and Principal Shopkeepers in Leicester, 1860–1914." Ph.D. diss., History Department, University of Manitoba, 1987.

Howard, Irene. *The Struggle for Social Justice in British Columbia. Helena Gutteridge, the Unknown Reformer*. Vancouver: University of British Columbia Press, 1992.

Howe, Karen, Deborah Romeyn, and Barbara Spence, songwriters. "Nothing Like the Freedom." In *Prairie Spirits*. Winnipeg: Grannyfone Records, 1986.

Hughes, William. *Indomitable Friend: The Life of Corder Catchpool 1883–1952*. London: Housmans, [1956] 1964.

Ingram, Kenneth. "Fifty Years of the National Peace Council: A Short History." London: The Council, 1958.

Jackel, Susan, ed. *A Flannel Shirt and Liberty: British Emigrant Gentlewomen in the Canadian West, 1880–1914*. Vancouver: University of British Columbia Press, 1982.

– "First Days, Fighting Days: Prairie Presswomen and Suffrage Activism, 1906–16." In *First Days, Fighting Days: Women in Manitoba History*, ed. Mary Kinnear, 53–75. Regina: Canadian Plains Research Centre, 1987.

James, Howard P. "Centenary of London Road Congregational Church, 1857–1957." Pamphlet. Leicestershire Record Office, n.d.

James, J. Ernest. *The Socialism of Jesus and Kindred Addresses*. Leicester and London: Adams Brothers and Shardlow, 1911.

Jarvis, Anthea. *Liverpool Fashion: Its Makers and Wearers: The Dressmaking Trade in Liverpool 1830–1940*. Liverpool: Merseyside County Museums, 1981.

Jensen, Joan. "All Pink Sisters: the War Department and the Feminist Movement in the 1920s." In *Decades of Discontent: the Women's Movement 1920–1940*, ed. Lois Scharf and Joan Jensen, 199–222. Westport: Greenwood Press, 1983.

Johnson, Dale, ed. *Women in English Religion 1700–1925*. New York: Edwin Mellen, 1983.

Johnson, Pauline. *Flint and Feather: The Complete Poems of E. Pauline Johnson (Tekahionwake)*. Toronto: PaperJacks, 1972.

Jones, Peter d'A. *The Christian Socialist Revival 1877–1914: Religion, Class and Social Conscience in Late-Victorian England*. Princeton, NJ: Princeton University Press, 1968.

Josephson, Harold, Sandi Cooper, et al., eds. *Biographical Dictionary of Modern Peace Leaders*. Westport, CT: Greenwood, 1985.

Kelm, Mary-Ellen. "Please Tell Emma that I Have not Forgotten her: Women, Families, and the Provincial Hospital for the Insane, British Columbia, 1905–1915." Paper presented to the Western Canadian Studies Association. Banff, 1990.

Kendall, Ernest. *Doing and Daring. The Story of Melbourne Hall Evangelical Free Church, Leicester.* Rushden: Stanley Hunt, n.d. [ca 1955].

Kennedy, Thomas. "Fighting About Peace: the No-Conscription Fellowship and the British Friends' Service Committee, 1915–1919." *Quaker History* 69, no. 1 (1980): 3–22.

– *The Hound of Conscience: A History of the No- Conscription Fellowship.* Fayetteville: University of Arkansas Press, 1981.

– "The Society of Friends and Anti-Militarism in Early Twentieth-Century Britain." Paper presented to the Southern Historical Association. Louisville, Kentucky, 1981.

– "The Quaker Renaissance and the Origins of the Modern British Peace Movement, 1895–1920." *Albion* 16, no. 3 (1984): 243–72.

Kent, Susan Kingsley. *Sex and Suffrage in Britain 1860–1914.* Princeton, NJ: Princeton University Press 1987.

Kinnear, Mary. "The Icelandic Connection." *Canadian Woman Studies* 7, no. 4 (1986): 25–8.

– *Margaret McWilliams. An Interwar Feminist.* Montreal and Kingston: McGill-Queen's University Press, 1991.

Koss, Stephen, ed. *The Anatomy of an Antiwar Movement: The Pro-Boers.* Chicago: University of Chicago, 1973.

Krebs, Paula M. " 'The Last of the Gentlemen's Wars': Women in the Boer War Concentration Camp Controversy." *History Workshop Journal* 33 (1992): 38–56.

Lancaster, Bill. *Radicalism, Cooperation and Socialism: Leicester Working-Class Politics 1860–1906.* Leicester: Leicester University Press, 1987.

– "Towards a Socialist Commonwealth? Cooperation in Leicester in the Late Nineteenth Century." *Midland History* 12 (1987): 48–66.

Leavitt, Sarah. *Victorians Unbuttoned. Registered Designs for Clothing, Their Makers and Wearers, 1839–1900.* London: George Allen and Unwin, 1986.

Liddington, Jill. *The Life and Times of a Respectable Rebel: Selina Cooper 1864–1946.* London: Virago, 1984.

– *The Long Road to Greenham: Feminism and Anti-Militarism in Britain Since 1820.* London: Virago, 1989.

– and Jill Norris. *One Hand Tied Behind Us: The Rise of the Women's Suffrage Movement.* London: Virago, 1978.

Linklater, Andro. *An Unhusbanded Life: Charlotte Despard, Suffragette, Socialist and Sinn Feiner.* London: Hutchinson, 1980.

Lytton, Constance. *Prisons and Prisoners. The Stirring Testimony of a Suffragette.* Intro. Midge MacKenzie. London: Virago, [1914] 1988.

McClung, Nellie. *Purple Springs*. Intro. Randi Warne. Toronto: University of Toronto Press, [1921] 1992.

McCormack, Ross. *Reformers, Rebels, and Revolutionaries: The Western Canadian Radical Movement 1899–1919*. Toronto: University of Toronto Press, 1977.

McGinnis, Janice Dickin. "The Impact of Epidemic Influenza: Canada, 1918–1919." *Historical Papers* (1977): 121–40.

MacKenzie, Midge, ed. *Shoulder to Shoulder*. New York: Alfred Knopf, 1975.

Mappen, Ellen F. "Strategists For Change: Social Feminist Approaches to the Problems of Women's Work." In *Unequal Opportunities: Women's Employment in England 1800–1918*, ed. Angela John, 235–59. Oxford: Basil Blackwell, 1986.

Mardiros, Anthony. *William Irvine: The Life of a Prairie Radical*. Toronto: Lorimer, 1979.

Marks, Alfred. *The Churches and the South African War*. London: New Age, 1905.

Martin, Janet D. "Elastic Web Manufacture." In *A History of the County of Leicester, Volume IV, The City of Leicester*, ed. R.A. McKinley, 326–7. London: Oxford University Press, 1958.

Mies, Maria. *Patriarchy and Accumulation on a World Scale*. London: Zed, 1986.

Millar, F. David. "The Winnipeg General Strike 1919: A Reinterpretation in the Light of Oral History and Pictorial Evidence." Master's thesis, History Department, Carleton University, 1970.

Minitonas Community Centre Committee. *Notes From Tent Town 1890–1979: A History of Minitonas and District*. Minitonas: The Committee, 1979.

Murphy, Emily. *Janey Canuck in the West*. London: Dent, [1910] 1917.

Myers, Sandra. "Victoria's Daughters: English Speaking Women on 19th Century Frontiers." In *Western Women: Their Land, Their Lives*, ed. Lillian Schissel, Vicki L. Ruiz, and Janet Monk, 261–81. Albuquerque. University of New Mexico Press, 1988.

Nash, David. "F.J. Gould and the Leicester Secular Society: A Positivist Commonwealth in Edwardian Politics." *Midland History* 16 (1991): 126–40.

– *Secularism, Art and Freedom*. Leicester: Leicester University Press, 1992.

Naylor, James. *The New Democracy: Challenging the Social Order in Industrial Ontario 1914–25*. Toronto: University of Toronto Press, 1991.

Nearing, Scott. *The Making of a Radical. A Political Autobiography*. New York: Harper, 1972.

Newton, Douglas J. *British Labour, European Socialism and the Struggle for Peace 1889–1914*. Oxford: Clarendon Press, 1985.

Newton, Janice. "The Alchemy of Politicization: Socialist Women and the Early Canadian Left." In *Gender Conflicts: New Essays in Women's History*, ed. Franca Iacovetta and Mariana Valverde, 118–48. Toronto: University of Toronto Press, 1992.

No-Conscription Fellowship. *Troublesome People. A Re-print of the No-Conscription Fellowship Souvenir Describing its Work during the Years 1914–1919*. London: Central Board for Conscientious Objectors, 1940.

Norell, Donna. " 'The Most Humane Institution in all the Village' ": The Women's Rest Room in Rural Manitoba." *Manitoba History* 11 (Spring 1986): 38–50.

Oldfield, Sybil. *Spinsters of this Parish: The Life and Times of F.M. Mayor and Mary Sheepshanks*. London: Virago, 1984.

Orme, Henry Gilbert, and William H. Brock. *Leicestershire's Lunatics: The Institutional Care of Leicestershire's Lunatics During the Nineteenth Century*. Leicester: Leicestershire Museums, 1987.

Osterud, Nancy Gray. "Gender Divisions and the Organization of Work in the Leicester Hosiery Industry" In *Unequal Opportunities: Women's Employment in England 1800–1918*, ed. Angela John, 45–70. Oxford: Basil Blackwell, 1986.

Owen, Wendy, ed. *The Wheat King: The Selected Letters and Papers of A.J. Cotton*. Winnipeg: Manitoba Record Society Publishers, 1985.

– "The Cost of Farm-Making in Early Manitoba: The Strategy of Almon James Cotton as a Case Study." *Manitoba History* 18 (Autumn 1989): 4–11.

Page, Stephen. "Emigration and Poverty in Edwardian Leicester." *Transactions of the Leicestershire Archaeological and Historical Society* 65 (1991): 68–84.

Palmer, Gwen, and Ed Dobbyn, eds. *Lasting Impressions. Historical Sketches of the Swan River Valley*. Swan River, Man: Swan River Valley Historical Society, 1984.

Pankhurst, Richard. *Sylvia Pankhurst. Artist and Crusader*. London: Paddington, 1979.

Pankhurst, Sylvia. *The Suffragette*. New York: Sturgis and Walton, 1911.

– *The Home Front: A Mirror to Life in England During the World War*. London: Hutchinson, 1932.

Patterson, A. Temple. *Radical Leicester: a History of Leicester 1780–1850*. Leicester: Leicester University Press, 1975.

Peterson, T. "Ethnic and Class Politics in Manitoba". In *Canadian Provincial Politics*, ed. Martin Robin, 69–115. Toronto: Prentice Hall, 1972.

Pettigrew, Eileen. *The Silent Enemy: Canada and the Deadly Flu of 1918*. Saskatoon: Western Producer, 1983.

Phillips, Ian. "A Study of Attitudes to, and the Impact of the Boer War in Leicester as Depicted in the Provincial Press." Master's thesis, History Department, Leicester University, 1988.

Pierson, Ruth Roach, ed. *Women and Peace: Theoretical, Historical and Practical Perspectives*. London: Croom Helm, 1987.

Pollock, Carolee. "Against the Tide: The Anti-War Arguments of the British Suffragists During the First World War." Master's thesis, History Department, University of Calgary, 1989.

Pratt, A.M. *The Story of Manitoba's Weekly Newspapers*. Winnipeg: Manitoba Weekly Newspapers Association, 1976.

Price, Richard. *An Imperial War and the British Working Class: Working-Class Attitudes and Reactions to the Boer War 1899–1902*. Toronto: University of Toronto Press, 1972.

Pritchard, R.M. *Housing and the Spatial Structure of the City: Residential Mobility and the Housing Market in an English City Since the Industrial Revolution*. London: Cambridge University Press, 1976.

Purvis, Jane. *Hard Lessons: the Lives and Education of Working-Class Women in Nineteenth Century England*. Cambridge: Polity Press, 1989.

Rauschenbusch, Walter. *Christianizing the Social Order*. New York: Macmillan, 1912.

Refvik, Kurt. *History of the Brandon Mental Health Centre 1891-1991*. Brandon: BMHC Historical Museum 1991.

Reilly, Catherine, ed. *Scars Upon My Heart: Women's Poetry and Verse of the First World War*. London: Virago, 1981.

Rempel, Richard. "British Quakers and the South African War." *Quaker History* 64, no. 2 (1975): 75–95.

Roberts, Barbara. "They Drove Him to Drink: Donald Creighton and the Wives of Sir John A. Macdonald." *Canada. An Historical Magazine* 3.2 (December 1975) 51–64.

– "A Work of Empire: Canadian Reformers and British Female Immigration." In *A Not Unreasonable Claim: Women and Reform in Canada 1880s-1920s*, ed. Linda Kealey, 185–202. Toronto: Women's Press, 1979.

– "No Safe Place: Peace Studies and the War Against Women." *Our Generation* 15, no. 4 (1983): 7–26.

– "The Death of Machothink: Feminist Research and the Transformation of Peace Studies." *Women's Studies International Forum*. 7, no. 4 (1984): 195–200.

– "Why do Women do Nothing to End the War? Canadian Feminist-Pacifists and the Great War," CRIAW Paper Number 13. Ottawa: CRIAW, 1985.

– "Doctors and Deports: The Role of the Medical Profession in Canadian Deportation 1900–20." *Canadian Ethnic Studies* 18, no. 3 (1986): 18–36.

– *Whence They Came: Deportation from Canada, 1900–1935*. Ottawa: University of Ottawa Press, 1988.

– "Women Against War 1914–18: Francis Marion Beynon and Laura Hughes." In *Up and Doing: Canadian Women and Peace*, ed. Janice Williamson and Deborah Gorham, 48–65. Toronto: Women's Press, 1989.

– "Women's Peace Activism in Canada." In *Beyond the Vote: Canadian Women and Politics*, ed. Linda Kealey and Joan Sangster, 276–308. Toronto: University of Toronto Press, 1989.

– "Ladies, Women and the State: Managing Female Immigration, 1880–1920." In Roxana Ng, Jacob Muller, and Gillian Walker, eds. *Community Organization and the Canadian State*. Toronto: Garamond, 1990, 108–30.

Rose, Michael, ed. *The English Poor Law 1780–1030.* Newton Abbot: David and Charles, 1971.

– ed. *The Rise of the Welfare State: English Social Policy 1601–1971.* London: Weidenfeld and Nicolson, 1973.

Rowbotham, Sheila. *Friends of Alice Wheeldon.* New York: Monthly Review Press, 1987.

Ruddick, Sara. *Maternal Thinking: Toward a Politics of Peace.* New York: Ballantine, 1990.

Sandall, Robert. *The History of the Salvation Army, vol. 3: Social Reform and Welfare Work 1883–1953.* London: Nelson, 1947.

Sargant Florence, Mary, Catherine Marshall, and C.K. Ogden. *Militarism versus Feminism: Writings on Women and War.* Intro. Margaret Kamester and Jo Vellacott, London: Virago, 1987.

Schults, Raymond L. *Crusader in Babylon: W.T. Stead and the Pall Mall Gazette.* Lincoln: University of Nebraska Press, 1972.

Schultz, Stuart, and Albert Lloyd Henderson. *Evaluation of Treatment, Brandon Hospital for Mental Diseases.* Report Series Memorandum No. 3. Ottawa: Health and Welfare Canada, 1957.

Showalter, Elaine. *The Female Malady: Women, Madness and English Culture 1830–1980.* New York: Penguin, 1987.

Simmons, Jack. *Leicester Past and Present, vol. 2: Modern City, 1860–1974.* London: Eyre Methuen, 1974.

Smith, Dorothy. *The Conceptual Practices of Power: A Feminist Sociology of Knowledge.* Toronto: University of Toronto Press, 1990.

Socknat, Thomas. *Witness Against War: Pacifism in Canada 1900–1945.* Toronto: University of Toronto Press, 1987.

– "For Peace and Freedom: Canadian Feminists and the Interwar Peace Campaign." In *Up and Doing: Canadian Women and Peace,* ed. Janice Williamson and Deborah Gorham, 66–88. Toronto: Women's Press, 1989.

Stanley, Liz, with Ann Morley. *The Life and Death of Emily Wilding Davison. A Biographical Detective Story.* London: Women's Press, 1988.

Stead, Robert. *Grain.* Toronto: McClelland & Stewart, [1926] 1963.

Steedman, Carolyn. *Childhood, Culture and Class in Britain: Margaret McMillan 1860–1931.* London: Virago, 1990.

Steinson, Barbara J. " 'The Mother Half of Humanity': American Women in the Peace and Preparedness Movements in World War I." In *Women, War and Revolution,* ed. Carol Berkin and Clara Lovett, 259–81. New York: Holmes and Meier, 1979.

– *American Women's Activism in World War I.* New York: Garland, 1982.

Stokes, John, Herman Beerman, et al. *Modern Clinical Syphilology: Diagnosis, Treatment, Case Study,* 3rd ed. London: W.B. Saunders, [1944]. 1987.

Strong-Boag, Veronica. *Parliament of Women: The National Council of Women of Canada 1893–1929.* Ottawa: National Museums, 1976.

- "Peace-Making Women: Canada 1919–1939." In *Women and Peace: Theoretical, Historical and Practical Perspectives*, ed. Ruth Roach Pierson, 170–91. London: Croom Helm, 1987.

Summers, Anne. "Militarism in Britain Before the Great War." *History Workshop Journal* 2 (Autumn 1976): 102–23.

Swan River Board of Trade. "Swan River Valley: The Garden of the Canadian West." Swan River: The Board, 194–.

Swan River Valley History Book Committee. *Eighty Years in the Swan River Valley.* Swan River: The Committee, 1978.

Tancock, Elizabeth. "Secret Trains Across Canada 1917–1918." *The Beaver* 71, no. 5 (1991): 39–43.

Taylor, Jeffery. "Dominant and Popular Ideologies in the Making of Rural Manitobans, 1890–1925." Ph.D. diss. History Department, University of Manitoba, 1988.

- "Professionalism, Intellectual Practice, and the Educational State Structure in Manitoba Agriculture, 1890–1925." *Manitoba History* 18 (Autumn 1989): 36–45.

Thane, Pat. "The Labour Party and State 'Welfare.'" In *The First Labour Party 1906–1914*, ed. K.D. Brown, 183–216. London: Croom Helm, 1985.

Thompson, Dorothy. *The Chartists.* London: Temple Smith, 1984.

Trofimenkoff, Susan Mann. "Feminist Biography." *Atlantis* 10, no. 2 (1985): 1–9.

Tuchman, Barbara. *The Zimmermann Telegram.* New York: Dell, [1958] 1965.

Turner, Barry. *Equality for Some. The Story of Girls' Education.* Glasgow: Ward Lock Educational, 1974.

Twilley, Fred. *Between the Hills: Life in the Swan River Valley 1787–1958.* Swan River: Author, 1958.

United Kingdom. House of Commons Law Commission. "Family Law. Report on Nullity of Marriage." Law Commission Report Number 33. *Sessional Papers 1970–71.* Volume 31. 359–420.

Valverde, Mariana. *The Age of Light, Soap and Water: Moral Reform in English Canada, 1885–1925.* Toronto: McClelland & Stewart, 1991.

- "As if Subjects Existed: Analysing Social Discourses." *Canadian Review of Sociology and Anthropology* 28, no. 2 (1991): 173–87.

Van Arx, Jeffrey. *Progress and Pessimism: Religion, Politics and History in Late Nineteenth Century Britain.* Cambridge: Harvard University Press, 1985.

Varley, Henry. *Private Address to Boys and Youths on an Important Subject.* London: Christian Commonwealth, 1884.

- *The New Theology and Mr R.J. Campbell's Teachings examined and Criticised.* London: Bible and Book Saloon, nd [1908?].

Vellacott, Jo. *Bertrand Russell and the Pacifists in the First World War.* Brighton: Harvester, 1980.

– "Feminist Consciousness and the First World War." In *Women and Peace: Theoretical. Historical and Practical Perspectives*, ed. Ruth Roach Pierson, 114–36. London: Croom Helm, 1987.

– *From Liberal to Labour with Women's Suffrage: the Story of Catherine Marshall*. Montreal and Kingston: McGill-Queen's University Press, 1993.

Vellacott Newberry, Jo. "Russell as Ghost Writer: A New Discovery." *Russell* 15 (Autumn 1974): 19–23.

Vicinus, Martha. *Independent Women: Work and Community for Single Women 1850–1920*. London: Virago, 1985.

Vincent, David. *Bread, Knowledge and Freedom: A Study of Nineteenth-Century Working Class Autobiography*. London: Europa, 1981.

von Petzold, Gertrud. *John Davidson: Und Sein Geistiges Werden Unter Dem Einfluss Nietsches*. Leipzig: Verlag Von Bernhard Tauchnitz, 1928.

– *Harriet Martineau Und Ihre Sittlich-Religiose Weltschau*. New York: Johnson Reprint, 1967.

Walker, Sonia. "Engineers and Secularists: Some Aspects of the Lives of Josiah and Sydney Gimson." Master's thesis, Leicester University, 1988.

Walkley, Christina. *The Ghost in the Looking Glass: The Victorian Seamstress*. London: Peter Owen, 1981.

Walkowitz, Judith R. *City of Dreadful Delight. Narratives of Sexual Danger in Late-Victorian London*. Chicago: University of Chicago Press, 1992.

Wallace, Archer. "History of Socialism in Toronto." nd [March 1916]. Typescript. Metro Toronto Public Library.

Warne, Randi. "Nellie McClung and Peace." In *Up and Doing: Canadian Women and Peace*, ed. Janice Williamson and Deborah Gorham, 35–47. Toronto: Women's Press, 1989.

Weiner, Gaby. "Vida Goldstein: The Women's Candidate." In *Feminist Theorists*, ed. Dale Spender, 244–55. New York: Pantheon, 1983.

Welch, Sharon. *Communities of Resistance and Solidarity: A Feminist Theology of Liberation*, Maryknoll: Orbis, 1985.

– *A Feminist Ethic of Risk*. Minneapolis: Fortress, 1990.

Weller, Ken. *Don't be a Soldier! The Radical Anti-War Movement in North London 1914–1918*. London: Journeyman Press & London History Workshop Centre, 1985.

Whyte, Frederic. *The Life of W.T. Stead, vol. 1*. London: Jonathan Cape, 1925.

– *The Life of W.T. Stead, vol. 2*. New York: Garland, [1925] 1971.

Willms, A.M., Ramsay Cook, et al. *Conscription 1917*. Toronto: University of Toronto Press, 1969.

Wilson, Barbara, ed. *Ontario and the First World War*. Toronto: Champlain Society, 1977.

Wiltsher, Anne. *Most Dangerous Women: Feminist Peace Campaigners of the Great War*. London: Pandora, 1985.

Wishnia, Judith. "Feminism and Pacifism: the French Connection." In *Women and Peace: Theoretical, Historical and Practical Perspectives*, ed. Ruth Roach Pierson, 103–13. London: Croom Helm, 1987.

Yeo, Stephen. "A New Life: The Religion of Socialism in Britain 1893–1896." *History Workshop Journal* 4 (1977): 5–56.

Young, Nigel. "Tradition and Innovation in the British Peace Movement: Towards an Analytical Framework." In *Campaigns for Peace: British Peace Movements in the Twentieth Century*, ed. Richard Taylor and Nigel Young, 5–22. Manchester: Manchester University Press, 1987.

Index